THE AMERICAN ALPINE JOURNAL

2022

[Cover] The snow pinnacle bivouac and crux traverse at 6,500 meters on Annapurna III's southeast ridge (p.12). *Vitaliy Polezhaiko* [This Page] Nicolas Favresse on the first ascent of Myope Tower, East Greenland (p.179). *Jean-Louis Wertz*

[Photo] Luka Stražar on an exposed lead during the first ascent of the 1,700-meter northwest face of Chobutse in Nepal (p.284). *Nejc Marčič*

2022   VOLUME 64 ISSUE 96

CONTENTS

RECON

HISTORY

CLIMBS & EXPEDITIONS

[Photo] Seen in profile from the approach to Passu Diar in Pakistan (see p.268), the magnificent northeast face of Ghispare (7,611m) was first climbed in 2017 (*AAJ 2018*). *James Price*

The American Alpine Club, 710 10th St., Suite 100, Golden, Colorado, 80401

E-mail: aaj@americanalpineclub.org
www.publications.americanalpineclub.org

ISBN (paperback): 978-1-7356956-6-2
ISBN (hardcover): 978-1-7356956-7-9

2021 GREAT RANGES FELLOWSHIP

[EIGER]

Jim Bodenhamer
Kevin and Leanne Duncan
Jerry and Sandy Gallwas
Kelson Foundation
Mark Kroese
Phil Lakin Jr.

The Lasky-Barajas Family Fund
Randy Luskey
Craig McKibben and Sarah Merner
Miriam Nelson and Kinloch Earle
Patagonia.com
Mark and Teresa Richey

Carey Roberts
Steve and Paula Mae Schwartz
Robert Weggel
Steve Whitaker

[ALPAMAYO]

John Berry
Dan Emmett
David Goeddel
Dr. Travis Hays
Thomas F. Hornbein, MD

David Landman and Marian
    Hawley
Steven and Lindsay Kafka
Mark and Samskriti King
Melissa McQueen

Vanessa O'Brien
Dr. Myung-Jin Oh
Bob Palais
John Parsons
Naoe Sakashita

George Shaw
Cody J Smith
Lawrence True and Linda
    Brown

[ROBSON]

Alpenglow Foundation and the John
    Hobby Catto Family
Peter Ackroyd
Marcio Avillez
Ryan Bouldin
Will Butcher
R.J. Campbell
Jerome Chin
Dan and Ilene Cohen
Joseph Davidson
Kit DesLauriers
The Duckworth Family

James Garrett and Franziska Garrett,
    MD
Dr. Roger Härtl
Rocky Henderson
Scot Hillman
Jennifer and Marley Hodgson
Richard E. Hoffman, MD
Rob Hutchinson
Syd Jones
Brendan Leonard
Liam Mac Sharry
August March

Edward Matthews
Morgan Family Foundation
Paul Morrow
Tadd Perkins
Ellen Sebastian
William and Barbara Straka
Theodore "Sam" Streibert
Glenn Thomas
Brian Weber
Richard Wohns MD

[TEEWINOT]

Lisa Abbott
Jon Anderson
Mark Andreasen
Anne Smith and Jim Herson
Mike Ashley
Mia Axon
Seavron Banus
George Basch
John Bird
Ronald Bixby
Fred Blau
Steve Bott
Tanya Bradby and Martin
    Slovacek
Dr. Michael Brandt
Pete Brownell
Paul Brunner and Coleen
    Curry
Thomas Burch
Edmund and Betsy Cabot
    Foundation
Kevin Cooney
Dr. Joshua Corsa
Billy Cox
Christopher Croft
Matt And Charlotte Culberson
Scott Davis
Rob DeConto
Lucia and Paul DeLia
Alvin DeMaria
Ed Diffendal
Christopher Downs
Jeff Dozier
Richard and Martha Draves
Don Luci
Ken Ehrhart
Stuart Ellison

Philip Erard
Rodrigo Espinosa de los
    Monteros
Timothy Forbes
Leonardo Franchi
Alexander Friedman
Jim Frush
Charles Galbraith
Ken and Rebecca Gart
Marilyn Geninatti
Charles Goldman
Jonathan Gopel
Russell Gray
Robert B. Hall and Sheila Matz
Jeff Hanks
Tim Harvell
John Heilprin
Audrey Heilprin
Janette Heung Memorial
    Foundation Limited
Holly Hollar
Alex Intermill and Lisa
    McKinney
Dennis Jackson
Lorraine Kan
John R. Kascenska II
Arthur and Diane Kearns
Adam Kilgus
Kendall Krause
Paul Kuchu
Paul Lego
Alison Levine
Daniel Lochner
Jamie Logan
Dave Lonack
George Lowe III
Conrad and Jenni Lowe-Anker

Chris Lynch
Brent Manning
Sara Maranowicz
Troy Martin
Bridget Martin
Scott McCaffrey and Rebecca
    Robinson
C. Wayne McIlwraith
Brad McQueen
Richard Merritt
Allan Mulandi DMD
Paul Muscat
Rod Nease
Hilaree Nelson
John and Alicia Nicholson
Sean O'Brien
Peter O'Neil
CJ O'Reilly
Joyce Palmese
Charles Peck
Allen Peery
Dr. Laura Peracchio
Eryn Phelps
Jeff Phillips, DDS
Keegan Potter
Mark Powers
Andrew Puhl
John and Mitzi Raaf
Randy Reddig
Dr. John Reppy
William Ricci
Wolf Riehle
David Riggs
Michael Riley
Joel Robinson
Vik Sahney
Alexa Saltzman

Charles Sassara III
Jacob Schonberg
Raymond VJ Schrag
Stephen Scofield
Karsang Sherpa
Will Shillito
Dr. Mark Simons
Curt Simonson
John Sirois
Martin Slovacek
Marne Smiley
Jay Smith
James Sneeringer
Katelyn Stahley
Rob and Jennifer Stephenson
Emerson Stewart and Parisa
    Tabriz
Bob Strode
Duncan Stuart
Steven Swenson and Ann
    Dalton
John Tedeschi
Andrew Tomko
John L. Townsend
Alexander Uy
Julia Wallace
Nick and Jenna Wathen
Chris Weidner
Ryan Whitted
Timothy J. Wilt, MD, MPH
Dr. Mark Woodard
Brian Young
Cheryl Young
T.C. Price Zimmermann

FRIENDS OF THE AAJ

Peter Ackroyd
Carla Firey
James Garrett and Franziska Garrett, MD
Richard E. Hoffman, MD
Dr. Myung-Jin Oh
Patagonia.com

[Photo] Ryan Driscoll at the fifth bivouac on the Medusa Face of Mt. Neacola in Alaska (p.70). *Justin Guarino*

THE AMERICAN ALPINE JOURNAL

EDITOR
Dougald MacDonald

ART DIRECTOR
David Boersma | Mojave Creative Lab

SENIOR EDITOR
Lindsay Griffin

ASSOCIATE EDITORS
Andy Anderson, Whitney Clark, Chris Kalman, Michael Levy, Erik Rieger

CONTRIBUTING EDITORS
Damien Gildea, Lauren Miller, David Stevenson (Books)

ILLUSTRATIONS AND MAPS
Glen Boles, Marty Schnure, Oleksandr Yurkovskyi

TRANSLATORS
Karen Freund, Rolando Garibotti, Monika Hartman, Anna Piunova, Pam Ranger Roberts, Lenka Strnadová

INDEXERS
Ralph Ferrara, Eve Tallman

REGIONAL CONTACTS
Steve Gruhn, Mark Westman, *Alaska*; Drew Brayshaw, Ian Welsted, *Canada*; Sevi Bohorquez, Nathan Heald, Sergio Ramirez Carrascal, *Peru*; Luis Pardo, *Colombia*; Damien Gildea, *Antarctica*; Rolando Garibotti, Camilo Rada, Marcelo Scanu, *Argentina and Chile*; Alex von Ungern, *Bolivia*; Harish Kapadia, Nandini Purandare, *India*; Rodolphe Popier, Richard Salisbury, *Nepal*; Hiroshi Hagiwara, Tamotsu Nakamura, Kaoru Wada, *Japan*; Peter Jensen-Choi, Oh Young-hoon, *Korea*; Anna Piunova, *Russia, Tajikistan, and Kyrgyzstan*; Xia Zhongming, *China*; Ben Dare, *New Zealand*

ADVISORY BOARD
Chantel Astorga, Kelly Cordes, Brody Leven (ski alpinism), Colin Haley, Mark Jenkins, Simon Richardson, Graham Zimmerman

WITH SPECIAL THANKS TO...
Christine Blackmon, Elizabeth Cromwell, Randy Cuccio, Jeff Deikis, Katie Ives, George Lowe, Max, Bruce Normand, Katie Sauter, the members of the American Alpine Club, and our hundreds of authors, photographers, and donors

United We Climb.

The AAC is the largest community of climbers in the country, and our members take pride in advocating for the public lands and conservation policies that protect wild landscapes and the wild people who love them. Join us in this mission—and simultaneously ensure you have the emergency rescue and medical expense coverage you need to dream big.

Ready to up your commitment to the AAC's advocacy work, and looking for 100% peace of mind in the backcountry? Consider upgrading your membership today. Learn more about the Club and join or renew at americanalpineclub.org/join.

American Alpine Club

📷 *AAC member Craig Muderlak*

MILESTONES

The climbs featured in the *American Alpine Journal* don't occur in a vacuum—they reflect the broader evolution of climbing styles and performance around the world. The following achievements in 2021 provide additional context for the longer rock and alpine ascents documented in this year's AAJ. —The Editors

FEBRUARY–APRIL

In February, Simon Lorenzi (Belgium) completed the sit start to The Big Island, a famous 8C+ (V16) boulder problem at Fontainebleau, France. Lorenzi called the new start Soudain Seul and tentatively graded it 9A (V17), which might have been only the second problem in the world of this grade, after Nalle Hukkataival's Burden of Dreams (2016) in Finland. However, in late March, French climber Nicolas Pelorson repeated Soudain Seul and said it was 8C+. Pelorson had previously repeated and downgraded another problem given 9A, No Kpote Only, also at Fontainebleau.

Janja Garnbret during the first 8c (5.14b) onsight by a woman. *Roman Krajnik*

Then, on April 2, Daniel Woods (USA) climbed the sit start to Sleepwalker in Black Velvet Canyon (Red Rock, Nevada), originally established by Jimmy Webb in late 2018 and graded V16. Woods' start added half a dozen moves to the problem, and Woods (who repeated Sleepwalker soon after the first ascent and eventually did it more than 15 times) said the extended problem deserved V17.

AUGUST

The COVID-delayed Tokyo Olympics took place in July and August, and for the first time in the modern Olympic Games, climbing was on center stage. The combined event calculated competitors' standings based on their individual rankings in lead climbing, bouldering, and speed. A victory in speed and a fourth-place finish in lead were enough to give Spanish climber Alberto Ginés López the first men's Olympic gold medal. In the women's event, Slovenian Janja Garnbret confirmed her status as the most dominant competition climber of our time (at only age 22), winning the Olympic gold. Garnbret won nine World Cup bouldering competitions in a row from 2018 to 2021.

A revised climbing competition will be part of the 2024 Olympic Games in Paris, with a combined lead-bouldering event and a separate speed competition. In December 2020, the International Olympic Committee (IOC) executive board recommended that climbing join the "core" Olympic program, meaning it is likely to be included in future Summer Games, starting with Los Angeles in 2028.

In another sign of sport climbing's commercial success, Planet Mountain reported in October that Norwegian climber Magnus Midtbø had surpassed 1 million subscribers to his YouTube channel.

OCTOBER

LAURA ROGORA (ITALY, age 20) repeated Erebor (9b/+ or 5.15b/c) at Arco, Italy, possibly the hardest sport climb done yet by a woman. In 2020, Rogora redpointed a 9b route, becoming the second woman ever to climb the grade.

Two other hard redpoints in October may rewrite sport climbing history. Near Rifle, Colorado, Matty Hong (USA) made the second ascent of Flex Luthor and said it deserved 9b/5.15b. (Hong climbed his first 9b in Spain in 2018.) Tommy Caldwell had established Flex Luthor way back in 2003 and did not grade the climb, saying only that it was harder than the nearby Kryptonite (9a/5.14d). Hong said some holds on Flex Luthor may have broken since Caldwell's ascent, making the route harder, but it seems likely the route was not only the first 5.15a in the United States but also possibly one of the first routes approaching 5.15b anywhere in the world.

In a similar development in England, at the very end of October, Will Bosi (Scotland) made the second ascent of Mutation at Raven Tor, first climbed in 1998 by Steve McClure. (At the time of Bosi's repeat, the climb was two months older than he was!) McClure rated Mutation 9a, but Bosi and other climbers who have ticked 9b and harder routes have said it must be at least 9a+ (5.15a). If the grade eventually is confirmed higher than 9a+, Mutation might have been the hardest sport climb in the world in 1998.

NOVEMBER

ENJOYING SOME TIME outside in Spain and away from her training walls, Olympic champion Janja Garnbret onsighted Fish Eye (8c/5.14b) in Oliana, giving her the first onsight by a woman. She repeated the feat just a few days later, onsighting American Hustle (8c), also at Oliana—an extraordinary end to a superb year for the young Slovenian climber.

PATIENCE

THE STUNNING SOUTHEAST RIDGE OF ANNAPURNA III IS FINALLY CLIMBED

MIKHAIL FOMIN

"Our plane is approaching Kathmandu airport. Please fasten your seatbelts."
Rubbing my eyes and looking out the window of the plane, I saw the familiar but still exciting view of the Himalaya in morning light. A beautiful mountain with a clearly discernible buttress drew my attention. I quickly snapped a photo, and after landing I showed it to Nikitos as a cool future objective, and he, accustomed to my sieve-like memory, calmly informed me that in a few weeks we would be climbing that very ridge. Half-asleep, I hadn't recognized our planned route up Annapurna III.

At that moment, the inner feeling that this would be the year we would summit Annapurna III by the unclimbed southeast ridge—a feeling that had been quietly ripening inside for a long time—suddenly strengthened, and that positive feeling did not disappear until we made it to the very top and back again.

Two years before, in the autumn of 2019, Nikita Balabanov, Viacheslav Polezhaiko, and I had descended to the base of the southeast ridge from around 6,300 meters. Various strong teams had been trying to climb this soaring buttress since 1981, and none had gotten much higher.

As we prepared to leave base camp in 2019, the three of us agreed this route definitely deserved another try. But we all understood that life is unpredictable. As it turned out, 2020 shattered all expectations with its unpredictability, but in 2021 a miracle occurred, and for the first time in our climbing careers, we returned to the same objective with the exact same team.

The steepest section of the southeast ridge of Annapurna III in profile. No team prior to 2021 had gotten higher than the obvious break in the ridge at 6,500 meters. This photo was taken during an attempt in October 2016. *Menk Rufibach | Red Bull Content Pool*

THE APPROACH

THE HELICOPTER, SKILLFULLY piloted by Sobit Gauchan, maneuvered through the cloudy Seti Khola gorge, trying to reach our base camp below Annapurna III. At 4,200 meters we ran into dense clouds, and after a quick discussion, we landed on the first available flat spot on the glacier, said good-bye to Sobit, and in a minute the roar of the engines was replaced with the silence of the mountains. Slava had kept the coordinates of base camp on his watch since 2019, and we knew it was still quite a distance away. It would take two days to shuttle gear along the glacier, but everyone reacted philosophically—after all, it was a great way to acclimatize. And, as Nikita correctly noted, in all of our previous successful expeditions together, our plans had never worked the way we laid them out in the city, so this was a great sign.

The ethical issues surrounding an approach by helicopter had bothered us since the 2019 expedition, since we try to use the minimum of external assistance on our trips and to finance them with a minimal budget. However, the most obvious option for an approach to the south side of Annapurna III on foot is now impossible—in 2003, Nick Bullock and Matt Helliker from the U.K. were the last to try that option. A landslide destroyed part of the trail, and there was a high risk that porters might be killed if they slipped on the steep slopes. Therefore, the British returned to Pokhara, chartered a helicopter to reach base camp, and recommended in their report that subsequent expeditions approach base camp the same way.

Nevertheless, before our 2021 expedition, we seriously considered another option: approaching Annapurna III from the opposite direction, starting from the Manang Gorge to the north and crossing a pass at an altitude of 5,500 meters. The descent from the pass to base camp at 4,600 meters is simple. But the ascent from Manang is an alpine climb of moderate difficulty, and there were no photos available to study the terrain. Plus, it was assumed the three of us would play the role of porters, making shuttle runs up and down the slope until we had brought up all the expedition gear. In the end we were forced to reject this option, since it would add at least eight to ten days to the schedule, which we did not have.

So, we chose to fly as far as we could, and we set up base camp in exactly the same place as in 2019. Even the stones we'd used for rigging our base camp tent still lay in a circle where we'd left them two years before.

ACCLIMATIZATION

To ACCLIMATIZE, we followed the same program we had developed during the 2019 expedition, first climbing south-facing slopes to the ridge running between Annapurna III and Annapurna IV and later climbing up Annapurna IV (7,525 meters). Few of our predecessors had considered Annapurna IV as an objective for acclimatization, most likely because of a short but difficult rock barrier that has to be cleared at 6,200 meters. We reasoned that if we could not climb these rocks on Annapurna IV, then there would be no sense in even trying to climb Annapurna III.

We arrived at base camp two weeks earlier than in 2019, and the monsoon was still blowing at full force. After we'd spent a night at 5,800 meters on the ridge between Annapurna III and IV, the weather turned really bad, and we sat for five days at camp.

We finally started for Annapurna IV very early on October 6. After spending a full day and night at 5,800 meters, we set out early again, and by 8 a.m. were starting to climb the rock barrier. Nothing had changed in two years—it was the same awful rock; fortunately, you're climbing diagonally the entire time, or else you would bombard the ropes and the other guys with stones. Atop the northwest ridge of Annapurna IV, our route converged with the 1955 first ascent, which started from the north in Manang Gorge; to this point, prior to 2019, our route may have been unclimbed.

Seen from about 6,000 meters on the southeast ridge, Annapurna IV (7,525 meters) is the main peak in the background, with Annapurna II partly visible behind. The 2021 team acclimatized with an ascent of Annapurna IV, completing a probable new route they had started in 2019. *Annapurna III Ukrainian Team*

All next day we tramped along the gentle and endless snow of the northwest ridge. We spent a restless night at 6,900 meters and woke at 4 a.m. (or, more precisely, we stopped lying down). We hadn't gone any higher than this in 2019, and we weren't set on reaching the top this time—the main goal was acclimatization. In addition, the weather wasn't conducive to "taking a walk" to the summit—by lunchtime the wind had begun to knock us off our feet. Since the terrain and conditions did not permit us to rest or talk, we just continued without discussion until, as we contoured around the north side of the mountain, the wind suddenly died. After another hour and a half, the three of us were at the summit.

Back in base camp, we anticipated resting for three days and then starting the main climb. But when we asked Slava's wife, Lena, for the forecast, the news wasn't good: five days of excellent weather and then a two-day storm with a meter of new snow. In practice, this meant we'd need ten days in base camp to sit out the storm and wait for the fresh snow to stabilize. At that moment, my hopes that I'd make it to Turkey to vacation with my family at the end of October collapsed, because we all agreed that we'd only go home after we climbed the mountain.

There was, however, a problem with the food and fuel. When we realized we would have to extend our expedition by two weeks, the first thing we did was separate out 12 days of food and gas for Annapurna III as an untouchable supply. Everything else would have to be rationed while we waited. As a result, when we finally set out for the climb, one month after leaving Pokhara, the only supplies left at base camp were a handful of crackers, 100 grams of bacon, and not a single gas cylinder. We joked that our trip was in the best tradition of Soviet climbers, who climbed mountains because they had better food up high than at base camp.

THE ASCENT

At 8 p.m. on October 22, we finally set out for the Annapurna III. Each of our packs weighed 22 to 24 kilograms as we left camp. There was a full moon and firm snow on the glacier, so we walked quickly, sometimes even without headlamps. By 10 p.m., at an altitude of 4,600 meters, we left the glacier and began to climb—first along a grassy slope and then firn, quickly gaining altitude.

Our progress soon slowed, however, because there was much less snow on the route than in 2019; steep mixed steps of five to ten meters interrupted the ice gullies, and these had to be climbed with a belay. As a result, we reached the snow ridge at 5,600 meters at 4 p.m., not at daybreak as planned—a 20-hour day of work. And despite the forecast for 12 days of perfect weather, it had started snowing at midday. We dug a site and set up the tent in a real blizzard, which left about 20 centimeters of fresh snow. Surprised, we messaged Lena for an updated weather report, and almost instantly received confirmation from her: "Twelve days of ideal weather!"

Because the snow was quickly becoming slushy once the sun appeared, we always moved at night on the lower part of the route and rested during the day. The next night, I climbed a rock barrier of about 30 meters and entered a steep gully, which on the last attempt had been completely filled with névé; we had gained 150 meters of altitude there in half an hour. This year, all the snow had melted, and the gully was a heap of unstable rock flakes and blades, covered with the previous day's fresh snow. It took me five minutes just to leave the belay station, because every

Mikhail Fomin on the chimney pitch at 6,250 meters *during the 2019 attempt, the rough rock shredded his clothes. Annapurna III Ukrainian Team*

The southeast ridge, seen from Annapurna IV. The steep buttress ends at 7,100 meters, leaving a 450-meter climb to the summit. The descent was to the southwest (behind and left). *Annapurna III Ukrainian Team*

rock I weighted with my feet shifted ominously or fell off immediately. I moved a little to the side and started up tensely, like a sapper clearing a minefield, tapping all the holds and pushing away everything unreliable. Dealing with such terrain, it took us another two nights to climb 400 meters and reach the snowy "pillow" at 6,000 meters, the most comfortable campsite of the route.

The next day, October 27, was Slava's birthday. In the morning, the birthday boy was given an off-the-books pack of *kissel* fruit drink, and was informed that a special holiday snow ridge was waiting for him to lead. However, our hopes that he would find firm névé leading up to the first rock band on the route came to nothing. The snow would not hold his weight as he walked, so Slava had to straddle the ridge as if on horseback or else squat, lop off the top of the ridge with a shovel, and tamp down the snow in front of him until it seemed possible to weight it. Then he would crawl forward less than a meter and start over. He would definitely remember this birthday!

As on all previous days, it started snowing in the afternoon and stopped an hour after we had dug out a campsite and pitched our tent. We didn't bother Lena, but simply accepted that whatever was happening around us was "ideal weather." The next day we started up the biggest rock buttress of the southeast ridge and, well after midnight, climbed onto the familiar ledge beneath the crux rock chimney.

We woke late the next morning and decided not to move the tent that day but just fix ropes on the chimney. For me, this pitch was like déjà vu: Despite the two years that had passed, the chimney felt as familiar as a training climb at home. The first time I led this pitch, the sharp, flaky rock had shredded my shell pants and jacket, and it looked like I had been fighting with a bull terrier. This time all my clothes remained intact. Slava aptly said the rock was like the Middle Eastern sweet called *halva*—it looked like a puff pastry, crumbling wherever it was touched. One dubious plus: Sometimes I could drive my crampons into that *halva* for a foothold.

The next morning we jumared the two ropes I'd fixed, and then Nikita continued up mixed ground along the ridge—probably the only place on the route where the rocks were more or less monolithic. We prepared for the night as usual, rappelling onto a drift of snow to the right of the ridge and building a tent site there. Ahead was a series of snowy ridges and very steep rock walls that were impossible to bypass—we had to climb them head on.

Tenuous snow traverses at 6,100 meters (top) and at 6,500 meters. See the cover of this edition for another view of the crux downclimb (lower photo). *Annapurna III Ukrainian Team*

On October 31, we climbed on top of a giant snow pinnacle at 6,500 meters with the last rays of the sun. There was no way to install anchors on the snow mushroom, so we simply dug the tent deeper into the snow, hoping that the entire structure was stable. This was the highest point anyone had reached on the southeast ridge before us, and it was easy to see why. To continue from the tent site, we would have to crawl across a 50- to 70-meter ridge of snow that was sharp as a knife. In the middle of this section, the ridge dropped sharply, and what the snow was like there we could only guess. The whole picture did not bode well, and everyone's spirits fell a bit.

Our snow specialist was Slava. No one, including Slava, knows where he got this skill. He just somehow feels the whole spectrum of snow conditions, knows how to position himself correctly on snow and interact with it. Plus, he really likes to use a shovel, and in this form of climbing, the shovel is the main tool.

Slava moved quickly across the first 15 meters of the ridge, but when it abruptly dropped, he looked beyond…looked harder… thought…stood…turned to us…and threw up his hands in confusion.

There was a long pause as each of us wrestled with his inner thoughts. If Slava couldn't get past this spot, we didn't see any other options—to the right and left, below the knife-edge, it looked even worse. Then, apparently, something occurred to Slava. He asked me to take the rope tight and gradually lower him beyond the bulge. My belay anchor was just me, sitting on a backpack where we'd set up the tent, but I carried out Slava's instructions, and he gradually disappeared from sight.

Over the next hour, unseen to us, an inspired Slava threw down several cubic meters of snow, descended and ascended the vertical snow wall a couple of times, and slowly constructed a set of seven broad and well-packed steps, so that Nikita and I could descend the steep snow with our heavy packs without the benefit of a top-rope. We couldn't see any of this, and tension lingered in the air. I remember telling Nikita that if Slava managed to reach the rocks beyond the knife-edge, we would descend only via the summit, and he agreed.

Satisfied with the result of his labors, Slava started moving forward again. He crossed another 15 meters of horizontal ridge, and then climbed another 20 meters to the rocks, where he shoveled off another few cubic meters of snow, built a belay anchor in the rock, and yelled the much-desired "belay on." Everyone exhaled happily. Looking back from that station, our previous night's bivouac looked even more magical than we could have imagined. [*See the cover of this edition for a view of the snow mushroom bivouac and the tenuous traverse.*]

Above Slava's belay, I climbed a pitch of steep ice, which seemed like a reward for previous troubles—just straightforward and fun terrain! But like all good things, it quickly ended. It was already our tenth day on the route, and we had realized long before that we would need to stretch our rations, which had been calculated for a total of 12 days. Our meals thus became briefer and less and less varied.

In the morning, an exceptionally chossy section awaited me. Slava and Nikita were right below, and there were no ways to climb to either side. The face was piled with large, trembling spikes. You had to climb with an ear for the music of the rock—you tap all the handholds and footholds, and when you find those that emit the highest-frequency sound, you make a move, simultaneously trying to ensure the rope below does not shift any low-frequency stones.

After another short but wicked overhanging wall, I climbed onto the ice slopes of the upper buttress, leading toward the ridge top. It started snowing as usual, and after a couple of pitches we built a platform under a huge snow mushroom and spent the night. The next day was much the same. By evening we were still not off the buttress, and through the blowing snow and darkness, we could see a vertical ice step that looked to be about 100 meters high and too difficult to climb at night.

It was time to deploy our "secret weapon"—a snow hammock, which up to then had been traveling in a backpack. We were in a steep icy gully covered with 20 centimeters of snow that had just fallen that day. We hung the hammock from ice screws,

Steep ice at 6,900 meters, one of the last barriers before the upper ridge atop the southeast buttress. *Annapurna III Ukrainian Team*

shoveled in all the snow we could reach, then chopped at the 50° ice slope for another hour or so. The result was a shelf about 50 to 60 centimeters wide—just enough space to crawl inside our tent and sit up throughout the night, trying not to slide off.

In the light of the morning sun, the ice wall turned out to be only 20 meters high, not 100 meters, but alas it was still just as vertical. Still, we were at 6,900 meters and we could see the finish line. After a couple more vertical stretches, it was already dark when I led the final vertical rock band. I climbed to the very top of this section, decided to have a little rest, hammered an ice axe into low-angle ice, and clipped in to it. I inhaled, exhaled, and then began to fall! Ten meters down, I hung from the rope next to a very surprised Slava. Under my weight, the spike had pulled out of the shaft of my ice tool.

Slava took over and finished the lead, and then we simul-climbed up an ice gully, before climbing a vertical ice tunnel formed by two snow and ice ridges, back-and-footing as if in a rock chimney. Sometime after midnight, we popped onto the ridge top at an altitude of 7,100 meters. The lights of Pokhara were visible far below. It was very beautiful and terribly windy and cold, and we immediately began to dig a site for the tent.

We huddled inside and sat silently for about 10 minutes, warming up and recovering after such a crazy day. Then came the realization: We had climbed the southeast ridge of Annapurna III! From here, it should be just a walk to the top. And then somehow we had to get down.

THE SUMMIT AND DESCENT

WE SLEPT LATE and then, putting on everything we had, set out at around 11 a.m. to climb up the south ridge toward the top. The forecast was for wind of 90 to 110 km/h and bitter cold of -35°C to -38°C. Though we were really freezing, we'd say the gusts were a maximum of 70 km/h. But that was still enough to greatly slow our already slow pace, and at times the gusts forced us down onto all fours, driving ice tools into the firm snow so we wouldn't be blown away. By evening we were still about 150 meters below the top. We found a small boulder sheltering us a bit from the wind, and after an hour of work with a shovel, the tent site was ready. Despite the high altitude, everyone slept like babies.

Early in the morning, we left everything at the campsite and headed for the top. The wind had not weakened, and although the ridge was not steep, it took us three hours to gain the remaining 150 meters. But everything ends, and this ridge too. The time was around 11 a.m., November 6, 2021. We had started climbing 15 days earlier. We yelled something into the camera, shot a couple of pictures, sent short messages to Lena and to Thaneswar Guragai, our expedition organizer, hugged each other, took a few more glances around, and started back down.

Initially, we had planned to descend along the route we climbed, and for this we had carried an extra 15 pound-in hooks and five titanium pitons for rappel anchors—that is, a total of 30 hooks and 10 pitons. But the higher we climbed, the more we understood how risky this would be, with all the loose flakes to snag a rope or pull down on your head.

Plan B was to traverse over the summit and along the eastern ridge and then descend into the Manang Valley (generally the route followed for the first ascent of Annapurna III in 1961). However, during the day that we struggled through the wind to reach our final bivouac, we abandoned this option as well. With such a headwind, we simply did not have enough strength to traverse 3.5 kilometers along a ridge at 7,300 meters. At that moment, one of us glanced down and to the left, toward the western slope, and voiced a new idea. *Why not go down this way?* We had no description or photo of this face. The terrain that we could see did not cause particular concern: It was mostly snow, with ice in some places, and though there might be surprises, we

The key section of the descent route on Annapurna III. The steep rock where the rappel rope got stuck is in center. Portions of the southwest ridge, climbed in 2003, are visible at left. *Annapurna III Ukrainian Team*

reasoned that we had a lot of gear and would deal with them. [*The west face of Annapurna III was climbed in 1979, far to the north (climber's left) of the 2021 descent route. The southwest ridge was climbed by an Anglo-American team in 2003, but from what they could see, the Ukrainians felt their proposed descent appeared easier.*]

In the end, our descent was a whole other chapter of this story, its level of uncertainty probably higher than that of the ascent itself, and it's an experience we hope to never repeat.

At first, the slope was simple and we walked down to 6,800 meters, alongside the south ridge. Below this point, the route would turn to the west on steeper ground; there were obvious icefalls below us, and, so late at night, we decided to put up the tent. In the morning we continued, sometimes moving together, sometimes rappelling off Abalakov anchors. By evening we were at 6,400 meters, but now we were at the top of an icefall with a vertical drop of about 100 meters. It became clear we'd need to spend another night here. We built a good ledge under a serac, which gave us excellent protection from the very strong wind. Still, this was possibly the coldest night of the expedition. The accumulated fatigue was having its effect, as was the fact that, two days earlier, before climbing to the summit, we had eaten our last real meal. Now we were each subsisting on one and a half bars a day plus a few cups of cold water and a pinch of electrolytes.

Intuition prompted us to look to the right in the morning, and it was not mistaken—we were able to rappel around the icefall. However, we soon got another surprise: a vertical rock wall with a drop of 80 meters. Well, we still had plenty of gear, so we set up a rappel and started down. At the end of the ropes, we all hung from an anchor in the middle of the rock face. Then, as dictated by Murphy's law, the ropes would not budge when we tried to pull them. Shit. We could have aided back up the face, but it might have taken a full day. We even discussed abandoning the two ropes and continuing down with just our 50-meter static rope. Thank God we didn't make that decision.

In general, what does not yield to brute force often yields to brute force plus technique. I snapped ascenders onto the rope we were trying to pull and began to jumar upward as Slava and Nikita hung onto me. It took five steps, but finally the rope, now as taut as a violin string, shifted half a meter. After another half an hour, the ropes were ours. We exhaled and rappelled down the remaining 25 meters to escape the rock. There we sat on gently sloping ice for a while, recovering and waiting for

Slava Polezhaiko, Nikita Balabanov, and Misha Fomin, just off the helicopter in Pokhara. *Sobit Gauchan*

darkness—the slope below obviously was raked with ice falling from the upper serac.

In the gathering twilight, the slope quickly froze, the pelting from above stopped, and we continued our descent. The last rappel was 55 meters of vertical ice. If we had left the stuck ropes above, we'd have had to make two rappels here, with a spicy hanging stance in the middle of the vertical ice. Finally reaching the icefall below the face, we saw the landscape around us littered with pieces of broken transparent ice, ranging in size from peas to a two-story house—we called it the "cocktail party," but it was definitely not a place you wanted to linger for a drink. We quickly stashed the extra rope in our packs and moved away from the ice cliffs, trying to escape this party where we were not welcome.

Once we were 200 or 300 meters away from the face, we decided to wait for dawn under the protection of a high serac. The altitude was 5,400 meters. While I melted ice with the remnants of our gas, the guys fell asleep. I woke them up, and we drank cold water and ate a handful of crackers, the absolute last bit of our food. I melted another half a liter of water, and the stove went out for good. Then I too closed my eyes. If we weren't eating, at least we'd sleep a bit.

Our preparations the next morning were lightning fast—just get dressed, put on the boots, and go. After a couple of hours we escaped the icefall and reached a flat glacier without crevasses. This was it, we realized—we were safe. We stopped, hugged, and sat down to wait for warm sunlight. Nikita called Thaneswar, told him our coordinates and also that we were a little hungry, and that his and Slava's fingers were slightly frostbitten. We agreed we would descend to 4,500 meters and a helicopter would pick us up there. No matter which side we had descended from the summit, we eventually would have needed a helicopter to collect base camp and get back to town. With no money or documents in our packs—and only 8,000-meter boots on our feet—it just made sense to ask for our ride here and now, rather than attempt to trek all the way down to Pokhara.

The moment the sun arrived, we remembered how hot it can be at 5,200 meters. Everyone's tongue instantly stuck to the roof of his mouth. The backpacks became heavier, the snow became slushy. As we started to move again, we spread far apart. I noted a large boulder below and walked in its direction. Even going downhill, I had to stop and rest every few steps. At an altitude of 5,000 meters, I sat in cool shade by the boulder and furiously nibbled icicles for a bit of moisture.

And then—at first I could not believe my ears—the sound of a helicopter. A couple of seconds later, a bright yellow Seven Summits Treks helicopter popped up from behind the nearest slope. I jumped out, waved my arms, and the helicopter circled and landed, about 50 meters above me. Where the strength came from I don't know, but I turned on my Ueli Steck and ran up to the helicopter. The doors opened and the smiling magician Mingma Sherpa, owner of Seven Summits, tossed a bag of Coca-Colas into my hands and told me to stay put while they flew up to get Slava. This suited me completely, because while he was finishing his sentence, I was already opening a second bottle. The helicopter door, window appeared and I handed him a bottle of the precious liquid.

Seemingly in no time, we were all at the Pokhara airport. It was hard for us to get used to the speed of events, but even if it was all just a dream, it was a good one. Nikita and I warmed ourselves on the grass of the airfield while Slava and Sobit flew off to base camp to retrieve our equipment and trash. An hour later they were back, and—another miracle!—Mingma said we would refuel and fly to Kathmandu. That evening, the very same day, having showered and shaved, we were drinking beer and eating steaks in Thamel.

AFTERWARD

ACCORDING TO THE weigh-in at the hotel, Slava lost 16 kilograms during the expedition, Nikita lost 13 kilograms, and I lost 12. One of our friends joked we had lost the equivalent of one (skinny) member of the team. As we prepared to travel home, the true meaning of the past two and a half weeks hadn't really sunk in. But after some time, I recognized that, in terms of experience, our objective had hit the bull's-eye.

For the first time, we didn't just climb a mountain, we learned to survive on it: 15 days up, three days down, a whole lifetime. We learned that we could endure uncertainty, cold, wind, and malnutrition, and at the same time continue to climb, belay, joke, share the day's last Snickers with a partner, give him a more comfortable spot at a belay or in the tent, offer to take over a lead or cook food when it wasn't your turn. The worse the conditions and the higher the level of uncertainty, the more we cared for each other. In the end, we felt we would not have climbed this route with a different team—each of us found his place, and each had a vital and irreplaceable role.

It did not take us long to come up with a name for the route: Patience. We all consider patience (with the mountain, with partners, with the weather and all other things that happen up there) to be one of the main qualities for a high-altitude climber. During each of those 18 days, we felt like the mountain was presenting us with intricate new puzzles that had to be solved, one by one. And each fresh puzzle extended the journey, so each time you had to be patient and find the inner resources to move on.

I am also sure that a large part of our strength came from the invisible support of spouses, relatives, and friends at home. Almost every day there was a situation in which each of us silently weighed the odds—could we continue to push or was it time to start rappelling back down our tattered ropes? I won't speak for everyone, but for me the scales were often tipped by text messages from my wife and family—by the understanding that they are waiting for you, that they believe you can do anything, and, if you can't, well, good job anyway, now come home and let's go to Turkey for a nice vacation together.

SUMMARY: First ascent of the southeast ridge of Annapurna III (7,555 meters) by Nikita Balabanov, Mikhail Fomin, and Viacheslav Polezhaiko (all from Ukraine). The trio summited by the upper south ridge and descended previously untraveled terrain on the southwest face. They left base camp in the evening of October 22, 2021, reached the summit on November 6, and were picked up by helicopter below the southwest face on November 9. The route was named Patience (2,950 meters, 6a A3 M6 80° ice and 90° snow). Balabanov and Fomin spoke about this climb on the AAJ's Cutting Edge podcast.

ABOUT THE AUTHOR: *Mikhail "Misha" Fomin was born in 1981 in Nikolaev, a small city in the south of Ukraine. Married, with two children, he lived in Kiev and headed the business analysis department for an Information Technologies company until the start of the war in Ukraine. As of press time in late April, the three climbers in this story and their families had survived the initial stages of the war. This story was translated from Russian by Karen Freund.*

A great bowl of steep granite rises above the third bivouac, at 6,600 meters, on the northwest face of Saraghrar Northwest. *Archil Badriashvili*

SARAGHRAR

A RARE EXPEDITION TO THE HINDU KUSH FINDS GREAT SUCCESS

ARCHIL BADRIASHVILI

As a prologue, it should be noted that all three of us—Baqar Gelash-vili, Giorgi Tepnadze, and I—feel grateful to have lived this adventure. The whole escapade felt like a return to a romantic era of mountaineering, yet in a natural, ecological style, with a small circle of friends, dishing out a powerful test of our capabilities.

When I first saw a photo of Saraghrar (7,340 meters), the king of the Rosh Gol valley, I felt enchanted. The 2,300-meter fortress wall of the northwest face was a natural wonder, with no routes nor any previous attempts. Saraghrar's main summit was first climbed from the east, in 1959, by an Italian expedition, and two teams had climbed routes from the Rosh Gol to other tops around Saraghrar's broad summit basin. But 7,300-meter Saraghrar Northwest remained unclimbed.

Catalan climbers had tried to reach this point three times via the southwest pillar—three huge efforts, starting in 1975. In 1982, three members of a large Catalan team completed the pillar and got to a point they called Saraghrar Northwest II, about 120 meters below the desired summit.

We chose a late-season attempt for the northwest face, believing a frozen wall would be safer; it was impossible to predict exactly what conditions we'd meet, as there had been no previous climbs or attempts in this area in autumn. It seemed likely there would be big temperature differences between day and night, and that the sun would light the face only for the last five hours of a relatively short day. We did not even know exactly what the face looked like, not to mention the quality of rock and other important details that a climber seeks to know nowadays before organizing a major expedition. Steep faces, isolation, undescribed areas, and neither an easy way up nor down—it felt almost like going to our home mountains in Georgia!

We decided to stay positive and prepare as if nothing was in our way, even when the situation did not give much grounds for hope: We faced

The south face of Languta-e-Barfi (6,833m GPS), showing (1) Deavoll-Todd attempt (2014) and (2) Georgian Route (2021), with a bivouac at about 6,400 meters on the east ridge. *Archil Badriashvili*

short deadlines for raising funds, and apart from that, the Talibs were taking over Afghanistan, immediately to the west and north of Saraghrar, and we had to wait impatiently for a permit in this border zone. It was a strange and stressful time to organize an expedition, but we gave it a proper try and it worked: The permit was issued, the training went quite well, we raised the bare minimum of funding a couple of days before departure, and off we went.

WE ARRIVED AT base camp at 4,204 meters in the Rosh Gol valley on August 20, five days after our arrival in Pakistan. From there we stared straight up at the southwest buttress climbed by the Catalans—a very nice place to be. Before attempting Saraghrar, our plan was to climb Languta-e-Barfi (6,833 meters GPS) at the head of the valley. This summit was first reached in 1963 but had never been climbed from Pakistan, although Pat Deavoll and Chris Todd came close in 2014—they climbed the left side of the south face and started up the summit ridge before retreating a couple of hundred meters below the top.

It took us two days to reach the foot of the south face over endless moraine and huge boulders. We started up on August 24, without pre-acclimatization. Giorgi and Baqar had done a couple of ascents earlier in the month, reaching 5,000 to 5,200 meters in our home mountains, but I hadn't been able to join them because of the pre-expedition frenzy.

Accompanied by a full moon, we crossed the bergschrund on the right side of the face and solooed up ice that gradually increased to 60° in the upper half. We gained 1,400 meters that day, and it was unexpectedly hot. Above a step of 70° broken rock, we cut a small ledge for a bivouac at 6,400 meters on the east ridge.

The next day we followed the ridge toward the top, overcoming a few very steep and unprotected snowy passages, with the right foot in Afghanistan and the left in Pakistan. On top it was very windy and cold. An amazing panorama opened before us, including Saraghrar and its northwest face, which was not well known to us before that moment. The view provided crucial information for our upcoming climb, especially of the terrain above 7,000 meters—its complexity was a revelation.

We descended the same day, parallel to our line, and after more than three dozen rappels and much downclimbing in bright moonlight, we found ourselves at the foot of the mountain, already celebrating Giorgi's birthday. Later that same evening we raised our cups for him in base camp.

Even though it was still August, it was already getting very cold at base camp. In the constant breeze, one couldn't stay outside the tent long. After a couple of days of proper rest and preparation, we set out for our main objective.

THE ROUTE UP the lower northwest face was obvious: a huge couloir leading more than 1,000 meters up the face. Above this was a rock headwall, and there appeared to be several options. We would decide which line to choose when we got there. We brought no special equipment: two ice tools each, light aiders, ascenders, a more or less standard rack, including pins and Pecker-style pitons, and a tiny bivouac tent. We were happy to pack mostly Georgian food—one week of rations.

We started up the face early on September 3 from around 5,000 meters. After ascending a steep icefall, we entered the couloir. A huge distance had to be covered, so we moved simultaneously all day. The ancient ice made the climbing a struggle, and the slope was approaching 60° when we entered the upper couloir. Inside the narrowing walls, it felt like stepping into the gates of a mythical castle. A bit earlier than planned, we started to dig a bivouac site in ice. We all felt the joy of being here. But at 6,200 meters it was obvious that, from now on, the cold would penetrate the last warm spot under the sky—our tent—and that the bivy sites would be even tighter. A big-wall sufferfest was about to begin.

We woke at dawn and resumed simul-climbing up the ice. At the start of an obviously climbable section of rock on the left, we gathered together. We had noted this place as one option to start up the rock wall, and it seemed more fun than continuing up the narrowing couloir.

I clipped a trad rack on my harness, and with axes but no crampons, started up the rock. I managed to free climb two hard mixed pitches of poor granite in this way, protectable but still

Two views from Languta-e-Barfi, showing (A) Saraghrar Main and (B) Saraghrar Northwest. The upper northwest face is in center, with the Catalan buttress falling to the right. [Inset] Koh-e-Langar (7,070m) in center and Saraghrar at far right. *Archil Badriashvili (both photos)*

A

B

[Opposite] **Day six on the route, pushing for the top of the headwall.** *Archil Badriashvili* [Above] **Climbing into the night at 6,370 meters.** *Baqar Gelashvili*

with the possibility of a big fall. Giorgi took the lead with about six hours of daylight left, and right there, on the third pitch, we faced one of those tough leads where dry-tooling, scary rock climbing, and hard aid combine. This short pitch soaked up the rest of the day, and at the top of it, we found a ledge only big enough for one person to sit. An open sitting bivouac at 6,400 meters—what a perfect way to spend our first night on the rock wall!

The area around us was so steep and snow-free that we could melt only a liter of water. Tired, without eating anything, we tried to get some brief shut-eye, with half of our bodies hanging in the air. Some moments in the cold night were so hard that I just wanted to stand up and scream, to frighten away the cold, but every move I made threatened to dislodge the stone on which two of us were sitting, and this thought somehow calmed me down.

In the morning, it took a while to recover from the torturous night and get moving. The air, which was drier than I have ever experienced at this altitude, caused throat problems that became an everyday struggle for Baqar and me. Plus, Baqar was suffering from a facial nerve inflammation that intensified soon after we started the climb. This would be manageable only as long as our tiny first-aid kit lasted.

As Giorgi climbed a very attractive and steep crack system, we waited eagerly for the sun to appear. Then for some hours we forgot the cold, and eventually we overcame the first rock wall, reaching a position high above the couloir. We could see the potential line ahead and a summit ridge far above, yet the way above constantly hid surprises from our eyes.

Starting our fourth day on the route as soon as the cold at 6,600 meters would allow, I completed two moderate leads and another hard mixed pitch. Although I tried to completely free the last one, a vertical stretch found me loading my protection. Following the leader on jumars, especially on pendulums or traverses, was exceptionally hard here; frequently the seconds had to climb as well, protected by their ascenders. The darkness and cold started to set in. After a false start and some downclimbing, Giorgi went off again and this time found a sharp ridge where we could create a relatively peaceful bivouac at about 6,750 meters. It was becoming obvious that our food, batteries, and gas were going to have to last longer than we had planned.

On the fifth morning I curiously opened the zipper and…. "Woah! We are starting the upper headwall today!" In the darkness the night before, we hadn't realized that a 250-meter

The northwest face of Saraghrar Northwest (ca 7,300m). The round-trip on the 2,300-meter route took nine days. The Catalan route climbed from the right to a high point near the final marked bivy. *Archil Badriashvili*

wall of vertical granite was right there above us.

The way ahead was everything but obvious—we just had to choose a line and climb whatever was in our way, as everything appeared equally bold and difficult. "Then let's just try the center," someone said. As I followed the third pitch that day, I remember wondering how Giorgi passed through the last 20 or 30 meters. I found almost no protection as I cleaned. Many times on the headwall, the leader would have to back-clean pieces to place them higher up, and here Giorgi had left us with a big pendulum swing around a corner. Baqar went last and burned his bridges by removing the only nut placed for horizontal speed control, making for a desperate start to this maneuver.

During the next pitch, a scary traverse above a huge drop, darkness fell again. Then another crack dead-ended, and Giorgi had to leave a precious piece of gear to lower off. Already we'd left two cams stuck in the cracks, and some titanium pitons had broken or deformed. Their absence was really felt in our small rack.

The rock above appeared simply unclimbable. Giorgi returned to the anchor at 6,850 meters, and we spent another three hours bending hard ice into a bivy site. I remember thinking that night that we could no longer afford the luxury of false starts. The days seemed to feel shorter and shorter, and gaining 100 to 150 vertical meters a day on a 2,300-meter line was not calming, especially when speeding up seemed to be beyond logic. With part of the tent waving in the air, as usual, our team had another tea-conversation: "We have to break through tomorrow, no matter what. There shouldn't be much rock left anyway!"

In the morning, our sixth on the face, a jaw-dropping sight appeared: A single crack split an otherwise blank wall. It was clear that another dead-end crack would finish our efforts, so close to our goal. The very hard first pitch took many hours, but on the plus side we were able to dry the sleeping bags for the first time. After a hanging belay, we watched Giorgi lead an amazing, overhanging pitch (the 18th of the wall), climbing for seven hours as he struggled to gain ground at almost 7,000 meters. For Baqar and me, the only joy was to watch it snowing upward the whole day, as updrafts blew flakes past the belay! It would have looked very funny if anyone could have seen us climbing this vertical wall in our thick high-altitude clothes. Some birds watched us from a distance, so we had to act boldly and stay cool.

When Giorgi finally finished his lead, Baqar and I happily yelled up to him and tried to get information about the ground above, hoping it would now be easier, as a reward for our struggles. But it was hard to make sense of Giorgi's replies. It became dark and we followed, spinning in space as we jumared. Our power of unity had been going through various tests; still, everybody kept up their spirits.

The pitch above looked horribly difficult, an overhanging wave-like rock, but our wall days appeared to be ending soon. Up Giorgi went. There were several hours of silence, and the rope barely moved. Baqar decided to follow and disappeared into the darkness for another silent hour. The weather had started to worsen, and soon I was covered with spindrift. The boys above shouted something too complex to understand. I started up, jumaring some of the time but mostly self-belaying with my ascenders. I found the rope stuck in a crack and understood why Giorgi had been unable to belay us. After another moment I stood up, alone in the darkness, and felt a mysterious sensation—the whole rock wall was below me. There was no celebration, just silence. I coiled the ropes slowly and then soloed up steep snow to help the others prepare a bivouac. Only at 3 a.m. did we get to crawl into the bags. We remained clipped in but finally slept without a helmet.

THE SEVENTH MORNING's warm-up session started by sharpening 78 points on our totally worn-out crampons and tools. Snow and wind gusts ruled the outside world. We packed half of our rack, one sleeping bag, the tent, and everything chewable that remained: a good bite of chocolate, a handful of dry fruits and nuts, and one delicious packet of soup I'd had in Tbilisi for a couple of years. We hoped to climb the remaining 300 meters in one day, but we were prepared for a bivouac if it took longer or if we had to descend another side of the mountain.

We soloed up high-angle ice and strangely deep snow to the ridge crest. From here, for the first time, we could see Saraghrar's main and central summits; our desired summit, the northwest peak, stood apart like a rock tooth.

The sharp ridge was loaded with unconsolidated and unprotectable snow, cornices on the left and a void on both sides. The only option to save a falling friend would be to jump off the opposite side. It looked terrifying. But this ridge was the only way to the summit! Step by step we started, over the first near-vertical snow wall, and then a second.... I heard snow collapsing behind me, the rope dragged, and I looked back so as not to jump in the wrong direction. Baqar was already some meters down on the north side, his tools biting into the snow—he waved with one hand, and a moment later we continued.

Before dusk—and without gaining much altitude—we had left the ridge and extreme tension behind us. The headwind increased as a moderate slope brought us to a point somewhere between 7,150 and 7,180 meters, where we finally could look down the southwest face. "Look, our base camp!" We called out in three voices, hoping the echoes would reach our friends at camp far below. Irshad and Hayat started blinking a lamp! A moment of laughter and joy. And we knew that they were happy too.

The people of Zondangram, the closest village, have kept alive the memory of all the expeditions that have visited the Rosh Gol. People like Karim Baig, father of Irshad, and his old friend, the father of our cook Hayat, had trekked with other alpinists or worked as mail runners for expeditions. "I have looked at the northwest wall—it looks possible to climb!" Karim had told us. We

It took two full days to traverse the ridge line to the summit of Saraghrar Northwest and return to the bivouac above the northwest face, and then a long day and night to descend the face. *Archil Badriashvili*

knew that no team so small had ever summited any of the Rosh Gol giants, but our new friends kept the faith, strongly believing in our chances.

Right after these torchlight greetings, we spotted the top of the Catalan route, very nearby. We stopped to bivouac, and after a cold night sharing our single sleeping bag, we snoozed the alarm a few times before preparing to move again. Symbolically, we ate our last meal on the mountain, but saved the remaining gas for that evening.

By midday Saraghrar's high summit basin, a kilometer long and wide, was all in view, and the answers to all the riddles about the various summits were now crystal clear. Clouds passed above us at high speed. We lay down to rest on flat snow, enjoying a moment of not worrying about falling—we could have danced here, but catching a breath would be a task.

The last lead up the summit pinnacle was moderate mixed, fun to climb. Slow like a fat lizard, I neared the top. On the eighth day of the climb, September 10, we celebrated the summit together. We could see Languta-e-Barfi in its full beauty. I called home to tell my dear family we were OK, and we all laughed and smiled, forgetting the difficulties for a moment. Then, within half an hour, we abseiled from the summit and landed back in reality.

After many discussions about descent lines, it was quite obvious now: We would return to the same face we'd come up. Before dark, we downclimbed the whole ridge that had taken us the previous two days to climb and stopped again at our bivouac above the wall. The next day we'd start a complete descent of the northwest face, dropping all 2,000 meters.

The ninth day was about dedicating all of our skills to completing what we'd started, despite the exhaustion we felt. The morning did not bring good weather, and communication and visibility were very poor. After just three rappels, we left familiar ground and continued straight down the wall toward the top of the couloir. The rappels continued all day and through the long night.

Somewhere in the night, we dropped two of the rappel devices, and all but one of our headlamps died. Only Giorgi, leading the rappels, had a good working light. Baqar had a small knife with a tiny light, and we'd use it to check our setup before each rappel—everything else happened in total darkness. At this strange stage of the

Badriashvili and Gelashvili relax on the summit. Languta-e-Barfi is behind on the right. *Giorgi Tepnadze*

climb, the wind calmed and it became totally silent. The contours of the walls and the couloir were barely visible. And the thirst! With no chance to drink anything, I felt my lungs greedily trying to absorb water from the cold, dry air. And—a happy discovery—it really seemed as if I could taste some water in the air, and this was my only satisfaction during the long night. I do not know how many rappels we did, but finally we stood at the bottom of the face—the beginning and the end.

In the morning light we found a way through the glacial labyrinth and to water. We had left half a pack of macaroni, some Georgian salt, and a bit of gas at our camp in the moraine, and Baqar made a meal of this that we happily ate. The sun thawed our bodies, and we all slept out on the rocks, under a chilly breeze, careless for a few hours.

Giorgi had some minor frostbite, and the walk down to base camp would not be easy for him. I, too, could barely walk. "Maybe I'll follow you guys tomorrow?" I joked in frustration. I had to remove the liners from my boots to fit my feet into them. We expected hours of struggle, and the long moraine and our numb legs did not disappoint us. That evening, though, we entered base camp, loudly singing, and reunited with Irshad and Hayat.

We decided to stay at base camp for several days to show gratitude to the surrounding nature and leave the valley calmly. All that remained to do was to think back on what had just happened. I have to admit, the most important insights and emotions, the grace of nature during all this, are beyond my words to express.

SUMMARY: First ascent of the south face and east ridge of Languta-e-Barfi (6,833m GPS) in the Pakistani Hindu Kush, by Archil Badriashvili, Baqar Gelashvili, and Giorgi Tepnadze (all from Georgia), August 24–25, 2021. The route gained about 1,800 meters and was rated TD (5A Caucasian), with 60° ice and 75° snow; the trio descended the same way. The same three then made the first ascent of Saraghrar Northwest (ca 7,300m) by the northwest face (2,300m, ED2 or 6B Caucasian), from September 3 to 10. They descended the northwest face until late into the night on September 11.

ABOUT THE AUTHOR: *Archil Badriashvili lives in Tbilisi, Georgia, and trains and climbs in the Caucasus mountains. His article about the history and climbs of Ushba is on p.78. Badriashvili spoke about the 2021 Hindu Kush expedition for episode 45 of the Cutting Edge podcast.*

GOLIATH

A STORY OF OBSESSION
IN THE HIGH SIERRA

VITALIY MUSIYENKO

What can I say about the Goliath traverse? I spent countless hours thinking about it, losing sleep, preparing myself mentally and cardiovascularly, learning about electrolytes, wondering how often I would be able to find water, how much weight I could carry and still feel light enough to free solo so much fifth-class terrain. Something like 60 mountains—it was crazy to think about that. Thirty-two miles of technical ridge, carrying all my gear, food, and water, knowing that every day I would be more tired than the last, but if I lost my concentration for even a moment, I could die. It was a goal that evolved into an obsession. An obsession that, by August 2021, I was tired of living with. I felt I had to climb the Goliath in order to be liberated.

IN 2010 I FELL in love with climbing through scrambling and peakbagging in the High Sierra. At first, I would be so nervous before a simple backpacking trip that I could hardly sleep. But with time and increased exposure to progressively challenging objectives, I became more comfortable. New friends helped me realize the endless possibilities climbing can offer, from bouldering in the gym to long routes in the mountains. Long ridges in the Sierra soon became attractive to me because they offer sustained technical terrain, the opportunity to tag multiple summits, and a much more enjoyable way to prepare for climbs in the Greater Ranges than hiking five gallons of water up a big hill.

In 2013, a year after my friend Ben Horne passed away in the Cordillera Blanca, I honored his memory (his motto: "magnificent failure is better than mediocre success") by onsighting the Evolution Traverse (VI 5.9) in the Sierra car to car, solo. For me, it was a glimpse into a future full of challenges with unknown outcomes—a 27-hour day spent way outside the comfort zone of a person who'd started his climbing career only three years prior. That was before FKTs became a widespread phenomenon, before I knew of anyone attempting routes as big as the Evo car to car.

After the bruises healed, I traced the Sierra Crest on a map while considering worthy objectives for the future. I was stunned to realize the Evolution Traverse was just a fraction of a 32-mile

Day eight and nearing the end.
Looking southwest from Mt.
Tom Ross toward Mt. Darwin.
Vitaliy Musiyenko

jagged ridgeline, covering approximately 60 summits over 13,000 feet. It was a natural objective—if you could describe traversing 32 miles of continually precipitous terrain high in the alpine as natural. I was sure other people were aware of it, but had anyone climbed it?

I came to learn the massive enchainment I envisioned was a combination of two known traverses, extending on either side of Bishop Pass. There was the Full Evolution Crest (16 miles, VI 5.9), which heads northwest from Bishop Pass, meeting up with the Evolution Traverse between the Clyde Spires (13,240 feet) and Mt. Wallace (13,377 feet), then continuing north to Mt. Darwin (13,831 feet), where the Evolution Traverse heads northwest and the Full Evolution Crest continues due north for many more miles. The Full Evolution Crest was first completed by Scott McCook and Kyle Sox in 2008 over eight days, with multiple food and fuel caches along the way.

The crenelated ridge extending south from Bishop Pass, meanwhile, had been dubbed The Full Monty (16 miles, VI 5.9), and at the time was an unclimbed extension of the Full Palisade Traverse (8 miles, VI 5.9), first climbed by Jerry Adams and John Fischer in 1979. In 2013, I read an article

SKI SEASONS

MODERN SKI ALPINISM IN THE ALASKA RANGE

SAM HENNESSEY

Like many questionable ideas, the idea of traversing the Alaska Range originated in extreme boredom. In 2018, Michael Gardner and I showed up in Alaska to one of the bleakest forecasts I have ever seen. For 12 days, rain poured down in Talkeetna, followed by a brief stretch of "decent" weather during which we flew in to Kahiltna Base Camp to help our friend Lisa Roderick, the camp manager, set up for the season. We hoped to do a bit of climbing afterward, but the window slammed shut, and for the next several days we were tent-bound, which allowed us to focus on our strength: talking endless amounts of shit.

At some point, amid a long stream of sophisticated jokes and intellectual discussion, came a question seemingly so pointless, it may never have been asked: "Which do you think would be harder? Climbing the Infinite Spur on Sultana's south side in ski boots or skiing down the north side in climbing boots?" A vigorous debate ensued, not to be resolved at that time and place, but the seed had been planted: Someday, we hoped, we would start on the south side of an Alaska Range peak, climb a technical route, ski down the north side, and exit across the tundra.

Sam Hennessey pauses during the 10,000-vertical-foot first descent of the Northwest Buttress of Denali. The Peters Glacier is hidden by the clouds, far below. *Adam Fabrikant*

Michael Gardner astride the Infinite Spur on the south face of Sultana (Mt. Foraker). After this ski-climb-ski adventure in 2019, the author says, "We were able to identify numerous other objectives, both in Alaska and closer to home, that made perfect sense to approach in this 'skimo' style." *Sam Hennessey*

The history of the Alaska Range is rich in adventure, with epic tales of storms, survival, and the unknown. Early climbers operated without the convenience of airplanes, and even some present-day expeditions (especially on the north side of the range) still walk, ski, or float in or out of the mountains. Our discussions were driven by a desire to play a part in this history, and to quiet the nagging voices in the back of our minds that said we hadn't been approaching the range with the same creativity and adventurous spirit as those who came before us.

That year, we weren't equipped to try a traverse, and when the weather finally cleared, we instead looked for adventure on the south face of Denali (*AAJ 2019*). However, when we got home, the idea wouldn't leave my mind. Would it be possible? Should I spend the whole winter skiing at Bridger Bowl in my climbing boots and Silvretta bindings? We spent the winter dreaming of spring in Alaska.

I'd like to say that all that time made us better organized, but although Michael and I purchased light ski boots and skinny skis, and even practiced climbing with them a bit, when the time came to head for Sultana (Mt. Foraker) in early June, we were still scrambling around base camp and trying to find crampon bails that would fit our boots. Once we were fully equipped (thanks to the efforts of friends Frank Preston and Adam Fabrikant), we left camp at midnight for the Infinite Spur. Forty-eight hours later, we were back. In between was a blur of wild adventure, made even more so by snowy conditions, a weak refreeze, and our lack of research about the route.

Originally our dream had been to exit the range to the north via packraft, but thankfully we were talked out of that idea by those who know the area better than we do—rather than the blissful paddle we were hoping to find, the area north of Sultana resembles a massive swamp filled with mosquitoes and grizzly bears. Visions of walking through knee deep murky water and dragging a raft convinced us instead to opt for skiing at top speed down Sultana's moderate northeast ridge—quite a good time, but the full traverse had eluded us. It did, however, make for an excellent test of our lightweight ski gear on a proper alpine route.

The COVID interlude of 2020 meant no Denali season. This period of forced distance from Alaska did have one positive, however. With perspective, we realized that our experience on Sultana was not just a novelty—it was in certain instances the best way to approach a climb. For example, the Infinite Spur's sheer isolation often makes getting to and from the technical climbing the crux of the whole experience. In the past, teams have either done shuttles of their skis or chosen the ethically dubious route of tossing gear in a crevasse so they didn't have to retrieve it after descending the mountain far from the start of the climb. Additionally, Sultana's descent is notoriously complex and threatened by crevasse hazard—skis make it safer, faster, and way more fun.

We were able to identify numerous other objectives, both in Alaska and closer to home, that made perfect sense to approach in this "skimo" style. We'd also discovered that it really completes the experience. Rather than the descent being a tedious affair, it can be just as challenging and enjoyable as the ascent.

When Michael and I met in Talkeetna in April 2021, the sky was blue and had been for almost two weeks. Conditions were perfect, but, unfortunately, barely 48 hours remained of this historic weather window. Picking the right objective for the right conditions is an art, and one at which I frequently fail, but this time we knew exactly where to go. The Isis Face, which lies on an obscure aspect of Denali's South Buttress, was first climbed by our friend Jack Tackle and Dave Stutzman in 1982. It has received only three repeats, and no one had ventured onto the face since 2005.

In 2015, I had spent several days staring at this face, along with Willis Brown and Seth Timpano, during our first ascent of the west face of Reality Peak (AAJ 2016). From this vantage, we could study an amazing looking unclimbed line to the right of the original route. In fact, this new line had been our primary objective that trip, but the weather did not allow for such a committing route. In subsequent years, Seth and I, as well as Michael and I, had this line on the top of our list, but again—weather. A large part of its challenge lies in the convoluted descent, which is time consuming and requires good visibility to be done safely, so we figured skis would be great to have along.

By this time, we had fully figured out our kit: a standard alpine climbing rack and bivy kit, plus skimo race skis and skins (162 cm, 60 mm underfoot, and 790 grams per ski); Scarpa Alien RS boots, which at 910 grams per boot are actually lighter than double mountaineering boots; and lightweight, durable, fixed-length poles. This equipment, we found, didn't actually change our climbing ability dramatically. Aside from the added weight, which definitely slows you down a bit, we found the main challenge to be remembering we had skis on our backs—occasionally, we'd accidentally whack each other in the head at belay stations. Our feet would get wet from snow coming over the cuff of the ski boots, but in Alaska, where there's extensive sun during climbing season, we were able to manage that.

Paul Roderick of Talkeetna Air Taxi dropped us off on the West Fork of the Ruth Glacier early on the morning on April 27, under clear blue skies, remarking that we both looked pretty "Euro," which we took as a good sign. The snowpack on the glacier had developed a stout crust, a testament to the warmth of the long early season window. We took full advantage and cruised over to the base of the wall in a little over an hour. The lower route took a convoluted and serac-threatened path up a pocket glacier, giving it a classic mountaineering feel before the technical climbing began. After a couple of dicey bridge crossings, we found ourselves at the base of the

[Top] **Steep mixed ground with skis on the pack on Anubis.** [Bottom] **The Isis Face, which tops out at 15,400 feet on the South Buttress of Denali.** (1) Isis (Stutzman-Tackle, 1982. (2) Anubis (Gardner-Hennessey, 2021). *Michael Gardner (both photos)*

opening runnel, which lured us in with 60 meters of fun, mellow ice. Soon enough, though, the angle reared up, and several pitches of proper climbing ensued: sustained but never desperate, with wide stemming around overhanging ice on perfect rock holds—these pitches were of the highest quality!

The middle of the route was more moderate, and several long simul blocks of wild flutings and snow climbing, interspersed with a short mixed section, brought us to the final headwall. It was getting dark, but we thought we were nearing the original line on the Isis Face—a deep chimney led invitingly upward. As it turned out, the original line went up moderate ramps farther to the left, and Michael soon was met with several lengthy leads on steep ice. I was happy to recharge for a couple pitches, but my peaceful stargazing at the belay was frequently interrupted by Michael's curses as his skis wedged in the narrow slot. Thankfully, the difficulties eased after a couple pitches, and I took the lead once again through moderate mixed climbing, finally finding a piton that reassured us we'd joined the original route and the end was near.

The rock band eased off into steep snow, and we pulled onto flat ground at 15,400 feet and crawled into our tent to rewarm our toes. The next morning, we lay shivering under our single sleeping bag, wondering where the sun was. As it turns out, if we'd set up our tent 20 meters further south, we would have been basking in warm sunshine all morning—classic!

The ski down left a little to be desired, with lots of blue ice, rappelling, and straight-lining under seracs, as we followed the South Buttress down to Margaret Pass, and from there took a pocket glacier down to the East Fork of the Kahiltna. Everything went smoothly, though, and a little over five hours after leaving our bivouac, we were cruising up Heartbreak Hill, feeling very psyched. We called the route Anubis (2,500m, WI5 M6), after the Egyptian god of the underworld, as a complement to the original Isis.

UPON ARRIVING AT base camp, we were happy to find an assortment of friends from across the country. Two days of rest seemed like barely enough, but a vague sort of weather window seemed to be on the horizon. We decided to take a lap up the classic Bibler-Klewin route on the north buttress of Begguya (Mt. Hunter). Our goal was the summit, so we carried a tent and some extra food, to wait out the cold night of early May. Thirteen hours after crossing the bergschrund, we set up our tent on top of the buttress in somewhat miserable conditions, which thankfully eased a bit by the morning. Typically, lenticular clouds on Foraker and Denali have us rappelling at top speed, but these had been hanging over our heads for days without anything more sinister happening, so we headed up. The strong winds made for scoured surfaces and easy trail breaking, and before we knew it we were on top. A quick walk and a couple of dozen rappels later, and we were back in camp for dinner. It started snowing the next day, delaying our flights out, and I almost missed meeting my clients in town for work.

While we guided trips on the West Buttress, the weather continued to be unsettled, but after eight days at 17,000 feet, I summited with a great group. Michael topped out the next day, and, feeling sufficiently acclimatized, we both headed down. After two days of "recovery" in the Fairview Inn, we weren't feeling all that sporty, but the weather coming up looked perhaps just stable enough for a bigger challenge on Denali.

View to the northeast over Sultana and Denali. [Blue Line] Infinite Spur on (A) Sultana/Foraker, via clockwise loop from Kahiltna Base Camp (BC). [Yellow Line] First ascent of Anubis on Denali's South Buttress (B), approached from West Fork of Ruth Glacier, with descent to East Fork of the Kahiltna. [Red Line] South-to north traverse of Denali (C) via Cassin Ridge on the south face, traverse to North Peak, and first ski descent of the Northwest Buttress (D), exiting via the Peters Glacier to Wonder Lake (E). (W) marks 14 Camp on Denali's West Buttress. *Google Earth*

Scarcely 48 hours after finishing our guided trips, we were back in the range and camped at the base of the south face. But then dark clouds rolled over the ridgeline and it began to snow heavily. It quickly became clear that we were going to have a tough go of simply navigating back to base camp, let alone moving in an upward direction, and we skied blindly back to camp in what was disturbingly close to rain. This unpleasant weather kept up for the better part of a week, which allowed us to recharge with the help of generous portions of Mountain Dew and corn dogs.

AS THE WEATHER improved, we were joined by our friend Adam Fabrikant, whose partners for various ski objectives had been unable to make it. Given the snowy conditions, Michael and I had abandoned our plans for a more technical objective, and the three of us packed skis along with our climbing gear. It seemed like it might be the perfect time for our old idea of traversing the range from south to north.

As an aside, this traverse was not entirely of our own design: Many others have had similar adventures, combining routes in creative ways, which definitely influenced us. To name a few, our friend Tyler Jones completed a Cassin Ridge to Muldrow traverse on foot with Kiel Hillman in 2005. A Japanese team, supported by a film crew and reportedly wearing traditional alpine ski

Denali's North Peak from slopes above the Peters Glacier. The upper Northwest Buttress generally follows the right skyline. During their 10,000-foot descent, the skiers exited onto the far side of the ridge (arrow), then swung around the base of the buttress to descend along the Peters Glacier. *Adam Fabrikant*

boots (!!), climbed the Cassin and skied the West Rib in 2018. Peter Dale and Aaron Mainer have been quietly doing the raddest ski mountaineering in the range over the last several years, including a top-down, alpine-style ski descent of the Wickersham Wall in 2019. And finally, much like Newton and Leibniz independently inventing calculus—but far less useful—our friend Chantel Astorga decided to use a skimo technique to approach and descend from her solo attempt on the Cassin, which she soon cruised (*see story on p.50*).

Our original plan for a new traverse was to climb the Cassin on the south face to the main summit, traverse to Denali's North Peak, and ski down the Pioneer Ridge and out the Muldrow Glacier to Wonder Lake. However, the glacial surge of 2021 had rendered the Muldrow an impassable maze of crevasses. As an alternative descent, Adam suggested the Northwest Buttress of Denali's North Peak, which drops around 10,000 feet from the summit to the upper Peters Glacier near Kahiltna Pass. First climbed in 1954, this route is rarely ascended but, according to one trusted source, was "probably" skiable. Although we had only Google Earth images and one crappy photo to go off, the plan was set. Once the sky cleared and the glacier refroze, we set off as team of three. To improve our motivation to continue to the tundra, we had all of our other gear immediately flown out from base camp.

We hoped the full traverse would take less than three days, and we planned just one bivy, on the Hanging Glacier at about 14,000 feet, which would allow us to rest a bit and set us up to arrive on the North Peak in the afternoon to catch perfect light for the ski down. We did not have sleeping bags, but instead carried puffy pants, a tent, and a stove. In "fast and light" style, we brought a tent with a bug net, thinking it could literally be a life saver when we arrived on the tundra!

None of us had done the Cassin before, and it exceeded our expectations for high-quality climbing. Because Adam is not as comfortable on technical terrain, we occasionally would fix our 6mm static rope for him on the tricky sections. The leader would solo, then the second would fix the rope while the leader continued to break trail. In this way, we were able to climb at an efficient pace despite being a team of three, and despite knee- to thigh deep snow below 17,000 feet. We set the tent up twice, bivying for nine hours on the Hanging Glacier and resting for about five hours at 18,000 feet, which allowed us to stay reasonably fresh for the entire climb. Arriving at the summit 36 hours after leaving base camp, in amazing wind-less weather, we were optimistic about our chances for good conditions on the descent. The quick ski down to Denali Pass was the social part of the trip—we passed numerous teams heading up on this perfect day, and were psyched to catch our friends Colby and Eric at Denali Pass. Their stoke for our adventure recharged our batteries, and we slogged up to the North Peak in about three hours. It was so calm on top that Michael and I took off our boots to dry our feet.

Around 6 p.m., we started down the Northwest Buttress. The skiing began as ice and sastrugi, but soon the snow began to get deeper, and it's hard to imagine having better conditions. Good visibility much of

Nearing Wonder Lake, with the north face of Denali a long, long way in the distance. *Sam Hennessey*

the way made the route-finding easier than expected, and we were able to ski continuously for most of the ridge. It felt very exciting to descend farther and farther into unknown, especially when a convection cloud and white-out conditions coincided with the trickiest skiing on the route, with thin coverage over blue ice that forced us to transition to crampons several times. We arrived on the Peters Glacier elated—the roughly 10,000-foot descent had taken only around five hours. Now, it was time to switch gears again and make tracks for Wonder Lake, more than 30 miles away.

The trip down the Peters was indescribably beautiful. In around 15 hours, we skied, walked, and waded our way from high alpine terrain to a dry glacier and finally through piles of morainal rubble to gain the seemingly endless tundra. A decade of staring at green grass dotted with countless lakes from up high on Denali had filled me with a romantic notion of what it would be like to experience this landscape, and although the blazing sun, swampy ground, and relentless mosquitoes quickly brought me back to reality, the experience was everything I could have hoped for. Sixty-four hours after leaving base camp, most of it spent awake, we arrived at the road just minutes before the last shuttle bus of the day departed. We were all spent, but I felt completely content. We had completed our objective in our preferred style, together as a team. Although nothing can compare to the early days of adventure in Alaska Range, I fell asleep confident that we were giving it our best shot.

The ski alpinism we've done on Sultana and Denali, along with many other people's trips, like those mentioned above, make me think that the future of mountaineering in the Alaska Range is bright. By combining skills in different disciplines, future adventure-seekers will find ever more creative ways to experience this special range. The only limits are our imaginations.

SUMMARY: First ascent of Anubis (2,500m, WI5 M6) on the Isis Face of Denali's South Buttress, by Michael Gardner and Sam Hennessey, April 27–28, 2021. North-to-south traverse of Denali, combining the Cassin Ridge and the first ski descent of the Northwest Ridge (North Peak to the Peters Glacier), with an exit to Wonder Lake, by Gardner, Hennessey, and Adam Fabrikant, June 12–14, 2021. The traverse covered a horizontal distance of approximately 50 miles.

ABOUT THE AUTHOR: *Sam Hennessey is a mountain guide living in Bozeman, Montana.*

FIVE YEARS ON THE CASSIN

TWO FIRSTS ON DENALI'S SOUTH SIDE

CHANTEL ASTORGA

On the 14th of June, I made the first ski descent of the Seattle Ramp variation to the West Rib of Denali, followed by the first female solo ascent of the Cassin Ridge, completing a longtime dream and a culmination of all the things I love about moving through the mountains: climbing a technical route alone, swiftly, in alpine style, using skis to approach and descend.

This wasn't my first climb of Denali, of course—I have a long history with the mountain. I first set foot on Denali in 2005 at the age of 19, when I summited by the West Buttress route and skied back down via the Rescue Gully. Four years later, I began guiding the West Buttress for the American Alpine Institute, and I did that for a few years. In the breaks between guiding trips, I went back up on the mountain and started ticking off ski lines that interested me.

In 2015, I started climbing difficult routes on Denali. I had climbed other challenging routes in the range—like the Colton-Leach and the second ascent (and first free ascent) of Polarchrome, both on Mt. Huntington, with Jewell Lund in 2014—but the first route I climbed on Denali, other than those in the West Buttress area, was the Denali Diamond on the southwest face, also with Jewell Lund, in 2015. This was the first time an Alaska Grade 6 route had been completed by a team of women.

Any time you climb a difficult route, the experience allows you to dream a little bit bigger. As someone who follows climbing history, I knew the Cassin Ridge had seen a number of impressive solo ascents. And that was something I was inspired to try. But what really excited me was the idea of adding skiing to the mix in an uncontrived way. In a way that made sense even. My vision was to ski down the West Rib, skin over to the base of the Cassin Ridge, free solo the route in a day with a light pack, and then ski down the Messner Couloir to return to the 14,000-foot camp on the West Buttress. My intent wasn't to set a speed record; I simply wanted to take the climbing and ski mountaineering skill sets I'd built over the years and combine them in the big mountains. The Cassin seemed like the perfect choice for an ascent/descent of this style.

In 2016 I flew into the Alaska Range with my eye on the Cassin, equipped with skimo-style skis and boots. I was quite fearful of approaching the base of the route solo, and I didn't

The author climbs toward Denali's summit, completing her ascent of the Cassin Ridge. *Zack Novak*

On the Denali Diamond in 2015, the first route up the southwest face climbed by women. Three years later, the author and Anne Gilbert Chase climbed the Slovak Direct on the south face. *Jewell Lund*

think much about the actual climbing. Heavy snowfall and strong winds had me tent-bound for most of the trip, and I had a lot of alone time to talk myself out of what I was there to do. I wasn't convinced I was fit or mentally prepared enough to climb in the style I was interested in. I also made the mistake of taking a super-light kit—small tent, no books, and mostly freeze-dried food—during my few weeks of acclimatization. This didn't help keep the spirits high. I ended up bailing before I had a chance to make an attempt. But I felt motivated to come back more prepared and try again.

Over the following years, a solo of the Cassin was always in the back of my mind, and I refined my ski kit for the project. I tried multiple race skis in an attempt to find a ski that was extremely light but skied well, and I went through the same process with skimo race boots. Each year I prepared to "maybe" climb the Cassin, but I also made other plans in the Alaska Range with climbing partners—if I felt motivated after completing that part of my trip, then I'd fly back in to try the Cassin. For example, in 2017, Anne Gilbert Chase and I attempted the Slovak Direct on the south face of Denali and got stormed off 4,000 feet up the route. In 2018 we went back and completed the Slovak Direct—another first ascent for an all-female team. In general, I came back from those trips feeling contented and tired, and didn't feel the need to go back in and continue to push hard. So, the Cassin had to wait.

Finally, in the fall of 2020, I got serious about climbing the Cassin and laid plans for the 2021 spring season. Beforehand, I planned to try a route on the North Buttress of Mt. Hunter with Anne Gilbert. I knew that if I wanted to climb both routes in the same season, I needed to increase my fitness so I could recover quickly from the first climb and still have the psych to go up on Denali and acclimatize. I live in Lowman, Idaho, which has great access to skiing and ski mountaineering, but very few winter climbing options. So I hired a local climbing coach who helped me discover creativity on my home wall, which I had built years ago but had rarely been motivated enough to use. I learned how to stay strong for climbing with very little time investment. I also hired a friend who coaches endurance athletes (and is a ski mountaineer himself) to help me with endurance. I'm an extremely motivated person, but I can also be lazy and inconsistent with training. I felt the need for accountability.

In May I flew into the Alaska Range with Anne Gilbert for three weeks. We attempted two routes on Hunter. However, we had mostly stormy weather, short windows, and often very warm temperatures. At the end of our trip, I flew out of the range for a few days to recover and then flew back in with a month of food and began the arduous process of carrying loads up the West Buttress.

Strong, cold winds persisted on the upper mountain, and the ski conditions never improved above 16,000 feet during my time there. At one point during an acclimatization run, I climbed up the Rescue Gully above 14K Camp, and clouds and wind moved in during my ski descent. I lost visibility and sight of my track, and found myself exactly where I didn't want to be: on skis in a vast patch of blue ice. I had a mountaineering axe in my hand, and I swung hard to try and penetrate the ice, without success. I carefully balanced and removed my pack so I could grab my technical ice tool, anchor myself to the ice, and switch from skis to crampons one boot at a time. (When I got off the headwall, I came across a Frenchman who had watched the maneuver and called it a French transition—a term that was new to me.) My goal had been to touch the summit ridge twice before attempting the Cassin, but I only made it up there once.

The biggest challenge was keeping my psych high. I had a lot of time alone in my tent to convince myself that what I was doing was pointless and even stupid. But somehow I managed to make myself believe that, if I was patient, I would pull it off. Finally, a two-day weather window was forecasted to begin on June 13. Some friends had just climbed the Cassin and broke trail through deep snow, which I knew would be advantageous. Everything was lining up as I'd hoped.

There are basically four approaches to the Cassin Ridge. Historically, the Northeast Fork of the Kahiltna Glacier (a.k.a. the Valley of Death) was the most commonly used approach, as it takes you from low on the mountain directly to the base of the route at 12,000 feet, but it has an immense amount of overhead hazards and many large crevasses. The East Fork of the Kahiltna, leading to Kahiltna Notch, is a long and relatively nice walk, but it is a heavily crevassed glacier. The other two approach options begin from the 14K Camp (where most people acclimatize anyway) and ascend to 16,500 feet on the West Rib route. From there you can descend the entirety of the West Rib to approximately 11,500 feet in the Valley of Death and walk a mile on the glacier to the base of the Cassin Ridge, or you can take the Seattle Ramp, which exits the West Rib at approximately 15,000 feet and leads directly to the base of the southwest face and the Cassin.

I had a lot of time alone in my tent to convince myself that what I was doing was pointless and even stupid. But somehow I managed to make myself believe that, if I was patient, I would pull it off.

Although I had descended the Seattle Ramp in 2015 en route to the Denali Diamond, it never really crossed my mind to ski it. I had mostly settled on skiing down the West Rib, but was still nervous about then having to walk a mile up the Northeast Fork of the Kahiltna alone. The Seattle Ramp is essentially an icefall, and though it is heavily crevassed and has overhead serac hazards threatening part of the descent, it is not nearly as crevassed as the other approach options. As my friend Colin Haley put it, "You can pick an option that has hundreds of crevasses or one that has less," and while I wasn't totally convinced, the Seattle Ramp did seem like the best choice.

Generally people approach the Cassin at night—with colder temps come safer conditions. I chose to leave late in the morning in hope of finding better skiing conditions in the warmth of the day than at night, when the snow surface would freeze into a breakable crust. I went to bed at 14K Camp in the evening of June 12 and slept through the night. The weather window was hold-

Astorga (the tiny dot in lower left) cruises toward the Japanese Couloir, start of the Cassin Ridge route, after descending the Seattle Ramp. *Vitaliy Musiyenko*

ing, and everything felt right. I never again questioned what I was doing.

I left 14,000 Camp at 11 a.m. and skinned and cramponed up the cutoff to reach the West Rib. From there I transitioned to skis and slowly started working my way down. Conditions were challenging, but after 1,000 feet, the slope angle eased up and I was able to open it up a bit more with my skimo setup. I ended up taking a pair of Atomic Backland Ultralight skis that were 78mm underfoot but only 149cm long—in other words, children's skis. I wanted them to be super short for climbing on the Cassin. I wore Atomic Backland Ultimate skimo boots, which ski quite poorly in funky conditions, but they were acceptable. I was concerned about keeping my feet warm enough during the climb in skimo boots that didn't have good gaiters, but I brought an extra pair of socks and took my chances.

A couple of hours after leaving camp, I made it to the Seattle Ramp. Suddenly, everything began to feel much more serious. I could feel my focus narrowing. Clouds moved in, I lost visibility, and it got quite warm. I couldn't decide if I was pleased by this or freaked out. I slowly made my way down in mostly good ski conditions, straight-lining over icy crevasses that fell deep into the dark abyss. I carried about 25m of 6mm rope specifically for rappelling over the big bergschrund at the bottom of the Seattle Ramp, but when I got there I realized my rope was way too short. I transitioned to crampons and downclimbed and traversed skier's left to look for a safe passage. Eventually, I found a feature I was able to downclimb to pass the 'schrund. I put my skis back on, traversed back skier's right, and navigated down through big crevasses. Needless to say, I was quite scared. But at this point I just tried to ignore my fears and tricked myself into keeping a cool and level-headed mindset.

After exiting the Seattle Ramp, I traversed the southwest basin through big piles of debris from the hanging seracs 5,000 feet above. With the last of the debris piles finally behind me, I felt a huge wave of relief. I looked up and saw a bald eagle—something I'd never seen so high in the Alaska Range—thermaling not far above me. I couldn't believe where I was, and I had an indescribable feeling of peacefulness. I skied powder down to a serac feature where I could drop into a shallow, protected nook to rest until it was cold enough to start climbing. The part of the journey that had concerned me the most was done, and now all I had to do was climb the Cassin, which, by comparison, sounded like fun.

In my pack I carried a small Reactor stove, a small gas canister, an extra pair of socks, a warm coat, a few pairs of gloves, 1.5 liters of water, and not enough food. I put on my jacket, burrowed into the tiny quilt sleeping bag and small bivy tarp I had brought specifically for resting at the base of the route, and settled in. I figured I'd get too cold at about midnight and I'd start to climb, but I comfortably slept through my alarm and woke up at about 4:30 the next morning. I drank coffee, ate a packet of oatmeal and a bar, and set off. I hit the bergschrund at the base of the Cassin at 5:30 a.m. and while I wasn't there to set a record, I set the timer on my watch, as I was curious how long it would take me.

I had been on the nontechnical terrain above 17,000 feet on the Cassin twice before, while finishing other routes, but I had never climbed any of the technical terrain on the lower Cassin, so I was, in effect, onsighting. I had hoped the Japanese Couloir would be covered in snow to make travel quicker, but it was mostly moderate ice climbing with some steeper water-ice steps. I moved through the Japanese Couloir quickly and got to what is supposed to be the crux of the route—a wide chimney-like feature—by Cassin Ledge. I had positioned my skis verti-

Selfie in the Japanese Couloir. The author skied onto the Seattle Ramp near the center of the big slope behind, then hugged the rock wall at far right. *Chantel Astorga*

cally on the center of the back of my pack, and never had any problems with them getting in the way. Once I got to the Hanging Glacier near 14,000 feet, I was happy to see there was still a track—waist deep in places—and I wouldn't have to do any deep trail-breaking. I continued through the first and second rock bands with some route-finding, as the previous parties' tracks had been blown clean at these elevations. Some of the short steps in these rock bands felt more difficult than any of the climbing on the lower route, but overall the climbing was very enjoyable.

When I reached 17,000 feet, I stopped to brew up some water and change my socks. Already bonking a bit, I ate my last bar and started the long hike to the top of Denali, knowing that I might suffer, given my shortage of food. It was easy trail-breaking, but still I had moments where I had to put my head down and mentally dig deep. I reached the summit just after 8 p.m., after spending 14:39 on the Cassin. It was a very quiet evening, and the only person up there was Zack Novak—a friend, but one I didn't know well. He gave me a hug and I started to cry in his arms. I was pretty tired, physically and mentally, but I was thrilled I had pulled it off. Zack made me a cup of tea and then skied off into the evening light.

The conditions on the upper mountain were too icy to consider skiing the Messner Couloir, but even had they been better, I'm not sure I would have tried. A mellow descent felt about right at that point. So I made my way down the West Buttress (a place I've skied many times), skiing or downclimbing as needed. I finally made it back to 14K Camp around 11 p.m., just in time for quesadillas prepared by wonderful friends I'd met during my time on Denali earlier in the season.

I honestly don't remember much about the climb. I felt like I was in a dream state throughout most of the day. The memories vanished the moment they were made. This has often been the case with my most meaningful climbing experiences—there are very few memories, just a sensation.

SUMMARY: First known ski descent of the Seattle Ramp (Bertulis, Wickwire, et al, 1972) on the lower southwest face of Denali, followed by a solo ascent of the Cassin Ridge, by Chantel Astorga, June 13–14, 2021. After a bivouac near the base of the Cassin, Astorga climbed the route in 14 hours 39 minutes to the 20,310-foot summit, the first female solo of the Cassin (and, incidentally, the women's speed record). Astorga spoke about this adventure on episode 44 of the Cutting Edge podcast.

ABOUT THE AUTHOR: *Born in 1985, Chantel Astorga lives in central Idaho and works as a highway avalanche forecaster for the Idaho Transportation Department.*

THE 10X PROJECT

EXPLORING THE INTERSECTION OF SKIING
AND MOUNTAINEERING IN THE ALPS

PAUL BONHOMME

The 4th of May, 6 o'clock in the morning. The halo of my headlamp guides me through the mixed pine and mélèzes forest on the slopes of Le Pouzenc in the south of France. I'm feeling fine, the air is cold, and I'm thinking about my project for today: a wild, steep, and magnetic face that I first saw in a picture a friend took a few years ago. The goal is to try to make the first ski descent.

I had already parked below Le Pouzenc twice this winter to have a look at the face through binoculars, but the conditions were not good. At the moment, I still have many doubts. Will there be enough snow ? And what will it look like? Or will there be too much new snow? Yesterday I saw a lot of fresh snow in the Massif des Écrins, farther north, and I'm worried about the avalanche hazard. But Le Pouzenc is a lot lower than the Écrins and this line faces southwest, and today it is cold enough for stability. I take some deep breaths to smell the spring forest's perfume. As usual, my doubts fade, leaving only one thought. I'm in the mountains I love, and no matter what happens, at least I will spend a wonderful day in the wilderness.

· AUTUMN ·

AUTUMN 2020, AT home in Cercier, about halfway between Lake Geneva and Lake Annecy at the foot of the Alps. We're in our second shutdown for the COVID pandemic. For one month, we are stuck in our homes, unable to travel beyond a 10-kilometer perimeter. But soon there will be a bit more flexibility, and, as often, my mind has been turning over the possibilities for the coming winter.

I'm always researching faces that might not have seen a previous ski descent—studying published reports, calling local skiers who know the history of their mountains—and I already had a few new lines in mind. One morning, I woke up with an idea for a grand adventure not far from home: I would try to open ten new lines of steep skiing throughout the Western Alps. Some very good French skiers had recently made similar achievements: Hervé Degonon had done more than 30 first descents a few seasons earlier (2016–17), but all of them were in the same range, the Massif des Écrins. Nicolas Jean had a huge season in the spring of 2018, also mostly in the Écrins.

I wanted to try something a little different: I would attempt new lines in many different ranges in Italy, Switzerland, and France. I also had a few self-imposed rules. I would climb and ski from summits and not just from shoulders or ridges; each line had to be at least 500 meters high; and I would not use any mechanical assistance on the mountain: neither cable cars nor snow machines nor helicopters. All the slopes would be reached by skiing and mountaineering.

The goal with all these requirements was to create a real adventure, which would demand a lot of research and preparation. Most of the obvious, logical lines in the Alps have been skied. Potential new lines may be very beautiful, but they aren't as obvious and you have to have more mountaineering knowledge. The weather, the avalanche risk, the date, the orientation of the slopes, the winds—all would be crucial to success. Over 80 percent of the time on this project would be spent looking at maps, at weather forecasts, at avalanche data—and, obviously, training hard.

· JANUARY ·

THE PROJECT STARTED on January 5, 2021, with a new line in the Aravis Range in Haute-Savoie, only about an hour's drive from my home. Le Jardin Suspendu was on the east face of the 2,362-meter summit of Pointes de la Blonnière. This is a 650-meter slope with a lot of difficult and quite hazardous traverses. I made the climb and descent with my friend Vivian Bruchez, after observing the slope a few days before.

Vivian also joined me for the tenth and final descent of the project, nearly five months later, on the southwest face of Täschhorn (4,491 meters), not far from Zermatt in the Pennine Alps of Switzerland. I called this descent "X," like the number 10 and like the unknown in a mathematical equation. It was a 950-meter descent, very technical, that began on the east face and ended on the southwest face, passing through gullies and over very steep hanging slopes. Leaving our tent

[Opposite] **The 950-meter line of X, final route of the project, on the southwest face of Täschhorn (4,491m) in Switzerland's Pennine Alps.** *Thomas Crauwels* [Right] **Vivian Bruchez and Paul Bonhomme glass the east face of Combin de la Tsessette.** *Christophe Angot | Linka*

though I had a list of objectives at the beginning of the project, it was the mountains that convinced me where to go. It was like, "Hey, I have a day free next week, let's look at the options." I'd check the weather forecast in France, Italy, and Switzerland, look at the avalanche bulletins, check social media to see what people had done recently, and only then start looking at lines that might be safe to ski and would meet my objectives. I felt like a prospector for gold.

In this way, the 10X Project was simply a way of evolving and learning in the mountains. Steep skiing is one of the best paths for this evolution because I believe there is no way to find steeper slopes than those that have already been skied. Therefore, in my opinion, it isn't possible or fruitful to compete, to argue about being a "better" steep skier than anyone else. To me, the only games that are still meaningful are about creativity and imagination, not about competition or difficulty. In fact, none of the lines we skied had the maximum grade for steep skiing (5.5/E4), nor were any of them particularly dangerous, at least with the conditions I found (or patiently waited to find). The way I thought about this project was more about exploration than difficulty.

I became a mountain guide not because I grew up in the mountains, nor with parents who were great alpinists. My education came in the cow pastures, with the smell of flowers and the sap from the pine trees—first walking gently through the forest, then climbing a little bit, then running and skiing. In fact, I would say I am not an alpinist at all—more a mountaineer. When I discovered the world of alpinism almost 40 years ago, I read a lot about heroism and conquest, and my first impressions of "alpinism" were of fear, as if the climbers were going to war, risking their lives (and sometimes losing them) because of their desire to conquer a summit. In my way of thinking, the mountaineer's primary goal is simply to be in the mountains.

I'm convinced the times of going to the mountains for personal glory have passed. We have to find other goals; we have to tell other stories than those about heroism, courage, and facing death. The 10X

[Top to bottom] North face of Le Chaperon; west face of Le Fouzenc, southwest face of Bietschhorn. *Emmanuel Abele, Jean-Pat Comba, Thomas Crauwell (from top)*

Project was a real commitment, but by that I don't mean a committing day or a committing style of skiing. This project was a way to illuminate what seems most important to seek up there—curiosity, imagination, respect, balance with nature, patience, renunciation—and what you can bring back home.

· MAY ·

MAY 4, 11 a.m. I pause to remove my skis and look back at the face on Le Pouzenc that I've just descended. As expected, it was very technical. The ascent took a long time. The lower rocky outcrop was really tricky, with an amazing traverse under an overhanging limestone band, an icefall, and a 30-meter mixed climb. After that, I had to cross the whole face from right to left, through many gullies, always looking for the best way to come back down. The crux of the descent was around 100 meters below the summit, an icy and very exposed traverse before a 15-meter dry-skiing section. As it was a traverse, abseiling wasn't possible.

Now, at the bottom, I'm feeling satisfied. Not with a feeling of glory ("Wow, I'm the first to do this!"), but more like, "Hey, that was really a wonderful journey." I strap my skis onto my pack and gently make my way back down through the pines, completely alone, deeply breathing the joy of wilderness.

ABOUT THE AUTHOR: *Born in 1975, Paul Bonhomme is a Dutch native living in Cercier, France. Married and with four children, he works as a mountain guide. Bonhomme and his skiing partners produced compelling videos of the descents described in this article. You'll find some of these at the AAJ website.*

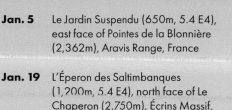

THE 10X DESCENTS

Jan. 5 — Le Jardin Suspendu (650m, 5.4 E4), east face of Pointes de la Blonnière (2,362m), Aravis Range, France

Jan. 19 — L'Éperon des Saltimbanques (1,200m, 5.4 E4), north face of Le Chaperon (2,750m), Écrins Massif, France

Jan. 26 — Il Segreto di Maïra (1,100m, 5.3 E3), east face of Rocca Bianca di Acceglio (2,950m), Alpi Cozie (Cottian Alps), Italy

Feb. 21 — Les Larmes d'Ulysse (500m, 5.2 E3), Mont Pélago (2,768m), Alpes-Maritimes (Maritimes Alps), France

Mar. 6 — La Cathédrale (1,600m, 5.3 E4), east face of Rochers du Rochail (2,853m), Écrins Massif, France

Mar. 10 — La Testa Tra le Stelle (1,100m, 5.3 E3), southeast face of Tête Carrée (3,732m), Monte Bianco (Mont Blanc) Massif, Italy

Apr. 1 — Les Piliers de Bagne (1,200m, 5.4 E4), east face of Combin de la Tsessette (4,141m), Grand Combin Massif, Pennine Alps, Switzerland

May 4 — La Traversée des Anges (600m, 5.4 E4), west face of Le Pouzenc (2,898m), Embrunais, France

May 9 — Merci Mumuns (900m, 5.4 E4), southwest face of Bietschhorn (3,934m), Berner Oberland, Switzerland

May 28 — X (950m, 5.4 E4), southwest face of Täschhorn (4,491m), Pennine Alps, Switzerland

A NOTE ABOUT SKI GRADES: The descents in this chart are graded for difficulty and exposure using the Toponeige system (a.k.a. Volo scale, named for skier Volodia Shahshahani, who developed it), which is in wide use in the Alps. The first grade covers skiing difficulty and ranges from 1 to 5, with the 5th grade currently subdivided into five levels, from 5.1 to 5.5. The second grade ranges from E1 to E4 and describes the exposure or fall hazard. A fall on E3 or E4 terrain is considered likely or certain to result in fatal injuries.

CHOOSE LAUGHTER

A WELL-TIMED ASCENT OF THE NORTH FACE OF DANSAM WEST

MARTÍN ELÍAS

We have been sitting in a cab for more than 12 hours, and we still have another 12 to go before we reach Islamabad. It's been three hours since darkness fell, hiding from view the gaping abyss to the side of the road. On the dash is a sticker that reads *Inshallah*— "God willing." The clock below the sticker reads 11 p.m. Our driver is showing signs of fatigue. He rubs his eyes incessantly, and his head drops forward in a weightless way. I try to put on my seatbelt, but there is no seatbelt. It has been removed, presumably to make something more useful. Jérôme must notice the driver's state of exhaustion too, because he also reaches for his seatbelt—also gone. With tenderness, I touch Jérôme's leg and tell him: "*Mon chéri*, we are about to endure the most dangerous moment of our Pakistani adventure." And yet the climb is already behind us. It's been four blurry days since we crested the West Summit of Dansam. We can barely stay awake, but we're far too scared to fall asleep.

LET ME GO back to the beginning.

Jeremy Stagnetto on day one of the six-day climb. *Martín Elías*

[Top] **Loading up for the journey from Skardu to Khor Kondus.** *Jérôme Sullivan* [Bottom] **Looking south from base camp toward snowy Dansam East and the huge rocky monoliths hiding the main and west peaks.** *Victor Saucède*

IT'S FEBRUARY 2021. The middle of the COVID crisis. Political hostilities between France and Pakistan are at a peak. Our work as mountain guides has slowed to a trickle, our income reduced by 60 percent. It is precisely at this moment, in the heart of global chaos, that my phone rings.

Jérôme Sullivan, a dear friend with whom I have shared unfathomable quantities of *vino tinto* and *mate* in the wilds of Argentine Patagonia, encourages me to open my email and look at a photo he has sent. It shows the upper third of a mountain. The shot is taken from so far away that it is impossible to zoom in without transforming the features of the peak into a meaningless jumble of boxy pixels. These kinds of vague photos are my favorite because they leave so much to the imagination. Jérôme knows this about me, and I suspect the low-res image is an intentional maneuver.

The photo was taken by American alpinist Steve Swenson, from the top of Link Sar, looking toward 6,666-meter Dansam—a.k.a. K13—a mountain believed to have never been climbed. The image shows the northern aspect of the Dansam massif, which is comprised of three summits: the highest central one and two others to the west and east, only 50 or so meters lower. The massif has been closed to tourism since the 1980s due to the war between Pakistan and India—the highest war in the world, at 5,000-plus meters—which takes place on the Siachen Glacier, only a few kilometers to the northeast from the Dansam peaks.

Many climbing teams have unsuccessfully applied for a permit to attempt Dansam. But during the last couple of years of ceasefire, the Kondus Valley, of which the Dansam group forms the southernmost rim, has been opened to foreign expeditions, and we manage to get the coveted permit. I am the last to join the team—Jérôme having already recruited Victor Saucède and Jeremy Stagnetto. Never in history, since my favorite Argentinian band, The Luthiers, got together, has such a team existed! As the famous French alpinist Yannick Seigneur, said, "You should always have a Pyrenean on your team." We will have two.

After scrambling to fulfill vaccine requirements, taking and failing multiple COVID tests, two flight cancelations, and long weeks of battling with airlines, we manage to take off from Paris on May 28. Two days later, under the blazing sun of Skardu and with the chant of the *muezzin* accompanying our preparations, we excitedly pack the yellow Hushe village bus to the brim and set out for the wild mountains of the Kondus Valley.

The view during an acclimatization climb above base camp, looking toward Dansam East's north face, lined with massive seracs. Dansam West is off-photo to the right. *Jeremy Stagnetto*

It's Victor's first time in Pakistan, and by the time we reach the village of Khor Kondus at the end of a long dusty road, the window is all greased up from having his face squashed against it, trying to glimpse the tops of the towering rock monoliths. As we drive past the first houses, at dusk, the inhabitants are waiting for us. They are excited to see visitors, as it has been many years since foreigners have come to their village. It is a sign that times are changing—and tourism is a good source of income. First the children come to meet us, running behind the vehicle, snotty-nosed and muddy, screaming wildly the few words of English they know. As we set up camp, curious adults come to see who we are. We are delighted and share gestures, smiles, and hugs. Very soon we are surrounded by half of the village. Everyone laughs and gesticulates, telling us stories in Balti we do not understand. But it doesn't matter—communication is somehow fluid, no matter the language differences.

Among those who welcome us that evening are the porters who will help carry our gear to base camp, just four hours above Khor Kondus, located at around 4,000 meters at a place called Minguli by the locals. It is a summer grazing area for the yaks, and its sparsely grassed pastures are a luxury compared with the arid and rocky surroundings.

Once base camp is installed, we begin to explore further up the valley. Finally, the awaited moment arrives, and we begin to put a tangible form to the imaginary world we had created from Steve's photograph. Our mountain of vapor morphs into cold brute mineral. For hours we've talked strategy, looked at maps and satellite images, conversed on the phone about our hopes and beliefs concerning the rock quality, the steepness. Now, below the formidable barrier and its three summits, we are ecstatic. Fractured hanging glaciers of a dark, healthy blue are split by massive pillars of granite. Paper-thin ridgelines are crowned with precarious snow mushrooms hanging dangerously over the edge. We watch in awe as falling ice triggers a massive avalanche, shaking the narrow valley and filling it with a cloud of snow and our souls with fear and excitement.

The main summit, our initial objective, seems too exposed to falling ice, so we decide to climb the pillar that leads directly to the western summit. [*See p.273 for a report about an attempt on the main summit later in the summer of 2021.*] A compact, north-facing granite prow, 1,600 meters high, scarred with a bone-white ice smear that dead-ends in a steep headwall. It is the line of my dreams: a logical route in the middle of a seemingly impossible wall.

We return to base camp only to be pinned down for ten days by multiple storms. The only possibilities for acclimatization have been placing a simple advanced base camp at the foot of our planned route and spending a night there, at 5,000 meters, along with short forays up snow gullies near camp, also to about 5,000 meters.

The long wait is difficult to bear, as our time is running thin. The thought of leaving without even attempting this masterpiece of alpinism is depressing, but there is reason for optimism. The 24th of June will bring a full moon. The farmers in my Spanish homeland of La Rioja often associate the change of the moon with a change in the weather regime, and sure enough, our weather forecaster's latest update seems to confirm the age-old wisdom. The team members quite like this Spanish remedy, and they joke that we should combine this lunar event with sacrifices to the yak god. On the 24th, with faith that our strategy will pay off, we depart from base camp in a flurry of snowflakes.

In the morning, we leave advanced base for what will be a six-day round trip. After climbing 400 meters of zigzagging snow ramps and wading through terrible and inconsistent snow, we finally set up camp on a snow rib dubbed "les pentes à Djamel," Djamel being Jeremy's nickname. Here, we wait out the snowstorm for the next 24 hours—it seems the yak gods did not believe in our intentions for sacrifices. Our line of ascent is a gully, and it channels the falling snow. Although our tent is not directly exposed, the snow aerosolized by the frequent avalanches shakes it violently.

On the 27th, we climb the central gully system under heavy spindrift. The ice quality is great. Between shouts of "Spindrift!" and "Hoods on!" we make good progress. Some pitches are quite steep and physical, and others more moderate and harder on the calves. The ice gully leads us to another snow rib we call "le Linceul" ("the Shroud"). We arrive quite late in the night and dig out a poor bivy site. The night is short, and at first light we are awake and ready for a big day.

Here we face the biggest question mark of our line: Above, 400 meters of abrupt compact rock guard the summit slopes. We make

The line of Harvest Moon on the north face of Dansam West (6,600m). The climbers descended approximately the same way. *Jérôme Sullivan*

Victor Saucède leads a steep, improbable, and short-lived ice smear at nearly 6,000 meters. *Jérôme Sullivan*

slow but unrelenting progress, discovering ephemeral ice smears on every pitch. Blots of ice allow us to keep a good pace in otherwise unclimbable terrain. Victor leads the most memorable pitch— an improbable ice smear pasted on an overhanging dihedral. We declare that, sadly, at only 26 years old, Victor has nothing left to look forward to, having just climbed what could be the best pitch of his life! We can thank the bad weather of the past weeks for the ice that has formed. As we will soon discover while descending the route, these good ice conditions are quite short-lived.

As night comes, we find a campsite on a ridge at around 6,000 meters. The main difficulties are behind us, and we crash into our sleeping bags. We have high hopes of reaching the summit the next day.

On the 29th we wake early to a starry night. Fatigue is showing, and it is difficult to get started. We leave our tents and depart for the summit. Behind us, far to the north, sunlit K2 drips pale golden light upon the blue canvas of the horizon. Our progress is slow. We had supposed the lower-angle terrain would be more easily overcome, but the bullet-hard ice hidden beneath 10 centimeters of powder snow is sketchy and time-consuming. We repeatedly build anchors, pitching out the 60-degree slope, and it takes a good part of the day to approach the summit.

The closer we get, the heavier our breathing becomes. I am leading up the summit pyramid when I am hit with an unexpected surprise. I blink my eyes and shake my head. A fixed rope in tatters runs down from the rocky pinnacle, shredded by the winds and time. A mixture of confusing thoughts runs through my head. I am stuck between laughter and frustration. This summit was supposed to be unclimbed! Error 404! Hypoxia and fatigue do not help with my confusion. Finally, I choose laughter, and with a smile I turn to my companions and tell them to hurry up.

Gathered at the foot of the small tower that separates us from the summit, we stare at the remains of what we later learn to be the Japanese expedition of 1981, which reached the summit of Dansam West by climbing the long western ridge. We joke about our situation: We are like dogs pissing on a lamp post, always wanting to be the first. And yet, we are satisfied with our

DANSAM WEST: THE FIRST ASCENT

JAPANESE STUDENTS CLIMBED THE WEST RIDGE IN 1981

BY KATSUSHIGE KOTERA *AND* SATOSHI NAGATA

IN 1981, MEMBERS of the Kindai University Alpine Club made the first ascent of Dansam West (6,450m). Our team was 14 undergraduates plus a doctor and senior observer. In that era, a captain from the Pakistan Army also had to join us.

Forty years ago, we had to hike six days up the Kondus Valley with 45 porters to reach the village of Chogoglong (Chogron, just east of Kondus village). Due to our tight budget and the weak Japanese yen, each student carried 30kg, which was more than the porters' loads. In high temperatures like we had never experienced in Japan, it was exhausting. Our porters kindly offered to carry more weight.

Three valleys extend toward Dansam from the north, and we chose the westernmost. Nowadays you can study mountains on Google Earth, but we had merely a rough map showing the largest rivers and mountain ridges. We made base camp at the tip of the glacial tongue on July 25. After overcoming a small icefall and climbing to the top of the ridge that divided our valley from the central valley, we had our first sight of beautiful Dansam on August 2. The great pillar that we called the "Elephant's Nose," climbed by the French team in 2021, looked magnificent but beyond our ability, so we would like to express our sincere respect for their route Harvest Moon.

[Top] The 1981 route up the north face and west ridge of Dansam West. [Bottom] Katsuhige Kotera dancing in the sun near the top; compare with photo on next page. *Expedition Photos*

We placed Camp 3 on the glacier in the central valley, and on August 3 we started to climb the right side of the north face, leading toward the main west ridge of Dansam. A slightly bulging snow ridge invited us with a comfortable double-axe climb. It started snowing on August 9, after showing us clear ultramarine sky for several days. We fixed ropes on the some of steeper slopes, but not all; I deeply regret that we left some of these when we descended.

On August 11 our first group reached the west ridge at 5,900m. The long ridge above was like winter climbing in the Japanese Alps—where we sometimes receive a couple of meters of snow overnight—except for the diluted oxygen level and doubled mountain size. In all, we placed six camps above base camp, the highest at 6,220m. On August 18, in a white-out, the first group believed they were going to make the summit. As the first climber reached the top, the sky opened up and he shouted, "There is another summit over there!" He was pointing to the main summit of Dansam (6,666m). On August 19, a second group reached the west peak. With not enough food or time, we had to give up plans to attempt the main summit—it was too far, even though it was right there in plain sight.

The members of the first team on Dansam West were Yoshimitsu Harada, Toshiyoshi Izumi, Satoshi Nagata, Masayoshi Otani, and Norio Yasui. The second team comprised Osamu Amagata, Fuminori Fujita, Kozo Ishigami (leader), Katsushige Kotera, Hideki Kubo, Etsuhide Nakase, Satoshi Okano, and Sachio Tochima. In base camp were Masahiro Horiuchi, Hitoshi Iida (doctor), and Katsuhisa Ota (senior observer).

climb. The yak gods have granted us good weather, and we've climbed an amazing line. To the east, the main summit looks temptingly in reach, via a snowy ridgeline, paper thin and fragile. But with all our bivy gear below and bad weather coming, reason calls us back.

The great Karakoram surrounds us, and striking Saltoro Kangri, 7,742 meters high, rises to the north, beckoning us to return to the Kondus Valley. Yet for now it is forbidden due to the damned war. I start humming John Lennon's tune "Imagine" as we turn our backs to the easy descent on Dansam's south side, also prohibited, and plunge back into the shadows of the steep north face.

We spend the next 36 hours descending our route. After a short night at our 6,000-meter camp, we start to rappel at first light for better protection from the heat and falling debris. The temperature is rising and we descend quickly, rappelling off V-threads and rock spikes. As the day goes by, we witness the line of thin ice we've just climbed slowly disintegrate.

We walk back into base camp at 10 p.m. on the last day of June, hungry, exhausted, and with no

[Top] **Surprise! The discovery of an anchor and fixed rope just below the summit brought the realization that Dansam West had been climbed before.** *Martín Elías* [Bottom] **Victor Saucede soaks in the view, looking to the north during the last day of the climb.** *Jérôme Sullivan*

food left. We are immensely satisfied that we've managed to climb this ephemeral line. The next day, at 6 a.m., it's time to pack up base camp. Our plane is due to depart in 48 hours.

We have a taxi to catch.

SUMMARY: First ascent of the north face of Dansam West (6,600 meters) by Martín Elías (Spain), Victor Saucède (France), Jeremy Stagnetto (France), and Jérôme Sullivan (French-American), June 25–30, 2021. Their route is called Harvest Moon (1,600m, M6/7 90°). This was the second known ascent of Dansam West; the main peak is still unclimbed.

ABOUT THE AUTHOR. *Martín Elías was born in La Rioja, Spain, and shaped in the Pyrénées. Today he lives in Chamonix, France, where he works as a passionate mountain guide. This story is adapted from an original piece of writing by Elías, with the assistance of Jérôme Sullivan.*

Nick Aiello-Popeo works up the headwall on day five of the first complete ascent of Mt. Neacola's north face. *Justin Guarino*

SURVIVING MEDUSA

SEVEN DAYS ON THE NORTH FACE OF MT. NEACOLA

RYAN DRISCOLL

My first thought, upon being violently shaken awake at 4:30 in the morning, is that I'm getting buried in an avalanche. My second thought is that I'm going to die. I press my hands against the nylon wall in front of me to brace myself as the tent flips end over end for what seems like an eternity. It comes to rest for a second and I have a glimmer of hope, but then I'm launched again, hurtling across the glacier. I can feel the repeated impacts on all sides. I wish it wouldn't end like this. I wish I could see my wife again. I hope Justin and Nick are okay. Finally, my body comes to rest. Miraculously, I'm not dead. I'm not even badly injured. I can move all my limbs, have feeling in all my digits. I'm breathing. I'm alive.

This was how April 4, 2021, began for Nick Aiello-Popeo, Justin Guarino, and me. The east face of Mt. Neacola in southwestern Alaska had released an avalanche so massive that the air blast sent our entire camp—which we thought we'd pitched a relatively safe distance from the wall—cartwheeling down the glacier. When that nightmare version of a magic carpet ride ended, and we each individually realized we were still on the surface, we yelled for each other, unsure if anyone else was still buried.

Ryan Driscoll angling up steep ground above the headwall in the evening of day six on the route. *Justin Guarino*

snow for a few hundred feet to a snow rib with spectacular views—a nice spot to excavate a platform.

We spent the morning of day four traversing a series of snow ramps. Arriving at our 2019 high point by midday, we paused to take a good look at the options above us. A perfect M6 seam was the obvious choice, so Justin took the rack and ventured forth, torquing, stemming, and aiding his way upward. On any climber's local crag, this would have been a classic pitch.

Justin led another pitch or two to an icy snowfield below a headwall. It was time to deploy our inflatable G7 portaledges, and we set to work building the best anchors we could. The gear placements were so uninspiring, though, that we only ended up setting up two of the ledges, and Nick—always the most willing to suffer—decided to hack a little ice bed above my ledge and go to sleep. As I crawled into my floating ledge I thought about what it would feel like if the anchor ripped and I plummeted down the face. The fear was overwhelming for a moment; then I bottled it up and put it deep down inside. "Fear won't do you any good right now," I told myself, and I did my best to sleep.

The next day our camp only moved a few hundred feet. We watched in awe as Nick, bare-handed in freezing temps, led us up 200 feet of 5.9 slab that reminded us of the climbing we often do back home on Cathedral Ledge, carefully smearing his boots and shifting his weight between small features. Above this we were back on lower-angle mixed terrain, and finally we arrived at the last bit of snow before the north face's 1,200-foot headwall. I dug out a ledge for the tent while Nick and Justin fixed a couple of pitches above. Our strategy of fixing ropes in the evening to discourage bailing in the morning was working quite well.

The complex wall prompted multiple solutions to the problem of where to sleep, including inflatable portaledges, snow hammock tent platforms, and an old-fashioned open bivouac. *Ryan Driscoll (top) and Justin Guarino*

The morning entertainment on our sixth day was to toss the haul bag containing our portaledges and some wet gloves off the wall. We were only about 500 feet from the top of the headwall and expected to be on snowier and wandering alpine terrain soon. To start us off, Justin skillfully led two pitches of hard mixed and aid in a chimney feature—the leads took forever, every move a question mark with potentially dire answers, and Nick and I steadily got colder at the belay.

"Off belay! Ropes fixed!" we heard Justin yell far above us. We were going to make it through the headwall! Surely there would be a wonderful spot to bivy just above. Nick cleaned the gear while I jugged, wearing my pack with Justin's pack dangling from my belay loop. As I passed piece after piece of sketchy pro, I appreciated the tremendous effort Justin had put in for the team. But when we arrived at his belay at 7 p.m., we realized we were in for a long evening—this was obviously no place to stop for the night. The weather was still clear, but the cold was coming, and, just like children, we feared the dark.

I led off on a rising traverse. One hundred feet into the pitch, around a corner from my friends, I found myself in a shallow dihedral with some suspect rock. I slotted the pick of my right tool into

Aiello-Popeo nods off in the Alaska sunset, just below the final bivouac. *Ryan Driscoll*

a thin seam, clipped my left tool to my harness, and used my hand to gently feel the left wall. I heard the rock move before I felt it, and to my horror realized that a sizable portion of the left half of the dihedral was moving. I fully loaded my right tool and tried to help an oven-size block clear my ropes below. Luckily they were under a little roof and trailed down and left due to the traverse. I nearly vomited with fear. For the second time in as many weeks I had thought: "So, this is how it ends."

After a couple more pitches, I built a belay at a stance with two fixed pitons and realized this must be the high point where Donahue and Harvey had "spent the short Alaskan night doing the dance of life on a tiny ledge chopped into the ice." Thinking about them standing there all night with spindrift pouring onto them "with the intensity of a waterfall" made us all appreciate the current fine weather. Nick took over and led one more rising traverse pitch to a small area of snow that, with some effort, yielded a bivy site.

At this point, given Donahue's description in the AAJ, we hoped things might get mellower. We were keeping an eye out for the easy-looking terrain he described, but simply couldn't see it from this vantage. The rock above us or out left looked loose, steep, and convoluted. We also believed that getting to the east ridge too soon wouldn't put us in a good position to summit, since it would mean more knife-edge ridge traversing to reach the top. The face seemed to be leading us up and right, so we decided to keep going that way and then punch it directly to the highest point of the ridge we could see.

Nick had the vision, so after a little moderate mixed climbing above the bivy and a low-angle snow feature, he led the final three rope-stretching pitches to the ridge while Justin and I followed with a mix of Micro Traxion seconding and proper ascending, feeling the commitment that traversing always adds. As Nick fired up the final pitch, the rock quality became very poor, and Justin and I cowered below a small roof. We heard Nick holler in excitement that he had reached the ridge, and began ascending the pitch to join our friend. Just 30 feet from his belay on the ridge, my rope shifted and a toaster-size rock skipped off and hit my leg. I can't remember who said it, but somebody joked that my leg would have been broken if it weren't for the vast quantities of ice cream I consume, keeping my bones strong.

Using the ice hammock again, we constructed a small, uneven platform to set up the tent, 30 feet below and 70 feet to the left of the gendarme we'd wrapped with cord for our anchor. We crawled in together and tried to sleep. The night was relatively calm except for one scare when I shifted to use my pee bottle and Justin thought that I was slipping off the ledge—If I *had* slipped, we all would have gone for a massive surprise pendulum in total darkness.

After a beautiful night, we woke with high hopes of traversing 1,000 feet to the summit (about 250 feet higher than where we stood) and then descending the west face, which had been climbed in 1991 by James Garrett, Lorne Glick, and Kennan Harvey. However, as soon as we climbed back up to the east ridge from our bivy down on the face, we were met with wind so intense that it stung our eyes through our goggles. We could barely stand upright, and verbal communication was totally out of the question. Reduced to head shakes and nods, we quickly agreed that going to the summit would be insane, impossible, or both.

The decision to go down is often tough, but in this case it really wasn't. Climbing the face was our goal and we had accomplished that. Going to the summit was always the ultimate dream, but down was the only choice to make if we wanted a good chance of making it out alive.

We had been staring at photographs of the mountain for two years now, and were somewhat sure that if we rappelled off a gendarme by the mountain's north summit and onto the east face, we could gain a system of snow ramps that would lead us back to the glacier. This was the same face that had avalanched on us two weeks earlier, but it was still early in the day and quite cold, and 98 percent of our descent route would be off to one side of the serac band that had tried to kill us.

I led the descent, hyper-focused on finding good anchors and getting us off the mountain. We rapped eight or ten times—I lost count. The usual anchor

After topping out on the north face, the team descended left along the sunlit east face. The summit of Neacola, behind, was reached in 1991 from the opposite side (west face). *Ryan Driscoll*

difficulties persisted: tied-off pitons, tight cracks, limited options. After a bit, we landed on snow that we could downclimb and enjoyed simple descending with tired legs. At long last we arrived at what would be our final rappel. In my depleted state, I dropped two pitons in a row while trying to make an anchor. Justin and Nick just watched wordlessly, too tired to care. We rapped again and landed on the lower snowfields of the east face. For our final exercise, we ran across the gully that was capped by the massive serac that had triggered the avalanche before.

Thirty minutes later, we arrived at our gear cache on the glacier and enjoyed some celebratory Pop-Tarts and candy. Stunned that we had pulled it off, we hiked back up to the base of the north face, grabbed our skis and haul bag, and stopped to stare at Medusa one last time. Sunlight had cooked the glacier surface and the evening shade had firmed it up, granting us some true New Hampshire snow conditions for our ski back to camp.

I am grateful for many things, but mostly that I shared this experience with my close friends— an adventure like this requires a real connection to your partners, and Nick and Justin are the best that anybody could ask for. We all question why we do this sort of thing: Is it really worth it? How will our families deal if we don't come home? I can never come up with any good answers. I love climbing mountains, and as I write this, the memory of the suffering and terror has already faded some and I'm starting to think about the next big objective. I guess there are worse things to be addicted to.

Summary: First complete ascent of the north face (Medusa Face) of Mt. Neacola (ca 9,350 feet) in southwestern Alaska, by Nick Aiello-Popeo, Ryan Driscoll, and Justin Guarino, April 11–17, 2021. The climbers measured the wall at about 4,600 feet high and graded the climbing at 5.10 A2 M6. They descended by the east face on April 18. Driscoll and Guarino spoke about their attempts and the climb of the Medusa Face on episode 40 of the AAJ's Cutting Edge podcast.

About the Author: *Ryan Driscoll is a trade worker and guide living in Tamworth, New Hampshire. When not climbing, he enjoys spending time with his wonderful wife, Angela, and two dogs. Driscoll received a 2021 AAC Cutting Edge Grant to help support this expedition.*

Oil painting of Ushba by Oleksandr
Yurkovskyi, from Kharkiv, Ukraine.
The artist has painted many of the
world's most beautiful mountains,
his Instagram is @oleksandr.art82.

USHBA

THE CROWN OF THE CAUCASUS

ARCHIL BADRIASHVILI

USHBA

rises near the west end of the South Caucasus Mountains, about 30 kilometers from Mt. Elbrus and entirely within Georgia, just south of the frontier with Kabardino-Balkaria (Russia). It is an extremely complex mountain, with two prominent summits and more than 50 different routes and variants. Both of Ushba's summits (South Peak, 4,710m or 15,453 feet; North Peak, 4,690m) have no easy access. The higher South Peak is considered the most difficult summit in the Caucasus, though it is not even in the top ten by elevation.

Ushba is associated with mystic legends and sacred spirits of the Svan, the people native to the mountainous region of Svaneti. The meaning of the name is unclear, even to locals, but it generally refers to a dangerous place.

The mountain has four flanks of steep granite and others of ice and mixed terrain. The microclimate is unstable, and objective danger is nearly always present. The mountain experiences a high incidence of accidents and fatalities, mainly due to objective hazards and the complexity of the climbs and descents, lack of detailed information about climbs or current conditions, global warming, and the failure of some parties to grasp the scale of the routes and their seriousness.

Ushba's dramatic appearance and huge relief made it very alluring to 19th-century European mountaineers beginning to look beyond the Alps. The English climber Douglas William Freshfield, just 23 years old, along with two English companions and a Chamonix guide, François Joseph Dévouassoud, visited the Caucasus in 1868, when few useful maps and no detailed descriptions of the mountains in English were available. They made the first recorded ascent of Kazbek (5,054 meters) and then undertook a long high-level traverse along the range to the west. In his subsequent book about the trip, *Travels in the Central Caucasus and Bashan*, Freshfield described twin-summited Ushba as the Caucasian Matterhorn, "Only here we had one Matterhorn piled on another, and then multiplied by two." Climbing either peak, he wrote, "seemed too insane to be as much as suggested." Nonetheless, Ushba's first summit route came just two decades later.

[Opposite Page] **Climbers on the Khergiani Route, the south ridge of the South Peak, first climbed in 1937.** *Archil Badriashvili* [Above] **Ushba's South Peak (4,710m, left) and North Peak from the east in April. (1) Khergiani Route (a.k.a. The Gabrieli, 1937). (1a) British Route (1937). (2) Cockin-Almer Route (1888). (3) North Ridge. In back is Mt. Elbrus (5,642 meters) in Russia.** *Capture from drone video by Tom Gaisbacher*

THE EARLY CLIMBS

IN SEPTEMBER 1888, Swiss guide Ulrich Almer and Englishman John Garford Cockin made the first ascent of Ushba's North Peak by climbing to the Saddle, between the two summits, from the Guli Glacier to the east. Cockin and his British companions, along with their two guides, had already had a hugely successful season in the range, making the second ascent of Dych-tau (ca 5,203 meters), the first ascent of Shkhara (ca 5,203 meters), and other climbs. After two previous attempts on Ushba—one cut short by guide Christian Roth's "severe arthritic pains" from all the step-cutting on the expedition, and a second attempt that ran out of time on the complex Guli Glacier—Cockin and Almer returned for a third try and reached the col between Ushba's peaks after 10 hours of work. "We were near to the south peak, but as the ridge heading to the top of this had much frozen snow and ice on it, whilst the rocks of the northern peak looked easy, we turned at once to our right," Cockin explained in the *Alpine Journal*. They were on top at 3:45 p.m. and returned to their tent at 11:20 "by lantern light."

Cockin and Almer's line only saw its first repeat 57 years later, during a tragic attempt to traverse the peaks in 1945. In the spring of 2017, this avalanche-prone route was followed to achieve the first ski descent from the North Peak, by Slovakian Miroslav Peťo.

The South Peak of Ushba is only about 20 meters higher than the north summit but was much more difficult to climb. Early probes discovered that steep rock barring access to the summit snowfields was likely to be the crux.

After two previous visits to the range, including an attempt on Ushba in 1895, Willi Rickmer-Rickmers from Germany brought a large international team of well-prepared mountaineers to tackle the problem in 1903. In July, three of these climbers and a local hunter quickly reached Mazeri Col on the south ridge, following a couloir on the southeast side. The next day, a larger group returned to the col, bivouacked, and then worked up the southwest face to a prominent

Climbing the Red Corner headwall on the southwest side of the South Peak. This passage was the key to the first ascent of Ushba's highest point in 1903. *Archil Badriashvili*

rock wall, the Red Corner. Above this, 23-year-old Adolf Schulze, who had done numerous first ascents in the eastern Alps, was leading the way when he fell off and plunged the length of their rope to a ledge. He lost consciousness, but his teammates were able to lower him all the way to their bivouac, and the next day they returned to base camp.

Four days later, amazingly, Schulze had recovered sufficiently to lead the final ascent, along with the German-Swiss team of Robert Helbling, Fritz Reichert, Oskar Schuster, and Albert Weber. This time, Schulze headed left where he had tried to climb to the right, and after surmounting an overhang he reached easier ground and brought the team up. They summited at 8 p.m., only to be trapped by a thunderstorm just as they started down. In the morning they staggered down to their camp, having completed what was certainly one of the hardest alpine routes climbed before World War I. Their route is graded Caucasian 5A today (roughly the equivalent of TD-/ TD) and is very rarely repeated because of rockfall danger.

Less than three weeks later, Ludwig Distel, Georg Leuchs, and Hans Pfann (Germany) made a five-day traverse over the north and south peaks, starting from the Ushba Glacier on the west. The trio climbed a new route to reach Ushba's north summit, then crossed the Saddle between the peaks, followed by difficult new ground up the south peak, before descending the Schulze route.

In all, during the three decades since the South Peak was climbed twice in a single season, there were two dozen attempts on the mountain, but only two teams were successful: German Willi Merkl and two other climbers, who made the second ascent of Schulze's "Red Corner" route in 1929, and Swiss climbers Lorenz Saladin and Werner Wickert, who in 1932 followed the same route.

August 1934 marked the first time an ascent was achieved by local climbers. Pioneering Georgian mountaineers and siblings Alexandra and Alexander Japaridze, together with Iagor Kazalikashvili, a guide from Stepantsminda, and Svanetian hunter Giorgi Niguriani, repeated Schulze's Route, climbing a variant to the Red Corner. After a cold open bivouac under the headwall, the team found themselves to the right of the original line. After several tries on the hardest section, Niguriani decided to climb in bare feet for more grip on the vertical granite—he managed to place a piton and overcome the headwall. The Georgians lit a fire on top to prove to residents of the Becho Valley below that it was indeed reachable. And with that, Alexander wrote later, "the last of local superstitions were burning in those flames."

The Japaridze family was marked both by great climbing successes and by tragedy. Simon, another sibling and a promising climber, died in 1929 during an attempt on Tetnuldi (4,858 meters), when one of his climbing partners slipped in a steep gully and Simon tried to grab him. Alexander and Alexandra made various first ascents in the range, and in the late 1930s and early '40s, they pioneered bold traverses—endurance climbs that seem barely doable even today.

Alexandra lived until 1974 and is considered one of the great figures in Georgian sports history. Alexander was killed in 1945 while attempting a complete traverse of the Ushba and Shkhelda summits, after a previous attempt two years earlier. After repeating the Cockin route to the North Peak, Japaridze and two friends were trapped by prolonged bad weather on the ridge and disappeared. Strong mountaineers united in a prolonged search for their bodies. Three of the team's letters—tradition required leaving detailed accounts of ascents inside summit cairns—were found, and one on the North Peak described their ordeal in an eight-day blizzard inside a tent. The note said they planned to descend the north ridge, but later evidence emerged that they had attempted to retreat by their ascent route and perished, likely in an avalanche.

It wasn't until 1950 that Georgians completed this demanding traverse. Led by Georgian climber Ivane ("Kako") Marr, the team took 26 days to traverse over Shkhelda's six summits and Ushba's two peaks, during which time the main avenue in Tbilisi, the nation's capital, sported a diagram updating the team's progress.

[Below Left] **Members of the team that made the first Georgian ascent of Ushba's highest top, in 1934, with some friends: siblings Alexander (far right) and Alexandra (center) Japaridze, with Iagor Kazalikashvili and local hunter Giorgi Niguriani (carrying a rope) on either side of Alexandra. [Right] In her long climbing career, Alexandra Japaridze completed many difficult routes and traverses in the Caucasus.** *Ivane Japaridze Archive*

From a camp on the Ushba Plateau (left) or the Pillow in center, the classic north ridge route finishes up the beautiful long arête near the right skyline. The rock wall on the left is the Mirror. *Vladimir Kopylov*

MODERN CLIMBS: THE NORTH PEAK

THE CLASSIC AND most frequented route to the North Peak is the north ridge, first climbed in 1935 by Boris Aleynikov and Vladimir Kiesel, who approached via the Ushba Icefall and the Ushba Plateau. The route is 4A (considered at least French AD+, but long and serious), and favorable conditions on the long summit arête are crucial to success. Previously, parties frequently approached this route from the North Caucasus, but the border crossing is no longer legal and the constant collapse of the Ushba Icefall makes this approach unviable. The north ridge is now approached via the Ushba Glacier, starting from the village of Mazeri in Upper Svaneti. A long glacier climb leads to a camp at the Ushba Plateau or the shoulder called "The Pillow," below the final ridge.

Other than the avalanche-prone original route and the now-standard north ridge, all of the other routes to the North Peak are very difficult.

The northwest face (a.k.a. "West Face") of the North Peak is a 1,500-meter-high ice and mixed wall, which has attracted very few suitors. Descriptions of the routes here are sparse. The first ascent was probably along the leftmost ice on the face, followed by exploration of logical lines on the right in the 1980s. Among hard the routes, the Kolomitsev Route (5B, 1982) has seen the most repeats, including at least one winter ascent.

The broad snow and ice lines leading directly up the west face to the Saddle were climbed many times, sometimes as part of a famous challenge called the Cross: ascending the Saddle from one side, climbing both summits of Ushba, and descending by the other side of the Saddle. Nowadays, the avalanche risk is too high.

The North Peak's 1,300-meter-high east wall, accessed by the demanding Chalaadi Glacier, is similarly unfrequented. The granite face looks impressive, but it is washed by rockfall in late summer. There are around five routes, from 5B to 6A. The first route, in 1960, was climbed by a team of six led by Andrey Chnoure. The Grishchenko line (6A), established by an eight-man team in 1982, was repeated in summer 2014 over five days.

The right part of the east face—the northeast wall—is named the Mirror and is the most remote part of the mountain. It was first climbed in 1964 by a strong Georgian team led by Mikheil Khergiani.

Mikheil, part of a distinguished family of accomplished climbers (see below), was the most renowned climber of Georgia. His broad range of interests included technical rock climbing and high-altitude mountaineering, as well as traverses, instruction, and, most importantly, numerous serious rescue operations. He was awarded many first-place prizes in the climbing championships of the USSR, and climbed on major peaks of the Tien Shan, Pamir, and the Alps. In North Wales, where he paired with Joe Brown, he was dubbed "Tiger of the Rocks."

Writing about the first ascent of the Mirror in his diary, Khergiani described a key moment when he was trying to free climb a wet, overhanging section with bad protection and few holds, with the rest of his team below at a poor belay. With retreat impossible, he shouted to his friends that they should untie from the rope. Instead, they began to sing a Georgian folk song, and, thus inspired, Khergiani continued to the top. The route was credited with bringing a new level of wall climbing to the Soviet Union, and it was done in great style. Sadly, in 1969, at age 37, Khergiani was killed by rockfall on the northwest face of the Cima Su Alto in the Dolomites.

There are five routes on the Mirror, and most have been repeated, but none has been free climbed. The direct routes have around 650 meters of climbing, and the wall is topped by "The Roof," an area with loose rock that requires excellent snow and ice conditions for safe progress. In August 2004, while attempting to complete a possible new line, an entire team of three from St. Petersburg, Russia, disappeared at or near the Roof. The wall has seen little activity since.

[Top] Mikheil Khergiani, Georgia's most renowned climber during the 1960s. [Bottom] The Khergiani Route on the Mirror, the northeast face of the North Peak, climbed in 1964. *Archil Badriashvili*

SOUTH PEAK CLIMBS

IN AUGUST 1937, British university students Bob Beaumont, Robin Hodgkin (a noted educator who was one of the best U.K. rock climbers of his generation), and Michael Taylor climbed the south ridge of Ushba from Guli, though at the steep section in the upper part they made a traverse across the east face to a large corner system leading back to the ridge, above the main difficulties.

A month later, Gabriel Khergiani, in a four-man team, climbed the south ridge directly, and their line (commonly called the Gabrieli) has become the standard route to the highest point of Ushba. Gabriel Khergiani was a renowned Svan mountaineer and one of several illustrious climbers in the family, including Mikheil (a distant cousin), and cousin Beknu, a mountaineering instructor and rescuer with many important first ascents, including the south pillar of Shkhara (5,203m) and the Shkhelda-Ushba traverse. They, along with other alpinists, played important roles in defending against the German army in the Battle of the Caucasus during World War II.

Ushba's west side, with the classic north ridge of the North Peak on the upper left skyline. (1) Kolomitsev Route (1982). (2) Georgian Route (1946, the original line up the west face of the South Peak). (3) Grigorenko-Prigoda (1972). (4) Mishlaev-Kosmachev (1960). (5) Monogarov Route (1960), finishing up the Red Corner. The 1973 Khergiani Route is near the right skyline. Other routes not shown. *Mikhail Golubev*

The Gabrieli is no pushover, at 5A or 5B, with the crux section generally climbed at UIAA V/VI and cracks that often are icy. The climb is usually started from a camp at the base of the peak, with two nights at a bivouac site high on the route.

The west side of the South Peak, comprised of walls with three aspects (northwest, west, and southwest) has the most routes and variants of any of Ushba's walls. Access to these faces is long and moderate via the Ushba Glacier.

The first route here (starting on the west face and finishing on the northwest) was in 1946, climbed by a Georgian team led by Kako Marr. They were looking for the Japaridze party, which had disappeared the previous year. No detailed description of this impressive alpine-style ascent has been published, and the route may be unrepeated.

The first ascent of the famous west face was made in 1960 by Oleg Kosmachev and Lev Mishlaev, one an exceptional rock climber and the other a visionary alpinist and author of many hard classics. They took 18 days in July to complete the line (the Mishlaev Route), which has become the most frequented on the face, being climbed more than two dozen times, several times free. In an era of grandiose ascents by very large groups, Mishalaev climbed in small teams, choosing obvious, beautiful, yet very difficult lines. On Ushba, Mishlaev and Kosmachev followed an obvious corner and overcame long barriers of difficult, wet, and broken rock, often with poor protection (including wooden wedges). The 1,700-meter route is graded 5B (TD+/ED), with pitches of F6/5.10 or above. The abs... to climb the... from the upper face soaks the wall; two experienced Georgian mountaineers died here due to hypothermia in July 2005.

Archil Badriashvili pauses below the daunting west face of Ushba South during an ascent of the Mishlaev Route (1960). Badriashvili and Giorgi Tepnadze climbed this route in 2020 in preparation for a new route up the west face that September. *Giorgi Tepnadze*

Starting in the 1960s, the motivation for many teams was to win prizes in the annual Soviet climbing championships. The central mountaineering committee studied the goals and experience of each member and gave permission to attempt specific lines. Apart from routes by climbers like Mikheil Khergiani and Lev Mishlaev, these climbs involved large teams, and many bolts were placed in hopes of winning "gold." (Many of these bolts were tiny and intended only for progress over blank rock, not for protection; they are now very old and untrustworthy.) Many of the climbers were Ukrainian and Russian, and included well-known activists such as Kensitskiy, Kustovskiy, and Monogarov. None of their routes on Ushba has been climbed free.

The South Peak's northwest aspect is about 1,700 meters high, with routes of 5B to 6A/B. The face has a very steep capping wall called the Rockband. All routes avoided the barrier until 1971 and '72, when large teams making two-week siege ascents overcame the Rockband—first a team led by Jury Artsishevskly, and a year later the Grigorenko Prigoda route. In 2015, Giorgi Tepnadze and I climbed a new variant to the Prigoda, made the first alpine-style ascent, and traversed both summits (*AAJ 2017*). In 2020, over five days, we returned to the wall and opened a new 6A/6B route by climbing directly up the center of the upper barrier (see *AAJ 2021*).

The southwest face was climbed completely for the first time in 1960 by Kavunenko, Kensitskiy, Monogarov, and Subortovich. There are few routes and equally few repetitions on this face, probably because of the vast, exposed nature of the wall and significant danger from rockfall. In the summer of 2021, a Spanish team unexpectedly opened a long variant on the right side of the southwest face to join the original Red Corner route (see p.243).

Routes up the rocky east side of the South Peak, between the normal route (Gabrieli) and

world, though it garnered the inevitable criticism at the time. Piaz was having fun innovating new ways of climbing, and he wasn't much bothered by other's opinions.

The following year, Piaz returned to this spire with Ugo de Amicis, the son of the political author Edmondo de Amicis, for whom Piaz had named the spire. The two prepared and crossed the Tyrolean, and on the top of the spire, after pulling over their equipment in a pack, they pulled their ropes, too, committing to an uncharted rappel descent. Only a climber like Piaz would have staked such a bet on anchoring technology at the time; he rigged three steep rappels and their anchors to reach the ground. In contrast to relatively safe descents down previously climbed ground, descending into the unknown eventually became a key strategy for climbers in the Alps and beyond.

Piaz's climbing endeavors were often controversial, and his wild rappels and Tyroleans were dismissed by one influential writer as "contrived (and) outrageous rope maneuvers, gymnastic exercises that do not belong in the mountains." Some also considered his piton use as excessive, and later in life he admitted to sometimes overdoing it—"to tame a huge wall by means of complete equipment from a blacksmith's shop," as Paul Preuss put it. By all accounts, however, Piaz was himself a purist in terms as climbing as free as possible and using pitons only for anchors and protection, not for "hook by hook" progress up the wall. He dismissed excessive use of aid pitons as "devoid of modesty and dignity."

GUIDING

PIAZ INITIALLY WORKED outside the official guiding system, risking censure in the guiding community. He eventually took the guide's course in Bolzano and became a sought-after Führer ("leader"), with many epic stories of hard guided climbs in his autobiography and in journals. The famous guide Guido Rey wrote in 1914 of Piaz's adventurous spirit: "Not satisfied with having ascended the Towers of Vajolet three hundred times, in sunshine or in rain, he wished to attempt them by night under the stars; therefore he persuaded an American lady to join him, and soon, in the heart of a beautiful summer night, his lantern could be seen shining, a newly created star, on the topmost pinnacle."

Mountain guides at the time referred to the "sack of flour" technique ("Mehlsacktechnik") for assisting clients with the rope—essentially early friction-braking techniques that eventually evolved into standard belay methods. If the terrain was too steep for a client to downclimb, guides generally lowered them with the rope tied around their waist. For such adventures, secure anchors were essential. Piaz described a client accidentally becoming untied at the crux of the Winkler Route on the Vajolet Towers. "In a flash I fixed the rope to a nail (piton)," Piaz wrote. "I slipped down and found him...barely holding onto the problematic hold with his head dangling in the void…. To tie someone up in such a situation, you would need at least three hands, and I from my birth had only two. Yet I tied him up which still remains a mystery to me."

The rope was not just useful to his clients: In addition to performing the longest rappels, Piaz experienced one of the longest leader falls (that was survived) on the ropes and gear of the time. While guiding the south wall of the Marmolada in 1907, "At one point I flew and fell perpendicularly into the void for about ten meters, until a strong tightening of the rope around the ribs told me that my life would continue as before." Despite the successful action of his "life-saving partner," Piaz subsequently had nightmares about the fall and its potential consequences for himself and his client, and swore he would never again fall while climbing.

It had become clear that Piaz's mastery of anchor techniques and rope work were not just stunts. With his extensive experience of rigging ropes for Tyrolean traverses and rappels, and his understanding of the complex terrain of the Alpine limestone, he was ready to lead a breakthrough climb.

THE TOTENKIRCHL

The Totenkirchl is a striking stone monolith in the Kaiser Mountains, about a hundred kilometers south of Munich. Totenkirchl translates to "Church of the Dead," and from a distance it is an imposing feature on the landscape. The steep west face of Totenkirchl was for many years "the last great problem" of the Eastern Alps, and several top climbers had made forays up the wall in search of a climbable route.

This area was considered the domain of the German-speaking "Munich School" climbers, and climbers from South Tyrol (today's Italy) rarely visited. Piaz was an exception. In October of 1908, Piaz began an epic 300-kilometer motorcycle trip from his home to Kufstein, traveling one of the first of the new roadways connecting the Tyrol regions, and with one of the first factory-produced touring motorbikes. He motored up to North Tyrol with Franz Schroffenegger, a Tiers mountain guide of repute, and in Kufstein they joined their North Tyrol teammates, a meeting of the tribes. Josef Klammer was an experi-

The Totenkirchl team, posing after the climb. Franz Schroffenegger (sitting left) and Tita Piaz (center); Rudolf Schieitzold and Josef Klammer standing. When Klammer gave a lecture on the ascent in Munich, Piaz was "dragged to the podium...to expose the smallest details of the heroic enterprise: The world had to know how many times we yawned or felt the need to pee!"

enced alpinist and founder of the first mountain rescue team from Kufstein, and Rudolf Schietzold from Munich had made a committing abseil of the Totenkirchl's west wall from its second terrace the year before. This top-down inspection, according to Piaz, provided only limited information for the route they eventually followed; Schietzold initially had reported the face was "impossible" and warned against any attempt.

Soon the team began their 16-kilometer trek from Kufstein to the small community of Hinterbärenbad, where the Totenkirchl dominates the view. Piaz wrote, "At a glance I was surprised the (west wall of the Totenkirchl) had not yet been won, and I did not even have a flash of doubt that the attempt would not be in vain." Exploring the wall with binoculars, he immediately saw the precise line: "Do you see the little wall on the right, with a crack barely noticeable on the left? Well, I tell you we will pass by there, and I promise, if we do not, then I will become a barefoot friar." Sure enough, the line that Piaz envisioned from below turned out to be the climbable line of weakness.

They launched their ascent in mid-October. The line they followed starts out steeply, right off the ground, then meanders up ledge systems to the Parete Piaz (in German, the "Piazwandl"),

The first route up the west face of the Totenkirchl gained about 450 meters, with 600 meters of climbing. The crucial leftward traverse is seen at about two-thirds height.

a difficult 5.7/5.8 pitch about 200 meters off the ground, requiring good crack and laybacking skills. (Although there is debate about when layback techniques were developed—and by whom—this climbing skill is still called "Piaz-Tecnik" or "Piazen" in some European climbing areas). Halfway up the wall, Piaz had envisioned a crucial 30-meter leftward traverse across a smooth wall to reach a chimney system. This pitch, which Schietzold led, was described as a long traverse up and left, then falling sharply downwards [with a "wall hook," or piton, to direct the rope] left into the chimney." Though Piaz himself preferred to focus more on the free climbing difficulty of the Parete Piaz in his recounting of the Totenkirchl ascent, this was the first tension traverse planned and executed as the key to a big-wall climb. Once they had regrouped in the chimney, the four men quickly reached the ridgeline atop the face.

Despite the first ascensionists' warning that "repetitions are not recommended for this route" due to its difficulty and danger, the west wall of the Totenkirchl quickly became a sought-after climb, with more than 30 ascents in the following five years. (The route is described today as having 16 or 17 pitches.) The key traverse was later free climbed without rope tension—as early as 1911, when Paul Preuss soloed the route, though it's unclear if Preuss used the rope he carried—but many still depended on tension for the traverse into the 1970s. Piaz and his companions had broken both technical and psychological barriers, and other difficult routes were soon established using ever-more complex rope and piton systems, including Hans Dülfer's more direct route up the west face of the Totenkirchl, climbed five years later in 1913.

Using ropes and anchors to move laterally across vertical rock eventually became known as the "Seilquergang" (the "rope traverse" technique), and in 1929, Karl Prusik referenced it as one of "six basic techniques" that should be taught to every climber. In the coming decades, the technique was used on other breakthrough climbs, including the first ascent of the north face of the Matterhorn in 1931 and of course the Hinterstoisser Traverse on the Eiger in 1936.

Perhaps a more important legacy than the rope traverse was the envisioning of a such a complex route through hostile, seemingly impassable terrain. After the Totenkirchl ascent, other big Alpine walls were eyed in a new way. No longer was a continuous line of obviously climbable rock needed. By connecting distant cracks and other features with rope swings and other tactics, the impossible was made visible.

The Totenkirchl route in 1908 was one of Piaz's most influential climbs, but by no means were his contributions over. Along with his involvement in local theater, military and civic service, and with his family, he continued to establish cutting-edge ascents and optimize climbing tools and techniques throughout his long and adventurous career. He ran the Vajolet Hut and later built the nearby Preuss Hut, named in honor of Paul Preuss, who died in a soloing accident in 1913. Though he was good friends with Preuss and greatly respected the famous climbing purist, Piaz was a key counterpoint to Preuss' strong opinions in the famous "Piton Disputes," published in the German-Austrian alpine journals in 1911-12.

Piaz was a bold and brash climber who loved the limelight (though the boastful language in his writing often was tongue-in cheek). His routes were held in high esteem among climbers in the Eastern Alps, and he was known to be generous with information about his climbs and techniques. Riccardo Cassin wrote of meeting Piaz in the Catinaccio group in the early 1930s and having "an immediate rapport." Said Cassin: "I grew to admire his limitless love of the mountains, his youthful spirit and his modesty about his own routes, his innovations in climbing techniques."

In 1947, the 50th anniversary of his first big climb on Catinaccio, Piaz's memoir was published and quickly sold out the first printing. He died a year later, at age 68, in a bicycling accident in Pera di Fassa. His legacy of exploration and innovation would long outlive him.

[Top] **Piaz with his second wife and a son.** [Bottom] **Piaz and friend.**

ABOUT THE AUTHOR: *John Middendorf has been interested in the engineering aspects of rock climbing equipment since he started climbing in 1974. Well-known for his big-wall tent designs, he personally tested his gear on some of the wildest walls of the world. His ongoing research and writing on the historical evolution of big-wall tools and techniques can be seen at bigwallgear.com.*

NOTES: *Roy McClenahan provided invaluable assistance with the editing of this article. The historical photos reproduced here were scanned from several older works, including the Piaz autobiography Mezzo secolo d'alpinismo (1947), Guido Rey's Alpinismo Acrobatico (originally published in 1914), and Meine Berge by Luis Trenker (first published in 1931). Other images were shared by Alfredo Paluselli, author of Il Diavolo generoso: La storia di Tita Piaz (2018).*

honors going to Phyllis Munday and then several others, including Helen Buck from New York, the American Alpine Club's second librarian.) That year, the pair made the first female ascent of difficult Hungabee Mountain, accompanied by Swiss guide Rudolf Aemmer.

With another well-known guide, Christian Häsler, Best and Shippam shared the first ascent of Iconoclast Mountain in the Selkirks and a new route on Popes Peak. A storm broke out on the latter expedition, and the *Minneapolis Star* wrote that all three "narrowly escaped death in an avalanche as they were descending on ice-covered slopes." As for Iconoclast, the *Selkirks North* guidebook says, "The original approach [in June 1924] was a very difficult three-day trip, through the bush and alder of Ventego Creek, in deep snow. The party…gained the summit by the long, badly corniced east ridge." They traversed the peak, descending by the northeast glacier, and also made the first ascents of two smaller peaks in the area.

Best and Shippam often climbed with paid guides—as did many highly experienced male climbers of the day—or with fellow participants in the ACC's annual summer mountaineering camps. But Best led many climbs herself, without a guide. According to Best's obituary in the *Canadian Alpine Journal*, written by Shippam, Best took the lead on Victoria, Lefroy, Huber, Odaray, Tupper, and other prominent Canadian peaks, "on these ascents graduating new climbers for the club on major peaks."

Indeed, Best's role as an early female guide is perhaps the most intriguing part of her story. In that era, the prominent guides in the Rockies were from the European Alps, employed by Canadian Pacific Railway to serve the growing tourism industry. There were no guiding organizations, qualifying standards, or tests like those of today's Association of Canadian Mountain Guides (or the AMGA in the United States). What distinguished Best from most female mountaineers active in the Rockies in the mid-1920s was her leadership role on ACC climbs and other outings. Early on, the ACC encouraged a few select women to lead all-female parties as a way of giving them freedom from male leadership. ACC co-founder Arthur Wheeler described Best as "a skilled mountaineer and competent to take charge of a rope." Best also guided men from the Minneapolis section, and *Canadian National Magazine* reported that she had at least one man on her rope during her failed first attempt on Robson, when her party was turned back by poor weather.

Best appears to have earned several other stamps of approval for guiding (though it's unclear if this involved mountain guiding or other forms of outdoor activity). In Best's obituary in the *Canadian Alpine Journal*, Shippam wrote: "She was accorded special privileges in all national parks by both the United States and Canadian Governments and was commissioned a fully licensed guide by the Department of the Interior of Canada." Newspapers also report she was a "registered guide of the Canadian National Parks."

Best's mountaineering accomplishments and many other feats helped her become a darling of the press and a popular lecturer around North America. The *Detroit News* described her as "a woman who has dared death in a dozen forms and undertaken feats of strength and endurance that few men could have overcome as smoothly and calmly." Breathless hyperbole aside, comparisons of her abilities to those of her male counterparts are a reminder that women who challenged traditional masculine roles in mountaineering were on the front lines of the burgeoning feminist movement. Although attitudes were changing, alpinism, especially at its highest levels, was still a predominantly masculine sport in the 1920s. Best told audiences that "mountain climbing is a science" and therefore, once armed with the requisite knowledge, being a woman was no impediment to being a climber. She stated unequivocally, "there is no sex in mountain climbing."

Off the mountain, Best eschewed female stereotypes by embracing physical challenges like white-water paddling and learning to shoot with a bow and arrow in order to hunt wild boar.

She also hunted whales and drove dog sleds in Alaska, dug up dinosaur bones in the Alberta Badlands, and learned to fly a plane. She told the press: "I'm just a rebel, I guess. I seem to have to do the things they say can't be done."

She and Shippam were among the original members of the influential group Trail Riders of the Canadian Rockies, where Best served in various leadership roles and logged more than 2,500 miles in the company of cowboys, poets, artists, and intellectuals. The club was founded on the progressive principle that "sex, age, race, creed, profession, or colour" had no bearing on membership, and Best evidently upheld that motto in her personal life. She backed efforts to include Japanese climbers as members of the ACC, and she used her growing popularity in the press to denounce gender barriers: "Life has undreamed of depths and heights, and women as well as men can experience them," she said.

Best's refusal either to be limited by or to renounce her femininity made her stand apart from her peers, and the press took notice of her

Cora Best leading up glacial ice on Farnham Tower in the Purcell Mountains, British Columbia, in 1923. *Audrey Shippam.*

open defiance of social norms. A reporter asked of her husband: "Does he let you go off on these expeditions whenever you want to?" She replied, "There's no such word as 'let' in this family." Both she and Shippam remained childless and traveled the world much of the year without their husbands.

The duo shot film and took photos in remote locations of rare plants and animals for use during Best's popular off-season lectures. Best took no profit from her lectures or films, and she eventually gave up medicine to climb and lecture year-round, with the goal of bringing more men and women into better health through communion with nature. This included being an advocate for equal and affordable park access and a promotor of physical fitness. She railed against the rise of obesity in America with the motto, "the longer the belt, the shorter the life."

Despite her shoot-from-the-hip verbal style, Best was a beloved member of the ACC. After Best's untimely death in 1930 from a lung infection contracted while climbing in Switzerland, Shippam paid tribute to her "poet's soul" and "vagabond heart," and Bliss Carman, author of *Songs from Vagabondia,* called her "one of life's music makers."

Best wrote in the *Canadian Alpine Journal* in 1923: "There isn't a mountain trip that isn't worthwhile." In celebrating her achievements, we celebrate a generation of women who pushed against the practical and social boundaries of their era to forge a prominent place in the alpine. Other remarkable mountaineering women are no doubt waiting to be discovered. It's up to us to make those worthwhile journeys to revisit their lives and give them their deserved place in our collective memory.

ABOUT THE AUTHOR: *Cheryl Jacklin-Piraino is a Canadian editor and poet who has spent 20 seasons exploring the Canadian Rockies.*

CLIMBS & EXPEDITIONS

CLIMBS & EXPEDITIONS reports generally are arranged geographically, from north to south, and from west to east, within a country or region. Unless noted, the reports cover climbs in 2021. The complete AAJ database, from 1929 to present, can be searched at *publications. americanalpineclub.org*. Online reports frequently contain additional text, photos, maps, and topos—look for these symbols indicating additional online resources:

FULL-LENGTH REPORT | ADDITIONAL PHOTOS | MAPS OR TOPOS | VIDEO OR MULTIMEDIA

Kwangde (left) and Tengkangpoche in Nepal. The very steep northeast pillar of Tengkangpoche, in center, was climbed in autumn 2021 (p.286). *Tim Banfield*

Viewed from the summit of Phantom Peak: Crooked Thumb and its subpeak Ghost Peak in the close foreground, with Mt. Challenger in the near background and wildfire smoke beyond. *Eric Wehrly*

WASHINGTON / CASCADE MOUNTAINS

PICKET RANGE, PHANTOM PEAK, WEST RIDGE

ON JULY 30, Rolf Larson and I completed a new route on Phantom Peak, climbing its west ridge. Phantom Peak (8,000+') is in the northern section of the rugged Picket Range of North Cascades National Park, and requires an involved two-day approach. After ten miles on trail up and over Hannegan Pass, we waded the Chilliwack River, navigated up and down the five-mile-long and scenic Easy Ridge, soloed exposed fourth-class to cross a chasm (the Imperfect Impasse), climbed through Perfect Pass and over the Challenger Glacier, then finally descended and traversed steep snow, talus, and more glacier to arrive at a bivy under Ghost Peak, Phantom Peak's neighbor to the north. From our scrabbly camp, the profile of Phantom's west ridge was finally in full view.

In the morning, we ascended to a 6,100' saddle in the ridge's lower reaches. A few hundred feet of hiking and scrambling up the ridge led to a notch with a convenient ledge for roping up. Friends and acquaintances had in previous years set out for the unclimbed ridge above us, but were either skunked by the area's notoriously fickle weather or, upon arriving at the base, reassessed their willingness to continue.

I led the first pitch, which began with a short and steep crack system, then gave way to rambling along the crest. The next four pitches were more of the same, and included some large corners, towers that we either bypassed or climbed directly, and exposed ridge running. The climbing was engaging but surprisingly moderate, mostly 5.7+.

Midway up pitch six, Rolf encountered a tough move over an airy four-foot cleft in the ridge. At the same moment, we spotted a plume of wildfire smoke erupting near the Chilliwack River, apparently threatening our return route home. Out of view, Rolf shouted, "We have a problem!" After a bit of back-and-forth banter echoing around the cirque, we concluded that bailing halfway up the ridge would not help us to deal with the soon-to-be-named Bear Creek Fire, so we continued upward.

The cleft on pitch six required a long 5.10-ish stemming move over the 100'-deep gap. Rolf created a handhold with a nut and a sling to tension across the gap. After removing the gear, and with the benefit of long legs and a top-rope, I was able to free the moves.

Two pitches later, we topped out on a tower and rappelled about 100' into a notch. Pitches eight through ten served up aesthetic face and crack climbing on solid rock, with outstanding views of the aptly name Picket Range immediately to our east and the sheer northwest-facing wall of Spectre Peak across the way to the south. As the difficulties eased off, we coiled the rope and soloed about 400' of fourth-class to the sharp summit ridge, followed by an exhilarating traverse to the final pinnacle. The descent by the southeast face route required methodical downclimbing and a sprint across a snowfield exposed to rockfall. (This would be more straightforward on snow earlier in the season.) We eventually circled back to our camp under Ghost Peak. The next day, bad weather scuttled our other plans in the Pickets, but also dampened the Bear Creek Fire's threat to our route home.

The west ridge of Phantom Peak is ten pitches plus approximately 400' of easy soloing, and involves much 5.7+ climbing with a single sequence of 5.10. 🔲

– ERIC WEHRLY

SNOQUALMIE PASS, CHAIR PEAK, THE UPPER WEST SIDE

SNOQUALMIE PASS HAS been extensively explored by skiers, but there is still plenty of untapped mixed-climbing terrain for those keen on adventure. On January 18, Doug Hutchinson and I skied around to the less-explored west face of Chair Peak (6,238') to see what we could find. A non-technical scramble in warmer months, the face is a jumble of rock buttresses and couloirs. To my knowledge, there were no established winter routes.

Our route climbed a 700' snow and ice gully capped by a cauldron of rock. An ephemeral pillar of ice flowed partway down the right face of the steep headwall. To gain access to the ice, I led an easy

mixed pitch up a series of left-facing corners to a comfortable ledge system. Doug took over the lead with a pitch of thin and technical smears and detached curtains. A perfectly placed tree provided a sturdy anchor. The remainder of the route consisted of steep snow and moderate but exposed mixed climbing up a bowl to a false summit, from which we followed the striking northwest ridge—first climbed in winter by Robert Harris and Kit Lewis in 1975—to the top.

The west face of Chair Peak, showing The Upper West Side, the first known winter route up the face. *Kyle McCrohan*

Our descent involved several rappels and downclimbing in the couloir on climber's right—what I believe to be the original 1928 summer route up the west face. We finished the day by skiing the remainder of the Chair Peak circumnavigation in the dark. I am not very creative, and all of Doug's name suggestions were too inappropriate. We settled on The Upper West Side (300m, WI5- M5 PG-13 60°).

This side of Chair Peak is anything but climbed out. Later in the season, friends tried a central plumb line, but conditions forced them to turn around. Several more mixed routes seem to exist on the various buttresses, and that plumb line still awaits an ascent. ⊡

– MICHAEL TELSTAD

SNOQUALMIE MOUNTAIN, NORTHWEST FACE, THE SNOSTRIL

DURING EARLY DECEMBER 2020, on a way-too-early ice hunting trip to the northwest face of Snoqualmie Mountain (6,278') with Tom Beirne and Christian Junkar, I spotted a plastered smear I had never noticed previously. This smear was much farther west (climber's right) than the established mixed lines on the face, of which there are at least five (including variations). It sits roughly halfway between the western exit chute of Thunder Basin (the bowl below the northwest face) and the Snot Couloir. The ice that grabbed my attention would not be called ice in most other places, but we take what we can get around here.

After about 40m of scratching verglas, with occasional rock gear, I pulled into an alcove on the left, happy to be done blunting my picks. Tom led a second 20m pitch, but the terrain above looked even more suspect. We bailed. When Christian and I returned a month later, we found slightly thicker ice and added a 60m rope-stretching pitch of WI4- above our first outing's effort. It ended in a cave beneath a massive chockstone; exiting the cave would require navigating an overhanging wall on the right. The lack of features and gear once again stopped us in our tracks.

Tom, Christian, and I returned a final time on January 29, 2021. Screw placements were finally frequent and secure. Even better, the crux overhanging wall to the right of the cave was both shorter—due to snow accu-

Tom Beirne climbing the mixed crux of the Snostril on the northwest face of Snoqualmie Mountain. *Doug Hutchinson*

mulation—and now plastered with ice. Tom led out of the cave via a 15m section of techy WI4 M5 climbing, and finished the 30m pitch on easier snow.

We were now in the bottom of a 50° snow couloir. Though the original plan had been to simul up this couloir, a mixed pitch 55m higher spoke to Christian. This 30m WI4 M5 alternative finish, which we named the Post Nasal Drip, had the best pure ice of the day. We topped out on a western subsummit of Snoqualmie. A steep walk off the south side brought us down to our packs.

Though the northwest face of Snoqualmie Mountain is not easy to reach, I was surprised no one had reported climbing our route before—rightly so, it turned out. We later heard from Mike Preiss, who told us he attempted the route in 1993 and backed off at the crux traverse out of the cave. In 2010, he rapped in and rope-soloed the crux. Therefore, Mike gets credit for the first ascent of the route, piecemeal; ours was the first integral free ascent: The Snostril (250m, WI4 M5).

– DOUG HUTCHINSON

ESMERALDA PEAK EAST, MOONLIGHT SERENDIPITY

ON NOVEMBER 21, Kyle McCrohan, Michael Telstad, and I approached an obscure and improbable line in the Cascades that Kyle had noticed on a condition reports webpage. The approach was fairly long for a route about which we had no further knowledge. In all likelihood, we would just be taking the gear for a walk, but a clear forecast beckoned. Off we went to poke our heads around in the Teanaway area.

About five miles before the Esmeralda Trailhead, we encountered some new deadfall covering the paved road into the area, so we parked and strapped our boots on. As we hiked up the Esmeralda Basin Trail and finally got an unobstructed view of our intended line, it was clear we wouldn't be getting on it that day. The ice appeared dangerously unstable, and the remaining approach was more than we had time for. However, we were struck by a nearby line that looked even more interesting. The northeast face of Esmeralda Peak East (ca 6,500', labeled as Esmeralda Peak–East Peak on some maps) looked like a classic alpine blend of thin ice, clean rock, and thoughtful mixed terrain. The abundance of possible rappel trees also caught our attention.

After crossing the North Fork Teanaway River and completing a steep treed approach, we pulled the ropes and pointy things out of our packs. A few pitches of ice with only sparse protection and easy mixed terrain led to a snow ramp. From here, we accessed a wide chimney that made for fun climbing on solid rock. Two more pitches of low-angle mixed climbing brought us to a headwall. The most plausible and direct line through it was a mixed corner. The rock deteriorated as we started

The upper northeast face of Esmeralda Peak East. Moonlight Serendipity (1,200', WI3 M5) follows obvious ice runnels, angling up ramps to the right near the top. *Kyle McCrohan*

up, crumbling beneath our picks and crampon points. Protection was hard to find on this pitch, but the climbing wasn't unreasonably difficult.

At this point we had run out of daylight. I didn't want to get into any dicey climbing in the darkness, so looked around a corner and found a perfect narrow snow ramp that led us to the snowfield above. Three more pitches of run-out mixed terrain brought us to the summit of Esmeralda Peak East.

Michael led the way for most of the descent, giving Kyle and me time to ogle the silhouettes of the surrounding peaks in full moonlight. I couldn't have been happier to be in such a beautiful position, especially after having my expectations for the day wildly exceeded. With that in mind, we named the route Moonlight Serendipity (1,200', WI3 M5). 📷

— KURT ROSS

Davy Crockett's Squirrel Gun (1,200' of climbing, IV M6) on the north face of Williams Peak. The June Couloir (1986) is partially visible to the right. *Kirk Bachman*

IDAHO / SAWTOOTH MOUNTAINS

WILLIAMS PEAK, NORTH FACE, DAVY CROCKETT'S SQUIRREL GUN

ON MAY 27, Ky Hart, Earl Lunceford, and I climbed a new route on the north face of Williams Peak (10,636'). Davy Crockett's Squirrel Gun is located climber's left of the super-classic June Couloir (a.k.a. Kitty Litter Couloir, III 5.7), first climbed in 1986 by Kirk Bachman and Ben Franklin. However, our addition covers a very different style of terrain.

The first pitch, at M6, is the crux. It begins in a gray dike and moves through an offwidth and chimney before heading left on thin face moves. The second pitch is M5 and starts in a number five–size offwidth. This pitch ends with some long runouts. After that, several long and much easier pitches bring one to the summit ridge. We descended the June Couloir, which was surprisingly difficult, leaving pins for rappel anchors. We encountered some nasty natural rockfall; future parties might find it more enjoyable to descend the south face of the mountain in an up-and-over style.

This was my second attempt at this route. I bailed on a solo attempt two weeks earlier due to a lack of wide protection and my usual fear of being alone in hard terrain, but I came back with the perfect crew and had an incredible day on a spectacular route. Davy Crockett's Squirrel Gun has 1,200' of climbing over eight pitches and is IV M6. 📷

— MATT WARD

SELDOM SEEN SPIRE

ON SEPTEMBER 8 and 9, Ky Hart and I climbed a new route on an unnamed spire in the Sawtooth Mountains. The north-facing wall of the spire rises above the cirque that drains the north face of Decker Peak, a four miles south of Redfish Lake and the Elephants Perch. The summit (9,880') is a subpeak on Decker's east ridge.

Our route's first two pitches were thin nailing and other aid through loose rock. The effort paid off, as the rock quality improved the higher we got. We bivied after pitch three—more for fun than necessity.

Pitches three through six went all free, around 5.9. They had excellent granite, as though it was meant to be climbed, with a great position high on the spire. The best pitch was the last: a perfect clean corner, 80' long, to the summit. We found a cairn on top but have not found any information on the tower; we presume it was climbed from the ridge. The spire is not visible from anywhere but within the cirque, so we named our route Seldom Seen Spire (650', 6 pitches, IV 5.9 A2). ◙

– MATT WARD

MONTANA/ CABINET MOUNTAINS

A PEAK, NORTH FACE, THE STUMBLING STONE

When I met Gunner Madsen in March 2021, he had only been climbing in the gym for 11 months, but was stoked to begin trad climbing. I decided to mentor Gunner with the intent of getting him ready for a route on the Elephants Perch in the Sawtooths of Idaho. We began climbing together every weekend, and by late June he had the confidence and skills needed to head into the alpine. We planned a trip to Blodgett Canyon in Montana to gauge our efficiency as a team.

About halfway through the drive from Spokane to Blodgett, an idea popped into my head: *What if we went into the Cabinets instead and tried to do a first ascent?* I had seen A Peak (8,634') in the Cabinet Mountains in 2019—ever since, I'd dreamed of climbing it. Now seemed like a good opportunity.

The Cabinets are about an hour southwest of Libby, Montana, and A Peak is the second highest mountain in the range. In 2018, Scott Coldiron and Jess Roskelley completed an ice and mixed route called Canmore Wedding Party (2,500', AI5 M7), which climbs the huge central gully on the north face. I'd been eager to explore the rock to climber's right of this. [*Editor's Note: Over three days in August 1962, Dan Doody and William Echo climbed a route up the north face of A Peak that likely started to the left of the line described in this report; it eventually entered the central couloir taken by Canmore Wedding Party and ascended that gully's right wall (AAJ 1963).*]

Gunner and I left the parking lot at 11 p.m. via the Granite Lake Trail and walked the 6.5 miles into Granite Lake. We bedded down for a couple of hours and then headed up to the base of A Peak's north face. We climbed four pitches up on new terrain, built an anchor, and rapped—we needed to make it back in time for work on Monday.

I called Gunner the next day and told him I had

The north side of A Peak (8,634') from near Granite Lake. (1) Feefyefoh (Gray-Mylan, 2021), which climbs the east face of the prominent subsummit. (2) Castor Sally (Gray-Marine, 2020). (3) The huge gully of Canmore Wedding Party (Coldiron-Roskelley, November 2018). (4) The Stumbling Stone (Godby-Madsen, 2021). The first known ascent of this face was in 1962 (Doody-Echo), starting left of (4) and moving into the central gully. All routes involve 2,000' to 2,500' of climbing. *Spencer Gray*

to go back. The peak was too inspiring to forget. This time, knowing what we were getting into, we planned with militaristic precision. We headed out Saturday evening, and again left the parking lot at 11 p.m. On Sunday, July 4, we reclimbed the four pitches we'd already done and added another six that day. The rock quality in the first six pitches was variable—at times absolute choss. But by pitch eight, after a long leftward traverse on broken terrain, the rock became quite good and remained so for the rest of the route.

We reached a giant flat ledge area, which we called Tier One, in the dark, and decided to bivy here. On our first visit to A Peak, there were no mosquitoes, but it was a different story this time. From pitch six to the summit, we had a permanent cloud of mosquitoes trailing us. The omnipresent buzzing made sleeping difficult.

In the morning, 300' of unroped easy terrain brought us to the base of a big, clean wall. Next came three rope-stretching pitches, all over 200', each with at least a few moves of 5.10—one sequence of which, on pitch 11, saw me about 40' run-out. The 13th pitch was classic: splitter hands, an incredible position, and a small roof to boot. I had thought it might spit us out on the summit, but how wrong I was: When we finished the pitch, around 1 p.m., we were on yet another big ledge, which we called Tier Two, with an 800' tower still looming above us.

Following a bit more unroped scrambling down and to the right, we climbed three more long pitches and reached the summit around 5 p.m. We had completed The Stumbling Stone (2,800' of climbing, V 5.10). It was more than either of us had hoped to achieve as climbers, but we didn't stop to appreciate that at the summit; after a couple of quick pictures, the mosquitoes got us moving again.

The descent went better than expected, but we were physically and mentally exhausted. We got back to the car around 1 a.m. and started driving home for work on Tuesday. We had climbed the route in 53 hours car-to-car, with four hours of sleep (two hours each night). If I did it again, I'd plan for 72 hours. [*A pitch-by-pitch description is included with this report at the AAJ website.*] 📄 📷

– KELTY GODBY

A PEAK, EAST FACE OF EAST SUBPEAK, FEEFYEFOH

IN LATE JULY, Kate Mylan and I climbed the high-quality fall line of the east face of the east subsummit (~8,400') of A Peak in the Cabinet Mountains Wilderness. Castor Sally, a route I climbed with Alex Marine in 2020, is to the right of this new line on the pillar that forms the lower right side of the subpeak. In the absence of another name, we've been calling this distinct subpeak "Gemini Point" to distinguish it from the main summit, of which it is almost a twin.

By following mostly dihedrals from bottom to top, we took advantage of the best rock and protection on the face. This was a direttissima, but the kind where a drop of water would linger on its way down. We lingered on the way up. The climb gets harder and more interesting higher up the beanstalk.

Three scruffy, moderate pitches off the ground (5.6–5.8) lead to 300' of unroped climbing up darker, water-stained rock. Here, just right of a bomb-bay chimney at the center of the face, the fun climbing begins. Footholds on the compact, rippled features combine with occasional jams and good protection in corner cracks to make for lovely 5.9 climbing. Sections of the colorful rock appear lifted from a confectioner's shop or sliced off an ice cream cake.

Easy pitches separate a committing chimney capped by a bell-shaped offwidth exit (5.10a) and two pitches with short roofs, one with excellent fingerlocks (5.10d), the other more awkward and a little loose (5.11a). Above the second roof and below a final tower, a long slab hosts a three-star

bivy at its upper edge. From here you can stare down the central maw that separates A Peak's main summit and the subpeak. We didn't smell the blood of an Englishman here, but others may.

The regal final tower, home, perhaps, to one or another grumpy giant, has the steepest climbing, with three separate roofs guarding the central dihedral and good protection through each crux. We split it into three pitches (5.11, 5.11+, 5.11a). Thoughtful route-finding on the face to either side of the corner, with crimps hidden by white lichen, reduces the need to simply grunt up it. The crux roof required directionals to keep the rope from knocking off blocks. A small set of pins is recommended on this route.

A deep notch separates the subpeak from the main summit, with roped and scrambling options to the top. A pleasant walk-off to the south, with one mandatory 80' rappel halfway down, follows mountain goat trails and the edge of snowfields through lush hanging valleys across from the remnants of Blackwell Glacier.

A car-to-car ascent of Feefye-foh (2,000' vertical, 14 pitches, 5.11+) would be doable, but the mandatory two- to three-hour bushwhack from Granite Lake to the small snowfields at the base would make it a bruiser.

– SPENCER GRAY

Kate Mylan in the big corner system (three pitches, each of them 5.11) on the final tower of Feefyefoh (2,000', 5.11+) on A Peak's eastern subsummit. *Spencer Gray*

Mt. Brown's northwest face. (1) Your Other Left (Bourret-Clark, 2020). (2) Complete Left Gully (Clark, 2020). (3) Mile of Smiles (Reardon, 2003). (4) Right Gully. Routes gain about 5,000 feet to the summit. *Adam Clark*

MT. BROWN, NORTHWEST FACE ROUTES

THE NORTHWEST FACE of Mt. Brown (8,565') in the center of Glacier National Park has two prominent—and in some years even popular—ice climbs. Known as Right Gully and Left Gully, they consist of thousands of feet of rolling WI2/3 with the occasional WI4 step. Both routes finish short of Brown's summit. In *Big Sky Ice*, Ron Brunckhorst suggests members of Montana's legendary Dirty Sox Club might have done the first ascents, but the dates or climbers remain a mystery.

In November 2003, after climbing the lower half of Right Gully, Blase Reardon—one of Glacier's alpine climbing pioneers—continued up 2,000' of unclimbed terrain, diagonaling up and climber's left, before joining the southwest ridge to reach the summit (*AAJ 2004*). His route, Mile of Smiles (IV 5.2 WI3+), is an excellent climb and endurance challenge.

Inspired by this long-ago precedent, I decided to see if Left Gully had worthwhile terrain above the traditional turnaround spot at roughly 7,000'. At this elevation the ice ends and the gully broadens into a rock-walled basin topped by a steep cliff band guarding the summit ridge.

On December 3, 2020, I started alone in foggy darkness. The climbing began at around 3,600'. Conditions were marginal, and I had to make some moves on wet rock and thin ice, but above 5,000' I enjoyed a ribbon of grade 2 or 3 water ice interspersed with steep snowfields. By midday I had reached the cliff below the ridge. After some false starts, I pulled a few steep M2 moves and continued on snow- and ice-plastered fourth-class rock to the summit ridge at 8,300'. Twenty minutes later, I was on top and basking in brilliant sunshine. I descended the shady northeast face to Avalanche Lake. The Left Gully taken to the summit (5,000', IV WI3/4 M2) is a superb fall or early winter alpine climb of moderate technical difficulty but demanding length. Several more difficult variations are possible, with ice up to WI4–5+ and stout dry-tooling challenges.

Blase Reardon had told me years ago, "You know, there is a third gully on Brown's northwest face. It is located left of the Left Gully. If you climb it, you should name it Your Other Left!" I finally set out to explore this mysterious third gully in December 2019 with Glacier ranger Ed Visnovske, but spindrift and dwindling daylight turned us around at 6,500'.

On December 6, 2020, three days after my ascent of the full Left Gully, the weather and avalanche conditions were still ideal for another big route, so I partnered with Sammy Bourret for a second attempt on the left-most gully. Temperatures had dropped since my climb of Left Gully, and the low-elevation ice had improved considerably. We began swinging tools at about 3,800' and moved quickly up several WI3 pitches and one short WI4 pitch. At 5,800' the gully narrowed to a few feet wide and offered passage through a formidable cliff band. Sammy then led a short but steep WI4 pitch at 7,000'. The final 800' continued up a deep cleft with fourth-class rock. We scratched our way up to a final snowfield and then the summit ridge at 7,900'. From the top, we descended the south face to Snyder Lake—definitely faster than going down to Avalanche Lake.

Your Other Left (4,800', IV 4th-class WI4) is another outstanding climb covering thousands of feet of moderate terrain in a beautiful alpine setting. 📷

– ADAM CLARK

MONTANA / MISSION MOUNTAINS

WEST ST. MARYS PEAK, SNYELMN PILLAR

In early September, Damian Mast and I hiked to a north-facing pillar above the south shore of Sonielem Lake in the Mission Mountains Tribal Wilderness. This pillar is an anomaly, pinched out of the northeast aspect of the northwest ridge of West St. Marys Peak (9,372'), like a crimp in a pie crust. The pillar appears to be made of thin beds of Precambrian limestone and siltite. It is generally steep, competent rock. The pillar varies from about ten to 80 feet wide, and the rock quality degrades quickly on either side. I'm not aware of other technical routes on this aspect of the northwest ridge.

After bivying above Vacation Pass to the south of Sonielem Lake, we scrambled to the base of the pillar at dawn. The first seven pitches, connecting ledge systems, were fairly moderate, with sustained difficulties from 5.7 to 5.10. Many small blocks and stacked flakes were piled on ledges and plastered on faces, so choosing protected belays was important. The underlying rock was sound, however.

The pillar is split into three tiers, the divisions coming at the end of pitches two and six. The climbing

Seen from the outlet of Sonielem Lake, the Snyelmn Pillar is the obvious central buttress. *Spencer Gray*

consisted of incipient cracks on faces, frequent horizontal breaks for hands and feet, and wandering corners. The line climaxed with a full-value 5.11+ pitch that shifted from a run-out face with finicky gear to an overhung corner capped with deep, reachy jams in a roof and a foot-cutting sequence. We walked off at dark after scrambling south over the summit of West St. Marys.

This line deserves repeating. Beyond quality climbing and attractive stone, much of it covered in lichen the colors of wood ash and neon daffodils, the route offers a unique technical passage out of a beautiful amphitheater. We called the route Snyelmn Pillar (1,300', 9 pitches, 5.11+). "Snyelmn" (anglicized on the lake and other landmarks as "Sonielem") is the local Salish word for "the place where you surround something," referring both to a place and a way of hunting. A full alpine rack, including small wires and pins, is recommended. 📷

– SPENCER GRAY

at dark after Spencer led a fantastic 70-meter 5.10+ pitch that had the most continuous splitter cracks of the entire route.

Spencer and I hiked back a final time after waiting out days of heavy rain at my house, an hour's drive from the trailhead. We jugged our lines to drill some key bolts and work the crux moves on the third pitch, then returned to the ground to mount a full free attempt. We went for it on August 23, the last day of climbable but still cold weather (the wall gets no sunshine after the summer solstice). Spencer dispatched the crux third pitch at 5.12b and then did the same with the fourth pitch at 5.11+. My contribution was freeing the eighth pitch, a chimney and offwidth, at 5.11-. After 15 hours, we completed the free ascent of Rite of Groot (V 5.12b or 5.9 A3-). We endured a marginal bivy near the top, and by the next afternoon the wall was fully cleaned up. Kyle, Jim, and Bill joined us to haul the huge kit back to the trailhead.

To our knowledge, this is the only rock climb in the Black Canyon drainage (and possibly in the entire Lake Fork drainage), aside from the standard four-pitch route on the Bears Tooth. (There are excellent ice climbs here, though.) Then again, this is the Beartooths, where over the decades people climbed but didn't report much of anything.

The route is equipped with stainless-steel belay anchors and rap rings, and was done with only seven protection bolts. (The aid variation has one bathook and two rivets.) Aid ascents will need pins, but it goes free without them. 📄 📷

— PETE DRONKERS

WYOMING / ABSAROKA RANGE

CLARKS FORK CANYON, THE MOUTH, LONG LIMESTONE ROUTES

TWENTY-FIVE MILES NORTH of Cody, Wyoming, at the mouth of historic Clarks Fork Canyon, stand imposing 2,000' slabs of pale blue Madison Limestone. Remnants of an ancient seabed that covered the Intermountain West, most of this rock is exposed through canyons and faulting in a cross-section of its layers. The slabs at the mouth of Clarks Fork, however, are actually tilted by the bulging of the Yellowstone Plateau. The rock is smooth and undulating like the sea floor it once was, and the quality is more akin to that of the Verdon Gorge than the broken crags of Rifle and Logan canyons.

My friends and I learned about Clarks Fork limestone some 30 years ago from Cody resident Bobby Model. Despite his claims about the high-quality rock, the notion that it was less than vertical kept our young, strong arms from turning the steering wheels in that direction. Bob tragically passed away after a car accident in South Africa in 2007, and despite the odd new route up obvious gullies and weaknesses (most with large runouts) at the mouth of Clarks Fork Canyon, there has been little real development.

Meanwhile, as the years and scar tissue accumulated during the last three decades, close friends Mike Lilygren, Shep Vail, and I have altered our primary focus in route development: Whereas once we wanted to create personal testpieces for our peers, we are now pursuing something a bit more egalitarian. The code has become: "The experience of the second ascent is more important than that of the first ascent." That is, the climbing experience doesn't have to be difficult, per se—it should be fun.

Our first route at Clarks Fork, in the fall of 2019, embodied this approach. It was a 12-pitch affair on a rib of extremely solid rock. For the most part, the rib had ledges every 25–35m, allowing for comfortable stances from which to belay and rappel. The odd crack or dihedral gave most pitches optional gear placements, and in a few places there were runnels that could be protected much like a crack. We bolted all the cruxes and then added additional bolts in several spots to make the climbing safer and more accessible at the grade (versus leaving long sections of unprotected moderate climbing). The crux of this route—which we named Colter's Rib, after trapper John Colter, who passed under the wall in the winter of 1808—came in at 5.10c. Most pitches were in the 5.7 to 5.9 range.

From the top of that route, we walked through forest and scree to reach the northeast ridge of an obvious spire, which we called Colter's Spire. The rock here was less solid, but some of the climbing was excellent, and the airy summit was worth a little choss. We topped out after four pitches, all roughly 30m, and none of them harder than 5.8. The route is mostly bolt-protected, but requires a light rack.

On our next trip, in the spring of 2020, we turned our focus to a much bigger spire to the north. Broken into four distinct bands of rock, each roughly 400' in length, this route got harder as we went higher. To complete this project, we used hundreds of feet of fixed line and bivied in a cave about halfway up. The route topped out on a tower we dubbed Chief Joseph Spire, for the Nez Perce chief who led his people away from the U.S. Cavalry via Clarks Fork Canyon. We named the route Forever (21 pitches, 5.11d), based on one of the chief's speeches. The hardest pitch can be climbed by a 5.10 leader by hanging his/her way through the crux on bolts.

[Top] Schlepping ropes, gear, and bolting equipment to the base of the slabs. *Sam Lightner Jr.* [Bottom] Sam Lightner Jr. climbing the 5.11a 21st pitch of M11, belayed by Mike Lilygren. *Kyle Duba*

Our third line, opened in the fall of 2021, ascended Buffalo Horn Spire, named for a Bannock chief who fought and lost a nearby battle with the U.S. Army. (This spire was first climbed by Justin Willis, by a different line.) Our route, M11, is 22 pitches with a 5.11c crux that can be climbed at C0; there are some obligatory 5.10 sections. M11 is named after the aforementioned Bobby Model. As with all the routes we have established at the Mouth, a light rack is useful despite ample bolts.

Mike, Shep, and I have a very tight relationship, and it seems to get stronger with each new route we do together. We always agree on the line, and generally begin answering each other's questions just before they get verbalized. It's a really cool camaraderie that comes from thousands of hours of climbing together, and makes the sport that much more enjoyable. I've come to realize that while the competitive days of youth were fun, doing moderates with my closest friends is even better.

We established all of these routes in a hybrid style, with some pitches climbed bottom up, others cleaned and equipped from above. We climbed many pitches in a run-out style, then added bolts later to make for enjoyable future ascents. All bolts are stainless steel, and all rappel anchors are set up so that they do not require parties to add or replace webbing. 📷

– SAM LIGHTNER JR.

EDITOR'S NOTE: *Pitch-by-pitch descriptions of these routes and other useful information are posted at Mountain Project. Lightner, Lilygren, and Vail also established an 11-pitch 1,400' 5.9 called Back Pain, but described it on Mountain Project as "a bad route that should not be attempted unless you like loose rock and fractured climbing. We note it because it has been climbed."*

WYOMING / GRAND TETON NATIONAL PARK

TABLE MOUNTAIN, SOUTH FACE, 29 FINGERS

MOST CLIMBERS WHO'VE spent significant time on the Lower Saddle between the Grand Teton and the Middle Teton have looked off toward the western edge of the park and seen the large swath of granite walls that make up the backside of Table Mountain (11,111'). Many have even considered making the journey out there to discover what these walls possess in untouched rock. Despite this, few have followed through, and Table Mountain has seen relatively little activity from climbers in the past 25 years. Paul Horton and Jon Stuart established Heartbreak Ridge on the south buttress in July 1995. In 2013, a route named Line of Fire (III 5.10c) was put up on the south buttress. Another route named Kindred Spirits (III 5.11) was established in 2021 on the north buttress.

After enough time dreaming about Table Mountain, Jamison Johnson, Thomas Ney, and I decided a trip was in order. Based in Driggs, Idaho, the three of us decided we wouldn't use the 8.5-mile approach via Cascade Canyon, but instead hike up Table Mountain from the west. On September 29, we reached the summit of Table in about four miles via the popular Face Trail. We descended an obvious gully to the south, which brought us to the bottom of the south-facing wall just left of the southernmost buttress.

Grant Burson warming up above the bivouac lodge on pitch 2 or run of 29 Fingers (9 pitches, III 5.10+) on Table Mountain. *Thomas Ney*

From the ground, we could see three steep golden walls, stacked one above the other, and decided to aim for them. Above the first pitch of standard Teton choss wrangling, we found a pitch with a beautiful splitter crack and engaging climbing. A stretch of low-angle loose terrain was followed by more solid rock on the fourth pitch, angling left at 5.8.

On the clean first headwall, an exceptional 5.9 hand and fist crack followed by a 5.8 pitch brought us to a large ledge below the second headwall. We bivied here, happy to take off our heavy packs filled with sleeping gear, food, and water.

The next morning, we were greeted by a sunrise over the iconic Cathedral group. The second headwall, directly above us, turned out to be the crux of the route. Pitch seven was a 5.10+ hand crack terminating in a small ledge in the middle of the face. On pitch eight, gear became sparse. Resorting to some aid to sort out the protection, we lowered back to the base of the pitch, leaving some of the gear preplaced, and climbed it on lead, also at 5.10+. We left one fixed nut behind to prevent ledge falls for future ascensionists.

Delighted, we followed another ledge system to the ninth and final pitch, which began in a corner filled with stemming and continued through a wild roof. We finished at the top of the last headwall at 10,826' (GPS). A short third-class scramble would lead to the true summit of Table Mountain, for those who want to tag the top. We called our route 29 Fingers (660', 9 pitches, III 5.10+) in recognition of the number of fingers used between the three of us on the first ascent: Earlier in the year, Jamison had lacerated a knuckle and severed a tendon in his pointer finger, forcing him to climb in a rigid finger cast. 📄 📷 🔍

– GRANT BURSON

WYOMING / WIND RIVER RANGE

ST. LAWRENCE BASIN, WOLVERINE CIRQUE, NEW ROUTES

ON AUGUST 7, Taylor Harmon and I left the St. Lawrence Basin ranger station on the east side of the Winds with the intention of establishing a few new routes in the Wolverine Cirque, sans bolt kit. This area was first visited in August 1988 by none other than Fred Beckey and James Garrett (*see AAJ 1990*); a number of climbers put up new routes in 2018 and 2019.

On our first day in the cirque, we ascended an unclimbed formation at the northwest end that we later dubbed the Good Buddy Buttress. Our climb started with 400' of exposed fifth-class up to 5.6, followed by three consecutive long 5.10 pitches to the top. We descended via the eastern ridge, rapping off chockstones that we hammered into cracks. The route is called Bad Larry (III 5.10).

Our second route was on an alpine tower just north of a formation called the Shield. We climbed six pitches on really good rock, varying in style from hands to fingers to offwidth to squeeze chimney to slab. At the crux, pitch four, I climbed a 5.11 face above my homemade bird beaks, which I'd pounded into thin cracks. On top of the tower, a gigantic golden eagle swooped above us and blasted out of sight over the horizon. We rapped the route, leaving four nuts and some 6mm cord behind.

We named our second route the CAC Route (6 pitches, 5.11), standing for Cashiers Alpine Club. The cliffs around Cashiers, North Carolina, are a favorite venue of mine, and the place where Taylor and I first shook hands and forged a climbing partnership. 📄 📷

– DYLAN VALVO

[Spread] Michael Abbey climbs while Gareth "Gaz" Leah belays on the Tail Feather headwall (5.12), during the complete ascent of Golden Eagle Feathers (IV 5.12c). [Inset] Abbey inspects some damage at the foot of Warbonnet Peak (behind him). *Will Saunders (both)*

WARBONNET PEAK, SOUTHEAST FACE, GOLDEN EAGLE FEATHERS

GOLDEN EAGLE FEATHERS are sacred to many and hold a place of prominence on a warbonnet. They carry strong medicine and guide the wearer toward courage, strength, and hope. In 2012, I witnessed two golden eagles dance together in the sky while I was climbing the "Eagle Feather," a feather-shaped band of rock partway up the southeast face of Warbonnet Peak (12,369', 42°45'40"N, 109°12'56"W; *"War Bonnet" is the official U.S. spelling*). The resulting route (III 5.11b) ended at a large gully directly below the higher "Tail Feather," and from there Nancy Bockino, Michael Kirby, and I descended.

It is said that the eagle flies highest of all birds, carrying our prayers up to the Creator. Hoping

to witness the eagles again, I returned many times to attempt the Tail Feather formation. In August 2020, Gareth "Gaz" Leah and I finally climbed this 11-pitch route in its entirety: Golden Eagle Feathers (IV 5.12c). The route shares the first pitch of Brown Cow and follows my 2012 climb to gain the Tail Feather headwall, which comprises exciting 5.12 climbing with a mix of bolts and gear. If combined, pitches seven and eight would make for a stellar 5.13.

The gift of a golden eagle feather represents honor, wisdom, and utmost respect. If you go to this place, treat it the same. As Black Elk of the Oglala Lakota said, "All things are our relatives; what we do to everything, we do to ourselves. All is really One."

— MICHAEL ABBEY

MT. WOOLSEY AND INNOMINATE: NEW ROUTES, 25 YEARS APART

The west face of Mt. Woolsey (12,978') , showing (1) Where the Animals Go (Ochenski-Schunk, 1996), (2) When Old Meets New (Parsons-Schunk, 2021), and (3) Candalaria (Richardson-Schunk, 1995). The normal route up the south ridge is on the right skyline. *George Schunk*

TWENTY-SEVEN YEARS AGO, when we shared the ripe age of 41, Kirk Richardson of Portland, Oregon, introduced me to the potential of Wyoming's Bighorn Mountains. He noted that my Wyoming cousin Edward Schunk had photographed the range for the Bonneys' guide in the 1960s and had a few first ascents of his own.

With Ed's guidance, in 1995, Kirk and I entered Wilderness Basin, a westside drainage north of Cloud Peak. We warmed up on the clean west face of the Innominate and the Gargoyle, two routes from Bonneys' guide. On the Innominate, we found an ancient braided-rope anchor, a possible remnant of a historic 1933 expedition, when W.B. Willcox and teammates made the first recorded ascents of Innominate, Mt. Woolsey, and Black Tooth.

Next, we put up a wandering free-solo line on the slabs comprising the north side of Cloud Peak, south of a tarn at 11,170'. Sufficiently emboldened, Kirk and I next chose a plum line falling from the prominent spire on the southern shoulder of the west face of Mt. Woolsey. A sliver of dark rock originates and cascades between the spire's twin angular summits, narrowing as it falls. Its right margin marks our four-pitch ascent route to the southernmost summit. Like other routes in this cirque, the quality of rock varied greatly. To our distress, the climb's hardest moves coincided with a patch of loose rock. We named the probable new route Candalaria (III 5.10), our neighborhood and stomping grounds in Salem, Oregon.

While the getting was good, I returned to the Bighorns in 1996 with George Ochenski and Hal Harper of Helena, Montana. Hal put golden trout on the table while George and I ascended a new four-pitch line, the Southwest Face (II 5.7), to the right of Wilcox's west face route on the Innominate. Six inches of snow had fallen at 11,000' on August 6, and melting verglas made the approach super dicey.

I then suggested to George that we try a line on the west face of Woolsey, just north and above Candalaria—it looked user-friendly and shorter. But George wanted to try the long line directly below the summit, south of the col between Black Tooth and Woolsey. The broken lower third of the wall is capped by a clean headwall with several right-facing corners, including a prominent dihedral in the middle. We started immediately below this dihedral, with a crux on pitch four involving blank ground linking two corners. We descended the route in four rappels and made it back to camp 10.5 hours after departing. We called our new six-pitch route Where the Animals Go (III 5.10).

I couldn't bring myself to publish our photos and routes. There was more work to be done on the west face of Woolsey, and I wanted to be part of it. I left Montana soon after these climbs and enjoyed many adventures in South America and work in Washington, D.C. By the time the pristine lakes and glacial cirques of Wilderness Basin began calling, the challenges of backpacking uphill 13 miles with climbing gear were real. Aging and it's close cousin, wear and tear, took their toll. Often when my partners were healthy, I was not, and vice versa.

George Schunk and Robby Parsons.

In the summer of 2021, 25 years after my trip to the Bighorns with George and Hal, I had the good fortune to team up with Robby Parsons, a robust 22-year-old athlete out of Bozeman. Upon our arrival in Wilderness Basin he announced, "The walls look bigger than the photos!" In a testament to previous climbers and fishermen, there were still no signs of camping.

We ascended unroped along the bowl to the right of the southwest ridge that splits the west face of Woolsey. I had saved a pound of backpacking weight by using a length of one-inch tubular webbing for my harness, 1960s-style. As we tied in Robby said, "That's *scary* retro!" I took the lead on the first pitch, planning to turn the sharp end over to Robby for the tough stuff. In hindsight, I probably had no business leading 5.7 at 12,700' in isolated wilderness. Everything felt awkward, and I stopped after only 100'. It was time to off-load the Ferrari I had trailered from Montana. Robby roared up to the belay and continued on. The swirling clouds lifted above the summit—today there would be no fear of afternoon showers. It was pure bliss and worth the long wait to return.

Robby's joy and confidence were captivating as I paid the rope out on the third pitch. I didn't as much clean this crux pitch as dirty it. Wild stems in a vertical open book led to a four-foot roof. Any residual off-the-couch stamina of my 68 years lasted about 30'. Thereafter I became the load for Robby's 3:1 pulley system. The fourth pitch was cake and we met 10' from the summit, following 400' of roped climbing. We were both grinning. We called our suspected new route When Old Meets New (III 5.10+). 📷

— GEORGE SCHUNK

CALIFORNIA / YOSEMITE NATIONAL PARK

YOSEMITE VALLEY, RIBBON FALLS AMPHITHEATER, SAWANOBORI

OVER THREE DAYS in early September, Chris Koppl and I completed a fun aid climb up the gut of the Ribbon Falls Amphitheater. On our first attempt, in 2020, we found beautiful seam nailing in otherwise mega-polished monolithic rock, climbing about two-thirds of the line. We were itching to return and find out if the high-quality cracks would continue to the top. They did. What surprised us is how much easier the climbing became on the pitches we had already nailed.

During the first attempt, on a key pitch, I ripped four consecutive micro-beak placements during a 30-foot fall. I got back up and kept placing a string of other micro-beaks and two RURPs, plus three hook placements on small natural edges, before getting good gear. It genuinely felt like A4-. However, after the pitch was climbed and cleaned, it felt A2-ish, thank God. It's hard to give this route an honest rating, but our best guess would be A3. There are no enhanced hook placements or bolts to get through blank sections.

Our route follows superb rock directly up the line of the waterfall, and we called it Sawanobori (1,612', 5.7 A3), the Japanese word for the art of climbing running waterfalls and streams. Despite the name, this route is only climbable in mid to late summer or fall, when the waterfall is dry. Don't try it if there is any chance of a storm unless you bring a kayak. We descended by rappelling the route with two 60m ropes. 📄

— VITALIY MUSIYENKO

CALIFORNIA / EASTERN SIERRA

The 1,100-foot ice line of Sacrificial Dread on the east face of Mt. Lewis. *Richard Shore*

MT. LEWIS, SACRIFICIAL DREAD

TAD MCCREA AND I stumbled upon the east face of Mt. Lewis (ca 12,350') in mid-November during a failed ice climbing foray to nearby Parker Falls. After finding not enough ice and too much snow, we wandered up to the Walker Lake trailhead. I'd been curious to see Mt. Lewis from up close—it's the only granitic peak in the netherworld of choss between Tioga Pass and June Lake, and I knew of only one recorded route (Fiddler-Keating, 1980, IV 5.10), which the first ascensionists described as "loose and not recommended." We were more interested in ice this time of year, so we hooted and hollered when we saw the winter potential in this hidden glacial cirque. A big October snowstorm in the high country had set up some fantastic ice and mixed climbing opportunities on this face. We spent Thanksgiving with our families drooling over turkey and our set of reconnaissance photos.

Tad and I returned on December 4, finding even better conditions than we had seen two weeks prior. The mostly dry approach took about two hours, with some post-holing in the latter half. We chose the most obvious line: a narrow ribbon of cascading ice and snow fed by a small sunlit bowl on the ridgeline above.

After a short solo up onto the buttress, we roped up and climbed eight pitches of moderate but sustained alpine ice, bullet-hard névé, and easy 5th-class mixed to the shoulder of Mt. Lewis' eastern subsummit. All pitches were engaging and delicate, with thin névé and tricky protection in the polished quartz monzonite rock. By the third pitch, I was trash-talking the classic Mendel Couloir, and by the sixth pitch we agreed this was one of the best winter routes either of us had climbed in the High Sierra. At the base of the final chimney, we traversed off right onto a mixed rock ramp to avoid a difficult overhanging chockstone exit.

A relatively quick descent along the north ridge looped back down east into the cirque, following a steep snow gully. We used an alpine rack of nuts and cams to three inches, a couple of thin pitons, and four short ice screws; a Spectre or two could have been useful. We called the route Sacrificial Dread (1,100', IV AI3+ 5.5). 📄

— RICHARD SHORE

WHEELER CREST, THE THIRD FIN, HOLE IN THE PUMPKIN

THE RUGGED PARADISE Crags Gully west of Aspen Meadow, roughly halfway between Bishop and Mammoth Lakes, is home to three orange rock walls that have the appearance of fins. The central of these was called the Big K-Mart in the 2001 *AAJ* and is also known as Paradise Point. Unimaginatively, the furthest of the three walls is known as the Third Fin. A Paradise local had climbed a short route on the detached tower at its toe, but no routes had been reported on the main wall.

On Halloween morning, Tad McCrea and I racked up at a series of orange flakes and corners leading up the center of the wall. We followed 5.9–5.10 climbing, with a few stance-drilled bolts that allowed us to face climb around a thin, mangy section of the main corner system. Near the top of our third pitch, we found a vintage drilled-out hex and fixed piton: evident bail anchors from a 1970s or 1980s attempt. Shortly above, on pitch four, lay the 5.11- boulder problem crux which connected two crack systems.

A wandering 5.8 pitch gained the shark-fin ridge atop the wall, where we now were confronted with the unappealing reality of having to walk off the formation in our climbing shoes. The exposed and narrow ridge eventually faded into tree-covered slopes without a proper summit block, completing Hole in the Pumpkin (1,000', IV 5.11-). We painfully descended the loose gully to climber's right. Trick or treat? 📄📷

– RICHARD SHORE

WHEELER CREST, THE SPACE NEEDLE, SELECTA RIDGE

ON MAY 23, Damien Nicodemi, David Pearson, and I trudged up the narrow Fifth Canyon to approach a previously unclimbed 9,600'+ summit near the top of the drainage. This formation, which we dubbed the Space Needle, sits a few thousand feet above the increasingly popular Rocketship and features one of the few enticing alpine ridgelines on the Wheeler Crest—most routes here climb smooth, slabby buttresses.

The steep approach went quickly, with much 4th-class scrambling high in the gully. The toe of the north ridge was littered with shrubbery and overhangs, so we began our climb with a long leftward traverse along a prominent horizontal crack to gain cleaner ground. A few steeper pitches up to 5.10 led onto the exposed and narrow ridge, which presented solid rock and moderate difficulty. A ten-foot overhang required a couple of A1 moves to surpass—this section would likely go free at 5.11+, but would be risky to both leader and second.

We climbed nine long pitches with some unroped scrambling to reach the summit. A tedious descent by the western gully landed us back at our packs, and we improvised a few rappels while descending the gully below. Selecta Ridge (1,500', IV 5.10 A1) was named after our favorite reggae DJ, who kept us thoroughly entertained for over 13 hours that day. Big up! 📷

– RICHARD SHORE

Selecta Ridge, a rare alpine ridge climb in the Wheeler Crest, with about 1,500 feet of climbing. *Richard Shore*

Southwest face of Notch Peak. (1) Southwest Face Left (Brown-Meinzer, 2018). (2) Witch Doctor (Brown-Marvell-Meinzer-Tuttle, 2021). (3) Airavata (Kvashay-Wickstrom, 2016). *Nathan Brown*

UTAH / HOUSE RANGE

NOTCH PEAK, WITCH DOCTOR

On April 9, Matt Meinzer and I made the first free ascent of Witch Doctor (1,400', IV 5.11+ R) on the southwest face of Notch Peak, after numerous earlier trips to establish the line. The route is located to the right of (and independent of) the Southwest Face Left (*AAJ 2019*), which Matt and I free climbed in 2018, and left of the route Airavata (*AAJ 2017*).

I made five trips to the wall to complete this route, the first in fall 2019. The bottom half was established ground-up with help from Jackson Marvell, Matt Meinzer, and Matt Tuttle. Initial exploration on the lower portion involved stressful leading and belaying while managing loose rock. It should be noted that Marvell made a bold lead of the crux second pitch before a few bolts were subsequently added to protect this difficult section. The upper half of the route was established solo and top-down with Micro Trax and trundle-and-clean tactics.

With four distinct 5.11 cruxes, this 13-pitch, majority-trad route provides a "desert alpine" challenge, and much run-out climbing remains. There are bolted anchors throughout, with additional rappel stations on the lower half to facilitate descent.

Establishing this route required a good deal of money, time, labor, and help from sturdy partners. In all, I logged 3,500 miles of driving, approximately 80 miles of hiking, roughly 6,000' of climbing, six books on tape, and one otherworldly trip to Mars with the Witch Doctor. 📷 🔍

– NATHAN BROWN

NOTCH PEAK, EASTERN SOFTBOY AND PROWD ENOUGH

In late May 2020, I met Sam England on the west side of Notch Peak in the West Desert. (I had spent a day hiking in gear and scouting route options as Sam finished the last leg of his drive.) Soon we were at the base of the lower north face, starting up the prominent buttress to the climber's left (east) of the routes Appetite for Destruction and Western Hardman. This wall is approximately halfway up Notch Peak Canyon.

Our line began with a pitch through cracks to reach a third-class ledge. Above this, we climbed three pitches up a right-facing corner and crack system. Encountering deteriorating rock quality, we traversed left and then back right for two pitches, then followed ledges and ramps to the upper headwall. Here, we angled left to a large corner and chimney, with face climbing and a bomb-bay slot to attain a ledge. Another 200' of choose-your-own-adventure scrambling got us to the top of the lower north face.

We fixed lines as we went, which we then used on our way down to clean loose rock, install an additional rappel anchor, and add a few key protection bolts. Eastern Softboy (1,200', 12 pitches,

IV 5.10) sports a reasonable 75-minute approach, moderate grade, and generally good rock.

As Sam and I hiked into Eastern Softboy each day, we stared at the prow at the head of Notch Peak Canyon, an obvious feature that ascends into the namesake notch of the mountain. (This prow is reached by continuing up after the fixed lines on the usual approach to the upper north face, entering a gully to the right of the prow where the normal approach cuts to the right.) We returned in May 2021 with Billyjack Cundiff to find a route up this striking swath of stone.

Our climb was beset with a litany of mishaps, from broken helmets to chopped ropes, largely owing to the decidedly mediocre rock in portions of the route. The middle pitches directly on the prow of Prowd Enough (1,200', 12 pitches, IV 5.10+) climbed nicely enough, but the detours to and from these pitches left something to be desired. A more direct start and finish would make the route more appealing. It's possible either to rappel from the top of the prow or hike down the east side of the mountain. 📷

– DEREK DEBRUIN

KOLOB CANYONS, TUCUPIT POINT, SKELETON KEY, FREE ASCENT

BRANDON GOTTUNG AND Karl Kvashay started up what would become Skeleton Key (1,400', 15 pitches, V 5.13a) on the north face of Tucupit Point back in October 2015. Over the next three years, they spent 26 days on the route, connecting stellar cracks with improbable sections of face climbing. They spent countless hours hand-drilling 75 bolts on lead and creating what I believe to be one of Zion's greatest free climbs. After several attempts, they freed all but 20' of pitch 12 and a single move of pitch 13.

Brandon and Karl had invited me to help finish a free ascent of another one of their Tucupit routes back in 2017. Morphology (8 pitches, IV 5.12+) provided pitch after pitch of quality climbing and opened my eyes to the work the duo was putting in on Tucupit Point. The potential was astounding, and Brandon was absolutely raving about the progress on Skeleton Key.

Sadly, after getting injured by rockfall during a rappel in the Organ Mountains of New Mexico, Brandon didn't see any scenario where he'd be freeing Skeleton Key in the near future, so he passed the opportunity of another first free ascent to me.

The line of the Skeleton Key (1,400', 15 pitches, V 5.13a) on the north face of Tucupit Point in Kolob Canyons. Other routes not shown. *Brandon Gottung*

Karl and I connected in October 2020 with the intent of freeing the missing sections. I had one week to put in before heading to Yosemite, so there was a fair bit of pressure.

On day one we climbed to the crux on pitch 12 to see if it seemed feasible. After a few hours of working out the holds, we decided it was worth a solid effort. After another day of sussing beta and fixing lines back to the ground, Karl took a rest day to hang out with his wife, and I went back out to

Kolob alone. I spent the entire day Mini Traxioning, chalking holds, and working out key sequences. At the end of the day, I succeeded on the crux boulder problem, but still hadn't linked the full pitch. As the sun started setting, I descended the wall and stripped all of our fixed lines for a free attempt.

Karl and I ventured back into Kolob two days later. We led in blocks, with Karl graciously letting me lead all of the pitches 5.12a and up. I surprised myself with a first-go send of pitch 12, which clocked in at 5.13a. Karl went for several attempts, freeing every move, but not quite linking the pitch.

The next pitch, which we hadn't worked on at all, had just that single sequence to be freed, and it looked to be about 5.12c. The move seemed like a dyno—not my forte. But after careful study, I saw a small, lichen-covered bump that could be a critical foothold. I scrubbed it clean, lowered, and climbed the crux from a stance using this little bump. Not the best style, but I was satisfied. We pushed to the summit and topped out to a classic Kolob Canyons sunset.

I'd argue this line should be high on any 5.12 or 5.13 climber's list. It goes reasonably at 5.12 A0 with only a handful of simple aid moves. There is a deluxe bivy just below the crux pitch. ◙

– **AARON LIVINGSTON**

KOLOB CANYONS, TIMBER TOP MESA, THE AVALON VALLEY CLUB

WHEN I WENT to Zion National Park for the first time, I intended to climb the Thunderbird Wall, on the north face of Timber Top Mesa (8,055'), in Kolob Canyons. I thought better of it after one glance at that monster face, and retreated to the main canyon to climb shorter trade routes. That was four years ago. Ever since, I've kept a topo of the Thunderbird Wall, now coffee-stained and covered with illegible scribbles, taped to my dashboard.

The north face of Timber Top has seen few ascents. Soaring 2,000' from base to summit, it was first climbed by Ron Olevsky and Earl Redfern, who completed the Thunderbird Wall route in 1986 after five attempts and called it Grade VI—a rarity in Zion. In 2006, the all-star team of Mike Anderson and Rob Pizem freed the Thunderbird Wall at 5.13- R. Until now, this was the only complete route up the face.

On a rainy rest day in April, I walked alone on the 3.5-mile approach toward the north face with a spotting scope, my excitement building the closer I got. In the preceding 12 months, I'd climbed five new big wall routes in Zion and was feeling ready. Soon I was looking at a nearly continuous crack system to the left of Thunderbird. There was only one noticeable blank section.

My friends Mike Dunn and Ky Hart were game for an attempt. We canceled appointments, sorted a rack and ropes, acquired permits, rationed whiskey, and stockpiled food and water for a seven-day mission. We fixed lines on some opening slab pitches, and on April 29 committed to the wall. When I found an old bolt on the first pitch, and a little higher above that an old anchor, we got discouraged. *Had this line been climbed and not recorded?* But it was soon apparent that whoever had been up there had retreated after one pitch. The climbing above was classic Zion aid: thin, dirty placements in sometimes rotten rock, and always spectacular.

After four pitches we were staring into the abyss of the blank section we'd seen from below. It was Mike's lead. He climbed straight up the wall until the crack died, drilled a bolt, and quested off on ten continuous hook moves (many enhanced), cracking the biggest unknown of the route. It was a heroic effort, especially on Navajo sandstone, so soft that even enhanced holes routinely blow out under weighted hooks. I don't recall him making a sound as he floated up the orange face, even as Ky and I swilled beers down at the belay and heckled him to hurry things up.

Later that evening, I retreated off pitch seven when rain and hail drenched us. A nearby lightning bolt got our full attention. We hunkered under a tarp while the storm blew over, then bivied for a third consecutive night at the sixth-pitch anchor. By the next night, we had reached a spacious bivy on top of pitch nine. For the first time on the route, we felt confident we would make the top.

On May 3, our fifth day on the route, we climbed three pitches, hiked through a burnt pine forest, and stood together on the summit. The views are always exceptional in Zion, but this one was transcendent. We could see from Cedar City to St. George, from the snow-capped Pine Valley Mountains to the streets of Toquerville. We named the route The Avalon Valley Club (2,000', 12 pitches, V 5.9 A3), after an insane asylum in one of my favorite books, a place to which the main character returns over and over. Two days later, when I drove north to start my seasonal river-guiding job in Idaho, I passed the turn to Kolob Canyons and noted that I still hadn't climbed the Thunderbird Wall. That route's topo is staying on the dash for now. 📷 🔍

— MATT WARD

EXTENDED TRAVERSE OF TOWERS OF THE VIRGIN

THE TOWERS OF the Virgin are a series of jagged summits that loom above Oak Creek to create a gigantic sandstone amphitheater. Dan Stih and Ron Raimonde envisioned and executed the first traverse of these towers in 1998, climbing south to north over the course of three days. The climbing begins on the 1933 southwest ridge route up the West Temple (7,810') and continues across the Sundial (7'532'), Witch Head (7,350'), Broken Tooth (7,242'), Rotten Tooth (7,390'), and finally the Altar of Sacrifice (7,505'; 5.9). Except for the West Temple, Stih and Raimonde had made the first ascents of all of these towers the year before. They finished their 1998 traverse by rappelling into Oak Creek between the Altar and then unclimbed Meridian Tower.

In the spring of 2021, Arthur Herlitzka and I spent three days on the second ascent

Looking back on (back to front) the West Temple, Sundial, Witch Head, Broken Tooth, and Rotten Tooth from the Altar of Sacrifice. *Mike Dunn*

of the traverse and extended it by six additional summits. On the first day we made it past the Witch Head. The next day we climbed the Teeth, the Altar, and Avalokiteshvara Temple (7,285'), before descending into Birch Creek to bivy near water. On day three we linked Meridian Tower (7,462'), Chameleon Peak (7,224'), the Point (7,144'), Big Red (7,200'), and lastly the Beehive (6,909'). That same day we took the Streaked Wall descent route back to the Zion Human History Museum. (The first known ascents of several of these summits include: Avalokiteshvara Temple in 2015, by Coutney Purcell; Meridian Peak in 2017, by Stih and Matt Mower; Chameleon Peak in 2008, by Stih and David Everett; the Point in 2019, by Stih; and Big Red, in 2019, also by Stih, via a route graded 5.9 A3.)

We climbed with a double rack of cams, nothing too big or small, and also had a rack of pins that we never used. We rated our extended traverse VI 5.9 R. There are no bolts, and we left very little tat behind. Expect countless rappels and downclimbs, and be prepared for soft, loose rock. 📷 🔍

— MIKE DUNN

OAK CREEK DRAINAGE, GAMBLER WALL, NEW ROUTES

IN NOVEMBER 2020, Earl Lunceford and I climbed a 1,300' new route on an unnamed wall in the Oak Creek drainage of Zion National Park. The wall is visible from the Zion Human History Museum, near the park's south entrance. This wall is deeper into Oak Creek than the Angelino Wall and The Shadow Line (9 pitches, 5.11 A3+).

The first half of the route contained high-quality aid climbing up to A2, and the upper pitches went mostly free on very good rock. One highlight was pitch seven, which climbs a glorious 5.8 chimney, then an incredible hand crack, then a steep offwidth, before finally finishing at one of the best bivy ledges—huge, flat, with great views—in Zion. We called the route Roll the Hard 6 (11 pitches, V 5.10 A2+).

In March 2021, I returned to the wall with Ky Hart. We climbed another new route that started with the same first pitch as Roll the Hard 6, which Ky was able to free at 5.11a. We veered right and stayed on an independent, parallel line, cutting left and crossing Roll the Hard 6 at the top of pitch four, then continuing straight up to the top. One of the best sections entailed leapfrogging number 5-size cams out a monster offwidth roof on pitch seven. To bivouac, we rappelled a rope length from the top of pitch seven to the excellent ledge on Roll the Hard 6, then jugged the rope the next day to continue up the route. We named this second route Splittin' Eights and Hittin' Straights (1,300', 11 pitches, V 5.11 A2).

Both routes have great rock, and both have bolted anchors on every pitch. To descend from either, rappel Roll the Hard 6.

As far as we know, these are the only routes that top out the wall, although there has been single-pitch activity at the base. If this face is in fact unnamed, we'd propose naming it the Gambler Wall. 📷

Roll the Hard 6 (yellow) and Splittin' Eights and Hittin' Straights (red) on the 1,300-foot "Gambler Wall." *Matt Ward*

– MATT WARD

BRIDGE MOUNTAIN, WEST FACE, FOR THE DOGGS

FROM NOVEMBER 1 to 3, Ky Hart and I climbed a new route on the west face of Bridge Mountain, which we dubbed For the Doggs (15 pitches, V 5.11 A2). The route starts 300' left of the popular ACL Arête (10 pitches, 5.10), established by Tyler Philips and Robbie Colbert in 2010, and follows a series of exquisite cracks in a black shield of rock. Ky had established the first four pitches solo the week before, and with a belay he was able to free the spectacular first pitch at 5.11. After these four pitches, the route intersects ACL Arête and then, via a difficult combination of rappelling and traversing, dives left into the massive gully that splits the west face, then back up solid easier terrain until crossing ACL again on the west ridge.

We believe we only climbed two pitches of ACL Arête, but that route's exact line is unclear high on the mountain. From the top, descend ACL Arête via its bolted rap anchors. 🖥️📷

– MATT WARD

Nat Bailey on the crux moves of pitch three on The Crack in the Cosmic Egg. The successful sequence that both he and Drew Marshall used to free the pitch ended up going right, not left. *Jérôme St-Michel*

THE CRACK IN THE COSMIC EGG
MIND GAMES ON A FIRST FREE ASCENT IN ZION NATIONAL PARK

BY NAT BAILEY, *CANADA*

In December 2004, American climber Mike Anderson did the first free ascent of the Lowe Route on the striking north face of Angels Landing. In an article in *Alpinist* 11, Anderson wrote, "For decades, climbers in Yosemite have been systematically eliminating aid from any route that will go. In Zion, apart from Douglas Heinrich, most climbers just don't bother. I decided to bother." I taped Anderson's article to the ceiling of my minivan.

Seventeen years later, on November 3, having decided to bother, I tied my rope around a coffin-size boulder at the base of The Crack in the Cosmic Egg, gave the rope a reassuring tug, and started up the first pitch alone, equal parts determined and terrified.

Les Ellison and Brian Smoot did the first ascent of The Crack in the Cosmic Egg (11 pitches, V 5.10 C2+) in 1984. The bulk of the route is a continuous five-pitch seam that rockets up Mt. Moroni's steep east face. A friend pointed it out once last fall and said it "might" go. I was in Zion alone and had the month of November free. I planned to aid solo the first five pitches to investigate the potential, and after seven afternoons the ropes were fixed and I began to see a possible free climbing path.

The first big question mark was the second pitch: a two-meter bolt ladder that connected a blank-looking section of sandstone to the route's dominant crack system. To the left of the bolt ladder I noticed a promising-looking secondary seam leading to a Braille trail of face holds that cut right, back to the major crack system. The second question mark was pitch three, a fierce 0.1 cam–size splitter with a few blown-out pin scars. For a few meters, it overhangs 20 degrees. There was just enough bomber gear to convince me to keep investigating.

The month rolled on. I toiled away at the slow, methodical, and very real labor of vision and dreams, speaking only to sandy holds and two California condors. It was coming together, but I was tired, eager to share the experience, and needed a proper belay.

Desperate, I called my friend Hoai-Nam Bui and offered to pay for her gas from Bishop if she'd come up on the wall with me. Her visit turned the page on the process. With new perspectives and a proper belay, the path forward became clearer. To avoid the bolt ladder on pitch two, I hand-drilled three bolts up the thin seam to the left. My variation then traversed back into the main crack system, which was pumpy, technical, and protected by very specific nut placements. Pitch three—where the seam kicks back—was proving to be the kind of pitch my teenage self only dreamed of finding: hard and scary, with just enough gear for it to be safe.

I returned with my friend (and hero) Drew Marshall for one final prep day. With some advice from Drew and motivation from The Pixies, I sorted out the moves on the pitch-two variation and felt confident I could climb the pitch. Drew, however, saw the original aid line engineering its way across a blank slab and was convinced it would go free. He quickly did all the moves. My personal definition of "blank" sandstone was redefined in an instant. Pitch two could go free two different ways: 5.13b using my variation or heinous 5.12+ slab following the original line.

It was finally time to try to lead all the pitches, bottom to top. On November 21, with my friend Steffan Hadeed on belay, I sent the 5.13b version of pitch two on my first try of the day, spending almost an hour climbing through the delicate and spicy seam after the crux boulder. It was late and the fall sun was already low. Steffan and I descended fixed ropes and returned the next day, gung-ho about sending pitch three and blasting to the summit. I gave everything I had on it, but came up short. I was bummed, but still determined to see my vision through.

I went back up two days later with Drew and our friend Jérôme St-Michel, whom I invited to take pictures. Once again, I couldn't do pitch three. Drew—an experienced technician—had found some alternate beta to my sequence, and he was looking smooth. His eyes met mine with empathy.

"You should do it, man," I said, breaking the silence. "You should lead this pitch."

Drew, a good friend, was hesitant. He said he didn't mind waiting for me to try again, but I had nothing left to give. I put on my puffy and a brave face and told Drew to go for it. He flipped the switch and fired it. To be honest, it hurt. I knew there was a lot to learn from Drew's graceful navigation of intense climbing and the nuances of friendship, but in the moment I felt more sad and conflicted than noble and wise.

Dejected or not, I was in for a ride on the next pitch, scrapping and screaming upward. Fearing more failure, I desperately yelled on the last boulder problem and slumped onto the anchor after clipping it, one of the best pitches of 5.12 I have ever climbed. The next day, we ascended our fixed lines to try pitch five for the first time. I was excited about the idea of a quasi-onsight and stepped off the belay ready to quest. I squeaked out a tricky traverse and groveled up an obligatory Zion chimney of sand, fear-screaming my way through the slopey exit. *We were going to the summit!*

Above this, pitch nine was the only one no one had yet freed. Drew and I took one look at the original aid line and knew that it wasn't the way. To our left, an easy looking sea of holds led to an arête. It was scrappy Zion climbing at its finest: tempting jugs held on by unknown forces, thorny bushes, and granular white rock that always climbs in a more engaging manner than it looks. We detoured around the aid line in two leads, dubbed the "Guide's Intuition Pitches."

On top we lingered as the sun set. I felt a warm wave of gratitude. For Zion. For Drew. In all, we had added six new free pitches: The Crack in the Cosmic Egg Free (10 pitches, IV 5.13b R).

Drew and our friend Meghan Denny graciously offered to come back with me after a rest day, and I sent pitch three with Drew's beta. I didn't feel euphoria so much as a sort of peaceful sadness. I'm learning that when you give something life, you inherently give it a death as well. I ran out of time to make a continuous free ascent that is someone else's dream, and I'm excited for them. To anyone reading this, I encourage you to tune out of the dogma of things that just *won't go* and tune into your vision. Go bother. 📷 🔍

FISHER TOWERS, KINGFISHER, THERMIC FEVER

THE FISHER TOWERS hold a special place in my heart—they are beautiful but barbaric, delightful but potentially deadly. Each year from 2002 to 2015, I spent at least one week-long trip in these towers; for ten of those years, Jeremy Aslaksen joined me. Our yearly Fisher pilgrimage gave me an opportunity to step back from my job as a trauma surgeon, turn off the cell phone, and enjoy some old-fashioned fun and fear. In 2015, after Jeremy and I put up the Hydraform Ridge, life changed. I moved to California to start a job, got married, and had a kid. Jeremy was helping his daughter get set for college and putting up routes throughout the Southwest. The years flew by. Discouraged that so much time had passed without a Fishers mission, we set an ultimatum: 2021 or bust.

Jeremy Aslaksen at the start of pitch five on Thermic Fever, traversing toward the main tower of the Kingfisher in back. *Joe Forrester*

As an objective for our summer trip, we picked the full southwest ridge to the top of Kingfisher. We planned to avoid Jim Beyer's 1986 route Jagged Edge (V 5.9 A4), on the upper left portion of the ridge, and minimize time on the Minotaur (IV 5.9+ C2), climbed by Duane and Lisa Raleigh in 1998. We saw a line, but it was largely on the south side of the formation—it would be a fry fest, to be sure, in the heat of late August.

Jeremy had spent two hot weekends in July soloing, hauling, and fixing the first two pitches to get to the ridge, so the third pitch was mine. It was an offwidth followed by a horizontal chimney through hot mud. The fourth lead followed a pitch of the Minotaur, and was gloriously rowdy, with one dicey mantel after another, high above old bolts. *This is what I had been missing for the past half a decade!* We returned to the ground to sleep, as we would each night.

The next morning we traversed under the head of the Minotaur on the north side, and then rapped 35' onto the south face. This set us up for a pitch the likes of which neither of us had ever climbed: a traverse over a gaping mud cave that disappeared into the depths of the tower. As we passed over the void, we dropped pebbles into the maw; they clattered down beyond the light from our headlamps. Guarding the start of the upper Kingfisher ridge was a chasm. I had two options: jump a gap and hopscotch on hoodoos to the opposite side, or lower down the face and aid back up. I decided to go for the jump. Jeremy gave me several large loops of slack. I shut off my brain, made a running start, and leaped for a barrel-sized hoodoo. I skipped to the next ledge, nearly skittering off, and finished on the opposite ledge.

Day three was filled with more heat-induced hallucinations and beak seams. But we were stoked come evening—only one or two pitches stood between us and the cap rock. At 4:30 a.m. on day four, Jeremy started beaking up an obvious seam. Eight hours later, he arrived at the base of the capstone and lowered down.

Day five. Our alarms rang at 2 a.m, and we hustled to jug our ropes. We saw lightning to the south beyond Castle Valley, but far enough away that we could justify starting up. I placed beaks to aid through a roof and started free climbing through the capstone. Light rain started. In the dark of predawn, we watched as lightning slammed Castleton Tower. I lowered off fast. Surrounded by lightning bolts, we rapped our fixed lines as fast as possible and walked back to the safety of our car. By 9 a.m., the storm had passed. Neither of us wanted to jug 600' of fixed line in the heat for the second time that morning, but we had to finish this thing off. Out we charged and up we went. I reached my high point and finished my pitch, then led a quick pitch to the top.

It had been five years since Jeremy and I had last roped up together. When I brought him up, we hugged, did an easy third-class scramble up the summit block, and then headed down.

We called our route Thermic Fever, as we are pretty sure we had heat stroke for much of the climb. Grades in the Fishers are fairly irrelevant, but we gave it VI 5.9+ A2+. It's not so hard that it isn't doable, but it's no cakewalk. [*A pitch-by-pitch description of the climb is at the AAJ website.*] 📄 📷

– JOE FORRESTER

NOT NOTCH CANYON AND PROSPECTORS CANYON, 25 NEW TOWERS

Some of the recently climbed towers in Not Notch Canyon (from left to right): Benjamin Putterman, The Toaster, The Fudgesicle, The Butter Sculpture, and Blocktop. *Cameron M. Burns*

FROM 2018 THROUGH 2022, a group of climbers from Utah, Colorado, Nevada, and Arizona converged on two small unnamed canyons in southeastern Utah and made the first ascents of 25 towers, the tallest being about 375'. The canyons lie about ten miles west of Blanding. We dubbed them Not Notch Canyon (after a geographical mistake we made, as the real Notch Canyon is farther north) and Prospectors Canyon (after old mining equipment we found there). Prospectors Canyon is just south of Notch Canyon, and Not Notch is the next canyon further south. Both are in an area sometimes called Chimney Park, north and east of a cleft called the Notch.

The main protagonists of this exploration were Trevor Bowman, Ben Kiessel, and myself. Others who took part included Jay Anderson, Benny Bach, Emily Bowman, Matt King, Danny McGee, and Jeff Widen. In general, we climbed by whatever means necessary, aid or free. Some routes required a few bolts in blank areas, but most followed obvious crack systems. Pretty much everything fell within the 5.10 C2 or A2 realm.

The most stunning towers were perhaps Prospectors Tower (5.10 C2), in Prospectors Canyon, and Mollies Bird (5.8 A2+), with its twin summits, in Not Notch Canyon. Prospectors started with a fist-size crack that turned into an offwidth. Trevor Bowman then led a wild chimney to a sprawling platform. Ben Kiessel led the final pitch on aid. These climbs had a mix of everything, from great yawning chimneys to hairline seams. On the first pitch of Mollies Bird, I went from beaks to number 5 Camalots within 60'.

Two towers that were especially aesthetic were the 250' Pencil (5.9 C2), in Not Notch Canyon, and Skellig Kerry (5.10 A2+), in Prospectors Canyon. Both involved stemming off the nearby buttes. One tower, which we dubbed Blocktop, had been climbed previously, but we could not find any information about this ascent.

Two other towers were climbed in the same time frame with the same folks, but in a very different location. In October 2021, Ben Kiessel, Matt Pickren, Jeff Widen, and I reached the summit of an unclimbed 500' tower in Arch Canyon, near its junction with Butts Canyon. We called it Marys Tower, after my mother, who passed away in July. The following day, Kiessel and Pickren made the first ascent of the Admirer, a 300' tower in the same vicinity.

– CAMERON M. BURNS

COLORADO / SAN JUAN MOUNTAINS

ROUND MOUNTAIN, NORTH FACE, MASON STANSFIELD MEMORIAL ROUTE

MAY 3, 2021. A friend and I were chatting in the kitchen when we got the message: an inReach SOS from Mason Stansfield and his girlfriend, Tessa. Soon came the news: Mason, 28, had died in a crevasse fall on the Eldridge Glacier in Denali National Park. The following hours, days, and weeks were a blur of tears, anger, and depression. Mason, an excellent climber and consummate guide, was a beloved member of the Ouray community and one of my closest friends. He was family.

Fast forward to January 23, 2022. Mason was to be inducted into the Ouray Ice Park climbers' memorial at 4 p.m. Steven Van Sickle and I decided this would give us enough time to scout an area up Arrastra Basin, southeast of Silverton, for new route potential, and still make it back for the induction ceremony.

After two hours of skinning and bootpacking, we were standing beneath the north face of Round Mountain. While the peak itself is mostly a large snow hill, the northern aspect holds a wall of steep and—for the San Juans—surprisingly good rock, varying from 800' to 1,200' in height. From our research, there were no known routes on the face. Steven and I identified an obvious line on the right side. It was 1:30 p.m. Mason's spirit was in the air, and we both knew this was an adventure he would've wanted to be on: a late start, no real plan, just going for it. We shared a knowing glance—we wouldn't be making it back for the memorial.

We started soloing up a steep snow gully guarding our intended line. Above was a narrow slot choked with a couple chockstones. Steven started toward the first chockstone while I quested onto the face to the right. Halfway up our respective solos, Steven was grunting and I was breathing hard through a vertical crux, scratching on small edges and frozen mud with my tools. "Little harder than I thought!" he shouted.

After this choose-your-own-adventure pitch, we roped up and Steven started the crux lead. At a large chockstone, he made a hard lock-off, cut his feet, and powered through a mantel. Over the next hour, he continued up nearly 60m of stemming and bulges, raining down rocks and snow. I took over for the next pitch, gunning up 40m of easier snow and mixed terrain. From here, we untied and soloed a gully leading up and right, with daylight fading into dark.

On top we hugged, laughed, and choked up. The Mason Stansfield Memorial Route (250m, M6) was complete. As we descended the western flank, I gazed skyward. Mason may be gone, but his spirit remains in the mountains, stoked as ever to accompany his friends on adventures.

– CHARLIE FAUST

DROP THE MIC
LONG MIXED TESTPIECE OUTSIDE OURAY

BY SCOTT TURPIN

ON NOVEMBER 21, Noah McKelvin, Phil Wortmann, and I completed the first ascent of Drop the Mic (10 pitches, V 5.11- M8 R), a 1,400' route accessed off Camp Bird Mine Road, above Ouray. This could be the longest and most sustained mixed climb of this difficulty in the Lower 48.

Drop the Mic is on the Dark Side, a large north-facing wall across Canyon Creek from the road. Despite its proximity to Ouray and the presence of over a dozen established routes, including the historic Bird Brain Boulevard, first climbed by Charlie Fowler, Jeff Lowe, and Mark Wilford in 1985, the direct line up the center of the wall, beginning in an obvious cave feature, had never been attempted. In 2018, Noah and I walked along the base of the cliff to investigate this cave. We identified an improbable line going out the roof—if it was climbable, it would be epic.

We returned later that season with Phil and established the first two pitches. Bolting ground-up on lead, we pushed as far as we could between pro. The short first pitch was wildly overhung and physical M8. The second required us to holster our tools and rock climb with crampons; it was hard to grade, but is roughly 5.11-. Later, with some creative ropework, we were able to link these pitches into one amazing 115' lead. One after another, we each climbed the mega-pitch with no falls, smiling the entire time. It stands on its own as one of the finest alpine pitches we've done.

As we stood on the road at the end of the day, we drew imaginary lines linking features above the cave and up the tallest part of the wall. But our vision would have to wait. We were each pulled in other directions in 2019.

In 2020, when the pandemic gave us reasons to refocus our efforts closer to home, we returned to the project. In November, Noah and I reclimbed the steep first pitch and the Shelf Road–esque second pitch. From there, we dispatched three moderate pitches and fixed lines back to the ground. Later, we added a bolt to pitch three to mitigate a horrendous runout that Noah had navigated.

Pitches six, seven, and eight became the second round of crux climbing. Each of these had a different flavor, and we divided the work of establishing them among us.

Phil onsighted the tricky-to-protect Mitten Pitch at M6 R, later opting to replace a number 2 Pecker with a bolt, again in a nod to the well-being of future ascensionists.

We dubbed the spectacular seventh pitch the F**k Average Pitch. It was a tenuous M8 horror show. Noah placed the first four bolts along an insecure traverse and up a slightly overhanging groove, getting pretty worked in the process. Phil took over, pushing above the last bolt on continuously steep and sketchy terrain. When our drill sputtered and died, and with his rope clipped to the bolt 50 feet below him, Phil summoned a heroic effort to hang on through the life-

Noah McKelvin starting pitch seven on Drop the Mic. This M8 pitch had a 50-foot runout on the first ascent; two bolts were added later, but it remains a heady lead. *Jason Nelson / Visualadventures.com*

threatening runout to the top. We later added two bolts, but this pitch remains serious and heady.

Pitch eight began with a low-angle chimney that brought me to the base of an overhanging offwidth. Stacked blocks and shards of loose stone hung in and around the crack, promising a harrowing experience for climber and belayer alike. I spent three hours tunneling through it, while Phil and Noah dodged trundled choss. Cleared of detritus, it became a surprisingly cool pitch.

We climbed another moderate but engaging pitch to arrive below a cool diving-board feature, which we'd hoped would provide a wildly exposed and difficult capstone pitch. Unfortunately, Phil found the rock to be more like loosely coagulated mud. He bailed and opted for an adjacent chimney and final finger crack.

We made our final ascent in November 2021 in team-free style, with someone from the team leading each pitch free and clean. Including that day, we spent a total of nine days on this adventure. We chose the difficult line at each turn, challenging ourselves to connect features the way we had envisioned from the ground. We bolted where necessary, placed lots of dubious gear, and punched it when there was no other option. I am honored to have shared Phil and Noah's company, grateful for our complementary skill sets, and in awe of the monster we created. ⌼

Base camp on the north side of the Maidens. The team climbed the north face of East Maiden (the left summit) and a new route on the Camel, the peak at right (route mostly behind the skyline). *Cameron Jardell*

EAST MAIDEN, THE SHIV, AND THE CAMEL, NEW ROUTES

In July, Mathias Gruber, Maya Humeau, Luke Shacter, and I ventured into the Arrigetch Peaks to fulfill our dream of a proper expedition-style adventure and explore the granite of the Alaskan Arctic. We spent 18 days in the area, most of them rainy. Based in the Aquarius Valley, our team made three failed attempts, three repeats, and four first ascents in what amounted to a spectacular trip.

On July 22, Brooks Range Aviation dropped us at Circle Lake near the Alatna River. We pushed through the sunlit night with 80-pound packs, bushwhacking the first few miles before finding the Arrigetch Creek Trail. After stopping for a rest, we made camp beneath the Maidens the next evening.

The next day Mat and Maya set their sights on the north face of the East Maiden, while Luke and I climbed two and a half pitches up West Maiden before bailing due to rain. [*Editor's Note: An NPS report written in 2003, titled "History and Route Descriptions of Rock Climbs in the Arrigetch Peaks," lists the north face of East Maiden as having been climbed by an unknown German party in 1998. Their exact line is unknown, though the 2021 party found bolts scattered on the face.*] Maya and Mat waited out the storm but lost steam several pitches up and traversed to a gully on looker's left of the face to descend. The next day, Luke and I soloed slabs to a col to attempt the south face of the East Maiden, only to be caught in fog and rain partway up the face, where we retreated.

Seven days of rain later, we were ready to send. The four of us walked up the Aquarius Valley to the east face of the Shiv, a fin-shaped peak between Wichmann Tower and Badile. Luke and Mat climbed to the left of Maya and me, and we simultaneously established two new routes on the 80° wall. Luke and Mat's Hunting People (300m, 5.11 R) climbs an open face with scattered flakes to a wide roof crack. Maya and I followed a left-facing corner system with intermittent slabs that we named Supernatural Apparition (300m, 5.10). Our route joins the last two pitches of Hunting People. We descended the north ridge, making just one rappel.

After 12 hours of sleep, Maya and Mat set off for another attempt on the north face of the East Maiden, while Luke and I did a link-up of the north ridge of Parabola Peak (5.7, 2002) and the Aquarius Wall (5.7, 2003). We soloed Parabola in two hours and then descended a heinous gully before climbing six pitches on the Aquarius Wall.

After 15 pitches on East Maiden, Mat and Maya completed a likely variation (based on the old bolts they encountered) to the unknown 1998 route on the north face. They found bolts on the upper route despite a consistent and protectable crack system. They dubbed the variation Gut Ripper (650m, 5.10).

Luke Shacter on Hunting People (300m, 5.11 R), a new line on the east face of the Shiv. *Matias Gruber*

With decent weather on the day before our scheduled pickup at Circle Lake, Mat and I left early to attempt the unclimbed northwest face of the Camel. A choss ramp took us to the bottom of a low-angle, slabby face, which we simul-climbed to the east ridge in three long pitches to gain the summit. We named the route Vasudeva (600m, 5.8). We rappelled the south face and then rappelled and downclimbed a gully west of the summit. During that time, Luke and Maya simul-climbed the Aquarius Wall in two pitches.

This trip was made possible in part by the AAC Live Your Dream Grant, as well as the wild mushrooms we foraged daily to supplement our meager rations. 📷

— CAMERON JARDELL

ALASKA RANGE / KICHATNA MOUNTAINS

PTARMIGAN SPIRE, WIZARD SLEEVE; THE ROOK, FRESH STEP

ON JUNE 6, Zach Lovell, Tad McCrea, and I flew to the Cul-de-Sac Glacier in the Kichatna Mountains. Six days later, we established a new route on the south face of Ptarmigan Spire. This tower is located along the ridge connecting Sunrise Spire with the Citadel, and had only one known ascent. In 1979, Jim Bridwell and Andy Embick climbed the huge snow couloir that separates Ptarmigan from the Citadel and then the east ridge of Ptarmigan (see *AAJ 1980*). Our line started up a deep couloir two gullies to the left; the gully we followed has a towering, slender pinnacle flanking its right side about 500' above the glacier.

Easy snow and a short step of water ice led to two steps of M4 mixed climbing. We had a loose plan to exit onto the rock face to the right of the couloir, but the mediocre rock and lack of attractive crack systems kept us following the line of weakness. A series of gullies with snow and

The south face of Ptarmigan Spire. Arrow marks the start of Wizard Sleeve (1,400', M4 5.8 70° snow). The climbers traversed the peak and descended the couloir on the right, separating Ptarmigan from the Citadel. *Zach Lovell*

some thin ice, linked by occasional short traverses on rock, eventually brought us to the crest of the ridge at a spacious, sandy col. We turned right and simul-climbed a couple of rope lengths of aesthetic mixed terrain along the ridge, with rock up to 5.8. We surmounted the exposed summit block at 3 p.m., just eight hours after leaving camp.

We made two long rappels—over some dangerously loose rock—down the northeast face and into the col between Citadel and Ptarmigan. An easy down-climb and a short ski brought us back to camp, 12 hours after leaving. Back at the col, as Zach and I were retrieving our rappel ropes, Tad had stepped around us to scout the gully below, and the tip of his ice axe snagged on my ultralight wind jacket and ripped an enormous hole in the sleeve. I now looked like an orange-clad wizard, and our route had a name: Wizard Sleeve (1,400', M4 5.8 70° snow).

Two days later, with nice weather holding, we started up a line we had picked out on Rook Spire, down the glacier from camp. Rook had only one known ascent, by Embick and Bryan Becker in 1978, accomplished by a ridgeline traverse from Bastion Spire to the north. (They then continued south along the ridge to Cemetery Spire; see *AAJ 1979*.) A sharp buttress on the west face, extending down from the peak's final headwall, appeared to have solid rock.

After a 10-minute ski approach from camp, we started up from the base at 6 a.m., climbing a large snow bowl between the Rook and Cemetery Spire. A few hundred feet up, we traversed left-ward off the snow and began simul-climbing up broken rock terrain, intent on climbing until we could outflank a blank, sheer cliff band and make a leftward traverse to the toe of the principal rock buttress. About 800' of moderate but extremely loose, nasty climbing on rock that closely resembled kitty litter brought us to a steeper step (fortunately more solid) of about 5.9 rock, which we belayed. Next, we made a long, undulating leftward traverse for a few hundred feet on snow and more crumbly rock that brought us to the foot of the main rock buttress beneath an obvious dihedral.

Here, we switched to rock shoes and climbed five steep and aesthetic pitches on much higher quality granite, starting in the dihedral and then continuing more or less directly up the prow or slightly to its right side. The climbing was exposed, sustained at 5.10 with good protection and belays, and followed very good cracks of all sizes. We reached the level crest of the buttress, where we had expected to find a moderate ridge to gain the final headwall of the Rook. Instead, the ridge was blocked by steep-sided gendarmes that lacked any cracks and thwarted our attempts to proceed. Descending the way we'd come seemed unthinkable, given all the loose rock.

Calling an audible, we slung a horn on the ridge and made a committing vertical rappel into a deep gully rising along the opposite (north) side of the ridge, intent on using the gully to bypass the gendarmed crest. A pitch of moderate mixed, a pitch of sloppy snow in the gully, and a final, fun rock chimney filled with ice brought us back to the ridge, above the section that had stopped us. An easy pitch along the crest led to the main ridge connecting Rook with Cemetery Spire, and an intersection with Embick and Becker's 1978 traverse. However, a pair of rock gendarmes flanked by steep isothermic snow blocked ready access to the col beneath the final 400' headwall of the Rook. From the glacier, this headwall had appeared low angle, with ample crack systems. Up close, however, only a very steep system of meandering offwidth cracks and flaky chimneys offered any reasonable hope of passage. We debated continuing, but with a rack that lacked wide-crack protection, we found that sitting on this perch in the evening sun, waiting for the snow to firm up while absorbing the stunning views, eating snacks, and telling jokes, proved to be the more appealing course.

Mark Westman leading a traverse beneath the gendarmed ridge high on the Rook's west face. *Zach Lovell*

Our plan was to escape by descending a steep mixed ramp to the north which dropped into the bowl between Bastion and Rook, at which point we could simply walk down the remainder of the way. At 11 p.m. we began the first of six rappels down steep snow that had been avalanching all afternoon, but which was rapidly firming. We made it back to camp at 5 a.m., and a few hours later Paul Roderick scooped us up for a beautiful flight back to Talkeetna.

Because our attempted route intersected a previously traveled ridge line, we're giving it a name, although what we did here was decidedly a failed attempt on the Rook. While the steep rock pitches on the buttress and the uppermost ridge were quite aesthetic, the lower portions of the route were memorable primarily for their disgusting rock quality, so we're naming our effort after a popular brand of kitty litter: Fresh Step (2,000', 5.10 60° mixed). With more stable snow conditions, the line of descent we used would provide a moderate way to regain our high point and find a passage up the final headwall, which would involve four to five pitches, at most. 📷

— MARK WESTMAN

CENTRAL ALASKA RANGE

WEST FORK OF RUTH GLACIER, CONDITION UPDATE

FROM MAY 8–12, Gabriel Messercola, Robert Paulson, Freddy Romero, and I attempted to climb through the icefalls at the head of the West Fork of the Ruth Glacier en route to the 1954 Thayer Route on Denali's South Buttress. [*Editor's Note: The most recent recorded ascent of this route was in April 1996, by Joe Puryear and Mark Westman.*] From the West Fork airstrip, we ascended to a camp at the base of the icefalls at approximately 8,400' and spent the next two days scouting a route to Margaret Pass. We found the lower of the two icefalls to be split, about halfway up, by a single, very large crevasse. After scouting this at numerous points, we realized the crevasse cleanly crossed the entire glacier. We investigated jumbled terrain to climber's right, but couldn't find a way around. The crevasse may have been passable on climber's left by traversing under a large cliff west of Mt. Huntington, but the avalanche hazard made investigating this option unsafe.

From our vantage in the lower icefall, the upper icefall looked similarly jumbled, and, notably, the headwall of the West Fork looked surprisingly icy and laden with seracs. We retreated to climb smaller objectives around the North Fork of the Ruth before flying out on May 17. 📷

— RYAN WICHELNS

Ines Papert climbing steep rock during the first ascent of Heart of Stone on the west face of Mt. Huntington. The route continues along the snow and ice ramps to her right. *Luka Lindič*

HEART OF STONE

TWO RAPID ASCENTS AND A NEW ROUTE ON MT. HUNTINGTON

BY LUKA LINDIČ, *SLOVENIA*

IN THE SPRING of 2021, my wife, Ines Papert, and I stayed in Alaska for three months, as the beginning of a larger journey down the length of the Pan-American Highway. At the beginning of April we headed into the Revelations, where we got totally shut down because of weather and conditions. After a short break in Seward, luck turned in our favor in Denali National Park.

On April 22, after flying through the Ruth Glacier so we could scope the walls, Paul Roderick dropped us below Mt. Huntington's west face, as it seemed to have the most promising conditions.

We set up our base camp and went to work on the Colton-Leach Route (1981) early the following morning. We were relieved to find good conditions and quickly progressed on moderate ice, many times stretching the pitches up to 150m. Being quick paid off, as the snow ramp in the middle of the route was still frozen when we reached it and enabled us to continue at a good pace.

At the end of the ramps, we zigzagged through the rocky section and climbed a short section of really cool steep cracks in perfect granite to the snow flank above. Here we followed a trail from a party that had climbed the Harvard Route a couple of days prior. It was really calm and warm at the summit, but we quickly started the descent, as we hadn't brought any bivy gear.

Rappelling the West Face Couloir, I kept looking at the steep wall to climber's left. The rock looked very solid and full of good cracks. This part of the wall seemed very attractive, but at that moment we didn't seriously think about it, as we were still preoccupied with getting back to our tent in the last light of the day.

The next day, while relaxing in the warm sun and thinking about what to try next, we got a very promising weather forecast for the next three days from Jack Tackle. The forecasted warmth seemed perfect for the steep rock wall that we'd seen on the descent. We even had climbing shoes with us in base camp, because we hadn't known where we would end up when we flew into the mountains. We quickly decided to try the new route after one more rest day. This time we packed bivy gear, and we decided on a late start to use the warmth of the afternoon sun for rock climbing.

Cloudless blue sky accompanied us as we left our camp for the second time at 11 a.m. on April 20. We found perfect conditions on the initial snow slope below the West Face Couloir and arrived at the steep rock wall, about 300m above the bergschrund, just when the sun hit it. At the place where we started climbing new terrain, we spotted a big heart feature on a blank granite face. It felt almost too sweet for us—a climbing couple—and we both laughed at the belay.

But to our surprise, the crack system that seemed the most logical was filled with ice, almost the same color as the rock because of all the dirt mixed into it—which is why we couldn't see the ice from a distance. The rock shoes stayed in the backpack and we continued in full mixed climbing mode.

The west face of Mt. Huntington, showing the line of Heart of Stone (1,050m, M7 90˚); the route begins on the West Face Couloir. Three days before starting this new route, Luka Lindič and Ines Papert climbed the Colton-Leach Route, which takes the most prominent diagonaling line to the left of Heart of Stone. *Mark Westman*

The climbing was steep and almost every pitch had a kind of a boulder problem crux. Some of them were quite powerful, but luckily had mostly decent protection. At that point there was already water running down the face and the ice became really rotten and slushy.

On the last pitch before reaching a right-trending ramp system we had a first little shock when Ines pulled off a loose hold and barely managed to catch herself. Then, after half a rope-length on the ramp, I got stuck for some time on one of those boulder cruxes. I underestimated it and started up with a backpack. After lots of cleaning useless snow and trying to find decent placements in thin ice, I hammered my lower tool as deep as I could into the ice and grabbed it at the head. With this extra reach, I could just barely get my tool into the next bit of ice. I thought I had it when the ice disintegrated and my tool ripped. I still don't know how I managed to catch my lower tool and not fall. After some breathing, I tried again, and that time I was able to sneak through this section.

The rest of the ramp went really well, with some great ice and good hooking in the cracks, until the very last pitch before the summit snowfield. This pitch took almost two hours of digging on the side of a huge mushroom, and with quite poor protection—definitely the most serious pitch of the route, especially as it was already dark. In two more rope stretchers we reached a perfect bivy spot below a big block. It was 3 a.m., but a full moon came out and we couldn't go to sleep for almost two more hours as the whole scene was so nice.

In the morning we left one backpack at our bivy site and reached the summit of Huntington at 11 a.m. We sat there for almost an hour, enjoying the warmth. In all directions we could see only wild Alaskan mountains, and we started wondering where our journey would take us next. The descent of the West Face Couloir went smoothly, and we reached our base camp in the afternoon for an early dinner.

After the initial snow slopes, we climbed 20 pitches of new terrain before joining existing routes on the summit snowfields. The rock feature that perfectly marks the start of our route gave the climb its name: Heart of Stone (1,050m, M7 90˚). We would like to thank Jack Tackle and Mark Westman for sharing their knowledge of Alaskan climbing with us.

PEAK 7,905' AND AVALANCHE SPIRE, SKI DESCENTS

ON APRIL 10, Paul Roderick dropped Ty Guarino, Zack Little, and me on an unnamed glacier east of the Lacuna Glacier. From there, we skied about four miles to establish a camp in the middle of the Lacuna, where we were treated to wolverine tracks, northern lights, and even a willow or two growing out of the lateral moraine. Over the next few days, we established a skin track to the base of the north face of Peak 7,905', located on the west side of the Lacuna (62°46'26", -151°34'34"). On April 14, a storm dropped 16" of light-density snow, covering part of the route we'd established.

Two days later, following what remained of our old skin track, we made our way up the ever steepening north face of 7,905'. We used Billy Goat ascent plates on the climb and found cold, dry powder up to 50° on the 2,500' descent. We believe this to be the first ascent and first ski/snowboard descent of Peak 7,905'.

On April 18, Paul and his Otter bumped us east to a camp at the base of the north face of Avalanche Spire (10,105'), south of Mt. Hunter. A ski descent had eluded Ty and me since our first trip to the area in 2016. We made a return trip in 2018. Both times we had targeted the northeast ridge and had been plagued with bad timing, bad weather, and accidents, including two large crevasse falls, one of which robbed me of a splitboard and my prescription glasses.

This time, after some scouting, we found the northeast ridge had become so broken with crevasses it looked impassable. The heavily glaciated northwest ridge appeared to be the most feasible route. [*Editor's Note: It's likely the first two ascents of the peak were made via this ridge; see two reports in AAJ 1965.*] We set out on April 21 and booted our way up the steeper lower slopes before switching to skis and skins between 7,000' and 9,200'. Above 9,200', we encountered mostly soft snow to 55° to the summit.

On the descent, Zack outclassed the "old guys" by making a complete ropeless descent of the entire mountain. Ty and I rappelled a 50' section of firm snow on the upper mountain, and I took a belay for 50', also on the upper mountain. We believe this to be the third ascent of Avalanche Spire, but recognizing that many Alaska climbs and descents aren't reported, we make this claim lightly. We would love to hear stories of other ascents of this seemingly constantly changing mountain. 📷

The north face of Peak 7,905', near the Lacuna Glacier, climbed and skied by the broad central line in April 2021. This was the first documented ascent of the peak. *Aaron Diamond*

— AARON DIAMOND

CROWN GLACIER, PEASANT PILLAR

ONE OF MY favorite parts of "going to school" in the Alaska Range is the annual lessons in adaptation. Both of my expeditions in June shared several elements: week-long weather delays, landing on backup glaciers, and healthy (or some may argue unhealthy) amounts of *Chappelle's Show*.

The first expedition was in the Kichatnas, where our Plan B objectives still yielded a great trip. (*See page 153.*) My second trip was also planned for the Kichatnas, but with questionable landing conditions, Joseph Hobby, Chris Robertson, and I ended up in Little Switzerland, focusing on objectives off the Crown Glacier, near the terminus of the Kahiltna. The Crown Glacier has several south-facing rock walls between Your Highness and Royal Tower that I had sighted while ski touring a few years ago. These walls are relatively small for Alaska (ranging from 800' to 2,000') but the most important landscape for us was having fun.

On June 28, Joseph, Chris, and I flew onto the Pika Glacier and headed due west to the Crown for two days of line-scoping and summer skiing. One shield of rock, in particular, caught our eye, due to the apparent quality of the rock and potentially connecting crack systems.

Two days later, the three of us skied to the base of the proposed route and climbed moderate snow into easy 5th-class rock for 500', until we reached the start of the shield. Seeing this up close revealed good rock but also a sea of question marks. These questions were answered with a comical effort involving a few starting attempts, a tension traverse, some wandering flakes, and a thank-god ledge to line us up with the main crack system.

Aside from a few brief bits of moss concealing the crack, we found wonderful splitters on the ever-steepening shield, starting with the 55m "Black Crack Pitch." The route's crux ended up being pitch 11, which started with some wild traversing shenanigans before reaching an exposed hands to offwidth crack near the prow of the shield. Under the glow of evening light, this memorable pitch put us on top of the main wall.

We climbed a few more pitches of blocky steps that ultimately led to the ridge running between Your Highness and Royal Tower, and then descended back the way we came via a few brief downclimbs and several rappels.

Peasant Pillar (1,400', 13 pitches, 5.10+ C2) took us 20 hours base-to-base and was climbed predominantly free, with approximately 10 percent of the route utilizing aid tactics to connect the route's dots. Like most of the neighboring walls on the Crown and similar routes off the nearby Pika Glacier, Peasant Pillar doesn't lead to a summit; it is, however, the first route up this wall. The route's high-quality rock surprised me in the Alaska Range, where so many routes have the proverbial "choss toll" in order to complete a line. 📷

— ZACH LOVELL

Joseph Hobby leading the steep "Black Crack Pitch" during the first ascent of Peasant Pillar (1,400', 5.10+ C2) above the Crown Glacier. *Zach Lovell*

ALASKA RANGE / HAYES RANGE

NENANA MOUNTAIN, SQUIDWARD DIRECT

ON AUGUST 25, Ethan Berkeland, Matt Capp, Brons Gerrish, and I flew with TEMSCO to the Hotel Glacier to attempt a new route on a satellite peak of Nenana Mountain (7,881'). Unfortunately, with a tight weather window, and having landed in over a foot and a half of fresh snow, our original plans were quickly abandoned.

With morale low, we opted for smaller objectives to test the conditions. Ethan and Matt explored an area where we'd done some cragging during a trip to the glacier the previous year (*AAJ 2021*), to the left of Nenana's South Buttress route, and found conditions to be quite good, albeit snowy and wet. With our enthusiasm reinvigorated, the next day Ethan and I went back to continue the line he'd started. Swapping leads through three more pitches of quality and varied climbing brought us to the base of a wonderful looking fingers-to-chimney crack that had a discouraging volume of water flowing from above. Ethan set off with little regard for the spray, and above this pitch the terrain mellowed to 4th- and 5th-class scrambling, luring us higher up the mountain.

Agreeing that rappelling from this position would be less than ideal, we decided to continue to the summit and attempt the descent taken by Jed Brown and Kevin Wright after their first ascent of the South Buttress in 2004. Eight 70m rappels brought us to the top of a snow gully where we had witnessed multiple avalanches the previous day. As our descent stretched deep into the night, the more stable snow conditions were a welcome silver lining. Back on the glacier, we were elated and proud to have completed a quality new line to the summit of Nenana via its southwest buttress: Squidward Direct (1,800', IV 5.10+).

On our last full day in the valley, Matt and I established an excellent corner pitch near the southwest buttress: Chef's Kiss (5.10b). We flew out happily, knowing the gamble on a late-summer weather window in the Alaska Range had rolled in our favor. Our trip was partially funded with an AAC Mountaineering Fellowship Grant. 📷 🔍

– TRISTAN O'DONOGHUE

MT. HAYES, SOUTHWEST FACE, SKI DESCENT

ON MAY 3, Adam Fabrikant, Beau Fredlund, Clark Henarie, and I made a ski descent of the southwest face of Mt. Hayes (13,832').

We began our trip on May 1, flying out of Talkeetna with Paul Roderick and establishing base camp at 7,000' on the upper Susitna Glacier, with 14 days of food. Our plan was to attempt the south buttress of Hayes, but I had done quite a bit of research and, after seeing a grainy photo in an old AAJ, I thought a gigantic couloir on the southwest face could be a possible backup. We spent the next day skiing around the area—the snow felt good, and the visceral feeling of being back in the big mountains is always special—and quickly ruled out the south buttress as a viable route for ascent or descent, as the glacier was shedding at an alarming rate.

Instead, we focused our attention on the southwest face. Brian Leo, Dougal McCarty, and Benno Ochenski first climbed the southwest face in 1976 (*AAJ 1977*), ascending the enormous couloir feature we had spotted; however, they stopped at the saddle between Hayes' north and south summits, leaving it to a later team to complete the route to the top.

Launching casually the next morning, we found easy travel up to the base of the couloir and then climbed steep névé for 3,000' until it was possible to exit climber's left. We had good photos

The southwest face of Mt. Hayes, showing the line to the higher north summit climbed and skied in May 2021. This route was first climbed in 1976 as far as the saddle and completed later. *Billy Haas*

from our flight in that showed a path to the 13,000' saddle plateau, through a feature we called the Smile Face. However, we hadn't seen the panel of steep alpine ice that separated the couloir from the Smile Face. Three horizontal pitches of ice (AI2/3) brought us into the mouth of the face, where interesting glacial route-finding landed us on the plateau. From here, easy travel led to the higher north summit of Hayes. Building clouds made for in-and-out views, but standing on top of Mt. Hayes is a fantastic position, with views to the tundra in almost all directions.

The upper summit headwall skied well, and we made the glide across the sastrugi-ridden plateau. Wild skiing through the serac-riddled Smile Face brought us back to the ice traverse. To return to the couloir, we made a few diagonal rappels on good V-threads and completed a single traversing pitch with ice tools and crampons. We had a spooky moment on the rappels when I was rigging a V-thread with the boys above, and a serac below them and right next to me calved off. The Smile Face was drooling, so we hurried up to get over to the top of the couloir, where we clicked back into skis.

We had hoped for some softening of the névé in the couloir, but the clouds kept the snow firm. No matter, we skied firm but edgeable névé for 3,000', down one of the most aesthetic couloirs any of us had ever skied. The angle stayed in the 50° range for almost the entirety of the run—fantastically sustained and enjoyable skiing. Back at camp we celebrated with cheese burgers and tequila.

With good conditions, we spent the next week touring around the upper Susitna and adjacent valleys. There is enough ski potential on the glacier to occupy any level of skier for well over a week. The military is very active in this area, and we would be greeted most days by fighter jets' sonic booms or Chinooks hovering overhead. Every day we'd see new wolverine tracks, but never actually saw a wolverine ourselves. They are intrepid creatures, dodging crevasses and scaling mountain passes, and our skin tracks would often follow theirs.

After ten days on the glacier, we called for Paul to pick us up, and a few hours later we were all drinking beers in the hanger. 📷

— BILLY HAAS

CANADA

Maarten van Haeren during the first ascent of Bogdar (1,000m, 5.3 AI4 50°), a new route up the southwest face of Mt. Logbard (3,609m). The peak in the center distance is Mt. Cook (4,196m). *Alik Berg*

EAST OF LOGAN
FOUR NEW ROUTES ABOVE THE HUBBARD GLACIER

BY ETHAN BERMAN

Before we arrived in the Yukon in mid-April 2021, Mt. Logan (5,959m) and the St. Elias Mountains already occupied a distinct place in my psyche. In the literature, the desolate, silent expanses of snow and ice were juxtaposed against the fiery human spirit of those pushing higher and harder on the complex, serac-ridden mountains. Every ascent seemed to chronicle a profound experience, pushing climbers to the edge of reason, ration, and survival, battling against fierce storms and the sheer vastness of the landscape. "The most *out there* you'll ever feel!" they said. I was intimidated, yet comforted by the combined experience of our team of four and the casual attitude we would bring into this stunning yet hostile environment.

Alik Berg, Pete Hoang, Maarten van Haeren, and I arrived in Whitehorse on April 6. We stayed busy for two weeks of COVID-19 quarantine by collecting daily drive-thru groceries, sharing meals, staying fit with beer-induced ski races, and prepping six weeks of meals for what turned out to be a delicious base camp culinary experience. We were released from quarantine in the midst of an unusually long high pressure system and flew to our base camp on the Hubbard Glacier on April 22. Our ultimate goal was a new route on the south side of Mt. Logan, and we had planned enough time to acclimatize well and to explore the mountains around camp.

The next afternoon we were skiing toward the east ridge of Logan with 10 days of food. We spent eight days on this classic route, pushing higher under clear skies and calm wind, and reaching the upper plateau at around 5,000m before descending to base camp in deteriorating weather to a delightful dinner of chicken vindaloo.

Over the next week, the weather was mixed but afforded us some opportunities to climb on the lower peaks surrounding our camp. On May 2, Alik and Maarten established Bogdar (1,000m, 5.3 AI4 50°) on the southwest face of Mt. Logbard (3,609m). A short section of snow led to a 60m one-pitch-wonder of WI4, above which easier snow slopes and mixed terrain brought them to the knife-edge southwest ridge and eventually an ice face leading to the summit. (Poor sedimentary rock on this aspect makes snow and ice recommended over rock climbing.) They possibly made the second ascent of the peak. [*The first ascent of Logbard was by the west face: John Chilton and Rich Prohaska climbed and then skied the face in 1993; see the 1994 Canadian Alpine Journal.*] To descend, Alik and Maarten followed the north ridge until they gained easy access to the west bowl, staying hard skier's right to avoid almost all overhead serac hazard.

After another two days in camp, Maarten and Pete headed to the last prominent unclimbed spur on the south face of McArthur Peak (ca 4,360m), the easternmost obvious buttress. Conveniently located directly above base camp, their route was Basecamp Buttress (1,000m, 5.8 AI3 60°), which they climbed in a long day. They found mostly good rock climbing, which would have been more enjoyable if they had thought to bring rock shoes instead of 6,000-meter boots. The two did not continue to the summit of McArthur, which was likely farther away horizontally than what they had climbed vertically! After gaining the high point of the buttress (just before joining the east ridge of McArthur), they descended the broad couloir directly climber's left of the buttress, making two rappels at the bottom.

On the same day, Alik and I headed to a snowier buttress on the south face of McArthur, intent on repeating AstroFloyd (Kay-Statham, 1992), following a system of snow ramps and ice steps up the buttress. After slogging up snow slopes all morning, we arrived at several pitches of steep ice, increasing in difficulty as we got higher. As Alik spent an hour methodically cleaning a vertical pillar of rotten ice, I doubted we were on Astro-

[Top] **The line of Bogdar on the southwest face of Mt. Logbard.** *Maarten van Haeren* [Bottom] **Van Haeren climbing on Basecamp Buttress, a long mostly rock route on the south face of McArthur Peak.** *Peter Hoang*

[Top] A major buttress on the right side McArthur Peak's south face, showing (1) AstroFloyd (Kay-Statham, 1992) and (2) Big in Japan (1,500m, AI6 50°, Berg-Berman, 2021). The summit is off picture to the left. *Peter Hoang* [Bottom] Steep ice on Big in Japan. *Ethan Berman*

Floyd, but rather an independent line to the right.

After following him up the steep pitches, I broke trail to the top of the buttress, a bump on the long east ridge of McArthur, and without hesitation we began our descent. We traversed the east ridge of McArthur away from the summit until reaching a long, mellow snow slope on the south face, which we downclimbed. After 23 hours on the move, we were happy to find Pete and Maarten had beaten us back to base camp by a couple hours, and therefore won the honors of leaving us some tasty quesadillas. Big in Japan (1,500m, AI6 50°) was a fun addition to the "alpine cragging" on McArthur.

(I also envision that the many spurs and ridges of Logan could be attractive for climbers focused on speed and endurance on moderate ground. For example, a link-up of the east ridge of McArthur, continuing over Dak Tower and Catenary Peak (4,097m), and following the Catenary Ridge (*AAJ 1968*) all the way to the east summit of Logan, would be a worthy objective for the right team.)

The weather looked mixed for the next week, so we decided to do another trip up the east ridge of Logan to further acclimatize; this would still leave us two or three weeks to attempt our main objective on the south face of Logan. We made good progress back to the plateau in three days and found ourselves above the poor weather, once again basking in sunshine. The next day our intended recon resulted in pushing to the main summit under blue skies and cold wind. After a rest day on the plateau, we descended to base camp where Pete, who had elected to stay behind, had endured snowstorms for the week.

With 14 days of total acclimatization on the east ridge, Maarten, Alik, and I felt well prepared to transition to the Seward Glacier and poke our noses into the south walls of Logan. Coincidentally, two friends were flying in to climb the east ridge (we hadn't seen a soul since arrival), so we luckily got a bump flight to the Seward, saving us many hours of glacier slogging, and Pete, who was not well enough acclimatized to join us for the Logan attempt, got a flight out. We rigged a modest ABC and set off to attempt the second ascent of I-TO (Okada-Yokoyama, 2010) on the southeast face. Although we had been interested in trying a new route, the south and southeast faces of Logan are mostly serac-ridden, and we couldn't envision an independent line that didn't look suicidal.

We started up in good weather, but on the second day, although it was still bluebird, we somehow found ourselves in a snowstorm, a most unusual and unfortunate microclimate. We reckon the heat on the south face, perhaps combined with the humidity from our fairly close proximity to the ocean, forced a very localized release of precipitation—precisely where we were on the mountain! We made slow progress, and as we entered a big gully system halfway up the face, with spindrift pouring around us, we decided to bivy and then retreat, not overly optimistic about the forecast. After a full day of rappelling, we reached ABC and woke up later to a foot of fresh snow (from an actual storm system that had moved in). After a rest day, we snowshoed back to base camp, cutting the epic journey from the Seward to the Hubbard in half by making use of a col we had spotted in the Hubsew Ridge, which we named "Sneaky Pete's Pass" (2,175m, 60°31'46.40"N, 140° 6'33.09"W).

Slowly deteriorating weather defeated any hopes of another attempt on the Logan face. During one break in the clouds, Alik and Maarten spent the day of May 26 making the first ascent of the southeast face of Hubsew Peak (1,000m, AI3 50°). They found just enough steep terrain to keep it interesting and noted the potential for 1,000m ski descents—possibilities that seemed to be quite plentiful around the range. Their descent (on foot) was via the blunt south-southwest ridge, until a large open snowfield facing east could be joined back to the start of the route. This is possibly the third route climbed on Hubsew Peak, after the east ridge (1995) and southwest face (2000).

[Top] A very unpleasant bivouac on the south face of Mt. Logan. *Alik Berg* [Bottom] The line up the southeast face of Hubsew Peak (3,569m). The descent was down to the left. *Maarten van Haeren*

Although we were thwarted on our attempt at the big show, and definitely spent more time walking and eating than climbing, we were satiated with six weeks of existence in some of the most remote and spectacular mountains around. We extend a huge thanks to the John Lauchlan Memorial Award for supporting this expedition. 📷

EDITOR'S NOTE: *The 2022 Canadian Alpine Journal will include an article by Maarten van Haeren with in-depth technical descriptions of the routes climbed.*

Duncan Pawson climbs a splitter hand crack on pitch five of Disaster Fauna (600m, 5.11 A0) on Chiq Peak. In back is the unclimbed north face of Gilt Peak. The glacier-topped Extinction Wall is on the right. *Nick Hindley*

FOCH-GILTTOYEES PROVINCIAL PARK, "PANGEA" VALLEY, NEW ROUTES

ON AUGUST 15, Harlin Brandvold, Duncan Pawson, and I loaded gear into a helicopter for a return trip to an isolated valley of glacier-clad granite walls in Foch-Gilttoyees Provincial Park. Having spotted the unnamed valley on Google Earth, and lacking any photographs or reports of prior human travel into the area, our initial helicopter flight in 2019 was a huge gamble. As we flew southwest from the town of Terrace, rocky foothills gave way to rugged, glaciated peaks. The unclimbed 1,200m north face of Gilt Peak (1,893m) soon crested into view, marking our destination on the horizon. The scale of the wilderness embodied a prehistoric aura that would later prompt us to give the valley a nickname: Pangea.

One result of that 2019 trip had been a partial route called Lizard King (300m, 5.10 C1, to the high point), which climbs a dike and splitter chimney perfectly bisecting the 700m face of Extinction Wall, along the northern flank of Gilt Peak, at the head of the valley. An incoming storm, which would ultimately end our trip, forced a retreat from our portaledge camp atop pitch eight. The initial objective for our 2021 return trip had been to complete this route. Unfortunately, we arrived to a wall soaked with the snowmelt, ending our bid before it began.

Through a spotting scope, we scanned kilometers of granite in search of a feasible new objective. We panned northward from Extinction Wall to Cambrian Wall, a smaller southwest-facing feature between Chiq Peak (1,741m) and Gilttoyees-Ecstall Pass. There was no shortage of potential route options, but having been humbled here before, notably on a 21-hour epic establishing Flight of the Dodo (350m, 5.10) on the Cambrian Wall in 2019, we tried to keep our ambitions in check. We decided to spend our first climbing day exploring a slab ramp up the east flank of Chiq Peak. The result was Planktonic Relationship (450m, 5.8) an easy ramble of mostly mid-5th class with some 5.8 moves to the top of the slab. Comfy shoes and bug spray are highly recommended.

The following morning, we felt ready to choose a larger objective. Through our scope, a prominent buttress on the south face of Chiq Peak caught our attention, with a succession of discontinuous cracks and corner systems. A promising line! We each loaded up ropes and racks and set out across the valley that same morning. About 600m north-northwest of our base camp, atop a snow slope and some fourth-class scrambling, we reached the base of what we came to call the Primordial Buttress (53°57'35"N, 129°14'04"W). Wasting little time, I tied in, pulled over a small roof, and pieced together the first pitch. Duncan and Harlin each led a pitch that involved slabby face climbing, bolting on lead as necessary. The 5.10 slab featured some of the most peculiar and undulating granite I had ever seen: ripples, chickenheads, and pods that we later learned could result from hydrostatic pressures at the interface of rock and glacial ice. We fixed lines to the base, and then returned to camp to wait out a storm.

As low clouds rolled past the seeping walls, we each peered through the scope to take stock of the terrain above our high point and set milestones for the following days. After many hard-earned lessons, setting achievable goals has proven to be one of the most important pieces of advice I have received for first-ascent climbing. With the weather improving, we gave the rock one more day to dry off. We packed up 200m of rope, an ungodly amount of rack, bolts, and drill batteries, as well as bivy gear, and then shuttled all the equipment to the base of the route.

Pawson leading pitch one on the unfinished Lizard King, with the Extinction Wall rising above. *Nick Hindley*

The next morning, we charged up the fixed lines under blue skies and climbed three more pitches. Pitch five began with some mossy hand jams before shooting out right through technical and adventurous face climbing. Duncan drilled a handful of generously spaced bolts between 5.11- moves, eventually leading into a beautiful, clean hand crack—a stellar pitch.

Black Sabbath roared through our portable speaker the next day as Harlin took the lead on one of the major unknowns of the route, questing across slab into a steep, shallow groove. A combination of free climbing, hooking, and bolting led him through the technical crux of the route. A drilled bat hook was used to surmount a short, particularly blank section. After two more pitches, we fixed the last of our ropes and headed down again.

The commute back up the nylon highway the next day took some time. Six more pitches of 5.9 rock mixed with heather scrambling then led us to a logical end to the route. We did not scramble the remaining few hundred meters to the summit of Chiq Peak. After a brief celebration, we bolted the final anchor on Disaster Fauna (600m, 5.11 A0) and rappelled to the ground.

We reclimbed the first nine pitches the following day in an attempt to free every move and clean up some of the vegetated sections. Only one move on the seventh pitch didn't go free; we think it would go at around 5.12-. An extra aid bolt was added in lieu of the drilled hook placement, creating a three-bolt ladder that goes at A0. In all, we placed 40 lead bolts and 26 anchor bolts on the line. Satisfied with our efforts, we cleaned our fixed ropes and returned to camp.

With bad weather on the horizon, we messaged our helicopter pilot. We spent our last day packing up, finishing off our whiskey in the sun, and taking in the views of the valley, just one of many untouched granite cirques nestled among British Columbia's vast Coast Mountains. 📷🔍

— NICK HINDLEY, *CANADA*

Not skiing that! Rappelling the serac band in the middle of the 800-meter Gold Card Couloir. *Steve Shannon*

ing the upper snow required three ice and mixed pitches (two WI3 and one M4 A0). We reached the top of the couloir just before 3 p.m. and found the only sun we'd felt all day, but the urgency of fleeting light helped for a quick transition.

The snow on the upper face skied well, with minimal sluff, just soft enough to enjoy the exposed turns. We skied to 20m above the ice and made a short rappel to an anchor we'd established on the way up. Two more rappels (60m and 40m) got us through the serac ice and into the lower couloir.

The snow here was firm and chalky. We linked turns to a traverse and one more 15m rappel through rambling ice. At 5 p.m., almost in the dark, we skied off the fan and onto the frozen lake below. By headlamp, we skied back to the sleds for the long, cold ride back to the vehicles. While bootpacking on the ascent, McNab had pulled out his phone to snap a photo, and we all noticed as a thin, shiny object sailed down the line—it was his Visa card. Hence the name: Gold Card Couloir (800m, 50–55°).

MT. THOR, SOUTH FACE With an arctic air mass embedded over British Columbia, it was time to take advantage of a big south-facing ski line. On February 10, Andrew McNab and I left the road 50km south of Revelstoke near the Shelter Bay ferry on Upper Arrow Lake. We bundled up with overboots, heated socks, and full down outfits for a terribly cold 24km snowmobile ride to reach the south face of Mt. Thor (2,939m) in the Monashee Mountains.

Starting at 1,200m, we skinned up the east-facing basin for the first 1,300m of vertical gain to the east shoulder of Thor. We then descended 200m to the north side to gain the north couloir, which would lead us to the top of our line. Dropping north with such cold temperatures made me nervous, but we moved quickly to the base of the couloir and found generally friendly boot-packing conditions. At the top we welcomed the calm and sunny conditions. Looking down the south face, the snow looked absolutely perfect: cold, dry powder on a huge face.

Testing the snow in the first few turns, we were ecstatic to encounter boot-top blower snow with minimal sluffing. Leapfrogging pitches, we took turns watching each other disappear behind the powder clouds of sunlit snow from each turn.

Arriving at a small step of rock and waterfall ice, we glanced around at options for anchors to rappel, then opted for some downclimbing with skis and some short mandatory air instead. Below was another 900m of sunlit cold-smoke skiing. After 1,300m of skiing up to 50°, we descended into the cold valley bottom and transitioned to skins for the long, flat walk back to the snowmobiles.

MT. NELSON, EAST FACE Both Ian McIntosh and I grew up in Invermere, a small town at the head-waters of the Columbia River, nestled between the Rockies and Purcell ranges. The iconic peak of Mt. Nelson rises to 3,313m in the Purcells, and its east face can be seen from most places in town. I grew up looking at this peak from my living room window, and around the age of 11 or 12, I started wondering if it could be skied. At that age, I didn't know anything about ski touring or first descents. It was just pure imagination, but it planted a seed. However, this is an intimidating line and a location with a tricky snowpack, and I procrastinated on any attempt.

Growing up in nearby Invermere, Christina Lustenberger and Ian McIntosh aspired to someday put ski tracks down Mt. Nelson's beautiful east face. This photo was taken about a week before the first descent. *Christina Lustenberger*

On February 23, Ian and I arrived in Invermere. Driving into the valley and seeing Mt. Nelson usually brings joy and a nostalgic feeling, but this time I felt nervous butterflies. We wanted to get eyes on the east face, so Ian and I headed up Panorama Mountain Resort with my dad and filmmaker Josh Lavigne. As we descended the resort piste, we scoped the face from different angles. The line looked good from a distance—and by good I mean incredibly intimidating—but at least it had snow. Later that afternoon we met at the Invermere airport to take a fixed-wing flight over a few objectives. From the air, Ian snapped photos of the approach up Nelson's south face and the grand east face while I hurled into the barf bag.

We spent the next week skiing around the area, familiarizing ourselves with the snowpack. A weather window presented itself and we mobilized a film crew. Two days before, I set a skin track from the Toby Creek Road to the alpine basin below the south face of Nelson.

We started skinning at 1:45 a.m. on March 4. From the trucks, it was just over 2,000m of vertical gain to the summit. At the base of the south face, we skinned up to the constriction of the rocks and transitioned to climbing. The dark night sky was lightening with orange and beautiful blues. The top quarter of the south face had little to no snow, so we continued scrambling up rock steps, mindful of rockfall. Finally breaking onto the ridge, we walked up toward the beautiful summit cross, reaching the top at 8:45 a.m.

Speed was crucial, as the east face had first light. With anxious parents and community watching from Panorama and ski patrol listening to our communications, we dropped in on a short rappel at 9 a.m. The snow on the face was very shallow and faceted (sugary), making clipping a rock a very hazardous possibility. We found the best snow in the main trough and skied one at a time, leapfrogging pitches. The snow stayed dry and cold, but just barely. We traversed skier's right over an exposed cliff band and regrouped. Due to the sugary snow, protruding rocks, and exposed terrain, we built an anchor using a pin, wire, and one screw in questionable ice, then rappelled 30m over the rocks to the final fan. Ian skied the fan while I coiled the ropes.

There was a sense of weight being lifted as we linked big turns exiting the face. Our line had been 750m of terrain up to 55°. A childhood dream realized with a good friend. Immediately after, the buzz of the descent had hit the community. We now get to look up from town with so much pride. [*Editor's Note: The online version of this report details another first descent in 2021, a direct line on the north face of Bagheera Mountain near Rogers Pass.*] 📷

— CHRISTINA LUSTENBERGER, *CANADA*

Mt. Niblock (2,976m) from the northeast, showing the 500-meter line of (1) Just a Nibble (April 2021) and (2) the 1976 summer route. Brette Harrington's March 2021 solo of the north-northwest ridge and upper north face traversed across the face (3) to finish on the 1976 route. *Brette Harrington*

MT. NIBLOCK, NORTHEAST FACE, JUST A NIBBLE

AMONG THE SKYLINE of giants around Lake Louise, Mt. Niblock (2,976m) had been hiding from me in plain sight all year, until finally I pulled my car over to take a closer look. Bands of black limestone shrouded the northern aspect of the mountain, revealing steep cliffs amid an otherwise white face.

On March 13, I soloed the north-northwest ridge and the upper north face in an 18-hour round trip. I brought along a half rope and some pins and wires for self-belaying. I climbed the final 200m or so using a self-belay loop to get through the cruxes of the climb.

About a month later, on April 16, I returned to Mt. Niblock with Dylan Cunningham to try the unclimbed northeast face. [*A summer route up Niblock's northern face was climbed in July 1976 (Calvert-Calvert-Gardner-Shank), with moderate snow and short rock and ice bands (AD-). The 2021 route climbs a steeper aspect left of a prominent buttress.*] We left the Lake Louise parking lot on skis, traversed under Mt. St. Piran (2,649m), and zigzagged up through the forest to the basin below the face, where we camped. Photos from my previous mission showed minimal overhead hazard compared with the other mountains in the area, where spring cornices hung heavy.

We began climbing by headlamp at 2 a.m. Dylan led us through a series of thin ice steps and deep facets. Navigating the fickle ice atop loose rock consumed more time than we had anticipated, and dawn had arrived by the time I took over the lead. The ice transitioned into tiers of WI4 and eventually into a 45–50° snow slope. About 150m of snow led to the base of the rock bands, where the face became vertical.

I slipped into my rock shoes, clipping my boots and crampons to my harness, and started up. The dark rock was fragile and splintered, making for very delicate, insecure climbing. After a few meters, I managed a beak placement and lowered back to the belay in search of a safer passage. I switched back into boots and crampons and began to traverse left. Soon I came upon a shallow chimney, which invited me up with one more transition into rock shoes. Dylan then led through the trickiest mixed section of the route: a bouldery overhang on insecure pick placements. I moved dynamically, cutting my feet as I seconded the pitch. We graded it M6.

Next came a compact low-angle slab dusted with snow, which I climbed in rock shoes; however, the snow I brushed off the rock melted underfoot and refroze into verglas. This was a unique experience—the climbing was no harder than 5.6, but the foot placements were coated in ice, making downclimbing impossible. I was quite afraid: unable to find a single placement of gear, knowing that the anchor below was an array of questionable pins. I angled toward the eastern skyline, where I landed a lucky strike and slung a frozen chockstone as my first piece of protection. Luck is a generous gift one cannot count on receiving, yet we rely on it every time we start up a big mountain.

The sun hung low on the horizon as we intercepted the east ridge. Complex terrain still loomed above to reach the summit, a couple of hundred meters up, and the descent down the ridge looked to be equally complex. We chose to start down while we had light.

We rappelled and downclimbed the ridge and traversed into a col, from which we opted to bum-slide the snow slope leading back toward camp on the north side. We cut away a small cornice to test the stability, then launched into the slide. We made it back to our camp by twilight, packed up, and skied back to the Lake Louise parking lot by 10 p.m. The climb was Just a Nibble (500m, 5.10- WI5 M6 R). 📷

– **BRETTE HARRINGTON,** *USA AND CANADA*

ROCKIES ANNUAL HIGHLIGHTS

WHETHER IT WAS the late effects of the COVID-19 chill or a very smoky summer, 2021 was not the most active year in the Canadian Rockies. Nonetheless, there were some interesting climbs.

On March 5, Alik Berg and Ian Welsted climbed a foamy, sticky ice strip on the northwest face of Mt. Vaux (3,310m), east of the Trans-Canada Highway, about halfway between Lake Louise and Golden. After a bivy at treeline, the two climbed a few vertical ice pitches, which led to 300m of moderate mixed ground, followed by 250m of technical ice before the northwest ridge, with Berg strolling to the summit in a storm: Western Névé (800m, WI5 R M5).

Western Névé (800m, WI5 R M5) on the northwest face of Mt. Vaux. *Ian Welsted*

About a week later, Berg teamed with Uisdean Hawthorn to make the coveted second ascent of the Mt. Wilson (3,260m) testpiece Dirty Love (V 500m, M7). They first climbed Totem Pole (200m, WI5) and then linked into Dirty Love for a 26-hour 1,700m car-to-car outing. Three days later, the same team added Amnesiac (500m, WI5 M7) on the northeast face of the east subpeak of Mt. Whymper (2,844m), visible from the Radium Highway (Hwy. 93).

Also in March, Luka Bogdanovic and Shawn White cycled 11km along the north shore of Lake Minnewanka to a drainage holding the incredible find of The Odyssey (200m, 7 pitches, WI4). With its remote yet easy-to-reach location, requiring only a 15-minute hike up the drainage after the bike approach, this south-facing route is bound to become a popular adventurous moderate.

In mid-April, Merrick Montemuro, Sebastian Taborszky, and Paul Taylor headed to Moraine Lake and found a striking line of ice in the bowl left of the Perren approach to Mt. Fay (3,235m). On the right side of the spectacular wall below the Fay Glacier, they climbed Play with Fay (345m, WI6). The same team added Last Harvest (110m, WI3/4) across Hector Lake, near Orion Falls, on April 20, at the end of the ice season.

The summer alpine scene seemed particularly quiet. In July, Berg and Juan Henriquez added a major summer-season line to the huge east face of Mt. Chephren (3,266m). Smoke and a Pancake (1,100m, 5.11-) was climbed over two days, and takes the buttress between the winter routes The Wild Thing (1,300m, WI5 M7) and The Dogleg Couloir (1,300m, V+ M7 A1). They found good quartzite for the first 600m, and the upper 500m alternated between limestone and shale ledges.

At the end of the summer, Berg and Maarten van Haeren completed the first traverse of the Trident Range outside Jasper. They began with the northeast ridge of Perevil Peak, the technical crux. The next day they moved counter-clockwise and completed Vertex Peak, Majestic Mountain and Mt. Estella. On the last day they went over Manx Peak and Terminal Mountain, down to Marmot Pass, and finally over Marmot Mountain, all on quality quartzite. The traverse is around

"Mt. Louis # 1" (2010), acrylic on canvas, by Glen Boles. The Diamond face is partially visible in profile in upper right. A treasured figure in Canadian mountaineering, Glen Boles died in January 2022 at age 87. He began climbing in the 1950s, and his experience ran the gamut from exploratory mountaineering to rescue and ski patrol; he was an honorary member of the Canadian and American alpine clubs. Boles was well-known for his artwork, and many of his paintings and drawings can be seen at *glenboles.ca.*

16km as the crow flies, highway to highway, and the suggested grade is III+, 5.6.

Dylan Cunningham had quite a summer, first climbing Smokeshow (IV 850m, 5.6 45°) on the northeast buttress of the north summit of Mt. Mummery (3,328m) with Tanya Bok. The peak is on the far western side of the Rockies, north of Golden, and the route was climbed at the end of August as part of the Alpine Club of Canada General Mountaineering Camp, hearkening back to an adventurous time in that venerable institution. Cunningham also snagged the third known ascent of the Cheesmond-Dick route on the east face of Mt. Assiniboine (V 1,200m, 5.9 A2), climbing with Ryan Richardson. Cunningham and Richardson joined Craig McGee for the final push up a new line on Mt. Louis (2,682m), which McGee established with various partners: Diamonds Are Forever (10 new pitches, 5.12) takes the right side of the sheer Diamond formation on the east face.

On October 5, Patrick Jones and Ryan Leavitt climbed a rock route up a likely unclimbed peak, Elevator #2 (referenced in the David Jones *Rockies South* guidebook), east of Elkford in the southern Rockies. They climbed 12 short pitches up to 5.8 and placed bolts for anchors due to poor rock quality.

The first new route in winter conditions, in October, was a moderate line on Mt. Whyte (2,983m), above the Lake Agnes teahouse. Whyte Noise (430m, AI3 M4) by Austin Goodine, Paul Taylor, and Taborszky became an instant classic. A few thin ice pitches lead to a romp up a snow couloir to a moderate mixed exit onto the ridge and the summit block; the route was repeated quickly by a few parties looking for early winter climbing.

Also in October, van Haeren and Welsted headed up to the north face of Storm Mountain (3,095m) looking for the mythical Thomas-Wallator route, a 500m line on the left side of the face, first climbed in 1988 and still unrepeated. They veered off right into easier ground when confronted by vertical cracks, resulting in a variation with ledge and corner systems and a sustained M5 dry-tooling pitch.

In a more conventional vein, Taborszky and Bruno-Pierre Couture climbed a three-pitch mixed route in Field just to the left of the thin ice of Big Sexy Yodel. Aggravated Turtles (130m, WI5+ M6) is a useful option when the ice next door is unclimbable, which is often the case.

Finally, in late January, the author finished a moderate dry-tooling project that follows weaknesses to the left of the classic Mixed Master along the Icefields Parkway. Astringent Apprentice (300m, M5) was started with Sam Eastman, then climbed to the last pitch with Uisdean Hawthorn, and finally completed in good mixed conditions with Raphael Slawinski. 🔲

— IAN WELSTED, CANADA

MT. TEMPLE, NORTH FACE, STRINGING UP THE LIGHTS

I LAY in my van as night fell on October 16 with nervousness in my stomach. Taylor Sullivan had worked a six-day week rigging Christmas lights in Calgary and wouldn't arrive until late. He'd spotted a beautiful vein of ice slithering down the north face of Mt. Temple (3,544m). It was probably formed by serac activity, as he'd never seen it before, despite living nearby.

We were inspired, but our limited experience on big Rockies walls and huge overhanging seracs made us feel inadequate and fearful. As a result, the easier, safer Elzinga-Miller (1974), which gains the north ridge to the left of the north face headwall, was our main plan, but we'd packed enough gear to keep the unclimbed and aesthetic direct line to the right an option.

At 4 a.m. on October 17, a bang on the door and blinding torchlight woke me. Fear turned to action, and dawn found us entering the Dolphin Couloir. Melt-freeze sn'ice saw us gain elevation quickly through stellar Scottish-style mixed pitches: tools in plastic ice and cams in splitter quartzite cracks. We soloed steep rock moves around a wind lip, finding our rhythm as I led the technical pitches and Taylor punched tracks through snow.

As we arrived at the top of the Dolphin snowfield, the October sky was clear blue and the mountain was sheltering us from strong southwesterly winds. A strenuous dry pitch took us to the decision point: escape technical difficulty and objective hazard by continuing on the ridge or head directly up the gorgeous tongue of ice that weaved up through the headwall and its ominous crowning seracs. With conditions near perfect and adrenaline in our veins, recklessness prevailed.

True to Rockies form, the first pitches of "ice" turned out to be unconsolidated crud on a chossy limestone band. About 150m of thin cascading ice, half a stubby thick, followed. The climbing wasn't steep, but insecure placements, illusory protection, and nonexistent belay anchors shredded our nerves. Then, midway through an unprotected simul-climb, a huge rockfall released above, sending microwave-size blocks rattling down the gully and forcing us to dive for cover. Darkness was closing in, the steep ice above looked cruxy, and we were tempted to retreat, but poor rappel options made continuing up the only choice.

As I led off, I found with relief that the ice thickened and the rock regained quality. Although progress was slow as night fell, temperatures dropped, and fatigue built, we were treated to fantastic climbing. First, a near-vertical WI4+ ice-choked gully, narrow enough for crampons to stem out wildly on the rock either side. Then, a thick smear of ice, which weaved up a slab and corner system and improbably around a roof.

Several snow and ice pitches later, we were ascending an alleyway through a maze of house-size seracs, clamber-ing onto a leaning block to escape the face, and plodding around crevasses to the summit. Despite a mammoth night-

Chris Petrauskas climbing thin ice on pitch three of Stringing Up the Lights, the first new route on the north face headwall of Mt. Temple since 2008. *Taylor Sullivan*

time descent ahead, the relief to be out from under seracs was palpable. The wind had eased, and in the calm silence, the Rockies spread out beneath us, bathed in moonlight. Self-doubt evaporated—we'd done it: Stringing Up the Lights (1,200m, WI5 M4 R), with 350m of new technical terrain, done in a 28-hour single push.

Another dawn broke before we returned to civilization. Taylor hotfooted to Calgary for another day of stringing up the lights as I contemplated how mountains are one of the few remaining environments which allow us to be reckless, where those who know better can't stop you from risking your life. We accepted huge risks, but in an age of mountain athletes and professionals, the fact a full-time accountant and Christmas light-rigger can still put up a quality line in a setting like Temple's north face shows how many incredible, accessible routes are still to be climbed, and how anyone can dream of climbing them. [*A full description of the 10 new pitches on this route is at the AAJ website.*] 📄 📷

— CHRIS PETRAUSKAS, *CANADA*

Charles Roberge leading the first pitch of Klondike (220m, WI6 R). *Yan Mongrain*

QUÉBEC

LA MALBAIE, GRANDS-JARDINS, AND GASPÉ, NEW ROUTES

THE HAUTES-GORGES-DE-LA-RIVIÈRE-MALBAIE saw a lot of action during the 2021 season, encouraged by unusual weather and travel limitations due to a province-wide COVID-19 curfew. The holiday season saw some major downpours, which contributed to the formation of new ice routes. Snow removal from the access road in the last couple of years also has been a game changer, since the former 30km approach on skis is now mostly done by car.

The most notable new line was Klondike (220m, WI6 R), opened in early 2021 by Jean-Philippe Bélanger, Yan Mongrain, and Charles Roberge. Back in 2017, Roberge had seen a tiny streak of ice high on the western side of the Malbaie River and 300m to the right of a route called Pomodoro. The torrential rain of Christmas Eve 2020 persuaded him to revisit the site and see if, maybe, a line had formed. The trio was in luck and launched the season with a smash.

A few weeks later, Bélanger and Roberge returned to the park and opened Tabasco (115m, WI6+) on the extreme left side of the cliff that holds the renowned Pomme d'Or. Despite being on the same face, it's a distinct and hard new route with quite difficult access, very high on the flanks of the mountain.

Also in early January, Vincent Demers and Patrick Gagné did the first ascent of C'est Pas la Mer Ciboire (120m, WI5). This route is between Triolet and Hystérie Collective, before the dam, on the west banks of the Malbaie River. A few days later, Carl Darveau and Jean-François Girard added an extension to the line to reach the summit: a 60m WI2+ and a 40m M7-. They have named their addition Inconscient Collectif (100m, WI5+ M7-).

In February, Patrice Beaudet and Sebastien Morin made a prolific trip to the valley, opening three new routes: Le Retour de Papy (90m, WI5), La Goulotte des Tropiques (70m, WI4), and Passion Hivernale (65m, WI4+). The duo also repeated Klondike during that trip.

The Grands-Jardins (located a bit west of the Hautes-Gorge) seemed a bit forsaken in 2021. However, the Gros Bras did see a major new route with the establishment of Baba Yaga (165m, M8 A1) by Jean-François Girard and Louis Rousseau. The ascent took 14 hours and combined delicate traverses, slabs, tiny cracks, overhangs, a chimney, and big loose blocks. The sixth pitch was the hardest (M8 A1) and completed with headlamps.

Also on the Gros Bras, Benoit Dubois and a partner made the second ascent of Folie de Jeunesse (240m, 5.11- M8+) in late March 2021; this summer rock route was opened in 2018 by Pierre-Alexandre Paquet and Jacques Lamontagne. Even though this wasn't officially a first winter ascent, it was a hard repeat in wintery conditions. It took the duo 13 hours to complete the route. Because of the curfew, they had to sleep in their truck on the return to avoid possible mishaps with the authorities.

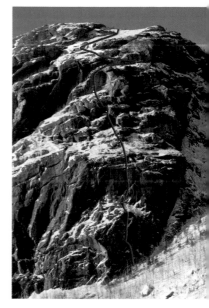

The north face of Gros Bras and Baba Yaga. *Louis Rousseau*

Out on the Gaspé Peninsula, Girard continued his season by opening Ad Absurdum (105m, WI5+ M6) at Gros Morne with Mathias Arroyo Bégin. The first pitch was on an ice-plastered slab with a vertical icicle at the end, and the second saw the pair climb some questionable rock, which also plagued the rappel.

Despite Québec's walls having been scouted by ice climbers for decades, this season confirmed there are still nice discoveries to be made, without having to drive for hours by car or snowmobile. 📷

— IAN BERGERON *AND* LOUIS ROUSSEAU, *CANADA*

NUNAVUT

BAFFIN ISLAND, INUKSUIT FJORD, VARIOUS ASCENTS

IN LATE JUNE, just before the sea ice starts to melt, Sarah McNair-Landry and I headed out from Clyde River and skied 100km to Inuksuit Fjord (sometimes called Inugsuin) and Perfection Valley, which lie approximately 70km southwest of Clyde River as the crow flies. We towed our kayaks loaded with 45 days of food, camping equipment, and climbing gear. Our kayaks and dry suits proved useful for crossing sections of rotten ice and open water.

Once in the fjord, our plan was to climb some of the impressive peaks around camp and then head inland, portaging our kayaks, to paddle waterfalls on four different rivers. The Nuksuklorolu Pinnacles towered over our small base camp, and we felt very small in this huge landscape of peaks and glaciers. It was an unusually cold and wet summer, and the weather tested our patience. Even in July, the weather alternated between snow and rain.

On July 3, we started up our first climb on Nuksuklorolu Pinnacle South. We approached via a long scree scramble that led to loose, easy climbing followed by several pitches of quality rock. We encountered a clean slab with a thin crack that we protected with a small piton, and the final pitch had a nice roof to a hand crack finish. We found no evidence of previous climbs on the feature, although, given its location, it is possible someone has climbed it. [*Editor's Note: A large Italian expedition in 1998 climbed nine routes in this area, including Welcome, Nunavut (800m, VI 5.11 A1) on Nuksukorolu Tower, the largest of the pinnacles, and a 1,000m 5.10 A0 route on the "Belluno Spur," which is likely very similar to a line climbed by Steve Sheriff, Gray Thompson, and Jon Turk in 1989, called Inugsuin Point Buttress and rated 5.9. See AAJs 1991 and 1999.*]

Our next objective was a beautiful arête, only accessible by a 2.5-hour ocean paddle to the northwest. We found great rock with sustained and varied 5.10 climbing. It drizzled throughout the day, and after nine pitches, heavier rain moved in, causing us to rappel back down to our boats. We got back to camp after 24 hours. We called the incomplete route The Road to Nowhere.

Next up was Nuksuklorolu Pinnacle Middle, which was climbed by a longtime friend Jon Turk, who did the second ascent in 1989; the first ascent was solo by Uwe Embacher in 1977. Our first attempt ended early, when it started snowing and we ran out of protectable cracks. On our second attempt we aided up wet, mossy, dripping cracks and climbed some hard free pitches (up to 5.11). Route-finding was the biggest challenge. Within a few pitches of the summit and after 32 hours of climbing, we came to a dead end and rapped back down. We were getting the adventure we wanted but were also being humbled by the climbing in this wild place. [*Editor's Note: It's likely they were climbing a new route, as the 1989 climb was rated 5.8.*]

Our last climb, Hotel Gina (320m, 6b+), was a route established by Hansjörg Auer, Ben Lepesant, and Matteo Mocellin in 2012 on the east face of the White Wall in the Perfection Valley (*AAJ 2013*). This was our favorite climb, following quality cracks and corners up a spectacular wall.

For the second part of our journey, we loaded up our white-water kayaks with 20 days of food and camping gear and headed inland, where we'd identified four new rivers to paddle. We completed 30km of the McBeth River (class IV+), 3km of Teacup River (V+), 10km of the Inuksuit River, and 3km of what we called Awesome River (class V+). We found huge waterfalls and high-quality rapids—Awesome River was the highlight, as Erik got to paddle 40- and 60-foot waterfalls. 🔲 🔍

– ERIK BOOMER *AND* SARAH MCNAIR-LANDRY, *CANADA*

Erik Boomer shuttling gear past sea ice that was too rotten for skiing, en route to Inuksuit Fjord. Cloud-capped Nuksuklorolu Tower is visible at far left. *Sarah McNair-Landry*

GREENLAND

Nicolas Favresse attempting the crux of Wall of Planck on Siren Tower. This section eventually was freed by Aleksej Jaruta at 8a. *Jean-Louis Wertz*

EAST GREENLAND / KANGERTITIVATSIAQ FJORD

MYTHICS CIRQUE, SIREN TOWER AND OTHER FIRST ASCENTS

WE DIDN'T KNOW where we were going as we sailed out of Brittany, France, on July 8. The course was set generally for the east coast of Greenland, but the specific destination would depend on where the other passengers of our two-masted, 24-meter sailboat, Kamak, would be able to fly in to join the boat. "Don't worry, if you drop us off in a fjord with some boulders, we will be happy. If there are big walls, it's a bonus," I told Jean Bouchet, the French guide and driving force of the Kamak project. Just to be in a beautiful wild setting for a long period of time would be a huge privilege.

We were a team of four climbers: Nicolas Favresse, with whom I have shared more than 25 years of adventures; Aleksej Jaruta, a talented 23-year-old Swedish climber with Russian roots, and Belgian climber and professional photographer Jean-Louis Wertz, who had joined Nico and me on previous expeditions in Venezuela and Pakistan.

Two awesome skippers and forces of nature were in charge of the boat: Gabriel from France and Vincente from Spain. The rest of the crew consisted of Bouchet, his 22-year-old daughter, Enora, and 75-year-old retired engineer Bernard, who gleamed friendliness. Once Bernard started talking, there was no stopping him. His favorite subject was physics. On one occasion he grabbed our attention when he mentioned the Wall of Planck. "Where is it? How big is it?" I asked. "No, you idiot!" he answered, "the Planck Wall is a principle of quantum physics!"

On July 20, after two weeks of sailing, lots of vomiting, and some wobbly hangboard sessions, we four climbers were dropped off below the imposing towers of the Mythics Cirque, our home for the next 45 days. The most obvious objective was the steep north face of unclimbed Siren Tower. Although we thought about "acclimatizing" with something easier, the approach to this face consisted of a steep snow couloir; in the current temperatures (more than 20°C), the couloir

North face of Siren Tower showing approximate lines of (1) Forum and (2) Wall of Planck, both climbed in 2021. *Jean-Louis Wertz*

would rapidly become objectively dangerous. We decided to fix ropes to an obvious ledge about 200m up.

As I lifted my heavy bag onto my shoulders, anticipating 10 days on the wall, I took a last look out to the fjord. Amid the icebergs I saw three dots moving toward us. We knew that Matteo Della Bordella, Silvan Schüpbach, and Symon Welfringer had also planned a climbing expedition to East Greenland, approaching their objective by kayaks. We ran down to the shore, stripped naked, and started playing and singing the Italian song "Ti Amo" ("I love you"). It must have been pretty cringy for them to paddle into a remote fjord and find four climbers singing in their birthday suits, but we got a good laugh out of it.

The climbing on the Siren proved to be sustained, with beautiful, physical cracks and big moves between good jams. The gneiss also offered surprising edges on the blank-looking sections, making the climbing easier than expected. On our third day we felt ready to push to the top. Until then we had onsighted most of the pitches, but one had resisted our efforts. A steep finger crack led to a disappearing seam, which offered a last piece of protection before a blank slab and a committing dyno. While jumaring the fixed rope, Jean-Louis noticed an easier line farther right. Before our attempt to reach the summit, we first climbed this easier variation.

The upper section of Siren Tower had decomposing stone, and every move required the delicacy of disarming a ticking bomb. "Erm, I'm a little bit out of my comfort zone," Aleksej admitted. Nico brought us safely to a ledge at the top of a broken pillar, from which I puzzled my way past the "Eye of Sauron," an intimidating big hole that looked like it had been blasted into the wall. After four more long, easy pitches, we stood on top of the tower, likely the first human beings ever there. We named the route Wall of Planck (700m, 16 pitches, 7b+; Aleksej freed the 8a Jaruta Variation during our descent).

Back at our portaledge camp, we were woken by the Italian-Swiss-French team climbing a line about 30m to our left. It might seem strange that in this extremely remote area, two teams ended up on the same wall of a previously unclimbed spire. On the other hand, maybe it's not so surprising, because it is one of the steepest and most spectacular faces in the area.

While rappelling Siren Tower, we had noticed two separate lines on Aurora Tower, the peak directly opposite. [*Aurora Tower was first climbed and named in 2016 by an international team that summited by the southwest ridge, outside the Mythics Cirque. In 2018, a French party climbed the right side of the southeast face and the upper northeast ridge.*] After a few rest days at base camp, we decided to split into two teams and make a race out of it. The rock, paper, scissors oracle put Nico and Aleksej up against Jean-Louis and me. We climbed all day in glorious sunshine above a sea of clouds, and when Jean-Louis and I reached the top after about eight hours, there was no sign of the others. The Olympic Games were taking place in Tokyo at that time, but big-wall speed climbing was not represented, so we were happy to have achieved The Olympic Speed Climbing Record (550m of climbing, 11 pitches, 7a+). An hour or so later we were joined by Nico and

Aleksej, who had completed the Russian-Belgian Route (550m of climbing, 10 pitches, 7b).

Back at base camp, we were able to catch up with the other three, who had finished their new route on Siren Tower (*see report below*). We opted to focus next on Ataatap Tower (a.k.a. Father or Daddy tower), the biggest feature in the Mythics Cirque, and decided to try the steeper wall to the left of Built Fjord Tough, the original Libecki-Pringle route on the northeast face (*AAJ 2013*).

Aleksej, Nico, and I switched leads on very serious climbing: big loose flakes, bad protection, runouts, and slimy rock. On one pitch we had to carefully climb around a huge, hanging tooth of rock. When we finally reached a big ledge at 500m, all three of us were mentally drained, and while it would have been nice to continue direct, we opted to traverse right along the ledge and finish up the dihedral of Built Fjord Tough. In comparison to what we had climbed, this was like a welcoming motorway, with straightforward route-finding, good protection, and even the occasional bolt. We ran to the summit, waited for sunrise, and then took the long walk down the far side, reaching base camp about 24 hours after leaving: Daddy's Sweet Tooth (800m of climbing, 17 pitches including the last seven of Built Fjord Tough, 7b).

By mid-August the nights were lengthening rapidly, and we had no clear idea when Kamak would return to collect us. While there were certainly challenges left in the Mythics Cirque, we were surrounded by unlimited wilderness and were hungry to explore. We therefore made three little "expeditions," on which we used our inflatable double kayaks to move deeper into the fjord.

On the first of those outings, I decided to stay at base camp because my knee was swollen from the long descent off Ataatap Tower. In 12 hours, Aleksej, Jean-Louis, and Nico climbed a spire we had spotted from the summit of Aurora. They named it Borsch Soup Tower and the route Borsch Soup (600m, 12 pitches, 6b).

[Top] Southeast face of Aurora Tower with approximate lines of (1) The Olympic Speed Climbing Record (2021), (2) Russian-Belgian Route (2021), and (3) French Route (2018). *Philippe Batoux* [Middle] Myope Tower. The first ascent generally followed the left skyline. [Bottom] Maculi's Ritual (600m, 7b) on the south side of Maculi's Tower, located about 10 hours up side valleys to the east of Kangertitivatsiaq Fjord. *Jean-Louis Wertz (two photos)*

Formations of the Mythics Cirque: (A) Ataatap Tower (a.k.a. Daddy Tower); (B) Hidden Tower; (C) Siren Tower; and (D) Aurora Tower. *Jean-Louis Wertz*

On the second kayak excursion, I realized I had forgotten my harness. I improvised one from a length of cord, but needless to say it wasn't comfortable. I stuck to seconding and ordered, "No hanging belays!" Nico and Aleksej insisted the route be called The Chastity Belt of Sean (250m, five pitches, 6c), and the unnamed formation Chastity Tower.

For the third little expedition, we kayaked for two hours and then walked up a big green valley. After about five hours, Nico and Jean-Louis found a spire that inspired them. They encountered some incredible pitches littered with big huecos, and in 13 hours reached the summit of what they named Myope Tower by the route Le Sentier des Myopes (650m, 14 pitches, 7a+).

Aleksej and I continued walking for another five hours until we found a needle with great rock and started up it. As I was climbing an easy offwidth, my foot slipped and I went flying through the air. I hit a small ledge and felt numbing pain shoot through my right ankle. I was unable to put any weight on it. The situation was serious. We faced 10 hours of hiking over difficult glaciers and moraine to reach our kayaks, followed by a two-hour paddle to the comforts of base camp. While Aleksej carried all the gear, I stumbled along with the help of my trekking poles. Even though there was a lot of pain, I accepted my fate and enjoyed the challenge.

A few days later, Aleksej and Nico returned and finished this climb on what they named Maculi's Tower. Gabriel, the French captain of Kamak, had insisted on performing the macoui ritual upon leaving Brittany to offset bad luck associated with the boat's name change; it included sailing three times in a circle, blowing the horn, and opening a bottle of rum. Maculi's Ritual (our interpretation of "macoui") was 600m, 7b, and climbed in 13 hours. [*Coordinates of all of these formations are at the AAJ website.*]

By September 9, when we finally boarded Kamak, night and day were of nearly equal length and a thin layer of ice appeared on the sea each morning. Twenty-three days after we left base camp, with the coast of Brittany almost in sight, the wind blew gently into our sails and the sun came out. A group of dolphins was playing with the bow, and now and again one of them would tilt sideways and look up at us. They were whistling, squeaking, singing. You would almost believe they were talking to us. You would almost believe that they knew. 📷

— SEAN VILLANUEVA O'DRISCOLL, *BELGIUM*

SIREN TOWER, FORUM; PADDLE WALL, SOUTHEAST FACE

OUR SWISS-ITALIAN-FRENCH TEAM headed to East Greenland in late July, planning to kayak to remote walls. Due to pandemic-related difficulties, we were a week late in reaching our starting point of Tasiilaq. Matteo Della Bordella, Symon Welfringer, and I were quite demoralized after the many bureaucratic hurdles. However, when we finally arrived in Greenland, our motivation increased immediately: The feeling of freedom and adventure was in the air!

We decided to visit the Mythics Cirque along Kangertitivatsiaq Fjord because it was quicker to access than our original objective. In addition, the north face of unclimbed Siren Tower seemed an attractive target. Only 36 hours after arriving in Tasiilaq, we had packed 200kg of food and equipment into three kayaks and headed northeast along the coast.

Our journey proved much easier than anticipated. The sea was mostly calm, and we were able to cover 40km per day. We were captivated by the beautiful, wild landscape, and soon everyday worries were left behind. After our hard kayak training, we were almost disappointed the journey was so smooth, but arriving faster meant more time for climbing.

When we arrived at the Mythics, guess who greeted us on shore? It was the Belgian climbers Nico Favresse, Sean Villanueva, and Jean-Louis Wertz and Swede Aleksej Jaruta. At first, I didn't know what to make of meeting other people on this wild expedition. But I quickly realized these guys were like soul mates, with the same passion. After setting up base camp, we made a reconnaissance of the imposing granite walls in the cirque and agreed that we still wanted to climb Siren Tower, even though the other team was already at work on it and would finish before us (*see story above*). We saw an elegant line to the left of the one being attempted by the others and, after confirming they wouldn't mind company, started up the next day.

After five days, we stood on the summit, and since we had the time, we dedicated the sixth day to climbing pitches we had not been able to free. The crux

Symon Welfringer working on the first ascent of Forum on Siren Tower. *Silvan Schüpbach*

pitch was a mix of wall and crack climbing, which we rated 7c. The climbing had been psychologically difficult due to inobvious gear placements. (We climbed almost the entire route with removable protection and belay anchors, placing just two bolts, along with some pitons to reinforce rappel anchors.) We christened our route Forum (800m, 22 pitches, 7c), because we are three strong personalities and every decision about what to do, where to go, and how to organize ourselves always required long discussions—constructive moments that allowed us to reach our goal.

With kayaks, you are not tied to one place in a coastal area like this. Wanting to make the most of the days still available to us, we packed our boats and explored the coast for more targets. Twelve kilometers south and the west from our base camp in the Mythics, we discovered a wall in a beautiful glacial landscape. It wasn't particularly impressive, but it got a lot of sun, was full of crack lines, and promised good rock. We named it Paddle Wall (66°15'19.38"N, 35°52'4.04"W), and our climb here was La Cène du Renard ("The Fox's Supper," 440m, 7a). A fox, the only animal that came close to us during the expedition, ate our cheese and crapped in our cooking pot the evening before we climbed.

In mid-August we paddled back to Tasiilaq. In all, we paddled 330km, taking four days to reach the Mythics and five to return. ◙

— SILVAN SCHÜPBACH, *SWITZERLAND*

Jacob Cook on the crux pitch (5.13b) of Los Naguales, which starts with full-body chimneying against a giant tufa and then breaks right across the big overhang just above. *Andrew Keating*

NUEVO LEÓN

LA POPA, NORTHEAST FACE, LOS NAGUALES

ONLY AN HOUR from the hustle of El Potrero Chico, La Popa has a very different feel. Way out in the desert, there's nobody home except the wild horses and endless, endless cactus. Whether or not you believe the local stories about evil spirits and shape-shifting horse-people, it's undeniable the place has a unique energy.

Despite having a great time climbing Super Blood Wolf with Tony McLane and Savannah Cummins in 2019 (*see AAJ 2019*), I decided afterward that I never wanted to go on another ground-up climbing adventure on La Popa. I did, however, miss the time out in the desert, with no distractions and the most spectacular night sky. When Drew Marshall and I returned to La Popa in December 2021, the plan was to camp on the summit and go fully top-down in order to create a good route through the steepest part of the wall.

We spent several days fruitlessly prospecting. We would fix our ropes from the top and then just hang next to each other out in space, slowly spinning. We found lots of amazing features, but nothing quite connected. Then one night I bivied at the base of the wall, and at sunrise I looked straight up from my sleeping bag and traced a line all the way through the lower wall on tufas and cracks. The only big question was some overhanging and blank-looking rock right at the top. The next morning we rapped in and were overjoyed to find a line of perfect pockets and jugs.

The line lies about 100m to the left of El Gavilan, the other steep sport route on the wall, put up by Kevin Gallagher and Jeff Jackson in 1997. Over the next month we worked like maniacs to develop it. We began with wild swinging to place bolts or cams all the way down—this was necessary to keep our fixed lines close to the overhanging wall. A tense couple of days followed, as we checked to make sure each section was actually climbable. We were thrilled to find it all went. Many days, around 150 bolts, and endless trundles later, we stood on the ground at sunset with a bolted and cleaned route above us. The only problem was I had a flight to Patagonia the next morning.

The whole time I was in South America, I couldn't stop thinking about the project back in Mexico. I was aware that hiking around the mountains and eating ice cream was terrible training for overhanging 5.13 pitches. By mid-February, I couldn't take it anymore. I messaged Drew and the next day booked my flight back to Mexico.

The crux of our line (pitch five) is around 5.13b, but the real difficulty lies in the route's extremely sustained nature, with five out of ten pitches being 12c or harder. We were both fairly certain we could free the route over multiple days, but decided to attempt the less certain goal of sending in a day. We fixed our ropes again and spent the next two weeks practicing on the route, each on self-belay.

In the past, especially on some of our hard multi-pitch routes around Squamish, B.C., Drew and I have developed what we like to call "send power." Something clicks in our partnership, allowing us to climb at our absolute best while maintaining a very relaxed approach. Drew blasted "Genie in a Bottle" from his phone as I set off to redpoint pitch eight, the "Christina Nagualera Pitch" (12d). Send power was clearly in full effect. High on the next pitch, the last 5.13 of the route, the doom-pump made it an all-out race to the belay. Fingers uncurling, I skipped the last bolt and slapped to the anchor with 300m of air sucking at my heels.

We decided to name our line Los Naguales (10 pitches, 5.13b) after those shape-shifting horse-people. We wondered if at some point in our time camped on the summit, we had in fact become the *naguales* ourselves? 📷

— JACOB COOK, *CANADA*

EL GAVILAN REBOLTING AND REDPOINT: *In late December, Bronwyn Hodgins and Kelsey Watts completed a team free ascent of El Gavilan (9 pitches, 5.13a), the first female free climb of the route, swinging leads with no falls. In 2019 and 2021, the two women and other climbers had rebolted the 25-year-old route and established an easier top-down approach to La Popa's climbs.*

LA POPA, COMO EL AGUA

I KNEW I was going to Mexico and that was about it. I had two haulbags full of bolting equipment, a fresh divorce, and all the time in the world. I decided to head to La Popa, and, without a partner, embraced a solo mission.

After a couple days of dropping in to inspect various sections of the five-mile-long wall, I found a line on the northeastern aspect with continuously quality stone. Though the wall is seemingly endless, the sectors that sport good rock from the dirt to the rim seemed limited. My line is about 500m to the right of the route El Gavilan.

I worked two to three days at a time, cleaning, working out moves, and equipping the line. Between these days I drove to Hidalgo to rest and charge batteries for my poor little Milwaukee 12-volt drill. By the time the route was ready for a send attempt, I had made friends in Hidalgo who were excited to give me a catch on the route. However, after spending so much effort working on the route solo, I decided the best style would be to send the route alone as well.

On March 20, 2022, I rapped into the wall, stashing food and water at both the crux belays. I then led the route from the ground up. The first pitches were awkward as I remembered how to free climb while belaying myself, managing slack, and clipping the right rope to the draws. By the time I made it to the base of the 5.12 pitches, I had the system dialed and sent both of them first go.

In total, it took me roughly eight hours car to car to hike three miles in, rap the route, climb and clean every pitch, and finally hike back to the car. I named the six-pitch route Como el Agua and proposed a grade of 5.12b, but that could be a sandbag because I wired the moves so well prior to sending. Or the grade could be soft, as things often feel harder solo. 📄🔍

— DAKOTA WALZ, *USA*

The summit of Pico La Cresta (5,200m) during the traverse of the Nevado del Huila massif. *Thomas Palmer*

VOLCÁN NEVADO DEL HUILA, COMPLETE TRAVERSE

VOLCÁN NEVADO DEL Huila (5,364m; 2°55'25"N, 76°1'41"W) is the highest volcano in Colombia. However, ongoing volcanic activity and sociopolitical conflict have limited access. In 2019, we attempted to reach the volcano via the town of Gigante to the southeast but retreated after supplies ran out on day nine of our trip. In February 2021, Timothée Callec (France), Alex Torres (Colombia), Luis Silva Pete, a guide from the local Nasa indigenous community, and I made a second attempt. Our goal was a complete north-to-south traverse of all four summits of Nevado del Huila, including Pico Norte (ca 5,300m), Pico La Cresta (ca 5,200m), Pico Central (ca 5,365m; a.k.a. Pico Mayor), and Pico Sur (ca 5,030m).

On February 8, we traveled from Cali to Tacueyo by bus. We then arranged transport with the Nasa, an indigenous people living in the surrounding area, and continued by jeep via a rough military road through the jungle. We spent the night at Luis' house (ca 3,600m), where wax palms give way to the *páramo*. The next day, five local porters helped us reach base camp (Campo Colombia, 4,500m). We first hiked on the road for a few kilometers, then branched left into the forest, crossing Río Paez, and made a long, steep ascent. After 11 hours, we made camp just below the glacier. Pico Central loomed above, covered by light clouds, and we could hear the volcano rumbling in the distance.

On the 13th, after three days acclimatizing in camp, Luis recited a prayer in the Nasa language, requesting safe passage for our team, and we set out for Pico Norte at 3:15 a.m. The climbing was on straightforward snow (50°), and we reached the summit at 8:30 a.m. From here, our route toward Pico La Cresta and Pico Central would cover new terrain. We descended from Pico Norte by crossing over a broad ridge and then rappelled and downclimbed to a col. Our ascent of Pico La Cresta was mostly on soft snow (60°) with a thin, meter-wide section to the pointy summit, which we reached at 11:30 a.m. Our next challenge, Pico Central, lay bathed in green volcanic smoke. Descending the south side of La Cresta turned out to be the crux of this peak, with steep, loose rock.

We climbed up and over a small ridge, with several ice formations to negotiate, before reaching the flat glacier between La Cresta and Pico Central. With soft snow, exhaustion, and one near miss from a failed deadman anchor, our confidence had taken a real hit. We needed to bivouac close to Pico Central that night to keep pace. At around 5:30 p.m., we reached a 10m, near-vertical section of snow and ice, which led to a narrow ridgeline. Pico Central has 14 active volcanic vents, and we snaked alongside them with little protection from the sulfuric fumes. Black smoke billowed above us. It was terrifying. At nightfall, we found a small rock ledge. Huddled together, we endured the night, falling in and out of sleep until sunrise.

At daybreak, we heated *aqua panela*, ate cheese, and tried to de-ice our equipment. For the next few hours, we navigated short, steep sections before ascending a gradually steepening slope (60°) to reach the summit of Pico Central at 10 a.m. As the clouds lifted, we glimpsed Pico Sur for the first time: a distant, low-lying dome. To our knowledge, this section had not been traversed before.

Descending from Pico Central, we navigated around large ice walls and crevasses, eventually making a 30m rappel to a vast glacier hugged by tall cliffs. We plunged up to our waists in the soft snow. At the end of the glacier, after climbing through a maze of rocks, we arrived at the foot of Pico Sur at around 2:30 p.m. To avoid the soft snow, we climbed on rock until we could reach the upper ridgeline, where the snow condition improved. We followed the ridge (40°) for several hundred meters, reaching the summit at 4 p.m. In all, our traverse of the massif (1,500m, AD) covered approximately 5km.

To descend, we moved along the west side of Pico Sur, hugging rocky cliffs prone to rockfall. Any water we found was undrinkable due to the sulphur, and we struggled for nine hours in the dark using a combination of GPS, moonlight, and the volcano's shapes to navigate. At Campo Colombia, we cooked up an almighty meal, recounting impressions from our climb—of the sound of dogs barking in the distance, voices on the radio, and whispers in the wind. It was strange to think of how, even together, our experiences could be separate, though that is probably the magic of this place. 📷

— THOMAS PALMER, *U.K.*

[Top] **On the Nevado del Huila traverse, with Pico Central** (ca 5,365m in back). [Middle] Luis Silva Pete descends loose rock bathed in eerie volcanic smoke. [Bottom] **The team rests at a rugged-looking bivouac en route to Pico Central.** *Thomas Palmer (three photos)*

GUYANA

Federico "Fuco" Pisani belays Alex Honnold on pitch three of the Sloth Wall. *Matthew Irving*

THE SLOTH WALL
BIOLOGICAL RESEARCH AND THE FIRST ASCENT OF A REMOTE TEPUI

BY MARK SYNNOTT, *USA*

THE SEEDS OF the 2021 "Lost World Expedition" were planted more than 20 years ago. At that time, my life revolved around new routes on the great walls of the world, but it began to dawn on me that expedition climbing can be a selfish pursuit. As I wondered if my skills as a climber and guide could be useful for something more meaningful than first ascents, someone at National Geographic introduced me to Dr. Bruce Means. A conservation biologist who specializes in documenting biodiversity in the tepui region of northern South America, Means needed someone to help him access tough terrain in Guyana's Pakaraima Mountains. I was a guy who could do just that.

In 2003, we spent a few weeks searching for new frog species in the cloud forest below the northern prow of Mt. Roraima. After Bruce flew home in a helicopter, John Catto, Jared Ogden, and I established a new route on the Prow, coming within a move or two of its first free ascent (*AAJ 2004*). Jared, Greg Child, Rob Raker, and I returned with Bruce in 2006, again finding more new species and establishing a new route on Roraima's east face (*AAJ 2007*). While flying home in the helicopter, we passed over a small tepui that wasn't on our map. Its summit was incised by a 600'-deep sinkhole with a thick forest in its bottom. Bruce grabbed me by the shirt and shouted, "Mark, I *need* to be in that hole." He called it "a lost world within a lost world."

In 2012, Bruce and I were helicoptered to the top of that tepui, called Weiasspiu (a.k.a., Wei-Assipu, 7,035', 5°13'22"N, 60°42'09"W), about one mile east of Roraima on the Guyana-Brazil border. I lowered us into the hole, where Bruce searched for a frog that he called a "missing link" in tepui evolutionary biology. On his fifth day in the hole, he found it: a species of pebble toad now called Oreophrynella weiassipuensis.

For years, Bruce had been trying to understand—much like Darwin with his finches in the Galapagos—how endemic species of amphibians and reptiles living on tepui summits got there. Did they become isolated on these islands in the sky millions of years ago as the sides eroded away? Or did frogs and lizards climb up these wild cliffs, propelled, perhaps, by some innate desire to explore their world? By comparing mutations in the weiassipuensis DNA to its closest ancestor, Bruce proposed the species diverged tens of thousands of years ago, not millions, as most scientists expected. This suggests weiassipuensis may have climbed up (and down) the sheer walls of the tepui.

To further study this hypothesis and others, Bruce proposed an expedition that would follow an elevational transect through the heart of the Paikwa River basin, culminating with the first ascent of Weiassipu's walls. According to my research, the only previous expedition to explore the headwaters of the Paikwa River was a British team in the late 1960s. In 32 previous tepui expeditions, Bruce had never studied the ecosystems on the vertical walls. As far as he knew, no one had. To help bring Bruce, who would turn 80 on this expedition, up the wall, I recruited two ringers: American Alex Honnold and Federico "Fuco" Pisani, a Venezuelan who is one of the world's most experienced tepui climbers. According to Fuco, Weiassipu was one of about a dozen tepuis yet to be climbed.

On February 7, 2021, we flew to the remote village of Phillipai, along with a filmmaking team. We loaded our equipment into handmade dugout canoes with outboard motors and proceeded 20 miles south via the Kukui and Ataro rivers to the tiny village of Wayalayeng. From here, we set off on a 40-mile trek across a swampy floodplain to the east of the Pakaraima Mountains, accompanied by 70 Akawaio porters and guides. It rained incessantly on the trek, and Bruce fell dozens of times. His safety soon became an ever-present worry for our team.

A week later, we established a base camp beneath a 200' waterfall called Double Drop Falls. Bruce and I had been to Double Drop twice before but had never explored the mysterious valley to the south that lay between us and the base of Weiassipu's north face. Bruce needed time to recover from the trek, so we decided to split up. The climbing team would move ahead to find a route to the base of Weiassipu, about five miles away, while Bruce stayed behind to collect specimens.

A group of Akawaios, including Troy Henry and Edward Jameson, who climbed the Prow with a British expedition in 2019 (*AAJ 2020*), led us into the valley. They slashed a path with their machetes through giant ferns and past old-growth trees held fast in the thin, sandy soil by colossal buttress roots. On our second day out from base camp, the ground steepened and we entered a maze of jumbled, greasy boulders cloaked in a thick blanket of moss. The firm earth gradually gave way to a lattice of deadfall that would occasionally break free like a trap door. When we finally popped out of the forest at the base of Weiassipu, it felt like being born.

[Top] **The north face of Weiassipu and the Sloth Wall route.** [Bottom] **Dr. Bruce Means taking field notes in the Upper Paikwa River basin.** *Renan Ozturk (both)*

The north face of Weiassipu is about 1,000' tall, split by a massive, vegetated ledge system 700' up. Our line followed a meandering path through bulletproof, horizontally banded quartzite on the 700' lower wall. (The 300' headwall above the ledge remains for future ascensionists.) We swapped leads and fixed ropes behind us so that we could haul Bruce up later. But when we got back to our hammock camp at the base of the wall on day three, we learned that our expedition doctor had pulled the plug on this hair-brained scheme: Bruce, now an octogenarian, would go no further. Instead, Bruce provided us with a drawing of a frog from the genus Stefania that he hoped we might find on the summit, one that likely followed a different evolutionary path than weiassipuensis. If we could find this frog, Bruce would be one step closer to understanding how life evolved on tepuis.

The next day, Alex repointed our six-pitch route, The Sloth Wall (700', 5.12b), eliminating the few moves of A0 we had used previously. We had placed 13 bolts, including anchor bolts and one piton and one bolt to protect the crux, a 25' roof on pitch two. We established a camp on the ledge system, and the next morning completed a 300' rising traverse up the ledge (to the southwest), fighting our way through strangle-thick vegetation to reach the summit plateau. Alex disappeared shortly after topping out, and Fuco and I spent the rest of the day searching unsuccessfully for frogs. Back at our portaledge camp that evening, Alex suddenly reappeared, barefoot, holding a pair of rock shoes in his chalk-covered hands. He had just free soloed our route in about 45 minutes. Fuco said it was the first free solo of a tepui.

We reunited with Bruce two days later. He was disappointed we hadn't found the Stefania or any other amphibians on top of the tepui, but staying behind had been a blessing in disguise. At the time of this writing, DNA analysis has tentatively confirmed that Bruce discovered six new species in the cloud forest below Weiassipu, including a cousin of the Stefania, a nonvenomous member of the Bothrops genus of snakes, and a spectacled lizard with a transparent lower eyelid. For decades, Bruce has nurtured a quiet dream that one day he might find a creature in the Paikwa River basin so rare and singularly beautiful that the Guyanese government would finally conserve this area as a national park. "Now," he says, "it's up to someone else to pick up where I've left off." 🔲

More information about this expedition can be found in the April 2022 issue of National Geographic magazine. Parts of this report were adapted from that article.

BRAZIL

PEDRA DA GÁVEA, WEST FACE, SEGUNDO SOL

IN AUGUST 2017, Marcos Dias, Pedro Salomão, Wayler Muiños, and I opened Segundo Sol (450m, 5.11a) on the west face of Pedra da Gávea (842m). This huge mountain, one of the largest coastal monoliths in the world, has several great climbing routes, mostly opened in the '70s and '80s. However, its imposing west face had never been climbed completely. Segundo Sol's 10 pitches are protected with a mix of bolts and traditional gear. The route ends at a forested terrace from which one can descend by trail or continue to the summit via Impressionismo Carioca (100m, 5.11a). [A full report is at the AAJ website.] ▤ 🔲

— CADU SPENCER, *BRAZIL*

Steep mixed ground on Knights and Days (1,000m, 70–90° VII M5) on the north face of Hualcán's west summit (6,107m). *Aritza Monasterio*

HUALCÁN: TWO NEW ROUTES
NORTHEAST RIDGE AND KNIGHTS AND DAYS ON THE NORTH FACE

BY MATEVŽ ŠTULAR, *SLOVENIA*

In July, the Slovenian Youth Alpine Team, comprised of Blaž Karner, Bor Levičnik, Matija Volontar, and I traveled to the Cordillera Blanca. After acclimatizing, we immediately started preparing for the north face of Hualcán (6,122m), which had been in our minds for over a year. Previously, the face had only been climbed by Alik Berg and Aritza Monasterio (*AAJ 2018*). Monasterio has a long history of climbing with Slovenians, and after contacting him, despite our age gap, he was keen to climb with us.

We departed Huaraz on July 15. The walk to the base of the face is usually done in two days, but we decided that we were all sufficiently acclimatized to do it in one long day. After eight hours of walking with a heavy backpack, we established camp on the glacier at the base of the wall. Looking at the face, we decided that Bor Levičnik and Matija Volontar would try to climb a new route starting on the left edge of the north face to reach the northeast ridge and east (main) summit. Blaž Karner, Aritza Monasterio, and I would try our luck on the right side of the north face, climbing a system of pillars, rock bands, and snow slopes leading directly to the lower west summit (6,107m). Both teams started climbing the following day. 📷

■ VIRTUAL INSANITY

On July 16, we started climbing on the far east (left) side of the north face, quickly reaching the northeast ridge. From the glacier the ridge line had looked easy, and we had envisaged that one day would be enough to reach the east summit. While climbing the first pitches of the northeast ridge, however, we quickly realized we were moving too slowly to get anywhere near our goal that day. The climbing was steep—sometimes overhanging—with poor protection. There were, though, a couple of pitches of very good névé and rock. We reached the top of the first part of the ridge in about 10 pitches.

The north face of Hualcán, with (1) Virtual Insanity, (2) Nadie Sabe Nada, and (3) Knights and Days. *Aritza Monasterio*

We expected the next part of the ridge to involve mostly walking along cornices, but we could not have been more wrong. Instead, we encountered massive snow mushrooms, almost impossible to cross. We traversed along the north side of the ridge, resorting to rappels in three separate spots to reach more solid ground. Exhausted, we set up our tent on a small plateau at around 5,700m.

On the morning of the 17th, we started at around 7:30 a.m., hoping to climb in the warmth of the sun. We were short on luck, as the sun was almost immediately covered by thick fog and a strong wind picked up. Without the photos of the upper route we'd taken from the glacier, navigation to the east summit would have been very hard. We mostly simul-climbed steep and variable snow and ice. What stands out the most from that day is the final pitch; mentally, it was the hardest, with at least 20m of near-vertical powder snow, very little to grasp onto, and no protection.

We reached the main (east) summit of Hualcán (6,125m) at around 3 p.m. Since it was almost a complete whiteout, and only getting worse, we descended immediately to the south. It took us eight hours across a complex glacier to reach Laguna Cocha, where we spent another night. From the lake, there is a nice path that took us to the road and back to Huaraz the following day. We called our route Virtual Insanity (1,500m, 70–90+° M5).

– BOR LEVIČNIK *AND* MATIJA VOLONTAR

■ KNIGHTS AND DAYS

ON THE MORNING of July 16, we made the approach across the broken glacier to the right side of Hualcán's north face. The initial pitches went smoothly, offering easy but interesting mixed climbing up to M5.

Above this was a steep, rocky pillar with a lot of dihedrals, none of which seemed easy. This was the obvious crux of the whole route, which we had spotted from the glacier the previous day. We planned to bypass the steep lower part of the pillar by the apparently easy couloir on the left; however, after observing significant rockfall in the couloir, we decided to traverse across smooth slabs to reach the middle of the pillar. These technical pitches were followed by steep and exposed climbing up to VII/6b on the pillar itself. We ended the day in search of a suitable bivy spot. After an hour of digging, we settled for a meter-wide snowy ledge.

The next day the technical difficulties eased up to M5 and we found some nice pitches with amazing ice. During the day the weather worsened, and fog provided some route-finding difficulties. We climbed the last mixed barrier at nightfall and pitched a tent on Hualcán's west summit (6,107m). On the 18th, we were quick to discard any hope of descending the normal route to the village of Hualcán due to zero visibility, snowfall, and strong wind. So, we spent a second day and night on top, awaiting better weather. On the 19th, after 36 hours on the summit, we quickly packed the tent in high winds and descended the glacier to the south and west to reach the village, ending our five-day adventure. We called our route Knights and Days (1,000m, 70–90° VII M5).

– BLAŽ KARNER, ARITZA MONASTERIO, *AND* MATEVŽ ŠTULAR

CORDILLERA BLANCA

URUS OESTE, NORTHWEST FACE

ON SEPTEMBER 3, Antonio Chinchay, Silio Chinchay (both from Peru), and I approached Urus Oeste (5,450m; 9°21'42"S, 77°27'21"W) via the Uruscocha Valley, starting from the town of Pashpa (3,450m). We camped near the second lake in the valley at 4,335m, just below the northwest face of Urus Oeste, which had no recorded routes. [*Urus Oeste was first climbed by its east ridge (AAJ 1964) from the col separating it from Urus Central (5,495m). The better-known Urus Este (5,420m) is typically climbed from the Ishinca Valley to the south.*]

The next day, Silio and I approached up the moraine from camp, reaching a tarn at the base of the face (4,800m). From here, we climbed decomposing rock with some vertical steps (UIAA III) for approximately 300m. We traversed left below the steep upper headwall to reach the hanging glacier, then ascended 45–50° ice slopes and, eventually, easier snow slopes to the summit. The route up the northwest face (600m, AD UIAA III 45–50°) took us approximately five hours from camp.

We descended to the east, climbing over a rocky subpeak, then down snow slopes to the broad col (5,100m) between Urus Oeste and Urus Central, and then on down to our camp in the Uruscocha Valley. 📷

– STEVE MEDER, *PERU*

JANGYARAJU, SOUTH FACE, CITA A CIEGAS

PART OF WHAT makes the Cordillera Blanca so exceptional for climbers is the proximity of stunning high peaks: Hire a taxi in Huaraz and within an hour or two you can be trekking toward your objective. Following an attempt on Alpamayo, I only had four days left in the Ancash Region when I ran into Adam Bielecki (Poland) at Monkey Wasi, a popular climbers' hostel. He had nothing to do for the next several days. Though we only knew each other vaguely—I'd written a feature for *Rock and Ice* on his and Dennis Urubko's 2018 rescue of Elisabeth Revol on Nanga Parbat, and we'd chatted at the Piolets d'Or event in Poland in 2019—we said *what the hell* and decided to partner up.

Based on a tip from local guide Micher Quito, we set our sights on Jangyaraju (5,675m, a.k.a. Jangyaraja or Jatuncunca), an oft-overlooked peak of the Ranrapalca massif, sandwiched between the more striking summits of Ocshapalca (5,881m) and Vallunaraju (5,686m). Climbing information about Jangyaraju—and even which peak is Jangyaraju—is convoluted. A 1975 expedition makes note of three unique summits: Jangyaraju Oeste (5,450m), Jangyaraju Este (5,675m), and Jangyaraju Central (5,630m); however, Evelio Echevarría's "Survey of Andean Ascents" describes these as Bolivar, P5,675m, and San Martin, respectively (*AAJ 1976*). It's unclear which top was reached on the 1958 first ascent from the north side. The 1963 second ascent (also from the north) claimed the correct name of Jangyaraju is actually Bolivar, coin-

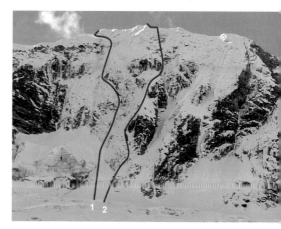

The south face of Jangyaraju showing (1) Árbol de la Alegría (2003) and (2) Cita a Ciegas (2021). *Adam Bielecki*

described here may share some terrain on the middle to upper portions with the 1995 climb.]

We climbed left of the gully, beginning with a demanding 25m pitch (M6+) consisting of quite challenging dry-tooling. We continued up and left with two 50m pitches of very nice, Tatra-style mixed climbing (M5+). After surpassing the rock band, snow interspersed with rock (70–75°) led us to the upper west ridge, where there is a straight path to the top of the mountain. Our climb, Polacos Banditos (500m, TD+ M6+), took us six hours to the summit. It took an additional three and a half hours to make nine rappels down the standard rock gully descent (Fear-Lahr-Malotoux-Ridgeway, *AAJ 1973*) on the southwest face.

— **DOMINIK CYRAN**, *POLAND, WITH ADDITIONAL INFORMATION FROM* **SEVI BOHÓRQUEZ**, *PERU*

CORRECTION ON 1999 SLOVENIAN ROUTE: *AAJ 2000 states that the Slovenian route Primorska Smer (Golja-Klanjscek-Kosuta-Markocic, 1999) ascends the northwest face of Churup Oeste. Although portions of the route may face west-northwest, it is actually located on the eastern margin of the southwest face (above Laguna Churup), a considerable distance to climber's right of the standard descent route (AAJ 1973) and Divina Providencia (AAJ 2016).*

The south face of Huamashraju Este (5,350m), showing part of the route Viva Perú Carajo, the first known route up this face. *Eneko and Iker Pou Collection*

HUAMASHRAJU ESTE, SOUTH FACE; HUANKA PUNTA, TWO NEW ROUTES; AND OTHER ASCENTS

IN EARLY JULY, Eneko Pou and Iker Pou made the first ascent of the south face of Huamashraju Este (5,350m), by a route they called Viva Perú Carajo (80° M7). Their route begins in a right-angling corner system and consisted of thinly iced slabs and mixed sections. It took about seven hours to cover the 600m of gain from base to summit. At the same time, Manu Ponce (Spain) and Micher Quito (Peru) completed a possible new rock route on the north face: Po-Quito Ponce (6c). [*Vitamina Huancaina (AAJ 2021) ascends the east face of this peak.*] The four climbers rappelled together, completing their climbs in about 15 hours round-trip.

In mid-July, the Pous and Ponce climbed a new route on the lower east side of Quebrada Llaca (a.k.a. Yaca), the valley southeast of Vallunaraju, which they called Mal de Panza (300m, 7a).

In early August, the three climbers opened two new routes on the limestone walls of the Cerro Tornillo basin, east of San Marcos. On the southwest face of Huanka Punta (ca 4,900m), they climbed Súper Canalizos (475m, 6c+), which begins a couple of hundred meters right of the trio's 2019 route Cabeza Clava (*AAJ 2020*). The route was climbed without bolts in six and a half hours. Next, they climbed Leire (300m, 6b) on Huanka Punta's southeast face. They completed this climb in seven hours, placing three bolts.

In mid-August, the Pous and Ponce traveled to the Quebrada Quilloc, where they made the first free ascent (7a) of the Eder Sabino Cacha route (originally graded 500m, 6c A2; *AAJ 2006*) on the west face of Huaketsa Punta (5,134m; a.k.a. Amahugaychu). 📷

— *FROM INFORMATION BY* **ENEKO POU** *AND* **IKER POU**, *SPAIN*

CHAUPI HUANCA, NORTHWEST FACE, ATTEMPT; CHAUPI JIRCA, SOUTHWEST FACE, EUPHORIA

FROM MAY 29 to June 6, our crew consisting of Simon Bustamante, Nicolas Davalos (both Ecuador), Austin O'Brien (USA), and I visited the Rurec Valley, establishing a base camp in the valley at 4,050m. Our goal was to reach the summit of Chaupi Huanca (ca 4,800) through a system of dihedrals on the left side of the northwest face. On our attempt, we encountered pre-existing anchors on a nearby route begun by an Argentine team in 2016. Our route initially climbs to the right of this line, then joins it for several pitches. We reached a new high point after three days, returning to our base camp each night.

On day four, we established three more pitches involving technical plant/mud climbing on decomposing granite to reach a ledge (4,475m) where we spent the night. Unfortunately, what had looked like cracks through binoculars turned out to be mere water streaks above the ledge. It appeared that many bolts would be required to continue, and without enough water or food, we decided to retreat the next morning. In all, we climbed 11 pitches, installing bolted anchors and some intermediate bolts to allow for free climbing and facilitate hauling. [*Editor's Note: This climb was completed to the southeast summit of Chaupi Huanca by* Álex *Gonzalez and Jaume Peiro in July 2021, after beginning on the Argentine line. See report below.*]

Following this, from June 11–18, Lee M. Krieger (USA) joined us in the Cerro Tornillo basin, located four to five hours from Huaraz, east of San Marcos. This zone was pioneered by a Spanish team in 2019 and offers an insane number of possibilities on walls up to 500m (*AAJ 2020*). Unfortunately, it is located along the boundary of the world's largest combined zinc and copper mine: Antamina. This mine threatens the future of climbing here; they do not like or welcome visitors.

We made our camp (4,400m) outside the mine's boundary, which belongs to the Huaripamba and Carhuayoc communities. The local people are friendly and can provide animals to shuttle gear, though, ironically, they live in extreme poverty just next to Antamina. The base camp has limited water.

There are three main peaks, all approximately 5,000m—Huanka Punta (ca 4,900m), Chaupi Jirca (5,012m GPS), and Cerro Tornillo (5,017m GPS)—and at least five secondary summits. [*These elevations listed are the author's estimates.*]

Our group made the second and third ascents of Burrito Chin de los Andes on Cerro Tornillo. [*This route was originally graded 700m, 6b; however, the author believes the route is closer to 500m, 6a.*] Next, we made the first ascent of Chaupi Jirca by a route we called Euphoria (500m, 5.10+ PG). The route ascends a crack

The southwest face of Chaupi Jirca (5,012m GPS), showing the route Euphoria (500m, 5.10+ PG), with the rappel route to the right (dashed), as seen from Cerro Tornillo. *Lee Krieger*

and dihedral system on the southwest face. This line can be identified by a single bolt (the only one on the route) at the pitch one anchor. To descend, we traversed the south ridge from the summit and made three 60m rappels (leaving bolted anchors) to access the valley floor.

Lastly, we opened a variation to Cabeza Clava (470m, 6c+) on Huanka Punta: 80m of technical crack and face climbing to the right of the original route, which it joins after a huge ledge in the middle. We named this Blood and Sand (5.11+/5.12). 📷 🔍

— FELIPE PROAÑO, *ECUADOR*

CHAUPI HUANCA, NORTHWEST SPUR, BIG FIGHTER

IN LATE JUNE, we traveled to the Rurec Valley to attempt Chaupi Huanca (ca 4,850m), after speaking with teams of Spanish and Ecuadorian climbers, who both had attempted the peak recently, about an unfinished route on the northwest spur, quite far left of the route Via Monttrek (Callado-Pedrochi, 1997). [*Editor's Note: The northwest spur was first attempted by Leandro Jochymek, Anibal Maturano, and Santiago Scavolini (all Argentina) in 2016. They climbed about eight pitches with difficulties to 7a+ and placed some bolts for protection and anchors. In June 2021, Simon Bustamante, Nicolas Davalos, Felipe Proaño (all Ecuador), and Austin O'Brien (USA) began just right of the Argentinian attempt,*

Felipe Proaño on the first pitch of Blood and Sand, Huanka Punta. *Nicolas Davalos*

joined it for several pitches, then continued up new terrain to a large ledge, climbing a total of 11 pitches, with difficulties up to 6c. See report above.]

On June 30, we arrived at our base camp in the Rurec with the spur as our target. We began next day by climbing the Argentine line, then continued up the new terrain climbed by the Ecuadorian team. After nine pitches, we reached the large ledge 300m up the wall, where we would spend the next three nights. On July 2, we opened the next three pitches, which were the most demanding on the route (6b+, 6c/A2, and 7a; it seems possible the section of A2 could be freed at 8a+). We fixed ropes and returned to the ledge.

The next morning, July 3, our alarm went off at 6 a.m. It was going to be a hard day. With little water on the wall and very little battery power left for our drill, we knew we had to summit or else go down. At 7 a.m., we began ascending the 150m of fixed ropes from the previous day. By 9 a.m., Jaume was leading pitch 13 (6b+).

After reaching a second shoulder on the spur, Jaume continued up a sporty pitch (6a), placing the first bolt of the day. Then Alex climbed a spectacular 60m dihedral and chimney (6b), placing a second bolt. We skirted the northwest summit, atop the main face, and Alex was able to reach the high point on the southeast top in a final 60m pitch (6c). In all, we climbed 10 new pitches (two very easy) from the bivy ledge. We placed 14 protection bolts in addition to anchors.

On the summit, we called home to celebrate our route, Big Fighter (750m, 19 pitches, 6c A2). The name is a tribute to Álex's brother, who, battling cancer, has been in a more complicated fight than reaching any summit. The route remains to be free climbed from the ground up—some bolts were placed using aid, not from stances. 📷 🔍

– ÁLEX GONZÁLEZ *AND* JAUME PEIRÓ, *SPAIN*

EDITOR'S NOTE: *Previous AAJ reports have incorrectly stated the summit elevation of Chaupi Huanca as 5,179m. According to satellite imagery and local sources, the tower is approximately 4,800–4,850m, with the southeast top (believed to be highest) visible from up- or down-valley and separated by a notch from the northwest top that caps the main face. The routes (from left to right) Via Monttrek, Caravaca Jubilar, Qui Io Vado Ancora, and Hasta Luego, Zorro all appear to have reached the northwest top.*

Previously unreported in the AAJ, in 2010, Anibal Maturano and Santiago Scavolini became the first to climb the Italian route Qui Io Vado Ancora (Palma-Pavan-Pedeferri, 2007) to the northwest top of Chaupi Huanca (the route originally finished at a junction with Caravaca Jubilar, below its upper dihedral); they climbed 200m of new terrain (to 6a+) to reach the top. Pedro Galan, Manuel López Ponoo, and Carlos Ly repeated the complete route to the northwest top in 2016, and then Ponce, Iker Pou, and Eneko Pou made the first free ascent of Qui Io Vado Ancora in 2017, at 7c+/8a-, but did not reach the northwest top due to a snowstorm.

CORDILLERA CENTRAL

NEVADO SULLCÓN , SOUTHWEST FACE

IN EARLY AUGUST, Steve Meder (France) and Edward Saona (Peru) climbed the first known route on the southwest face of Nevado Sullcón (5,650m, 11°53'41"S, 76°3'5"W). One month prior, in July, they made a reconnaissance of the face and climbed to the north summit (5,500m). [*The first recorded ascent of Nevado Sullcón was in 2001, though ascents in the Cordillera Central are not well documented (AAJ 2002).*]

On August 8, they began their approach from Yuracmayo (4,300m), where the road ends, and then trekked to a 5,000m base camp along the Sullcón Glacier. On the 9th, they began climbing early up the center of the southwest face. The route consisted of good ice and mixed climbing. It took them 10 hours to reach the upper northwest ridge (normal route). After a rest, they continued south along the penitente-covered ridge, reaching the summit at 5:30 p.m., where they enjoyed a superb sunset. They descended the normal route down the northwest basin, reaching their base camp in 17 hours round trip (700m, TD WI3+ M5).

— **MARCELO SCANU**, *ARGENTINA, WITH INFORMATION FROM* **STEVE MEDER**, *FRANCE*

CORDILLERA VILCABAMBA

NEVADO PADREYOC, NORTHWEST RIDGE

THE MAJOR MASSIFS of the Cordillera Vilcabamba were ascended in the 1950s and 1960s. The last of these to be climbed was Nevado Padreyoc (5,771m, 13°22'39"S, 72°44'31"W, a.k.a. Quishuar or Kiswar); Japanese climbers Tetsuju Kawada and Takeshi Rito ascended its north face in 1965. An Australian team repeated the north face climb in 1969, but the peak had no known ascents since then. While some things have changed—the glacier and, notably, the new dirt road from Santa Teresa to Yanama over Yanama Pass (4,600m)—the massive east and south sides of the mountain remain completely untouched.

In June 2021, Kody Boos, my brother Taylor Heald, Andres Marin, Anna Pfaff, and I teamed up to climb Padreyoc. The northern approach via Yanama Pass seemed to offer the simplest access to the glacier. From Urubamba we drove over Malaga Pass (4,400m) then descended barf-inducing roads through a twisting jungle of thick, humid air, plantations of tea, mango, banana, and coffee, and dogs sunning themselves in the middle of the road. From Santa Teresa (1,500m), we gained altitude rapidly, nervously crossing many landslides from the rainy season. After a few hours, we parked the trucks at a curve just below Yanama Pass and spent the night.

The next morning, we found a cow trail traversing below Puerto de Yanama (5,596m, a.k.a. Quellucocha) and Yanaccacca (5,700m), which extend from Padreyoc's northwest ridge. After five hours we found a nice camp (4,800m) a few hundred meters below the receding glacier.

We left the tent at 12:15 a.m. on June 26. Half an hour later, we donned crampons and began climbing up and right toward the northwest ridge. After a few hundred meters, crevasses began to block our route. Some of these were totally solid ice, though only 50cm wide, while others were like an icy web veiled in snow. Eventually, we navigated to a broad snowfield below the northwest ridge.

At dawn, the cornices atop the face lit up one by one. Looking northwest, the sharp, diffi-

cult-looking Yanaccacca crowned the ridge, with Lasunayoc (5,936m) behind, its summit like a giant ocean wave. We climbed 60° slopes of hard snow well below the crest to avoid any danger of a cornice collapse. Just below the summit, we pulled up under a giant overhanging serac. Around the corner, a final 60° slope brought us to the wide summit plateau at 9:30 a.m. I climbed up a 4m-tall cornice to make sure we tagged the highest point (900m, AD+).

Instead of descending our route on the northwest ridge, we decided to rappel straight down the north face and rejoin our tracks near the crevasse field. It was careful work remembering which bridges we had crossed. We were all back at our tents around 4 p.m. The next morning, we hiked down to the trucks and then relaxed in the sleepy town of Santa Teresa. 📷

— NATHAN HEALD, *PERU*

[Top] On top of Nevado Padreyoc (5,771m) after the first ascent of the northwest ridge. Pumasillo (5,991m) and Lasunayoc (5,936m) are behind on the left. *Nathan Heald* [Bottom] View from Cerro Chaupiloma, first climbed in 2021 (see report below), to the southeast slopes of Padreyoc (5,771m), with the highest point on the left. The only routes, including the northwest ridge, are on the opposite side. *Lukas Steffen*

CERRO CHAUPILOMA, NORTHEAST SLOPES TO SOUTHWEST RIDGE

ON MAY 1, Jens Hassfeld (Germany), Matthias Rehder (Germany), and I left Curahuasi, where we live and work, to climb Cerro Chaupiloma (5,339m; 13°25'12"S, 72°41'40"W), which had no recorded ascents.

After one hour of driving, we passed Mollepata, then drove another two hours west on a dirt road. At Marcopucro (3,300m), we left our car due to a landslide blocking the road. A few hundred meters further, after crossing Río Comas, we entered the beautiful, uninhabited Valle Comas and hiked north. At the end of the valley, we walked in the riverbed and had impressive views of the south face of Amparay (5,408m). Eventually, we turned westward toward our goal and made camp at 4,400m.

We started at daylight on May 2, continuing for 30 minutes on a path toward the pass at Chalan (4,700m), which crosses north into Valle Santa Teresa. At about 4,600m we left the path, hiking southwest. Most of our ascent was on the easily accessible northeast-facing scree slope. At the end, a short, steeper passage gained the glaciated southwest ridge. We ascended hard snow on the west side of the ridge and reached the summit at 11 a.m. to find great views of Padreyoc to the northwest and Amparay and Salkantay to the east-northeast. Our GPS read 5,348m.

We descended the same route and reached our camp around 2 p.m. By about 6 p.m., we were back at the car. 🔲

— LUKAS STEFFEN, *SWITZERLAND*

CORDILLERA URUBAMBA

NEVADO VERONICA, EAST FACE TO NORTHEAST RIDGE

OVER THE LAST decade, I've climbed Nevado Veronica (5,911m GPS) a handful of times via the north face to northeast ridge. This afforded me a view of an alternative approach to the unclimbed east face; I just had to wait for the opportunity to climb it.

On September 12, Urs Jermann (Switzerland), our porter and friend Macario Crispin (Peru), and I traveled to Collpa (via the road to Malaga Pass). Locating the usual herder's path was difficult, though once we did we gained altitude quickly. With rain and clouds at the level of the glacier, we made camp at 4,500m in a big flat area. The next day we followed an exposed rock ridge to reach the edge of the glacier and a perfect, well-protected campsite (4,900m).

Urs and I got moving at 1 a.m. on the 14th, and the technical climbing started right away with a full pitch of ice (AI3). Above, we followed the path of least resistance through seracs. At 5,300m, we turned up and left, weaving through big seracs with short, steep sections, and even a tunnel to gain the upper icefield (5,500m). From here, I'd hoped to climb directly up the final part of the east face; however, we opted to finish up the northeast ridge, reached by a short traverse to the right. We reached the summit at 9:30 a.m. in great weather but with a blanket of clouds below (900m, D).

On the descent, clouds made it difficult to find our tracks, and our pace slowed considerably. After several short rappels through the serac maze, we came to the debris field around nightfall. Eager to descend, Urs slipped from above me after stepping into a shallow crevasse. With the slack in the rope, he slid 25m before the rope went tight, thankfully catching on an ice horn above me. After securing two screws to transfer the load, I found Urs hanging upside down, rope wrapped around his feet and his face all bloody, but otherwise relatively unhurt. After a short rescue, we were able to continue, this time with only a few meters of rope between us. About an hour later, after a final rappel from a V-thread, we reached camp again at 9 p.m. after 20 hours on the mountain.

The next day, we descended the rock buttress below our camp, making one rappel down a steep section. It took only a couple of hours to descend the remaining 1,600m to the road. 🔘

– NATHAN HEALD

CORDILLERAS VILCANOTA AND CARABAYA

CONCHA DE CARACOL, SOUTH FACE, CERVEZA, PAN Y ÁCIDO; MARIPOSA, SOUTH-SOUTHWEST FACE, ATTEMPT

ON JULY 5, Andres Marin, Alex Torres (both from Colombia), and I met up with Cordillera Vilcanota local climber Luis Crispin in the small town of Pacchanta, at the foot of Ausangate. There, Luis helped Andres, Alex, and I organize logistics and horses for an exploratory mission into the range. With information and photos of unclimbed alpine lines from our friend and local guide Nathan Heald, we were stoked to see what was ahead.

On July 7, we started the trek around Ausangate and arrived at the base camp of our first objective, the south-southwest face of Mariposa (5,842m; 13°47'7.92"S, 71°12'35.94"W). After climbing a huge portion of this face, we were forced to turn around approximately 150m below the summit because of an unprotectable slab of sugar snow. [*Mariposa was first climbed from the north-northwest (AAJ 1958) and has since seen numerous ascents and variations on that aspect. The complete south-*

east ridge (700m, D) was climbed in 2020 by Luis Crispin and Thomas Schilter (AAJ 2021). The approximately 600m south-southwest face remains unclimbed.]

With an array of other objectives nearby, we decided to backtrack and move our base camp north, just below (ca 4,800m) the Jampa Pass. Early on July 13, we set out for a new route on the south face of Concha de Caracol (5,640m; 13°45'16"S, 71°10'38"W). With a light alpine rack, we started up the face to the right of the 2019 route Via Pirenaica, each of us leading in two-pitch blocks. [*Via Pirenaica (550m, TD+, Baró-Rodriguez-Sancho)*

South face of Concha de Caracol (5,640m), showing (1) Via Pirenaica (550m, TD+, Baró-Rodriguez-Sancho, 2019) and (2) Cerveza, Pan y Ácido (700m, ED 90°, Marin-Pfaff-Torres, 2021). *Oriol Baró Collection*

ascends the central part of the south face (AAJ 2020).] The climbing quickly became steep and thoughtful, with a variety of ice, mixed, and snow conditions. The last pitch required everything of Alex to dig through the sugary snow on the summit ridge.

The limited daylight in Peru left us concerned about the descent, so we opted for an open bivy (5,500m) just below the ridge, hoping to continue to the top in the morning. After an extremely long, cold night with little sleep, we continued up the summit ridge to reach the top of Concha de Caracol. We rappelled the same line of our ascent and reached our base camp again around noon on July 14 with cold toes and an amazing adventure to remember: Cerveza, Pan y Ácido (700m [*climbing distance*], ED 90°). 📷

— ANNA PFAFF, USA

EXTENDED BIKE TRAVERSE AND MULTIPLE ASCENTS

AFTER A 2019 trip to the Cordillera Central (*AAJ 2020*) and a 2020 mountain bike tour of the Pyrenees combined with ten climbs throughout the range, I wanted to unite both concepts. My goal was to cycle through little-visited massifs of southern Peru, opening alpine routes along the way.

I left the town of Juliaca (3,800m), near Lake Titicaca, at the beginning of July, loaded with 45kg of gear and more weight for food and water. From there, I crossed the Carabaya and Vilcanota mountain ranges until reaching Urubamba in mid-August. In all, I traveled about 750km, having ascended five 5,000m peaks (three alone, and four by probable new routes.) The daily cycling stages were limited to around 30–35km due to the average altitude of 4,000m, the low nighttime temperatures, and the great effort of moving a bicycle and load totaling 60–65kg. Approximately half of the route was on dirt tracks. [*The author's complete trip report, with maps and topos detailing the ascents, is at the AAJ website.*]

On July 6, looking for a suitable peak to acclimatize in the Cordillera Carabaya, I hoped to ascend Pumaqulluni (5,225m). However, I was met by the strong mistrust of pastoralists living at its base, so I continued down the trail to the huts of Atompampa instead. Early on the

[Top] The 2021 route up the southeast face and northeast ridge of Jurcay Cuchillo (5,570m) in the Cordillera Vilcanota. [Middle] Southwest face of Sargentuyocc (5,120m), showing El Sueño de los Meteoritos (370m, D UIAA V). A second route was climbed up this face, farther right, in November 2021. [Botttom] Camp in the Cordillera Vilcanota. *Sergi Ricart Ibars (three photos)*

7th, I hiked west through a valley until observing the wide northeast spur of a peak the local shepherds call Cerro Apacheta Queroni (5,125m; 14°3'9"S, 70°16'40"W). My route was on mostly decent rock: Rigabor Sanes (250m [climbing distance], AD UIAA III+). I descended the south ridge and east slopes.

From Atompampa, I descended by bike to Macusani. After a break in nearby Mazuko, I retraced my way by taxi to the end of the Antajahua Valley, below the south face of Allinccapac (5,780m). My objective was the south face of Japuma (5,543m; 13°55'3"S, 70°26'2"W). At first light on the 15th, I ascended the east slope of the valley to 5,150m. I then ascended the southern glacier (55°), avoiding crevasses, until the southeast ridge, where low-angle snow and rock led to the summit (700m climbing distance, PD+ 55° II). My route may follow the path of the 1954 first ascent (*AAJ 1955*), though, with glacial retreat, they were likely quite different ascents. I descended the north face.

After riding to the town of Phinaya, in the Cordillera Vilcanota, I took a vehicle back to Abra Chimboya (5,100m) on the 29th. From there, I descended past the old mining huts of Mina Chimboya and walked along vicuña paths to reach the southeast face of Jurcay Cuchillo (5,570m; 13°49'5"S, 70°51'39"W; a.k.a. Chimboya or Chabuca). I chose a line trending up and right with great ice gullies (65–70° III) to reach the northeast ridge and then the summit: Go Girls! (650m climbing distance, AD+ 70° III). I descended the south ridge to the end of the south glacier then through rocky steps and moraine to reach Abra Chimboya.

On my next climb, I was joined by Aris Ramos and Jorge "Cocor" Sirvas. On August 5, we left the town of Pitumarca, traveling by vehicle on poor-quality dirt roads into the Quillita Valley. Once there, we walked for one hour, making our base camp at 4,950m. On the 6th, we left the tents at around 4 a.m. to reach the northeast face of Kunturt'uqu (5,554m; 13°50'56"S, 71°8'9"W). [*This peak, a.k.a. Cóndor Tucco or Condortuco, was first climbed from the north (AAJ 1969)*]. At first light, we reached an icy couloir below a large serac barrier. We climbed the couloir up and right (45–65°) until reaching milder slopes (30°) and varied terrain on the three summit towers (II–III). The highest point appears to be the third tower (westernmost), where there were extraordinary views of Ausangate and the entire Vilcanota. The route was El Laberinto Del Cóndor (900m climbing distance, PD+ 65° II). We descended east down the same path until the upper glacier, then diverged to the east summit (5,500m), which we reached without difficulty (30° UIAA II). From there, we descended north, this time passing under the serac barrier on the climber's left.

For my final climb, the southwest face of Sargentuyocc, a rocky peak of 5,120m (13°54'36"S, 71°24'55"W; a.k.a. Alcaldillocc/Alcaldiyocc and Coscocawarena), I was joined by Diana Gómez and Cocor Sirvas. We left the rock climbing–rich area of Chacco Huayllasca on the morning of the 11th and first hiked up to a col at 4,700m, which had stunning views of the mountain, then descended into the valley, from where we scrambled up grassy and rocky slopes (III) to the foot of the southwest face. From there, we climbed eight pitches (III–V) on very compact rock that was difficult to protect; we mainly used narrow pitons, a few cams, and nuts. Despite the moderate grades, the climb was entertaining and highly aesthetic: El Sueño de los Meteoritos (370m, D V). We descended carefully to the north peak, north through the valley, then east toward Chacco. [*Editor's Note: On November 11, 2021, Berna Weigand (Spain) and Jack Sierralta (Peru) climbed a second new route on the right side of Sargentuyocc's southwest face: Tayta Parawayra (240m, TD 6b).*]

Reflecting on this journey alone by bike, the sharp cold and the intense effort did not allow me to nose around everywhere I would have liked. However, there is an incredible sense of freedom that one experiences when cycling. The sensations of crossing the mountains by my own means, coupled with improvised, exploratory alpinism, made this my almost-perfect adventure. 🖼 🔍

– SERGI RICART IBARS, *SPAIN*

SCREWDRIVER, SOUTHWEST RIDGE, AND OTHER ASCENTS

DURING THE 2021 season, I repeated two lesser known routes and made one first ascent in Peru's southern ranges. On May 30, I made the fourth known ascent of Callangate (6,110m) in the Cordillera Vilcanota with Macario Crispin (Peru). We followed a similar route to that of the 1960s first ascent, ascending a glacial ramp on the northwest face to the northwest shoulder and finishing on the north ridge.

On June 24, I soloed a prominent peak in the northernmost region of the Cordillera Vilcabamba. On my map, it is called Chaupimayu (5,330m), but previous ascent parties referred to it as Nevado Blanco. I ascended the southwest face to the south ridge to reach the summit. Mine was the fourth known ascent and possibly the first in about 50 years; I followed a similar route to previous parties. [*Recent photos of these peaks are with this report at the AAJ website.*]

On July 3, Derek Field, Giselle Field, and I climbed a new route on Screwdriver (5,543m) in the Cordillera Carabaya: the southwest ridge (330m, 5.7+ AI3 M4 80°). Screwdriver had prior ascents via its northwest rib and face (see AAJ 1965 and AAJ 1968) and north ridge (Alpine Journal 2008).

Derek Field in 2016 on Mamaccapac, with a view of Screwdriver's southwest ridge (left side of the face shown). *Aaron Zimmerman*

[*Editor's Note: Tragically, Giselle Field died in a rappelling accident on July 13 while the Fields were descending from the first known ascent of a previously unnamed rock tower they called Kawri Orcco (5,185m, Quechua for "Monster Peak), also in the Cordillera Carabaya. The two climbers have contributed numerous reports to this journal.*] 🖼

– AARON ZIMMERMAN, *USA*

Traversing the summit ridge toward the south top of Illampu. *Matt Ward*

BOLIVIA

ALL-NIGHTER
A NEW LINE UP THE WEST FACE OF ILLAMPU IN THE CORDILLERA REAL

BY MATT WARD, *USA*

AT AROUND 8 a.m. on July 30, Brad Ward (no relation) and I stood together on the summit of Illampu (6,368m), having arrived there by a completely independent new route on the left side of the west face.

Illampu is the fourth-highest peak in Bolivia and has a reputation as the most difficult 6,000m peak in the country, at least on the standard routes. Our route was the first new line on the west face in 30 years, and we found very different conditions than those visible in old photos. The glacier below the face has receded, and the lower snow and ice pitches of routes such as Alpos Secret (1991) appear to have disappeared. In some ways we benefited from changing conditions, as we found good water ice in places where in the past only snow existed.

From the road head at Lackathiya (ca 4,010m), we used burros to reach base camp at Aguas Calientes. We then made a reconnaissance trip to the west face and left a gear cache at the edge of the glacier. On July 29 we left base camp at 1 a.m., arrived at the bottom of the face at sunrise, and began climbing.

Low on the face, nearly every pitch had lovely alpine ice and often perfect névé for step-kicking. Protection and anchors were plentiful. There were several pitches of water ice, including high-quality WI3 and WI4, and several mixed pitches on good granite up to M5.

High on the face, we climbed pitch after pitch of steep Andean flutings and struggled to find a suitable bivouac site. Any attempt to dig into the steep, sugary snow struck ice after 30–60cm. As we gained altitude the flutings often dead-ended, forcing unprotected traverses into new ones. It was often only possible to place one or two ice screws in 70m. Around midnight I climbed the worst of the flutings while Brad froze at the anchor; I've never understood how near-vertical powder snow stays on those faces, nor how humans manage to cling to it, but there we were, slowly gaining ground.

We were exhausted, having been on the move for 24 hours and gained over 1,600m from base camp, and I had led more than 20 pitches. Nearing desperation, I suddenly climbed out of a fluting and found myself on the summit ridge. Moving onto the leeward side, we were able to dig a shallow bench with a backrest at around 6,250m. Sheltered from the wind, we made a brew, got into our thin sleeping bags, and began spooning and shivering through the rest of the nearly sleepless night.

Five hours later, the sun had warmed us enough that we could move. Brad led off and very quickly took us to the north summit. He ran the rope out again and again through the morning as we traversed the long, corniced ridge that leads to the higher south summit. We celebrated in warm sunshine and congratulated each other for not dying during the preceding night. Then we started down the standard route of the southwest ridge. The descent took most of the day and many rappels before we arrived in base camp.

Our route lies between Nada Mañana (1991) and Koroska Smer (1986). We called it Mental Ward (850m, WI4 M5). Our trip was funded in part by the McNeill-Nott Award from the American Alpine Club and the Mazamas Adventure Grant. [For a history of climbing on the west face of Illampu, see AAJ 2018.] 📷

[Top] Part of the west face of Illampu (6,368m), showing (1) Nada Mañana, (2) Mental Ward, and (3) Koroska Smer. For all the routes on this face, see AAJ 2018. *Matt Ward* [Bottom] Matt Ward on the west face of Illampu, climbing good ice below the upper flutings, during the first ascent of Mental Ward. *Brad Ward*

Chachacomani West (W) and the higher east (E) summit, seen from Jankho Laya to the southeast. The northeast ridge starts from the col (C) between Chachacomani and, to the right, the Tres Marias. The Tummon–von Ungern traverse followed the skyline from the col to the west summit, and then descended the far side. The idea came during von Ungern's earlier traverse of Jankho Laya, and this photo formed the "topo" during the ascent. *Alexander von Ungern*

CHACHACOMANI, NORTHEAST TO SOUTHWEST TRAVERSE VIA COMPLETE NORTHEAST RIDGE

ON AUGUST 20, Fiona Tummon (Dutch/Irish, resident in Switzerland) and I left La Paz at 5 a.m. Before reaching the little village of Peñas, we took the road to Laguna Khara Khota and then over the Paso Mullu, which crosses the Cordillera Real at a little over 5,000m. A long descent took us to the village of Amaguaya at 3,600m. We then drove up the valley to the northwest to an altitude of 3,800m before stopping, five and a half hours after leaving La Paz.

We hiked up a valley to the southwest for four and a half hours to reach the lake of Leche Khota (4,500m on IGM 5946-III). Our packs were heavy, but we persevered for another hour and camped on a fine, white sandy beach, close to a stream just below 4,750m. Our goal was the unclimbed lower rocky section of the northeast ridge of Chachacomani (6,074m), and we decided not to get up too early the following morning, so that we could enjoy the first rays of sunshine when we touched rock.

Reaching the glacier leading to the col at the start of the ridge proved a real ordeal, crossing a huge, very unstable boulder field left by the rapidly retreating tropical glacier. However, the granite on the ridge was excellent, with sublime views of the neighboring glacier-covered summits and the cloud-covered Amazon basin. We overcame a series of granite needles, overhanging on their far sides, in the middle of this rocky section. We used counterweight and other "cowboy" rope techniques to rappel quickly, without leaving gear, but at one point managed to get a core shot close to the middle of our rope.

We took care to summit all the gendarmes, needles, and other spires on the ridge and finally reached the snow at around 5,600m, with the afternoon already well advanced. Contrary to expectations, we didn't move any faster now. I had first been introduced to the fun of snow penitents (névé penitentes) a decade ago, but had always crossed them while they were well frozen. I now discovered they become even more tiring when melting and soaking wet, especially in the steeper sections, where we had to repeat the same step several times to bulldoze our way forward.

Around 100m below the summit, we stopped to make some tea and enjoy a spectacular sunset, before reaching the top under a full moon. We then continued to the lower western summit, before heading down toward the north. [*Above the rock gendarmes, the snow section of the northeast ridge had been traveled previously, both in ascent and descent, reached from either the north or south flank.*] As there hadn't been much traffic on the normal route, we couldn't find a trail and decided to head straight down. Once we finally reached the huge, flat glacier on the western side of the mountain, we continued until we reached some rocky outcrops, where at 10·30 p.m. and still above 5,300m, we bivouacked for a second night, too tired to eat a proper meal. Next day we quickly found our way off the glacier and at 2 p.m. arrived in the little village of Alto Cruz Pampa.

The idea for this climb had been born earlier in the summer on Jankho Laya, where the south side of Chachacomani formed a backdrop throughout a northwest-to-southeast traverse that Thomas Wilken and I did on July 24. This traverse was first done (in both directions) by the 1973 Austrian expedition that made the second ascent of the mountain. Given how little the peak is visited, it may not have been repeated since. Even by Bolivian standards, the area between Jankho Laya and Chachacomani is wild, with not a single road or mine (abandoned or otherwise) in sight. 📋 📷

– ALEXANDER VON UNGERN, *ANDEAN ASCENTS, BOLIVIA*

WILA LLOJE, NORTH-NORTHWEST TO SOUTHWEST TRAVERSE; WARAWARANI AND JANKHO PEQUE, POSSIBLE NEW ROUTES

ON AUGUST 7, Fiona Tummon (Dutch/Irish) and I left Peñas in a taxi with a completely worn-out hand brake—probably due to not replacing the real brakes for far too long. Fortunately, our destination was uphill, close to the Paso Mullu col at 4,730m, just short of Lago Jankho Kkota. From there we hiked up the valley to the west, crossing a pass a little over 5,300m below Wila Lloje (5,596m), and after a total of four hours of walking we camped in the middle of the glacier plain beyond.

The following day we left the tent at first light and approached the long north-northwest ridge of Wila Lloje, which starts from col southeast of Peak 5,604m. Motivated for our first climb from this glacier, we didn't skip a single gendarme on the ridge, although most could easily have been circumvented on solid névé. Up to the first significant summit—unnamed Peak 5,580m—we climbed generally sound rock.

Continuing over peaks 5,560m and 5,575m, mainly on hard snow, we reached a steep rocky section below Wila Lloje. Progressively deteriorating rock on this 100m passage made for delicate climbing. From the top we descended the southwest ridge (55° in the upper section) to the col we'd crossed the previous day and regained our tents less than six hours after leaving.

The next day we decided to climb a gully on the east face of Warawarani I (5,542m) that had attracted our attention while setting up camp. We began climbing at sunrise on an initial

(A) Part of Jankho Peque. (B) Col at the start of the 2021 traverse of Wila Lloje, below the north-northwest ridge. (C) Peak 5,530m. (D) Peak 5,580m (the west face—then a snow and ice couloir, now primarily rock—was climbed in 1996 by a two-man British team, arriving on the ridge just left of the summit). (E) Peak 5,560m. (F) Peak 5,575m. (G) Wila Lloje. (H) Col at base of southwest ridge. *Alexander von Ungern*

The difficult crossing of Arroyo Chorrillos en route to Cerro del Salto. *Glauco Muratti*

CENTRAL ANDES

CORDILLERA FRONTAL, CERRO DEL SALTO

In late March, Ramiro Casas and Glauco Muratti (both from Argentina) began a long trek south from the town of Punta de Vacas along the Río Tupungato and then southeast along one of its tributaries, Río Salto, to an area of remote and rarely visited 5,000m peaks in the Cordillera Frontal. The only previous known ascent in this zone is Pico Vivi Lofti (5,264m; *AAJ 2014*).

During the first one and a half days, they made two difficult river crossings (Arroyo Chorrillos and Río Tupungato). It took two more days for them to ascend the Quebrada del Salto, eventually making a high camp at 4,600m below the western slopes of their intended peak.

On March 26, they ascended a mix of glaciers, scree, and hard snow (40°) up the west side of the peak to the summit. They suggest calling the mountain Cerro del Salto (ca 5,350m; 33°08'13"S, 69°36'49"W). It took them two more days to retrace their route to Punta de Vacas, covering about 80km in all. 📷 🔍

– MARCELO SCANU, *ARGENTINA*

CAJÓN DEL ESMERALDA, MORRO DE LOS CASTAÑOS, WEST FACE, CERRO EL PLOMO, SOUTHEAST FACE

East of the popular Cerro El Plomo (5,424m), near Santiago, Cajón del Esmeralda stands out for its rugged beauty: threatening (and threatened) glaciers, imposing rock faces, massive moraines, and steep river valleys. Since the area does not reach great altitude, the landscape is decorated with colorful shrubs and flora. Being hidden from view by Cerro El Plomo, Cajón del Esmeralda has remained mostly ignored by mountaineers.

On November 1, David Cossio, Agustín Ferrer, Catalina Medina, Emil Stefani, and I (all members of Club Andino Universitario) made the first known ascent of Morro de los Castaños (4,736m; 33°14'24"S, 70°11'3"W). We started from Alfalfal on October 29, approaching via the Río Olivares, and then traveled west up the scarcely explored Estero Esmeralda. We made base camp at 3,100m and bivouacked again at 3,900m. From there, we ascended by a short and easy couloir on the west face. The final step to the summit required us to cross a narrow and exposed ridge, but it didn't require the use of ropes (1,600m, F).

For lovers of the unexplored, this area has several more interesting challenges. The steep, unclimbed south face of Cerro Chávez (4,830m; 33°11'6"S, 70°10'41"W) offers incredible, varied lines up to 500m, and its lower wall holds several ice cascades. The upper east face of Cerro El Plomo presents numerous steep snow and ice gullies up to 600m. El Plomo's southeast face was only just recently climbed by Carlos Fouilloux and Nicolás García-Huidobro, in December 2021, over a five-day trip (1,700m, D+ 40–70°); they followed the snake-like Glaciar Castaños to the top.

The Sierra Esmeralda and the hills to the east of Morro de los Castaños offer unclimbed peaks and new routes, including rocky Cerro Esmeralda Central (4,520m; 33°12'21"S, 70°8'20"W). The slopes of the unnamed hill just east of Morro de los Castaños could be skied in a good winter. 📷 🔍 ▶

— DAMIR MANDAKOVIC, *CHILE*

[Top] The upper southeast face of Cerro El Plomo and Los Castaños Glacier. The obvious snow and ice ramp was climbed by Carlos Fouilloux and Nicolás García-Huidobro in December 2021. [Middle] Unclimbed south face of Cerro Chávez (4,830m), with varied lines up to 500m. [Bottom] The Río Olivares with a view northeast to Cordillera Ferrosa and (A) Nevado del Plomo, (B) Point 5,363m, (C) Morro del Fierro, (D) Cerro Risopatrón, and (E) Cerro Tronco. *Damir Mandakovic (three photos)*

CERRO SAN FRANCISCO, SOUTHEAST FACE, NEW VARIATION

IN LATE JULY, Rodrigo Diaz, Nicolás Gutierrez, and I climbed a new variation on the elegant southeast face of Cerro San Francisco (4,345m; 33°44' 52"S, 70°5' 17"W), located in Monumento Natural El Morado, just southwest of Cerro Morado (4,647m). Our route climbs an incredible narrow couloir that diagonals up and left, eventually reaching the southwestern shoulder via the upper part of the Krahl-Meier route. [*Editor's Note: The initial section of this couloir is shared with the 2015 route Antiparkes (Baró-Farré, AAJ 2016); however, that route exits the couloir to the right and zigzags up the wall well to the right of the 2021 route.*] We descended the other side of the mountain via Embalse del Yeso, 24 hours in all. 🔲

— CRISTÓBAL SEÑORET, *CHILE*

PICO COLINA SUR, INDIRETTISSIMA

The unclimbed west face of Pico Colina Sur. *Damir Mandakovic*

IN OCTOBER, FEDERICO Caballero, Rafael Reinoso, and I made the first known ascent of Pico Colina Sur (4,620m; 33°53'54.9"S, 69°51'45.6"W) in the Central Andes. This peak is the highest of the Picos Colina group, on the border between Chile and Argentina, which includes (from north to south) Pico Colina Norte (4,296m), an unnamed 4,448m summit, Pico Colina Oriente (4,490m), and Pico Colina Sur. Despite their proximity to Santiago, mountains in this area have few ascents.

Starting from a camp at 4,000m below the northeast side of the mountain, we climbed an indirect route up steep slopes and gullies comprised of snow and rock for 600m. Eventually, we reached a 20m section of technical rock (5.8) on the north face of the final summit pyramid. We accidently dropped Federico's backpack before the final pitch, watching it fall down the steep west-side gullies, but he finished the climb anyway. On the summit, we didn't find any signs of previous attempts.

Our route is Indirettissima (600m, PD+). To descend, we followed a more direct couloir on the northeast face, which would make for a better "normal" route. 🔲

— DAMIR MANDAKOVIC, *CHILE*

TORRES DEL BRUJO, NEW ROUTES

THE TORRES DEL Brujo (34°42'10"S, 70°22'22"W) comprise a little-visited area of granite spires near the terminus of Glaciar Universidad (ca 3,000m), 50km east of San Fernando, Chile. [*Editor's note: See AAJ 1999, 2003, 2008, and 2010 for more background on the area; a number of routes are not well-documented.*] In December, Isidora Montesinos, Alexis Rojas, and I climbed a new route (230m, 5.11+) on Aguja de la Paz, located in an unglaciated sector below the main spires. After this, Isidora and I continued up to the main spires, which are at the base of the steep, narrow glacier extending southeast from Cerro El Brujo (4,740m). For our second climb, we completed a new route on La Aguja Dama, on the east side of the glacier. Le Pusimos Espíritu Del Brujo (400m, 5.11) climbs to the left of A Ultima Dama (*AAJ 2008*). [*There are at least two other routes to the right of A Ultima Dama.*]

I returned to the spires with Isidora in January 2022 to climb a route on the area's principal spire, on the west side of the glacier (sometimes referred to as Brujo Falso or Torre Grande). Our route, Los Guardianes Del Brujo (650m, 5.10+) begins in the notch formed by the adjacent 300m spire, Aprendiz del Brujo (home to several routes), and then ascends a line to the left (east) of previously established routes on the 500m northeast face; these include Los Últimos Días De Inocencia (5.11+ A2; Brewer-Richter), Clandestino (5.12d A1; *AAJ 1999*), Gandalf y Saurón (5.11 A3+; Globis-Martin-Zegers), and Linea de los Suenos Sueltos (6b A3; *AAJ 2010*).

Our route required several days of portering gear, cleaning, and climbing. The approach was the crux for us, with constant rockfall and avalanches setting a threatening tone. However, once established on the wall, we were protected. With approximately 650m of free climbing never exceeding 5.10+, Los Guardianes could easily become the "normal route" on this beautiful granite needle. 📷

— NICOLÁS GUTIÉRREZ, *CHILE*

NORTHERN PATAGONIA

REGIÓN DE LOS LAGOS, CERRO COHETE, EAST FACE

CERRO COHETE IS in Cerduo Alto, which is about 30 minutes southeast of the town of Pucón and just north of Volcán Villarrica (2,847m). The approach is both easy and beautiful. I started opening a route on the east face with my brother Juan Señoret and finished the climb with my friend Andres Zegers. The route is eight pitches and 5.11d R.

— CRISTÓBAL SEÑORET, *CHILE*

The east face of Cerro Cohete, climbed in eight pitches (5.11d R). *Cristóbal Señoret*

COCHAMÓ, CERRO CAPICÚA, SOUTHWEST FACE, RAICES

IN MARCH 2022, Alexis Rojas and I managed to finish a route on the far right side of Cerro Capicúa, which I had started one year ago with the help of Isidora Montesinos and Benjamin Lira. In all, the route took me 11 days spread across these trips.

Our route, Raices (1,100m, 5.11+ A1), is located to the right of the lines Los Tigres del Norte (*AAJ 2009*) and Adios Michi Olzowy (*AAJ 2006*). We approached the climb via vegetated slabs on a hill below and right of the main wall. At least half of the 26-pitch route consists of continuous cracks. We did not free climb the route entirely due to lack of time; however, I did make all of the moves on pitch 12, which I expect to be 5.13a/b. We left bolts at every anchor. 📷

— NICOLÁS GUTIÉRREZ, *CHILE*

Snowy view of (A) Llave de Granito (1,902m), with the 2021 route, and (B) Cerro Choss (2,067m), climbed in 2009. The peaks were much drier during the 2021 ascent. *Linde Waidhofer*

LLAVE DE GRANITO, NORTHWEST ARÊTE TO NORTH RIDGE

SITTING ON JIM Donini's deck in Patagonia, a world of peaks can be seen, many of them unclimbed. Jim has taken to saying, "Climb the view." In this spirit, Weston Boyles, Max Schilling, and I made the first ascent (to our knowledge) of one peak visible from Jim's deck in austral summer 2021. The peak is the northernmost in Parque Patagonia, above Lago General Carrera, and is located along the same ridgeline as 2,067m Cerro Choss (*AAJ 2009*), which Donini climbed with Morgan Boyles. [*These peaks are on the east side of Lago General Carrera, approximately halfway between Puerto Guadal and Chile Chico.*] Since the rock changes from volcanic choss to Llaves pluton granite at the nearby Paso Las Llaves, we informally named the 1,902m peak Llave de Granito ("The Granite Key," 46°37' 53"S, 72°19' 27"W).

We approached from Paso Las Llaves in February. A week prior to our successful climb, Nadine Lehner and I had pioneered the first part of the route up the northwest arête: four pitches of easy rock (up to 5.6). Weston, Max, and I repeated this portion and then continued via a long section of talus bashing to reach ice-covered rock on the upper northwest arête. Two pitches of spicy 5.6–5.8 led us past a perfect perch of a bivy site and onto the northern summit ridge, which had a few sections of 5.6–5.7 and snow leading to the top.

We reached the summit at sunset and descended 100m to the bivy spot in the twilight (about 11 p.m. at this latitude). With mini-Tabasco-sauce dinners, no wind—for two of us (*sorry, Weston!*)—and great views down to the lake, it was a beautifully planned night out. Coffee, down-climbing, two double-rope rappels, and scrambling got us back to the ground the next morning. We continued to Puerto Guadal, taking in excellent views of soaring condors along the way, and, eventually, fulfilling our dreams of cold beers and pizza.

– GREGORY DE PASCALE, *CHILE*

NORTHERN PATAGONIAN ICEFIELD, CERRO SILVIA, NORTHEAST FACE

IN LATE OCTOBER, Rebeca Caceres, Isidora Llarena, and I met in Puerto Guadal with the goal of climbing of Cerro Silvia (2,770m; 47°10'4"S, 73°29'33"W) on the Northern Patagonian Icefield. We departed for Valle Colonia on the 26th with three 75-pound backpacks, brimming with packrafting, mountaineering, skiing, and camping gear and 14 days of food. Although Isidora and I knew this multi-day approach well from our expedition to Cerro Nora (*AAJ 2021*), Patagonia quickly reminded us to leave expectations behind. We parked the car four miles earlier than expected due to a chest-deep, swollen river. Two hours in, wind gusts caught our skis and paddles during a river crossing, leading to two swims and four lost trekking poles. On day two, we arrived at Lago Colonia to oceanic waves and persistent winds, forcing us to delay our paddle.

On October 28, we paddled four miles across Lago Colonia through a building headwind and reached the far shore with renewed momentum. We spent the next two and a half days making

Bushwhacking with a tremendous backdrop, en route to the Northern Patagonian Icefield—Cerro Arenales is behind. *Nadine Lehner*

our way toward the icefield: crossing Cachet Dos lake by packraft, hiking along Glaciar Colonia, and bushwacking through lenga forest. At last, on October 30, we reached the dazzling expanse of the icefield and put on our skis. We crossed Glaciar Colonia and established our base camp on a nunatak (1,750m). The following day brought bluebird weather, and Isidora and I skied to the 2,750m plateau between Cerro Garcia and Cerro Arenales to scout the area.

On November 1, we used a short weather window to attempt the northeast face of Cerro Silvia, located between Cerro Buscaini and Cerro Garcia. Leaving early, we skied two miles to the base of a snow ramp leading to the col between Silvia and Buscaini. We left our skis and bootpacked to the col, crossed a sizable bergschrund, and then climbed 60–70° ice and snow to the summit ridge (200m, AI2). From there, we traversed to the summit. The ascent had views to the Pacific Ocean, but clouds quickly moved in at the top. After the obligatory selfie, we began the descent in whiteout conditions. On our ski back to camp, Rebeca fell and injured her knee.

We spent the following three days hunkered in our tent as Patagonian winds howled outside. We passed the time by reading aloud from Pema Chodren's *When Things Fall Apart*, building a massive wind wall, and sponging up the increasingly flooded tent. On November 5, the storm cleared. Isidora and I began an attempt on Cerro Arenales but turned back early due to wind and snow conditions. As a team, we decided to descend and begin the four-day journey back to Puerto Guadal. 📷 🔍

— **NADINE LEHNER**, *USA*

SOUTHERN PATAGONIAN ICEFIELD, CERRO ILSE VON RENTZELL

THE CORDÓN ILSE von Rentzell, located on the Southern Patagonian Icefield about 50km northwest of the Chaltén Massif, contains numerous beautiful and challenging summits, all of them believed to be unclimbed prior to our 2021 expedition. The range is named after German-born Ilse von Rentzell, who, after emigrating with her family to Argentina, became a standout writer,

Looking west from a helicopter, the Cordón Ilse von Rentzell includes all of the distant, snow-capped peaks from left to center. Cerro Ilse von Rentzell (2,506m) is the tallest peak on the left, capped by a mushroom of rime ice. The other peaks in the group are believed to be unclimbed. *Camilo Rada*

painter, photographer, mountaineer, explorer, and plant geographer. She participated in several expeditions to the Andes, including a few adventurous weeks exploring the Lago O'Higgins/San Martín region of the icefield in the summer of 1933.

The 1933 expedition accessed the icefield from the east via Glaciar O'Higgins, which is flanked to the south by a then-unknown mountain range they called Cordón GAEA, after the Argentine Society of Geographical Studies, which sponsored the expedition. Further into the icefield, they observed and mapped for the first time a chain of peaks southeast of Cerro Pirámide. This is where Cerro Gorra Blanca (2,907m) and Cerro Falso Ilse (2,512m) are located; Camilo Rada and I climbed both in December 2008 (*AAJ 2012*).

To the north of Glaciar O'Higgins, they discovered yet another unknown range, an episode described by Ilse as follows: "We saw to the northwest, for the first time, in all its extension, a chain of mountains that still did not appear on the maps. Among this new mountain range, which presents the typical forms of pointy summits, runs the main glacier with a width of 40 or 45 kilometers."

In 1959, Hugo Corbella, Marcelo Costa, Jose Marticorena, and Pablo Schiffini made a notable expedition connecting Lago O'Higgins with Fiordo Eyre to the southwest, and then crossing eastward back to Lago Viedma. During this exploration, they named the most well-defined summit of the range described above after Ilse von Rentzell to remember the first woman known to have set foot upon the icefields of Patagonia. Cerro Ilse von Rentzell was coveted for decades, but it remained unclimbed until April 9, when Camilo Rada and I reached the summit. In practice, it is difficult to define which of all the peaks along this range is Ilse von Rentzell, so we went for the highest, which is approximately located where Corbella's maps placed it.

We achieved this long-awaited ascent on the only good day of weather offered to us during two weeks at the Greve hut (having reached it by helicopter as part of a maintenance crew). The hut is located at the very center of the icefield and to the southwest of Cerro Ilse von Rentzell.

Once we reached Ilse, we ascended the south face on skis until we reached the southeast ridge. There, we crossed the bergschrund and gained the last couple of hundred of meters using crampons on an icy 40° slope. The climb ended with a crux 15m climb over a voluminous mushroom of rime ice; after 5m of vertical climbing, the angle gradually eased until we stood atop a flat little summit.

Our GPS gave us an altitude of 2,506m (48°43'50"S, 73°25'17"W), and the summit gifted us with expansive views of the icefield, surrounded by amazing mountains, so many of them unclimbed that our fingers run short to count them. 🔲 🔳

— NATALIA MARTÍNEZ, *ARGENTINA*

LA NORTE

A NEW LINE UP THE NORTH FACE OF CERRO TORRE, WITH A TRAGIC CONCLUSION

BY **TOMÁS AGUILÓ**, *ARGENTINA*

IN 2013, NICOLAS Benedetti and I attempted the north face of Cerro Torre for the first time. We did not have a clear strategy nor much information. We reached the north face via the American Torre Egger route [*the 1976 route, which began up the east face of Cerro Torre*], and managed to open six new pitches on the left side of the north face. We found a natural and very aesthetic line, which proved to be quite difficult and varied. We retreated due to high temperatures and unpromising weather ahead.

The next year we tried again, and this time Jorge Ackermann joined Nico and me. Conditions were challenging, with a lot of rime, which, combined with high temperatures and wind, forced us to retreat quite early, at the height of the English box. [*This "box" is the ruin of a rigid bivouac shelter that was installed at the base of the prominent dihedral on the right side of the east face by English climbers in 1978.*]

In the beginning of 2019, we were back at it again. Nico could not join us, so Corrado "Korra" Pesce took his place. With a better strategy, better conditions, and a strong team, Jorge, Korra, and I decided to follow a different line, Un Sogno Inter-rotto (Giarolli-Orlandi, 1998), in the lower third of the east face, and then managed to open three new pitches beyond our previous high point on the north face. We reached an obvious shoulder on the upper left edge, solving yet another crux. We bivouacked there, and in the early morning, when the wind increased—and since Korra had broken

Cerro Torre from the northeast. (1) Brothers in Arms, climbed in 2022 (see p.223), follows the 1976 Torre Egger Route and El Arca de los Vientos on the lower east face, then climbs the huge dihedral on the right side of the face before joining La Norte to the top. (2) La Norte, starting with Un Sogno Interotto (1998) and the 1976 Torre Egger route and then climbing about 550 meters of new terrain on the north face. *Rolando Garibotti*

Korra Pesce gunning for the top of the north face on La Norte. *Tomás Aguiló*

a finger in a fall the day before—we decided to retreat. In early 2020, Jorge, Korra, and I joined forces again, but bad conditions did not allow us to get even close to the peak.

With Jorge busy with life pursuits in the Northern Hemisphere, Korra and I met in Chaltén in mid-January 2022. Within days, a good weather window showed up in the forecast. There was no time to lose. The mountain conditions looked optimal, and the forecasted temperature was promising, being lower than in previous attempts. The weather window spanned January 25 to 28, so on the 24th we hiked to Noruegos, the advanced camp near the base. When we arrived, we were surprised to find the lower wall was snowier than expected, so we decided to wait an extra day to let some of the snow and ice clear off. To gain some time for the next day, we fixed the first three pitches.

On the 26th we woke up at 1:15 a.m., jumared those first pitches, and continued climbing. There was some ice and verglas in this section, so we were slower than expected. Around noon we reached our bivouac site, at the height of the English box but 50m to the right: a ledge with a large granite flake in the back. Leaving our bivouac gear there, we climbed one more pitch to the base of the north face and then fixed the first pitch on the face. This is the crux pitch and has a potential ledge fall, so we wanted to avoid doing it in the early morning.

On the 27th we woke at midnight and started moving at 1 a.m. We decided to leave our bivouac gear on the ledge and climb to the summit non-stop, planning to descend at night. Having led them on our two previous attempts, I took the first seven pitches. Despite the darkness and verglas on some of the cracks and slabs, I managed to move quickly, reaching the Burke-Proctor traverse in only six hours. [*This left-to-right traverse was a key part of the 1981 British attempt on a long new route up the east and north faces.*] I continued leading two more pitches to the base of an ice gully. Upon reaching that belay, I could see Italian climbers David Bacci, Matteo Della Bordella, and Matteo De Zaiacomo pop onto the north face from the east end of the Burke-Proctor traverse; they had climbed the big corner on the east face, and after moving onto the north face, they followed our line. (*See report on p.223.*) Korra took over the lead, his skill set being well suited for the mixed terrain that lay ahead.

At 11 a.m. we reached our previous high point. From here up it was virgin terrain, but having studied the wall, we knew where to go. Korra climbed a crack, then negotiated rime, reaching a comfortable belay ledge. The next pitch looked amazing—parallel cracks splitting immaculate granite—and Korra progressed quickly.

The following pitch was a bit easier, navigating from right to left and passing under an intimidating mushroom to reach another comfortable ledge. From there Korra continued, wearing rock shoes initially and then switching to boots, crampons, and ice axes. The last pitch before joining the Ragni Route (west ridge) was a very nice 90° ice gully that deposited us at the base of the final rime mushroom on the ridge, which Korra dispatched in barely 20 minutes. At 5:20 p.m. we were both standing on the summit of Cerro Torre.

After so many attempts, so much effort, our dream had finally come to pass. We had completed a direct route up the longest portion of the imposing north face. We thought of Jorge and Nico, who had been with us in earlier attempts, and gave a loud cheer, beckoning them from afar.

At around 7 p.m. we started rappelling our route. At the small shoulder partway down, we decided to wait until around 10 p.m. for the temperature to drop and for the wall to stop dripping. Then we continued down to our bivouac, which we reached at 2 a.m. We were tired, so we stopped to hydrate and eat. We discussed continuing down, but changed our minds, deciding to get some rest. We covered our legs with our sleeping bag and dozed off....

EDITOR'S NOTE: *The conclusion of this story was prepared by Rolando Garibotti, after conversations with with Tomás Aguiló.*

At around 3:30 a.m., a few minutes after dozing off at their bivy site, 600m above the bottom of the east face, Korra and Tomy heard falling rocks. Within a few seconds, rocks started hitting their surroundings. Soon there was a massive crash. They both were thrown downward, their safety lines cut, but somehow they both stopped on small ledges 2m to 3m below the bivy

ledge. They were in extreme pain. Tomy's upper left side was badly injured, and Korra could not move his lower limbs. A 4m-by-1.5m rock flake that had been behind them at the ledge—sheltering them—was gone. Although it might have protected them from a direct hit, it's also possible it was the flake rolling off that caused their injuries.

Their equipment had fallen down the steep wall or was scattered around them. Tomy could not find their inReach communicator. He started making an SOS signal with his headlamp. Several hours passed, and he never saw a reply. Close to daybreak, Tomy, who was able to move with great difficulty, found one crampon and put it on for added safety. Beneath some snow he discovered some food and the inReach. He typed several distress messages, but because of a weak satellite signal on the vertical face, they did not get sent. Nonetheless, Tomy encouraged Korra to maintain hope. Korra in turn encouraged him to go down. Tomy, who eventually was diagnosed with a broken collarbone, five broken ribs, and a punctured lung, thought he would be unable to descend. He could not move one hand and could barely move the other. Korra insisted, and at the same time expressed his intention

Aerial photo of Cerro Torre's upper north face. (1) Brothers in Arms (2022), coming up the east face and then following (2) La Norte (2022) which joins the Ragni Route to reach the summit. (3) Burke-Proctor attempt (1981), ending just below the west ridge. (4) Directa de la Mentira (2015). (5) El Arca de los Vientos (2005), joining the Ragni Route to the top. *Rolando Garibotti*

Priti Wright leads a traverse under the summit mushroom on Punta Herron. *Jeff Wright*

AGUJA STANDHARDT TO TORRE EGGER TRAVERSE

IN JANUARY 2022, my husband, Jeff Wright, and I completed a successful Patagonian "smash 'n' grab," when an excellent forecast prompted us to make an 11-day round-trip (Seattle to Seattle) to El Chaltén, during which we enchained three of the four peaks in the Torre group: Aguja Standhardt, Punta Herron, and Torre Egger. This was the first time a woman has completed this traverse or climbed Punta Herron. [*Editor's Note: Priti Wright was the third woman to summit Torre Egger, after Steph Davis and Brette Harrington.*]

This was our fifth climbing trip to El Chaltén. In 2019, we climbed Cerro Chaltén (Fitz Roy) in a 10-day smash 'n' grab from Seattle. In early 2020, during two months in Chaltén, we climbed Cerro Torre on the route Via dei Ragni. Urgency and several parties in line behind us compelled us to join the conga line and accept a top-rope on the final pitch of the summit mushroom. We now have stood on all four summits of the Torre skyline [*another first for a female climber*].

Our traverse from Standhardt to Egger took four days and three nights, with two bivouacs on Standhardt and then climbing through the third night up-and-over Torre Egger.

After arriving in El Chaltén, we approached the standard Niponino camp for the Torres the next day, spent the night, and cached our tent there; we carried a tarp and a double sleeping bag for the traverse. After a night at the Torre Glacier bivy site, waiting for icy conditions to improve, we started up Aguja Standhardt on January 18, climbing the route Festerville (400m, 6c 90°), which follows the spine of the north ridge for approximately 13 rock pitches. Another team of two (Michał Czech from Poland and Agustín de la Cerda from Chile) started up the route ahead of us, and we effectively joined forces, climbing symbiotically, with each team helping the other along the way.

We bivied 11 pitches up and then summited Standhardt via two more pitches and 30m of 90° ice and rime. Michał and Agustín rappelled the Exocet route while we bivied near the summit (a short day).

In the morning, we made seven rappels down the south face of Standhardt, then climbed 30m of the route Tobogán to gain the Col de los Sueños. The traverse continued up to Punta Herron via Spigolo dei Bimbi (350m, 6b 90°), with five pitches of fantastic rock climbing and another two pitches of beautiful vertical ice and rime to the summit. A single rappel led down to Col de la Luz under the north face of Torre Egger.

From here we continued up Espejo del Viento (200m, 6a+ 80°), often referred to as the Huber-Schnarf Route, in the dark. Three rock pitches end in a long, run-out and wet technical slab traverse under Torre Egger's overhanging summit mushroom. Two more moderate pitches up the mushroom on 70° snow and ice brought us to the summit of Egger at 2 a.m.

Through the night, we descended along the route Titanic on the east pillar, with 27 rappels and downclimbing. We reached Niponino after 44 hours of continuous movement since our second bivy on Standhardt.

We collapsed in our tent, realizing we were too late to catch our planned flight home. Unfortunately, we neglected to notify anyone that we would miss our early-morning airport taxi ride, which led to the driver waking climber Korra Pesce, who was sleeping in the room we had previously used. Korra notified the hostel owner and Rolando Garibotti, who proceeded to notify rescue teams. Later that morning, however, Rolo successfully contacted us via our inReach, halting any rescue plans and teaching us a valuable lesson.

A week later, a large team of volunteers attempted an unsuccessful rescue of Korra Pesce, who had been seriously injured on Cerro Torre. Jeff and I, who were already back in the United States by that time, just wished we could have been present to aid in the rescue efforts.

– PRITI WRIGHT, *USA*

CHALTÉN MASSIF 2021–2022 SEASON SUMMARY

THE CLIMATE CONTINUES changing. Weather patterns in Patagonia are strongly influenced by the north-south location of the low-pressure belt surrounding Antarctica, and from 1980 on, this belt has trended southward—more pronounced during the summer—which is leading to drier, warmer weather (*see "Sunny Patagonia" in AAJ 2018*). Some of the changes—long stable weather windows—are welcome; others—regular rock and ice fall and serac collapses—are less desirable.

In the Chaltén Massif, some of the affected places this season included the southwest face of Poincenot, from which large blocks reached the Polacos camp, the glacial approach to the east side of Cerro Torre, swept several times by a serac, and the couloir below La Brecha on Cerro Chaltén. In Torres del Paine, the affected areas were the east face of Cerro Catedral, the southeast face of Torre Norte, and the north face of Cuerno Central.

Due to glacier recession, the approach to Niponino camp, below the Torres group, has become increasingly problematic. The original route, contouring around the lake via its northeast side, is a lottery of sorts, involving more danger than most climbs. Several groups have turned around, others have taken falls, and some have had to rappel after getting stuck on steep, hard mud. In February, Luka Krajnc and Luka Lindič explored the south side and found a safe, albeit longer way. Where the trail used to drop down to the glacier, they went up and then traversed horizontally before dropping straight down to the grassy meadow before the glacier. A month later, a group of volunteers marked the route, making it easy to follow.

The new south-side traverse around Laguna Torre, an easier and safer route following glacier recession. *Luka Lindič*

What other lessons will the climbing community draw from this new climate landscape, and how will we adapt? In the Alps, climbers have been forced to shift objectives drastically. Climbs that previously were done in summer are now only done in winter or spring. Is the same sort of seasonal adaptation necessary here?

On Cerro Torre, Vitto Messini, Gabriel Tschurtschenthaler, and Matthias Wurzer climbed the Ragni Route on the west face in late December 2021. Theirs was the first ascent of the peak since

Pain and Gain on the east face of Aguja Desmochada. The route finishes along Puerta Blanca, which comes up from the icy saddle at right. *Rolando Garibotti*

February 2020. Notable about their climb is that Gabriel is legally blind. If light conditions are optimal, he can see the shapes of the peaks, but no details. Harder than the climb itself was the approach, especially contouring around Lago Eléctrico. Earlier, the three climbed the Cochrane-Whillans route on Aguja Poincenot. These are the first ascents by a blind person of both peaks.

Over four days in late January 2022, Jeff and Priti Wright climbed Aguja Standhardt, Punta Herron, and Torre Egger. Priti's ascents are the first female ascent of Herron, the third of Torre Egger, and possibly the third of Standhardt. (*See report above.*) In addition, four all-female rope teams in the same season climbed the Northwest Ridge (Afanassieff Route) of Cerro Fitz Roy (in chronological order): Ramona Volken and Anne Flechsig (CH), Laura Tiefenthaler and Babsi Vigl (AT), Fanny Schmutz, Lise Billon and Camille Marot (FR), and Rocio Voumard and Delfi Fainguersch (AR). Prior to this, there had been only five all-female ascents ever.

Ondrej Húserka and Jozef Kristoffy (Slovakia) opened a new route on the east face of Aguja Desmochada, to the right of Circus Pets. They approached via the Poincenot Couloir (700m, 3), a climb in its own right, which took them seven hours. Their 14-pitch route, Pain and Gain (500m, 7a+ C1), climbs a line on the right side of the face. A pitch below the summit, they improvised an open bivy, reaching the top on day two. The climbing is sustained, and pitch 11 required aid, but with dry conditions it might go free. They rappelled Circus Pets.

On the far left side of Aguja Saint-Exúpery's south face, Esteban Degregori, Horacio Gratton, and Pedro Odell (Argentina) climbed El Zorro y la Rosa (450m, 6c+ C1). They joined the Austrian route on the south spur and continued to the summit of Punta Cristina (700m in all). Around the corner, to the west, Kiff Alcocer and Jordon Griffler climbed four new pitches (5.11b C1), connecting Last Gringo Standing to the Brooks-Crouch, finishing on the Austrian route.

In late February 2022, Jenny Abegg (USA) established the fastest known time (FKT) for "La Vuelta al Hielo," the circumnavigation of the Chaltén Massif via the Southern Patagonia Icefield, which covers 55 miles with 10,000' of vertical gain. Twenty of those miles are on glaciated terrain, on the eastern edge of the icefield, following the approach commonly used to reach the west side of Cerro Torre. Beyond the danger of solo-glacier travel, the biggest difficulty is navigating sections of very unstable moraine. Abegg completed the "closed, trails loop," counterclockwise, solo, and unsupported, in a blazing 15:29:58, beating the previous FKT by more than four hours. Twenty days earlier, Kaytlyn Gerbin and Fernanda Maciel did a partial version of this traverse, the "U variation" (47 miles, 8,600'), supported by two porters, in an incredibly fast 13:15:11.

In late 2021, to the north of Río Eléctrico, Julián Casanova and Joaquín Paul skied several new lines, some with Pablo Torres Mash: the east faces of Cerros Milodón Norte (500m, 45°) and Central (400m, 50°), the east face of Cerro Neumeyer (500m, 50°) with one 30m rappel on the lower part, and the south face of Cerro 30 Aniversario (600m, 45°) with a 15m rappel.

There were three fatalities in the Chaltén Massif this season. One involved an avalanche, another massive falling debris, the third a lone falling rock. Two of the climbers were conscious after the accident and died alone. These brutal details are included here to underscore how serious it is to climb in a remote wilderness area where there is no professional rescue team with helicopter support. There were other close calls, some of which involved a lack of planning that was staggering. Some takeaways:

- Risk management protocols commonly used for ski-mountaineering are often ignored in summer alpinism. While one might not need to carry beacons and other avalanche equipment, after big snowfalls it's essential to assess the stability of a slope before getting on it, move one at the time between relatively safe spots, and consider turning around.
- Peaks that are crowned by huge, overhanging rime mushrooms should be considered off-limits when the freezing line is well above the summit.
- Plan your climbs based on the forecast, set a turnaround time, and respect it. In 2019, three climbers died of exposure for pushing their luck against a serious forecast. This season five people came mighty close to suffering the same fate.
- A communication device (inReach or VHF radio) can be crucial for speedy and effective response during an emergency. (The frequencies and phone numbers to program on your device are at pataclimb.com. Share your contact info with other climbers in the vicinity of your route.) If possible, do not push the SOS button on your inReach; it results in cumbersome, delayed communication. Instead, contact the local authorities or friends directly.
- When an accident happens, send an alert, but then do everything you can to carry out a self-rescue. Do not sit around and wait.

The south face of Aguja Saint-Exupéry, showing (1) Austriaca (1987) and (2) El Zorro y la Rosa (2022). *Rolando Garibotti*

Pay for rescue insurance, and make sure it includes body recoveries. Although rescues here are done on a free, volunteer basis, insurance may cover additional resources that could make a difference in your survival. Body recoveries are not done for free, and cost a minimum of $10,000. Before climbing, register with the national park (free; link at pataclimb.com).

The local volunteer rescue team, the Comisión de Auxilio Fabio Stedile, continues to do a superb job, mobilizing people and resources to help those in need. This season two of their interventions were life-saving.

— ROLANDO GARIBOTTI

The line of Dos Hermanos (800m, 5.11+ A0) on Cerro Cathedral. *Cristóbal Señoret*

TORRES DEL PAINE, CERRO CATEDRAL, NORTH FACE, DOS HERMANOS

WE STARTED THINKING about Cerro Catedral after seeing its 1,000m east face from Trono Blanco in 2019. Over January 18–19, 2022, we ventured to open the first route on the north face of this jewel. [*The north face is accessed from Valle del Francés, via the Irish Couloir, but the face actually rises one valley to the west, above Glaciar Perros.*]

Our route up the left (east) side of the face required a lot of navigation to connect crack systems. On day one, we climbed 12 pitches and then found an incredible ledge to bivy. On day two, we climbed eight more pitches, finishing this unforgettable climb and the first Chilean route on this wonderful mountain. To descend, we rappelled our route. We placed three protection bolts in all, and two short wet sections required us to pull on gear (A0). We called our 20-pitch route Dos Hermanos (800m, 5.11+ A0).

— CRISTÓBAL SEÑORET *AND* JUAN SEÑORET, *CHILE*

EDITOR'S NOTE: *Cerro Catedral was first climbed by a British team in 1971 via its west ridge. The east face is home to three independent routes (from left to right): the 1993 Italian route Il Volo Del Condor (1,000m, UIAA VII+, A3+), which finished at a lower subsummit; the 1992 American route La Escoba de Dios (1,000m, 5.10 A4+); and the 1994 Spanish route Cristal de Roca (6b A4). La Escoba de Dios was free climbed with significant variations in 2013: The Belgian route (1,000m, 7c+) shares pitches 1–6 and 18–19 with La Escoba de Dios, but mostly climbs to the left. Refer to AAJs 1971, 1992, 1993, 1994, and 2013 for more info. — Erik Rieger, with information from Rolando Garibotti*

TORRES DEL PAINE, LA HOJA, EAST FACE, CUARZO MENGUANTE

IN LATE JANUARY 2022, Pepo Jurado (Ecuador) and I ventured into Valle Bader hoping to climb a new route on La Hoja. I had attempted a line on the east face a few years ago but was shut down due to a bottoming crack and an icy roof.

This time, we climbed a line on the far right side of the wall. We started on the first two pitches of the route Andúril (650m, 5.11 A1; *AAJ 1997*) before heading right into a continuous crack system we had spied in photos. We climbed sustained and sometimes very closed-off cracks (consistent 5.11). A section of aid (A2) got us past a finger crack that shrunk into an almost nonexistent seam. That night, we bivied on a small ledge laden with gigantic diamond-like quartz formations.

The next day, we continued up sustained vertical terrain to the summit ridge, before traversing around to the west face and finding easier ground leading to the top. We named the route Cuarzo Menguante (650m, 5.11+ A2), after the quartz ledge and the *menguante* moon that accompanied us through the night. 📷

— SEBASTIAN PELLETTI, *AUSTRALIA*

Pepo Jurado on Cuarzo Menguante (700m, 5.11+ A2) on the east face of La Hoja on day one of his and Sebastian Pelletti's two-day ascent (*report on previous page*). The two climbers, along with Romano Marcotti, made the first ascent of Cuerno Este (*report below*) just a week prior. *Sebastian Pelletti*

TORRES DEL PAINE, CUERNO ESTE, FIRST ASCENT BY NORTH FACE

In mid-December, Romano Marcotti (Chile) and I ventured into the Valle Bader to check out a project of mine. After discovering that conditions weren't great for that climb, we decided to attempt a stellar-looking line on the north face of Cuerno Este. We climbed pitches up five-star cracks and perfect rock until we reached the end of the granite. Looking up at the metamorphic rock comprising the summit tower, we descended, assuming this part had been climbed before.

Arriving back in town, we learned the first three pitches of our route are shared with the 2002 route by Hesleden-Nadin, which climbed only the lower granite portion, and that Cuerno Este had no complete ascents. [*Editor's Note: The 2002 route was repeated by Frédéric Degoulet, Jean-François Reffet, and Romaric Pellicier in 2009; they continued for an additional five or six pitches to the western subsummit, calling their climb Bailar con el Viento. In 1998, Tom Dauman, Alan Kearney, and Jack Lewis climbed a five-pitch route further to the right, stopping where the granite ends (AAJ 1998).*]

Curiosity got the better of us, and on January 18, 2022, Romano and I headed back into the valley with Pepo Jurado (Ecuador). We climbed the same five pitches of incredible splitter cracks and then simul-climbed a 200m-long ridge to the base of the summit tower. We first checked our options on the north ridge but then decided

Vacaciones Metamorficas (600m, 5.11-) on the north face of Cuerno Este, the line of the peak's first complete ascent. The route shares some terrain with Bailar con el Viento (Hesleden-Nadin, 2002), which climbs to the western subsummit (right). *Joe Feltham*

on a system of ledges and overhangs to the left that seemed to have a crack for protection. The crack disappeared after the first relatively easy pitch. We continued by climbing four more spicy pitches, composed of loose rock and ledges interspersed with vertical to overhanging sections, to reach the small, pointed summit. The view was incredible, with turquoise lakes in all directions.

We descended by rappelling the north ridge, leaving one piton below the summit and carving out natural anchors in the rotten rock until reaching the lower route. We named the route Vacaciones Metamorficas (600m, 5.11-) after a rest day spent swimming in a "heated pool" of glacial meltwater warmed by giant granite slabs, and in honor of the terrible metamorphic rock that crowns Cuerno Este. ▣

— SEBASTIAN PELLETTI, *AUSTRALIA*

[Top] Cerro San Luis from the southeast. The 2021 route was near the center of the photo. Once on the ridge, the climbers traversed left (west) about 500 meters to the highest point. *Sebastian Pelletti* [Bottom] Bushwhacking through the dense forest; it took eight hours to travel 5km. *Nicolás "Nico" Secul*

CORDÓN MONUMENTO MOORE, CERRO SAN LUIS, SOUTH FACE

ON AUGUST 30, Camilo Pedreros, Nicolás "Nico" Secul (both Chile), and I kayaked west from Estancia Perales (30km northwest of Puerto Natales) across Fiordo Última Esperanza to reach Península Antonio Varas in the northern Cordón Monumento Moore. We left our kayaks along the bay and camped at a small shelter. On day two, we began our approach through very-dense subpolar forest, at times progressing on our hands and knees. It took approximately eight hours to travel the 5km to the base of the broad south face of Cerro San Luis (ca 1,500m; 51°34'39"S, 72°58'54"W).

On day three of the trip, we began our climb up the center of the south face, climbing a technical ice pitch above the bergschrund at dawn. This was followed by a few technical pitches both above and below a long snow ramp. The snow ramp allowed for quick progress and the only safe passage among large hanging seracs. Near the top, Nico led a beautiful dihedral plastered with a thin strip of ice, and I excavated a tunnel through sugar snow for us to crawl onto the summit ridge. We traversed west for approximately 500m to the summit and then descended the east face back to our camp. We kayaked back to Estancia Perales the next day.

We named the route Memoria Kawésqar (750m, AI4 80°) in honor of the Kawésqar, an indigenous people who navigated these fjords by canoes thousands of years ago. Cerro San Luis had one prior ascent by Gabriel Mancilla Jipoulou and a friend in 2015 or 2016; they ascended the north ridge. ▣

— SEBASTIAN PELLETTI, *AUSTRALIA*

The north side of Grupo La Paz, showing the west-to-east traverse over (A) Aguja Yeque, (B) Aguja Oeste, (C) Aguja Central, and (D) Aguja Este: Ayayema Wesqar (1,000m, 5.11-). *Hector Diaz*

CORDILLERA RIESCO, GRUPO LA PAZ, NEW ROUTES AND TRAVERSE

AFTER A CHANCE encounter with Don Guillermo, a generous local fisherman, Jose Navarro, Nicolás "Nico" Secul (both from Chile), and I sailed west from Puerto Natales into the Canal Santa María on October 28. After a six hour boat ride, we made base camp on the east shore of Península Roca in a lush forest surrounded by swamp. Our objective was Grupo La Paz (51°58'59"S, 73°12'18"W; a.k.a. Los Dientes del Diablo), a mystical looking group of three rock towers situated in the southern Cordillera Riesco. The towers are seldom seen, and we had only a few photographs for reference.

After a storm broke on day two, we walked northwest for about 4km amid deep clouds and camped below the northeast face of the east tower, Aguja Este. On day three, we began traversing up and left along a glacial ramp on the northeast face. At the upper rock portion, we climbed rock and mixed terrain up a left-trending weakness to reach the east shoulder and then followed a snow ramp to the summit.

Descending west from the summit, we decided to bivy on a small ledge above the col between the east and central towers. The next morning we rappelled to the col, and from there climbed the right side of the east ridge of the central tower, reaching the summit by early afternoon. We later learned this was the first ascent of Aguja Central. We descended by rappelling and downclimbing along the north ridge.

We named our enchainment El Poder del Ahora (700m, 6b M4) after a book that Nico was reading in base camp. The route feels like a traverse, but with significant vertical gain and moderately technical terrain.

I remained drawn to this group of towers and hoped to complete a full traverse. So, on February 20, 2022, Antar Machado, Hernán Rodríguez, and I left Puerto Natales with captain Hector "Chino" Diaz and disembarked on the shore of Fiordo de las Montañas on the west side of the Cordillera Riesco. That evening, we made a high camp below the west ridge of Aguja Oeste, ready to start a complete west-to-east traverse.

We first tackled the westernmost subtower (150m, 5.7), reaching it by 7:30 a.m. We thought of calling it Aguja Yeque (meaning "small" in Kaweskar). We then rappelled to the col between it and Aguja Oeste and continued up a white pillar (300m, 5.10), generally following the upper part of the Quesada-San Vicente route (2000). We reached the summit by early afternoon, blown away by the beauty of the Cordillera Sarmiento to the west.

We descended east toward the col between Aguja Oeste and Central with five rappels down the Chouinard-Donini route (1988), then two traversing pitches and one rappel on quite bad rock to finally reach the base of Aguja Central. We found only a trickle of water after a dry summer and spent two hours hacking a ledge into the steep moraine for our tight two-man tent. At nightfall, clouds began to form unexpectedly on the summits of La Dama Blanca and Cerro Trono to the west.

A restless night made for an even gloomier morning, as we awoke to intermittent rain and tent-shaking wind. We decided to wait patiently and begin climbing the two remaining towers at midnight. The wall remained totally soaked, but the weather report was promising, and so we ventured up the first pitches of wet, abrasive rock, immersed in the bubble of our headlamps' glow. The improbable-looking third pitch was a smooth, wet slab, with no gear and little holds, guarding the entrance to another crack system (5.11-). One more steep pitch, scrambling, and a long traverse with two steep sections brought us to the top of Aguja Central at first light.

We made three rappels to the col below Aguja Este. From there, two high-quality pitches (5.10+) got us to its summit. For a moment, we basked in the beauty of this place: turquoise lakes, rumbling glaciers, and shimmering fjords. To complete our line, we descended the steep east face, making eight rappels. With our gear dwindling, we make it to the valley floor, exhausted, hungry, sunburnt, and euphoric. Still, we hoped to make it to Canal Santa María on the east side of Cordillera Riesco before nightfall. Some trail running ensued, our legs on autopilot. Our captain Chino, faithful as ever, rendezvoused with us on a small, pristine peninsula at sunset, and we cruised back to Puerto Natales.

We called our traverse Ayayema Wesqar (1,000m, 5.11-), which means something to the effect of "spirit of the mountains" in the language of the Kawésqar, who still inhabit corners of this Patagonian archipelago in total harmony. 🖸

— SEBASTIAN PELLETTI, *AUSTRALIA*

HISTORICAL NOTES ON GRUPO LA PAZ: *These mountains are in the Cordillera Riesco, on Península Roca, which is formed by Fiordo de las Montañas to the west and Canal Santa María to the east. The Cordillera de Sarmiento lies just west across the Fiordo de las Montañas.*

Aguja Oeste (1,190m) is the highest in Grupo La Paz. The tower was first climbed in 1988 by Yvon Chouinard and Jim Donini. They approached from the south to reach the large col between Aguja Oeste and Aguja Central and then climbed seven pitches to 6a (AAJ 1988). Rafael Quesada and Iñaki San Vicente made the second ascent of Aguja Oeste in 2000 (not Aguja Este, as stated in AAJ 2000). They began on a north-facing snow ramp, climbing a narrow couloir to reach the col on the west spur. From there, they climbed three pitches of rock and mixed terrain (5+) to the summit.

Aguja Este was first climbed by Carsten von Birckhahn and Andrew McAuley in 1998. Their 14-pitch route, Cuando Cambia la Luna, climbs the east face with difficulties to 6a (AAJ 1998). In 2020, Erwan Le Lann, Marko Prezelj, and Gerald Veniard made the second ascent of Aguja Este via a new route (450m, 6a) on the east face, parallel and to the right of Cuando Cambia la Luna.
— *Erik Rieger, with information from Rolando Garibotti*

ANTARCTICA

SANDNESHATTEN, NEW ROUTES

THE FRENCH GROUPE Militaire d'Haute Montagne (GMHM) once again sent a team of mountain soldiers to Queen Maud Land for exploratory ascents during November and December. Jacques-Olivier Chevallier, Didier Jourdain, Sebastian Moatti, and Jordi Nogeure used kites to help ski the 37km from their landing site, near the well-known spire Ulvetanna, eastward to the Conrad Fjella peaks at the northern end of the Orvin Fjella massif. Their primary objective was a striking granite prow on the east side of twin-summited Sandneshatten (2,200m, 71°41'57"S, 9°41'20"E).

Sandneshatten's eastern and highest peak was first climbed in 2006 (*AAJ 2007*) by a Norwegian team led by Ivar Tollefsen, the climbing pioneer of the region, and it received a second ascent in 2009 by Austrian guide Christoph Höbenreich with Karl Pichler and Paul Koller (*AAJ 2010*). Both parties climbed moderate terrain on the south side. When the French were researching potential new lines in the area, it was Höbenreich who suggested the impressive wall beneath the east summit.

On December 3, the four French climbed the moderately angled and sweeping northeast arête of the east summit, which gave 800m of rock climbing (French 5), followed by steep snow (up to 60°) and mixed terrain up the northern side of the summit tower.

[Top] Le Pilier du Contrevent on the left edge of the east face of Sandneshatten's east peak. The climb took four days. [Bottom] The climb up the northeast side of the east peak. *GMHM photos*

Six days later, Chevallier, Jourdain, and Noguere set off for the main objective: the prow on the east face, zigzagging up a line of tafoni. (Tafoni are giant pockets in the granite formed by a combination of chemical and physical weathering, with the strong wind of the region removing rock softened by temperature and salinity changes.) At the top of the pillar, they moved left across the upper south face and up mixed ground to the summit. The climb took four days. The 750m line, with climbing to 6a A2 M4, was named Le Pilier du Contrevent ("Windbreak Pillar").

The GMHM has an impressive history in Antarctica: skiing to the South Pole in 1998-99, climbing new routes in the Ellsworth Mountains—Mt. Tyree (4,852m) in 1997 and Mt. Vinson (4,892m) in 2011—and putting up several new routes in Queen Maud Land in 2008 (*AAJ 2009*). In 2018 they visited the remote Pirrit Hills (*AAJ 2010*), climbing several new routes and implementing kite-skiing to access this isolated area.

— **DAMIEN GILDEA**, *WITH INFORMATION FROM* **DIDIER JOURDAIN** *AND* **CHRISTOPH HÖBENREICH**

Misha Mishin follows a pitch of Ørneeggen on the west face of Storskiva. *Juho Knuuttila*

EUROPE

LOFOTEN, STORSKIVA, WEST FACE

IN 2020, ON satellite images, I spotted the cool looking west face of Storskiva (848m) on the island of Moskenesøya, in the far west of Lofoten. It seemed very hard to reach due to steep sea cliffs guarding the approach on both sides. I was able to find only one photo of this face, taken from a boat. It showed a magnificent spur splitting the wall.

In August 2021, Misha Mishin and I drove to the village of Reine and took a boat to Vindstad, from which we planned to start hiking to the face. It was very rainy, and in the end we decided to sleep in a waiting room at the Vindstad harbor instead of in our tents.

The following morning, we started hiking at 6 a.m., carrying only daypacks. We followed a faint trail over a mountain pass to the Hermannsdalen valley in order to reach the west coast of Moskenesøya. Then we followed the shoreline northward for a kilometer, climbing above saltwater canyons and over steep grass slopes. By sheer luck it was doable, and way less tiring than we'd imagined.

The face looked quite intimidating from below. Its left side is probably the steepest in Lofoten, while the right side presented an imposing slab with some roofs; in the middle of these two lay the spur, with the only continuous-looking crack system on the entire face. That was our line.

To reach the spur we climbed four pitches on broken slabs, heading slightly left—not difficult technically, but they were very compact and with poor protection.

It was noon when we started up the main spur. The next 11 pitches provided some of the best rock I have seen, but the grass in the cracks made the climbing slow and poorly protected. On some pitches we needed to dig out every gear placement, and on some we were hand jamming and pinching grass tufas or scratching mud pockets to stay on the wall. The nut tool was our best friend.

Here and there we encountered faster free climbing pitches, but the going mainly alternated between easy aid and bold slabs. Often we needed to lower the leader back down to retrieve gear in order to complete pitches only 30m long. We were also very lucky the crack system ran straight up and that we didn't have to do any big traverses.

This would be a three-star free climb without all the moss in the cracks. The location was amazing, with eagles flying above our heads, the waves of the Atlantic Ocean raging all the way from the North Pole, and no mobile phone reception anywhere. True adventure climbing.

At 11 p.m. we reached a big grass ledge and thought the climbing would be over, but we still needed to do one exit pitch to reach easier terrain. Once again we were lucky and got through the rock barrier on our first try, as it was already pitch dark and we had no clue which crack would lead us to the top.

After midnight we hiked to the top of Storskiva and started descending straight away. It was misty, and navigating by GPS was the only option. We returned to the harbor at Vindstad at 4 a.m., after 22 hours on the go, and crashed on the floor in the waiting room, only to be woken up by hikers few hours later.

We named the route Ørneeggen ("Eagle Spur"); difficulties were up to N7 (5.11) C1 in 15 pitches of climbing. No gear was left behind. [*Editor's Note: In June 2016, Catalan climbers Guille Cuadrado, Jordi Esteve, and Pau Gómez climbed the east shoulder (Point 551m) of Storskiva, adjacent to Bunes Beach, possibly the first technical route on the peak; see AAJ 2018.*] 🔘

– JUHO KNUUTTILA, *FINLAND*

SWEDEN

STORA SJÖFALLET NATIONAL PARK, NIERAS ICE ROUTES

DURING A WEEK in March in Laponia (the Swedish part of Sápmi or Lapland), Johan Lindfors and I had great ice conditions and were able to put up five routes on Nieras (1,424m), one of the beautiful peaks of Stora Sjöfallet National Park. With a convenient place to sleep and eat at Stora Sjöfallet Mountain Lodge, we explored the southeast and northeast faces of Nieras, which turned out to hold lots of potential for new lines.

Our first route was on the southeast side, where we hoped we'd be somewhat protected from the strong storm winds blowing at the start of our visit—which it turned out to be, as long as you didn't object to the spin-drift pouring down the route. We took a full day to climb a quite interesting three-pitch WI5+ line. In the following days, we climbed on the northeast face, putting up three more routes, from four to six pitches, with climbing up to WI6. Then we had to return to the southeast side for a thin, steep line of ice that looked just amazingly

Steep ice on Nattsud (7 pitches, WI6 M4), one of several new routes on the northeast face of Nieras. *Johan Lindfors*

good: Den Tunna Blå Linjen (4 pitches, WI6), with technical ice formations over very steep rock. Starting in beautiful blue-sky weather, we finished in beautiful spindrift and full-on storm, again!

In March 2022, Johan and I returned to Stora Sjöfallet and climbed another new route on Nieras' northeast face, called Nattsudd: a major line with seven pitches and WI6 M4 climbing.

Stora Sjöfallet is reached from the road between Gällivare and Jokkmokk. This area was the site of massive hydroelectric development, which drowned many traditional Sámi villages and changed the environment in many ways. It also provided a good road into these mountains, making it possible to access the ice climbs. The winter season is very long, usually from October/ November until May. [*Photos of these routes are at the AAJ website.*] 🔲

— **KRISTER JONSSON**, *SWEDEN*

The east face of Mont Blanc showing (GP) Grand Pilier d'Angle, (1) Cascata Major, and (2) Route Major with Gobbi-Ottoz finish. *Lindsay Griffin*

THE ALPS

ALPINE 2021 – AN OVERVIEW

LATE WINTER SNOW that took longer than normal to clear, ongoing COVID-19 restrictions in the first half of the year, and a surprisingly cool summer, when the mountains mostly escaped the intense heatwaves that plagued the rest of Europe, characterized the Alps in 2021. A small representation of the most interesting ascents follows.

Mont Blanc Massif

A NOTABLE ASCENT took place on Mont Blanc on November 20 when Francesco Civa Dano and Guiseppe Vidoni pioneered a partial new line on the historic Brenva Face, the first new ground to be climbed there for many years. The face's Route Major (TD, Graham Brown–Smythe, 1928) is one of the great classics of the range but is climbed far less frequently these days; the approach is extremely exposed to serac fall.

In 1971, Pierre Mazeaud and Roberto Sorgato traversed left from a point low on the Major and climbed a buttress between the Major and the Pear routes, eventually finishing well left of the normal Major finish or the Gobbi-Ottoz and Seigneur direct variants. This route is highly dangerous, ED, and is thought never to have been repeated. Immediately left of the Mazeaud-Sorgato on the lower buttress is an open depression at over 4,000m, and Vidoni, who lives in Courmayeur, saw that a steep, 170m-high icefall had occupied this groove in November.

Starting early from the Col de la Fourche Bivouac, in excellent weather and snow conditions, the Italian pair followed the approach to the Pear Route until they could climb directly to the smear, which they reached at dawn. They found the ice to be good quality but thin, with even short stubby screws not penetrating fully at times. They completed this section in five pitches, then slanted across the snow slope above to finish up the Gobbi-Ottoz variant to the Major. They continued to the summit and down to the Gouter Hut that night, naming their route Cascata Major (1,300m, VI/5).

On the south face of the Grandes Jorasses, left of the Hypercouloir, stands a fine triangle of rock, its right edge a perfect pillar of seemingly compact granite. It is known variously as the South Pillar, the Pilier du Glacier Suspendu, and the Ghiglione Pillar. Piero Ghiglione and Arthur Ottoz made the first ascent in 1948, climbing more broken ground left of the true pillar but working right to finish near the crest (TD VI). There have been few repeats—possibly none of the original line—and the long access to the base has become objectively dangerous in recent decades. In May 2019, Jon Bracey and Enrico Bonino climbed an ice/mixed line that is probably quite similar to the middle-upper section of the 1948 route (5b WI5+ M6+).

The true crest of the pillar, an obvious and logical line, had been considered by many over the years, including Matteo Bernasconi, who throughout the last decade was a regular climbing partner of Matteo Della Bordella. In 2020, Bernasconi perished in an avalanche, and Della Bordella was motivated to complete one of Bernasconi's dreams

Della Bordella, Giacomo Mauri, and Luca Schiera skinned up to the Boccalatte Hut on February 23, set off at 4 a.m. the following morning, and in four hours had reached the foot of the pillar. Two 60m pitches (6a and 5+) on the left side of the initial buttress took them to the compact pillar crest.

Contrary to expectations—they were carrying bivouac gear, expecting a two-day ascent—the granite was extremely weathered and well-featured, and the three were able to climb fast over moderate difficulties (4+ to 6b). The pitch below the summit of the pillar was completely vertical but with great holds, and the temperature throughout was warm enough for bare-handed climbing. From the top, an easy ridge led to the glacier plateau and the Grandes Jorasses normal route, which they descended to the Boccalatte, arriving at 7 p.m. The 450m route (excluding the approach) was named Il Regalo di Berna.

The west face of the Petit Dru now has a hard new free route. Four members of the Groupe Militaire de Haute Montagne (Thomas Auvaro, Léo Billon, Jordi Noguere, and Sébastien Ratel) took four days to complete the climb (February 18–21) and a fifth to descend to the valley. (The ascent was live-streamed on social media by a cameraman filming from Montenvers.) With the Grands Montets lift closed, the team had to make the more arduous approach via Montenvers, and they ferried loads to the bottom of the face a week earlier.

When the four set off up their chosen route, which approximated the former Harlin-Robbins Direttissima (much of which was destroyed in a 2005 rockfall), they were unaware that in winter 2015 two Spanish climbers, Josep Maria Esquirol and David Palmada, had spent 14 days on this line before bailing a little over 300m from the top (though they still gave their attempt a name: Abdruits, 6a M5 A5 70°). The French followed the Spanish line for the first third of the face, then made a vari-

The Petit Dru and the line of Base (1,000m, 7a M8+) through the huge rockfall scar on the west face. *Lindsay Griffin*

The south face of the Meije above the Etançons Glacier. (A) Pic du Glacier Carré. (B) Grand Pic. (C) Doigt de Dieu and the line of Athée Pieds. (P) Promontoire Ridge, the normal route, reaching the left side of the hanging Glacier Carré then climbing the left skyline ridge of the Grand Pic. *Lindsay Griffin*

ant, before rejoining the last seven pitches of the Spanish line. Almost immediately above the 2015 high point, they found the crux: a dangerously loose pitch of 7a. A further five pitches of sustained 6b/6c led to easier ground and eventually the summit.

The rock was generally sound, and the climbers felt the hard dry-tooling pitches would have been very much harder climbed conventionally with hands and rock shoes (perhaps 7c). The route was largely protected with nuts and cams, and was named Base (1,000m, 7a M8+).

Écrins Massif

CYRIL DUPEYRÉ, Benjamin Ribeyre (France), and Erin Smart (USA) are three active guides based in La Grave on the north side of the Écrins. Over three consecutive days in August 2020 and a fourth in late August 2021, they opened the first new route in six years on the south side of the Meije (3,984m). Athée Pieds (700m, 970m of climbing, 20 pitches, 7c 6c obl) lies entirely to the right of the historic but infrequently climbed south face of the 3,973m Doigt de Dieu (700m, TD+, 5+, Chaud-Walden, 1951. (The route's original finish contained—remarkably for the era—a short section of 6b.) The Chaud-Walden route, with mixed quality rock, was soloed in 2016 by Ribeyre.

The new route weaves up the steep, compact wall below the shoulder immediately right (east) of the Doigt de Dieu. Most of the belays are bolted, and around 40 protection bolts remain in place, of which 14 were placed in the compact rock of the crux sixth pitch.

Dolomites

IN THE FIRST week of March, stable high pressure sitting over the Dolomites prompted a flurry of activity on the vast northwest face of Civetta.

Lorenzo d'Addario and Nicola Tondini made the first winter ascent of Dulcis in Fundo (ca 400m, IX-, de Blasi–dal Pozzo, 1988) on the Torre di Alleghe. Neither had previously climbed the route, but they completed it in a day. On Punta Civetta, Titus Prinoth and Alex Walpoth made the first winter ascent of Chimera Verticale (600m, 15 pitches, IX, Bau-Beber-Geremia-Matteraglia, 2008). The pair required two bivouacs. Walpoth had previously repeated the line, situated between the classic Aste and Andrich routes, in summer 2014. Another first winter ascent was completed on W Mexico Cabrones (1,150m, 33 pitches, VIII-) on Punta Tissi, first climbed in 2001, solo, by Venturino de Bona. Alexander Baù, Thomas Gianola, and Giovani Zaccaria, who had all climbed this route at various times in summer, combined forces to make the winter ascent with two bivouacs.

The Dolomites continue to be explored for ephemeral ice and mixed climbs, for which there still appears to be great potential for those able to snatch good conditions when they arrive. One of the foremost protagonists is Emanuele Andreozzi (Italy), who with various friends climbed three big new lines in the spring.

On the first day of April, with Matteo Faletti, Andreozzi tackled the north face of the Cimon della Pala (3,184m), an elegant spire in the Pale di San Martino group that is often referred to as the Matterhorn of the Dolomites. The pair followed a logical line up an obvious series of chimneys, gullies, and ramps to create Elements of Life (900m of climbing, AI5 M6). The ice was in excellent condition; the face receives no sun at this time of year, keeping the temperature well below freezing even when warm elsewhere.

The new route, to the right of Via degli Allievi (AI5 M4, Colomba-Vidoni, 2019), begins with a 100m icefall first climbed by an Italian team in January 2020. Above, it links lines of weakness and at one point traverses a spectacular shark's fin snow crest in the middle of the wall. The pair reached a notch on the summit ridge only 20m below the top, but, disappointingly, conditions prevented further progress—it was, after all, April Fool's Day. They rappelled and downclimbed from this point along the left side of the north face.

On the 20th of May, with winter long gone but the Dolomites still covered in deep snow, Andreozzi, Faletti, and Santi Padros (Spain) took advantage of the unusual conditions to climb a huge ice/mixed line on the north-northeast face of Cima Tosa (at 3,173m the highest peak in the Brenta Dolomites). This is the rock wall left of the

Santi Padros leads the M7 pitch 18 of Pazzione Primavernale on the north-northeast face of Cima Tosa. *Emanuele Andreozzi*

famous Canalone Neri (AD and skied from time to time). After camping below the face, the three left at 2:15 a.m. and took 16.5 hours to complete Pazzioni Primavernale (around 1,000m of climbing, 19 pitches, AI6 M7 90°+) to the summit plateau. They slid and downclimbed the Canalone Neri, regained the tent and skis, and were back at the road by 11 p.m.

The first half of this route follows the 1933 Castiglione-Detassis (IV and V), then traverses left to cross the Piaz Route (IV+/V, Michelson-Piaz, 1911) before leaving it to climb the right-hand of two huge, previously untouched chimneys. No gear was left on the route.

Ten days later, Andreozzi and Padros were below the northwest face of the Cima de Gasperi (2,994m) in the Civetta group. They had walked up to the Vazzoler Hut in relatively warm temperatures above green valleys, but when they stepped out of the winter room at 2:15 a.m., they met a hard frost. The goal was a huge gully/depression left of the northwest arête (750m, Andrich-Bianchet-Zancristoforo, 1935), and they were surprised to be able to climb the first 300m unroped. Things then became more intense, with a few hard and sometimes unprotected pitches. The climb finished up a large chimney, which proved to be easier than it had appeared from below. At the exit, they traversed left across the 1934 Benedetti-Zanutti route for three pitches to a col on the northeast ridge, which they reached after 9.5 hours climbing. From there it was a straightforward descent on snow to the hut. The route was named Alchimia (800m, 11 roped pitches, AI5+ M6+).

Swiss Alpine Rock

TWO NOTABLE FREE ascents of alpine rock routes took place in the summer/fall, both in Switzerland.

The steep, monolithic north face of the Petit Clocher du Portalet (2,823m), at the east end of the Mont Blanc Massif, has always been a forcing ground for free climbing. In 1989, Philippe Steulet climbed the old Darbellay aid route at 8a, the first time that a climb of the eighth grade had been established in the Western Alps. In 2001, Didier Berthod and Francois Mathey climbed a splitter crack on the orange wall left of the fourth pitch of Etat du Choc, the Remy brothers' 1983 strenuous crack feast (280m, nine pitches, 7a). Graded 7c+, this fantastic new pitch ended in the middle of nowhere.

Twenty years later, Fabian Borter and Bertrand Martenet bolted a continuation of the 2001 line, called Histoire sans Fin, on or close to the arête left of Etat du Choc. With the help of Berthod, who had recently returned to climbing after a long absence living in a monastery, they climbed the line but were not able to free it. This fell to Sébastien Berthe (Belgium), who redpointed the full route on August 6. After the first three pitches (6b+) of Etat du Choc and the 7c+ fourth pitch, the six new pitches are graded 7c, 8b+, 7c, 8b, 8a+, 6b+. His partner on this ascent was Siebe Vanhee, who returned on the 9th for his own redpoint. The two feel it may be the finest long granite route of this level in Europe.

Seeking little-frequented corners of the Alps during the early days of COVID-19, Peter von Känel and Silvan Schüpbach investigated the unclimbed west face of the Dündenhorn, above (and northeast of) Kandersteg in the Bernese Oberland. In the spring of 2020, the Swiss pair established an eight-pitch route on excellent limestone, protected entirely by traditional means.

Schüpbach came back in the fall to look at a better and more direct finish, checking out the final pitches from the top. In September 2021 he equipped the route with fixed ropes so he could work on a redpoint ascent. This took place on October 15, with the support of von Känel, when Schüpbach completed the sustained route Tradündition (8a, 7b+ obl), climbing the final pitch (6b) for the first time—the first free ascent was therefore also the first complete ascent of the route. Apart from cams and nuts, a few pitons and Peckers were used, all left in place to facilitate repeat ascents. The climbers feel their new line is probably the most difficult trad multi-pitch route in Switzerland. They would like to see the Dündenhorn remaining a bolt-free zone. 📄 📷

— LINDSAY GRIFFIN, AAJ

[Top] The Petit Clocher du Portalet and the superb arête taken by Histoire sans Fin. Immediately to the right, the prominent corner system is Etat du Choc. *Claude Remy* [Bottom] Silvan Schüpbach on pitch one (7c+) of Tradündition on the west face of the Dündenhorn. *Vladek Zumr*

POLAND / HIGH TATRAS

THE EXPANDER IN WINTER

SPRĘŻYNA ("SPRING") WAS the nickname of Polish climber Maciej Gryczyński—the name given because of his curly hair. In the 1960s he put up now well-known and classic routes on four mountains, and all four routes are called Sprężyna: the northeast face of Mały Młynarz (350m, climbed variously in 10 to 16 pitches, VI-/VI); the northeast face of Kocioł Kazalnicy (200m, 8 pitches, VI/VI+); the east face of Mnich (160m, 4–5 pitches, VII-); and the short but high-quality west face of Kościelec (90m, 3–4 pitches, VI+).

In the late 1980s, legendary Polish climber Krzysztof Pankiewicz came up with the idea of linking all four Sprężyna in a nonstop push. He achieved this with Piotr Panufnik in just 17 hours during September 1989. The routes are located in three separate valleys, and the link-up involves a total distance of 32km, crossing four passes, and 3,000m of ascent. The four Sprężyna have been thought of as the four springs on an old-fashioned "chest expander" exercise device, and the linkup is thus called The Expander.

The Expander was repeated in 23 hours during August 1996 by Krzysztof

Maciek Ciesielski on the first pitch of the 350-metetr Sprężyna route on Mały Młynarz, the start of the winter Expander link-up. *Kacper Tekiekli*

Bełczyński and Marcin Tomaszewski; by Czesław Szura, solo, in 23 hours during August 2014; and most recently by Łukasz Mirowski and Kacper Tekieli in 15 hours 52 minutes during July 2019. Although each route was climbed in winter decades ago, no one had completed the winter link-up. This fell to Maciek Ciesielski, Piotr Sułowski, and Kacper Tekieli, who completed The Expander in winter in 43 hours 50 minutes, from March 2–4, 2021.

The three took no bivouac gear, opting to travel as light as possible. On the first day they climbed Mały Młynarz free, and during the night Kocioł Kazalnicy, free at M7. The following day they climbed Mnich with some aid, and that night Kościelec, also with some aid. They had no support or preplaced caches. They had one hour of sleep and a few short breaks (a total of around three hours), and employed a strategy that involved the climber who was neither leading nor belaying having a nap.

Although all three were experienced at climbing long routes in a single push, they all "hit the wall" on this outing, fortunately not at the same time. 📷

— INFORMATION FROM **KACPER TEKIELI,** *POLAND*

TURKEY

Northeast face of Vayvay. Nessuno (2012) is off-picture to the left. (1) Turkish line (1997). (2) Ceschia-Perotti Route (1986). (3) Sessizlik (2021). *Misha Utkin*

VAYVAY MOUNTAIN, NORTHEAST FACE, NEW VARIATION

IT's HARD TO believe that in such a densely populated country, it is still possible to find places where there are no humans. We didn't see anyone during the five days we were in the Torasan group of the eastern Aladağlar. The only traces were cairns, a couple of pitons, and old descent slings.

Before our trip, we understood there were two routes on the northeast face of Vayvay Mountain (ca 3,600m): Nessuno (470m, 8a+, Giupponi-Larcher, 2012), located on the far left side, and the Ceschia-Perotti (1986), which weaves up the center of the wall. My partners Vitaly Todorenko, Egor Tsvetkov and I examined the wall with binoculars and saw what looked to be a solid new line.

We approached the face on August 1 and climbed the first pitch, fixing it for next morning. The next day, we jugged our rope and climbed eight more pitches (sending the crux 7a pitch in the dark). We fixed a line and descended to a big ledge to spend the night. The next morning we topped out on the ridge. We decided to skip three or four hours of ridge climbing to reach the summit and instead made one 60m rappel and then headed west and then north to Vayvay Pass. We descended a couloir and talus back east to reach our base camp.

Our route follows a natural line, but some sections required blade or beak pitons; we placed two bolts on the route. We named the route Sessizlik ("Silence," 500m, 7a) because, for all three of us, the silence of this place was very impactful. [*Editor's Note: In 1997, Turkish climbers Doğan Palut and Emre Altoparlak found a new start to the 1986 Italian route, angling in from the left and then climbing more directly in the middle (TD+). The 2021 ascent followed the Turkish line through the start and middle of the face, and then climbed independently to the top (about five or six new pitches) to the right of earlier ascents.*] 📷 🔍

— MISHA UTKIN, *UKRAINE*

ALADAĞLAR AND DEDEGÖL MOUNTAINS, NEW ROUTES: *In the autumn of 2020, Ukrainian climbers climbed several probable new routes in the Aladağlar and Dedegöl mountains. On the north face of Mt. Kaldı (3,734m), they climbed two routes on the same day in October: Nikita Balabanov and Slava Polezhaiko on one line, and Igor Chaplynksky, Mikhail Fomin, and Vitaly Todorenko on the other. Both teams bivouacked near the top of the wall and summited the next day; the routes were around 550m and D/TD 6a.*

In November 2020, Fomin and Todorenko traveled to the Dedegöl Mountains, northeast of Antalya, and climbed a very prominent chimney line on the main massif; they saw pitons early on their route, below the main difficulties, but nothing higher. The two climbed through the night and topped out at 6 a.m., making it back to the seacoast in time for dinner with their families. They called the 600m route Turkey Never Sleeps (TD+ 6c). — *Information from Mikhail Fomin* 📷

GEORGIA

Searching for the exit pitches high on Ushba during a Spanish team's first ascent of the Southwest Spur. In back is Mt. Elbrus, the highest peak in Europe. The rock tower in the background, directly above the climber, is the main top of Shkhelda (4,360m), also climbed by the Spanish group. *Spanish Mountaineering Team*

CAUCASUS MOUNTAINS

USHBA, SOUTHWEST SPUR; GULBA, SOUTH FACE, KHACHAPURI

WE HAD A fantastic trip to the Caucasus in June, undoubtedly helped in our goals by some very good weather. Our primary objective was to climb the main (south) summit of Ushba (4,710m), starting from the south via the Ushba Glacier. Our group consisted of four members of the Equipo Español de Alpinismo (Spanish Mountaineering Team)—Javier Guzmán, Mikel Inoriza, Rubén Sanmartin, and Bernat Vilarrasa, along with Roger Cararach, Alberto Fernández, and team director Mikel Zabalza. In the Caucasus there is very little infrastructure for climbing, with no lifts, so everything must be carried up from the valley. Logistically, it was interesting preparation for future expeditions.

With a lot of recent snowfall and warm temperatures, we found that some of the routes we had considered climbing on Ushba were running with water. We had to come up with another goal. We saw a very long spur on the southwest face that apparently was dry, and we decided the whole group would try the same route in three independent rope teams. Without any information other than our own intuition, we began to climb on June 19, always seeking out the weaknesses of the wall.

In the first 400m or more of ascent, we didn't find any evidence of previous climbers. [*The Spanish line was to the right of earlier routes on the lower southwest face; they likely intersected other routes in the vicinity of the upper ridge.*] The leader wore climbing shoes, while the seconds wore boots and carried the heavy packs. The rock was good in general, with decent protection except in a few sections. When we moved around the spur, we discovered a piton in an overhang, 500m

[Top] The line of Khachapuri (14 pitches plus scrambling), possibly the first route up the full south face of Gulba. *Spanish Mountaineering Team* [Bottom] Bernat Vilarrasa leads the crux 7b pitch on the south face of Gulba. Part of Ushba is seen behind. *Mikel Inoriza*

above the glacier. We finished the day in a perfect spot for a bivy at around 4,000m. We were all able to unrope and lie down—a total luxury.

We started very early the next day and traversed left through snow and ice in search of weaknesses. Here we climbed three magnificent pitches of nearly vertical rock and another mixed pitch before reaching the final ridge, which was covered in variable snow and corniced. With great caution, we got through this section and reached the summit at midday.

We descended via the Gabrieli (south ridge), which is the most common summit route. It wasn't easy to find the descent, since many of the rappels were covered in snow. On the way down, we met up with a team of Kyrgyz who were climbing the Gabrieli. They had a tent and were very surprised that we had climbed without one. We bivied lower than them under a rock that sheltered us from the annoying wind. The next day, with more rappels and downclimbs, we reached the Guli Glacier and then the village of Mazeri. The Espolón Sur-Oeste (Southwest Spur) was 1,500m, 6b+ M5.

We rested for two days and prepared for our next climbs. The weather continued to be excellent, but we knew change was brewing. One of our teams, Mikel Inoriza and Bernat Vilarrasa, went to the head of the Guli Glacier, where they completed a magnificent and difficult rock route on the south face of Gulba (3,725m). [*The history of climbing on Gulba is not well-documented, and it is possible this was the first route up the south face.*] Their route, Khachapuri, named for a Georgian cheese bread, was about 700m long (14 pitches plus scrambling), on solid rock, with difficulty up to 7b; they climbed completely clean.

The rest of the group decided to finish the trip by climbing Shkhelda (4,360m). The main peak of this complicated mountain appealed to us because of its big rock tower, which we approached via the southern flank. Toward the top we found a lot of old pitons and had to climb about 300m of rock with difficulties up to 6a/b. It seemed to have been many years since this peak had been climbed.

Visiting Georgia had been a great success. It felt a little like what climbing in the Alps might have been years ago. Without a doubt this was a fantastic experience on all levels.

— MIKEL ZABALZA, SPAIN, TRANSLATED BY PAM RANGER ROBERTS

TETNULDI, WEST FACE, FIRST WINTERTIME ASCENT

TETNULDI (4,860M) IS a beautiful peak in the Svaneti region of Georgia. The mountain's classic route is the south ridge, and the pyramidal west face is very attractive; its white profile can be seen from many places, even from Svaneti's administrative center in Mestia. For such an aesthetic face, it seems strange it was only climbed for the first time in 2011, by a large Georgian team.

After a lot of research on winter attempts on Tetnuldi, I discovered a single sentence in an Ivane Japaridze book describing an ascent in February 1958, following the original route up the south ridge. The mountain is well defended in winter by large amounts of snowfall, avalanche-prone slopes, and high wind.

The Czech Route on the west face of Tetnuldi (4,860 meters). The ascent in December began from a bivouac at 4,000 meters, at the base of the face . The descent was by the south ridge (right skyline). *Archil Badriashvili*

Giorgi Tepnadze and I tried to climb Tetnuldi in February 2019. We nearly got trapped at around 3,550m after two heavy snow days, and, still far from the summit, started our retreat. In the key couloir we triggered two avalanches, and with great effort we skied down hip-deep snow in the direction of Adishi village. To ski from 3,550m to 1,650m took two days.

In December 2021, I observed that recent stable weather likely had brought good conditions to Tetnuldi. I called Giorgi and Baqar Gelashvili, and we drove to Mestia. According to the old Georgian Orthodox calendar, it was the first day of winter.

On the 14th, starting at 2,600m, Giorgi and I snowshoed up the approach, while Baqar skied. It took us a day to reach 3,600m. On the second day we reached the bottom of the west face at around 4,000m. We decided we would climb the remaining 850m of the face directly by a steep, icy line first climbed in 2013 by Czechs.

We left behind our bivouac gear, hoping to make a round trip in a day. I led the first half of the face, and we all simul-climbed. We could see Mestia waking up at first light as Giorgi started to lead a diagonal traverse to the left, into the upper face. We climbed several pitches of steep ice (60–65°), really hard to penetrate. The wide upper bergschrund led to a continuously steep face, loaded with snow at first, then ice all the way up to the summit ridge.

A forecasted storm had arrived, and we suddenly were exposed to snow blowing from the northeast. The remaining 150m up the ridge were climbed in very poor visibility. After a total of nine hours, all three of us reached the top at 2:15 p.m. on December 16.

We climbed down the south ridge quickly but carefully to the shoulder and then to our bivouac. Baqar skied all the way down from 4,000m to 2,600m non-stop and very fast. Meanwhile, Giorgi and I put on our headlamps and struggled for the next several hours to find the way in blizzard and snow. By midnight we reached Baqar, who had waited for us, and drove together to Mestia.

– ARCHIL BADRIASHVILI, *GEORGIA*

KYRGYZSTAN

North face of Svarog (ca 5,000m) with (1) 2014 route (first ascent of the face) and (2) 2021 route. The face is about 1,000 meters high. *Expedition Photo*

ASHAT GORGE, SVAROG, NORTH FACE, NEW ROUTE

THE ASHAT GORGE is interesting not only for its natural beauty but also for its wall routes. The logistics are quite simple: Fly to Osh, get to Uzgurush by ground transport, say hello to Nurudin, load 265kg on five horses, pay the carriage for three days of travel, and end up walking two days. A base camp can be set up by the river, three to four hours of walking from the walls.

The highest peak in the region is Sabakh (5,300m), which has five routes of 25 to 30 pitches up its north wall. Our objective in 2021, Pik Svarog (39°34'41.0"N, 69°55'22.8"E), is about 300m shorter than Sabakh, but its north face is steeper, rising more than 1,000m above the bergschrund. On the left side of the wall is a huge roof. [*Svarog's elevation has been given as 4,960m and 5,100m; the 2021 team measured the summit as 5,000m with their GPS.*]

Until last summer, only one route had been climbed up the face: The Russian team of Vladislav Dubrovin, Vadim Kalinkin, Konstantin Markevich, and Dmitry Skotnikov spent 10 days in the summer of 2014 on their route, which they reported as having 1,250m of climbing (6B A3+). In 2014 and 2015, there were two attempts to climb this wall in winter by a team of Krasnoyarsk climbers, led by A. Zhigalov. Quite recently, a team of Chelyabinsk climbers made the second ascent of Markevich's route.

Even in midsummer, there is a lot of ice on the wall, and in some places there is snow on the ledges. It is best to climb in lightweight two-layer boots, comfortable for all kinds of technical terrain.

We were a combined team from Krasnoyarsk, Novosibirsk, and Moscow, consisting of Ratmir Mukhametzyanov, Alexander Parfyonov, Alexey Sukharev, Nikolai Stepanov, and Vyacheslav Timofeev. We packed the standard equipment: a dozen of that, a dozen of the other, and a drill and a bunch of bolts. We left bolts with nuts in especially difficult places, but without a hanger, because they are valuable and we had few of them. We used portaledges on the wall; there was snow or ice along the entire route, so we didn't have to carry water.

We began climbing on August 10 and reached the summit on August 13. Our route ascends the north face to the right of the 2014 line and completely independent of it.

The route began with a 500m ice slope (60–70°), interspersed with two rock bands of 20m and 30m, respectively, climbed in boots (no harder than 5c). The rock at the very bottom of the main wall was not as reliable as we would have liked. Once I had to drill holes in the wall to bypass loose blocks. After about 100m of rock climbing, we reached the site for our first bivouac.

The next day, aid climbing prevailed along a system of broken cracks and flakes. On the third day, we managed to overcome the prominent arching roof, overhanging 100° to 110°, with some drilling. Above this, we found vertical walls with fine cracks and inside corners with thin flows of ice. We spent a third night under a roof with a chimney. Above this, we began to encounter more snow-covered ledges and some corners with ice, making it possible to move faster. Before the ridge, there was a good pitch of ice (50m, 50–55°). After 36 pitches, we reached the ridge and continued easily to the top, returning to our high wall camp on the night of the 13th and to base camp on the 15th.

My personal impression is that I would not go back to this route. But I want to return to this wall! If I am lucky enough to be in this gorge again, I will climb another first ascent on this mountain. 🖸🔍

– **RATMIR MUKHAMETZYANOV,** *RUSSIA, WITH ADDITIONAL
INFORMATION FROM* **ANNA PIUNOVA,** *MOUNTAIN.RU*

KARAVSHIN REGION, ORTO-CHASHMA GORGE, PIK OSTRYI

IN THE SUMMER of 2021, Maria Dupina, Marina Popova, and I (all from Russia) made the first ascent of Pik Ostryi ("Sharp Peak," 4,818 m), located in the Orto-Chashma Gorge. Our expedition was supported by a Grit & Rock grant.

The Orto-Chashma Gorge is located between the better-known Karavshin and Lyailak gorges. There is a good path to the confluence of the Ak-Tyubek and Dukenek rivers. The latter is the easterly of the rivers flowing into the gorge, and higher along the Dukenek only local shepherds and their flocks walk; climbers rarely visit. Unnamed Pik 4,818m (39°35'06"N, 70°07'53"E), a beautiful granite needle, had caught our attention in a photo taken by trekkers. The mountain projects from a ridgeline extending to the southeast from Pik Alexander Blok toward Turo Pass, part of the frontier with Tajikistan.

After setting up base camp, we placed an assault camp right under the wall, by the glacier. We spent several days carrying loads to this camp, and after looking at various options, we decided to climb the steep east ridge.

On August 4, we left camp at about 4:30 a.m. and climbed up the shoulder under the ridge. At 6 a.m. we began the technical climbing, at first mostly easy but with short difficult passages (up to 6b), leading toward a huge roof line, which we skirted on the right. The terrain here was quite difficult, and due to bad weather (including falling snow) and wet rock, it was not possible to free climb it—a 50m section was aided. Above this, good cracks led back left and then up again; some additional aid was used in icy cracks here. No bolts were placed. In good weather, the entire route could be climbed free.

On top of the ridge, we leveled a site for a tent and spent the night. The next morning, at 8 a.m., we began to move along the ridge, passing to the left around gendarmes. Before the second

The first ascent of Pik Ostryi (4,818m) by the east ridge. The team traversed over the summit and descended to the col below Pik Alexander Blok (5,239m, partially visible behind), then back east to the glacier. *Oleneva Collection*

gendarme, we rappelled 20m to the left and then climbed back to the ridge. The length of the ridge was 400m (II-III). We were on top by 10 a.m.

Neither on the wall nor on top, nor on the descent, did we find any traces of other people, so we can say with confidence this was the first ascent: Russian 5B UIAA VII+ A3. The vertical gain was 550m, with a total length (including the summit ridge) of 1,020m.

We descended to the west toward Tro-Block Pass, then continued down to the glacier under the walls of Pik Alexander Blok, making eight 50m to 60m rappels in all.

— NADYA OLENEVA, *RUSSIA*

AK-SU VALLEY, PIK SLESOVA, AMERICAN WAY, SECOND FREE ASCENT

EMILY HARRINGTON AND husband Adrian Ballinger (USA) repeated The American Way on Pik Slesova (a.k.a. Russian Tower, 4,240m), a free line established by David Allfrey, Brent Barghahn, Nik Berry, and Eric Bissell in 2019. Climbing alongside a three-person film crew, Harrington freed the 950m, 5.13a route with only two falls; she led every pitch harder than 5.12a, and swapped leads with Ballinger on the rest of the climb.

— *INFORMATION FROM* EMILY HARRINGTON

KICHIK-ALAI, PIK SKOBELEV, NORTH SLOPES OF WEST TOP

IN AUGUST I led a team to the Kumtor area, where we climbed two summits in 2018 (*see AAJ 2019*). This time, we climbed the western top of the range's highest mountain, Pik Skobelev (5,051m, 39°47'33"N, 72°37'01"E), by what might be a new route. We followed a glacier coming down from Skobelev's north face and then up to the western shoulder, reached by a short, steep section with a bergschrund. From there we proceeded directly to the western top (4,986m) after a tiring ascent through fresh snow, with short sections of ice up to 35° (Russian 1B). We were thankful it had snowed every day for a week, because in dry weather the slope would be an ice shield and much more difficult.

From the western top you could follow the heavily corniced ridge to the main summit (perhaps two hours), but we did not try this. The team comprised myself leading Stanislav Cmiel, Marketa Rusniokova, Rostislav Slouf, Tomas Walach, and Lucie Zaklasnikova. 📷 🔍

— MICHAL KLESLO, *CZECH REPUBLIC*

PAMIR / ZAALAISKIY RANGE

KOMANSU VALLEY, PIK 5,265M

A GROUP THAT I led visited the Komansu Valley in August and climbed a minor peak of 5,265m (39°23'59"N, 72°49'15"E) between 60 Years of October Pass and 30 Years of Uzbek SSR Peak. Its icy summit is clearly visible from the last pastures in the valley, at 4,050m, and the western ridge is the obvious route to the summit. In good

Pik 5,265m (Czechoslovak Legions Peak). *Michal Kleslo*

snow conditions you simply follow the ridge (up to 45°, 2A). If there is ice you might need a rope, ice axes, and ice screws in steep sections, and it could be 2B. We found large crevasses under the summit that we passed on the right-hand side. From the summit you get fantastic views over the Komansu Valley to the west and across to nearby Lenin Peak (7,134m) in the east.

Back in Osh we discussed our climb with Kyrgyz and Kazakh climbers who think this peak might have remained unclimbed in previous years, as it is not very high. We gave it the name Czechoslovak Legions Peak. The altitude on the old Soviet map is 5,265m, but according to our GPS it was 5,245m. The group was Antonin Borovka, David Brezovjak, Stanislav Cmiel, Leszek Kocurek, Marketa Rusniokova, Zdenek Skorepa,Tomas Walach, and Lucie Zaklasnikova. 📷 🔍

— MICHAL KLESLO, *CZECH REPUBLIC*

TIEN SHAN / ALA ARCHA

PIK SIMAGINA, NORTH FACE AND EAST RIDGE, AQUADISKOTHEQUE

ON FEBRUARY 18, Anatoly Syshchikov from Yekaterinburg, Pavel Tkachenko from Chita, and I from Irkutsk (the latter two cities close to Lake Baikal in Siberia) climbed a new route on the north face of Pik Simagina (4,400m), the summit immediately east of Svobodnaya Korea (Pik Free Korea, 4,778m). Although this was a great time for winter ascents in the area, there were few people, and the huts were almost empty. High flight costs within Russia and Asia due to the pandemic were leaving their mark.

We began to the left of the lowest point of the bergschrund, then slanted up left for five pitches, following the ice slope between the bergschrund and the walls above. On the fourth pitch we needed to make a pendulum across steep ice around the base of a rock spur. We then climbed a broad snow couloir through the lower rocks of the face for more than 200m. A ramp led up left toward a big chimney system slanting in the same direction to the east ridge. Four mixed pitches up this chimney system (70° M5, 70° M5, 80° M5 A2, and 80° M5) led to the ridge. For the belay below the last of these pitches, we placed two bolts, and on the pitch below this we found it necessary to climb very carefully due to large loose blocks.

The north face of Pik Simagina, showing Aquadiskotheque (5A, 2021). Two routes (Belinski and Polivoi, both from 1969) climb the buttress just left of the big couloir. *Alexey Boyko*

We climbed along the loose east ridge for around 300m (moves up to III+) to the summit, from which we continued to follow the 1990 Rodikov Route (4B) steeply west to the col before Free Korea, then down the north couloir to the glacier.

The new route, which we named Aquadiskotheque, has a vertical interval of 550m, a climbing length of 995m, and a grade of 5A M5 A2. We think a fit and competent party should manage the climb in 15 to 17 hours (not including the approach and descent, which will add a further five or six hours). Winter is a logical time for this route; in summer it would be too threatened by rockfall.

— ALEXEY BOYKO, *RUSSIA*

Pik Kosmos (5,942m) from the north, showing the first ascent route (red line). The 1,800-meter climb took five days, with another two days to descend (yellow line). At right is Pik Rototayev. *Alexander Gukov*

PIK KOSMOS
FIRST ASCENT BY THE NORTH FACE

BY DAMIEN GILDEA *(AAJ) AND* ALEXANDER GUKOV, *RUSSIA*

RUSSIAN CLIMBERS ALEXANDER Gukov and Victor Koval made what is almost certainly the first ascent of Pik Kosmos (a.k.a. Pik Schmidta, 5,942m, 41°00'16"N, 77°37'01"E), by a difficult route on the impressive north face. The peak rises at the head of the western branch of the Grigoriev Glacier, along the frontier with China, near the center of the Western Kokshaal-too range.

In mid-September, the pair acclimatized by camping on the summit of Pik Uchitel (4,540m) in Ala Archa National Park and then traveled to the Kokshaal-too over the next two days and approached up the Grigoriev Glacier. Like other parties who had eyed Kosmos, the pair found the seracs on the face to be extremely active and thought it might even be too dangerous to attempt, but eventually scoped a route in the center of the lower face that connected the lower and upper glaciers. Their line also bypassed difficult rock, as they knew the short days of late season would preclude slow aid climbing.

After bivying below the wall at 4,100m, the pair started up on the morning of September 26, simul-climbing through the lower section and pitching ice up to 75°, before reaching the first glacial serac, where Gukov was hit by falling ice but not seriously hurt. Climbing left and then back right around the serac, they ascended the 50° slope above and reached their first bivy site around 5 p.m., at 4,600m. They placed the tent under a protective rock wall, but it was damaged by rockfall in the night.

The next day the pair chose the left of two possible ice couloirs and climbed 10 pitches before again stopping at 5 p.m. to bivy, at around 5,060m. Early on their third day, one of the large seracs in the upper right-hand side of the face released with a roar, but they were out of range. The two moved up steepening ice, including a 20m overhanging stretch. Realizing they would not reach the ridge that day, they stopped early at 5,460m to cut a small ledge in the ice for a sitting bivouac. They nested their two sleeping bags and shared them for warmth, but spindrift began hitting them in the middle of the night, and eventually Koval got too wet and decided to stand on the ledge until dawn.

Day four saw them continue all day in the central gully before exiting onto the west ridge at

5,820m at 5 p.m. Disappointingly, they found the ridge very sharp and again needed two hours to dig a site for their tent, which was buffeted by high winds through the night. The two braced the walls with their bodies and attempted to dry their sleeping bags over the flame of their stove.

On September 30, they continued up the summit ridge, finding it very difficult along broken rock. At one point they dropped down onto the north side to traverse, before being forced back up onto the ridge. At 4:50 p.m. Gukov and Koval reached the summit, where their GPS read 5,957m, then began descending the east ridge, needing numerous rappels to reach the high northeastern plateau, where they eventually stopped at 10 p.m. and camped in a crevasse. The next two days were spent in an increasingly exhausted and desperate state, rappelling and navigating down through steep and crevassed terrain to finally reach their camp, friends, and safety, a week after leaving. The pair rated their 1,800m climb ED WI4 (2,600m climbing distance).

This mountain has officially been called Pik Schmidta, but it is popularly known as Kosmos. Earlier, it was known as Pik Dankova. In the 1960s it became apparent that another mountain 8km northeast across the Grigoriev Glacier, at 5,982m, was the highest in the area, and the name Dankova was transferred to that peak while the 5,942m peak became Pik Schmidta.

For some years there has been conjecture over whether Kosmos/Schmidta had been previously climbed. Research in the 1990s seemed to indicate it was climbed in the 1980s by a Soviet military team, but it now appears at least two old images in Soviet mountaineering archives with routes marked on the mountain were likely showing *proposed* routes—one a traverse, one a direct route up the north face—which needed to be submitted for approval before departure, and not lines that had actually been climbed.

Various unsuccessful attempts were made in the post-Soviet era, via the southeast ridge (2019), the north face (1998), and the northwest ridge, between Kosmos and Pik Rototayev (1995 and 2014; see AAJ 2015). It seems most likely the Gukov-Koval climb was the first ascent of the mountain. 📷

EDITOR'S NOTE: *This report was adapted from a longer story by Alexander Gukov, with his assistance.*

[Top] Day one of the climb involved navigating around and over dangerous serac bands. [Bottom] Once on the summit ridge, the difficulties did not end, with a long traverse over technical terrain and very loose rock. *Gukov Collection*

Joris Korevaar below In Libido Veritas VI (5,030m GPS), showing the first ascent up the south face and west ridge. *Arjen Pieters*

The Kayindy has been explored by a number of expeditions over the years, with the first Western team arriving in 1995. Most of the summits that have been reached are located toward the upper (east) end of the valley. We decided to explore some mountains farther west.

We took a 4WD from Inylchek to a settlement at about 2,720m in the Kayindy Valley, where we were able to arrange for a horseman and three horses (this felt like a lucky break) to carry gear to our base camp at 3,200m at the base of the main glacier. This was about a 10-hour walk. The same horseman picked us up—one day late—at the end of expedition.

For our first climb, we placed a high camp at 4,100m alongside a glacier running up to the south from the main valley, which we called the Schuur Glacier after our weather guru back home. On August 20, we departed this camp and climbed 600m, keeping mostly to the left side of the glacier, to reach the col at its head. From here, we climbed the east ridge of a summit marked 5,449m on the Russian map (42°00'39.0"N, 79°37'00.9"E), mostly on steep snow with a few icy patches. During the last 200m we were surprised by some ups and downs in the ridge, but at 8:30 a.m. we reached summit, which we measured at 5,360m on our GPS watch. We called the mountain Pik Nooter, named after a climbing mentor, and graded our route AD. We descended the way we came.

We started our next attempt on August 22 from a high camp at 4,050m below an unclimbed peak (42°05'55.1"N, 79°34'33.5"E) on the north side of the Kayindy Valley. We started up the southeast face but retreated because of avalanche danger. Before heading back to base camp, we inspected the south face for a later attempt.

On August 30 at 2 a.m., starting from the same high camp, we climbed the steeper south face, finding extraordinary 50–60° ice, for which we roped up on the last 100m. We reached the west ridge at 4,600m and continued up through deep, soft snow. We summited at 9 a.m. and descended the same way, rappelling the south face using Abalakov anchors. We called the mountain In Libido Veritas VI (5,030m GPS) and graded our route D.

We also made an attempt on Peak 5,061m (42°02'04.0"N, 79°34'57.7"E), starting from the Merzbacher Glacier, one valley to the east of the Schuur Glacier. The Irish QUBMC expedition had attempted this mountain in 2016 three times but failed because of poor conditions and steep seracs on the east ridge. We had more or less the same plan, and from a high camp at 4,100m on the glacier we climbed to 4,900m, just below a steep serac, where the snow conditions became very poor. With limited options for belaying, we decided to turn around.

For our final climb of the expedition, we headed west from base camp toward a peak marked 4,669m on the old Russian map, located on the south side of the valley (42°01'13.3"N, 79°29'28.5"E). The climbing was mostly boring deep snow in beautiful scenery until the last 50m, where steeper ice and a few meters of loose rock made things a bit more spicy. We descended the same way after completing the first known ascent of Punta Margarita (4,590m GPS, AD). [*Editor's Note. These climbers have prepared an excellent online map of the Kayindy Valley, labeling climbed and unclimbed peaks. This can be found at the AAJ website.*] 🔗 🔗

— ARJEN PIETERS, *NETHERLANDS*

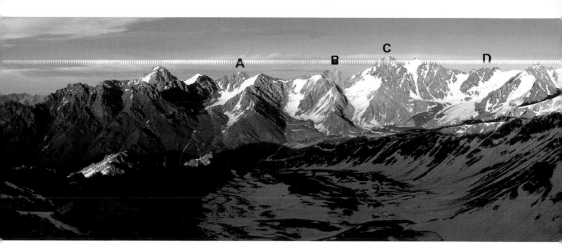

Looking east to high peaks of the Tuyuk-su basin, including (A) Manshuk Mametovoy (4,194m), (B) Mayakovskogo (4,208m), (C) Ordzhonikidze (4,410m), and (D) the pinnacles of Igli Tuyuk-Su (4,213m). The first day of the 27-kilometer traverse crossed rocky peaks on the left of the photo. *Kirill Belotserkovsky*

KAZAKHSTAN

TIEN SHAN / ZAYLIYSKIY ALATAU

TUYUK-SU TRAVERSE

FROM SEPTEMBER 14–16, Kirill Belotserkovskiy completed the first known traverse of the rugged crest of the Tuyuk-Su cirque, 25km southeast of Kazakhstan's ex-capital, Almaty. As a guide in the area, Belotserkovskiy has climbed all of this group's peaks and most of its routes, and he had previously attempted the traverse once before with a partner who was not sufficiently acclimatized for the effort.

Starting from the Tuyuk-Su base camp, Belotserkovskiy moved clockwise around the cirque. He gained the crest and headed south on day one, climbing seven peaks and using the rope only to rappel after one of the summits. Following a bivy at Manshuk Mametovoy pass, his route took him over seven peaks and several technical routes, including the north ridge of Manshuk Mametovoy (4,194m, Russian 3B), the north ridge of Mayakovskogo (4,208m, 3A), Pik Ordzhonikidze (4,410m), and Pik Partisan (4,390m). His second bivouac was at Igli Pass.

The final day started with the most technical climbing of the route, crossing the rock spires of Igli Tuyuk-Su (4A), where he hauled his pack twice. However, the non-technical terrain that followed would prove to be the most exhausting, as he continued late into the evening, climbing 10 summits over nearly 14km. He returned to Tuyuk-Su base camp 20 hours after starting the day at Igli Pass.

Belotserkovskiy carried an "anorexic" rack and free soloed most of the routes on the traverse. In all, he covered 27.3km and gained 3,742 vertical meters. 🔍

— *INFORMATION FROM* **KIRILL BELOTSERKOVSKIY,** *KAZAKHSTAN*

Tiphaine Duperier on the lower section of the northwest ridge of Darchan, one of three peaks skied above the Bulche Glacier, northeast of Gilgit. *Boris Langenstein*

DARCHAN AND GARMUSH I AND II: NEW ROUTES AND SKI DESCENTS

AFTER FOUR CANCELED flights and a week in the hot atmosphere of Islamabad, waiting for our skis to arrive, Boris Langenstein, Aurelia Lanoe, Guillaume Pierrel, and I finally reached Gilgit on June 2. Our main goal was a ski descent of Gasherbrum II (see p.267). However, we didn't want to get bored going up and down on the same route for acclimatization, and we also wanted to experience new places, so our plan was to acclimatize during 15 days split between two different areas.

We had hoped to explore the Chiantar Glacier in the Hindu Raj, but a transport strike forced us to change plans. Instead, we went first to the Bagrot Valley, 30km northeast of Gilgit, on the south side of Diran (7,266m) in the Rakaposhi Range, hoping to ski new lines. Half a day's walk along the Bulche (Burche) Glacier took us to a base camp at 3,342m on a fine meadow. In order to see the possibilities, we climbed and skied a 4,800m summit, directly above base camp, via the west ridge. We found late-spring conditions, with the snowline at around 4,000m, and spotted two interesting summits a little over 5,000m. We decided to leave base camp for four days to attempt these two peaks.

Everything worked as planned, despite high temperatures. First, we climbed Darchan (5,347m GPS, 36°1'35.32"N, 74°42'35.38"E). [*Labeled as 5,500m on the Polish orographic map "Rakaposhi-Malubiting Mountains," this summit was first climbed in 1976 from the east by an Italian team; the 2021 ascent is likely a new route.*] We climbed the northwest ridge and skied down. The snow conditions were horrible, and the top section was relatively steep (45°).

We then moved camp to 4,573m on the west ridge of an unnamed 5,040m summit, immediately south of Darchan. We climbed to the summit and skied the airy west ridge. It was 55° at the top, decreasing to 45° at the base, and gave us a breathtaking view of the Bulche peaks (6,950m and 6,700m) and Diran. Happy to have seen this cool spot quite close to Gilgit, we moved on toward Darkot in the Hindu Raj.

We arrived in Darkot village on June 11 with only five days before our scheduled journey to the Baltoro. To make the most of this short time, we opted not to take porters; slow and heavy, we walked 10km on good shepherds' paths to the northeast of Darkot. At first it was disappointing. The mountains looked very dry, with the snowline up at 4,700m. At least snow conditions would be safe. We stopped for the night at the last flat place with clear spring water (3,674m) and made our second camp at 5,142m on the snow-covered glacier at the base of the west flank of Garmush Zom I (6,244m).

On the 13th we climbed directly up the northwest couloir of Garmush Zom I, finishing up the north ridge. Fortunately, the snow was hard enough not to be exhausting, but monster cornices on the summit ridge blocked any view of the Chiantar Glacier on the other side. We needed to wait for the sun to soften the snow in the couloir, but the cold and altitude made us leave the summit earlier than desirable. Our descent

Southwest face of Garmush Zom II with the line of the ascent and ski descent, seen from the approach. *Tiphaine Duperier*

therefore was far from how we had dreamed but proved a good exercise in steep skiing—1,100m between 55° and 45°.

Excited by our success, we moved camp to the south, at 4,711m on the glacier directly below Garmush Zom II (a.k.a. Garmush Zom South, 6,180m). There was a 1,400m leftward-curving couloir on the southwest face. The ascent was harder and more technical than the day before, with the first 500m on steep avalanche debris. The following 200m had icy sections, and then we started to break through the surface to calf depth. A final 30m of mixed led us to the summit ridge, where we could finally see the Chiantar. We skied from the summit, crossing the mixed section with a rappel. The ground below was again a good technical exercise. The snow proved hard to anticipate—sometimes firm, sometimes crusty.

Going down the beautiful valley, beside a powerful river, I thought how lucky we had been to find what we came for: steep skiing in remote locations. 📖 📷

— **TIPHAINE DUPERIER**, *FRANCE*

HISTORICAL NOTES ON GARMUSH PEAKS: *Garmush Zom I was first climbed in 1975 via the southwest ridge by three Austrian climbers. In 2007, a Korean team climbed a similar line, crossing the toe of the southwest ridge and climbing more on the northwest flank. The 2021 French party climbed the northwest flank directly from the glacier, possibly following much of the same ground as the Koreans.*

Garmush Zom II was first climbed in 2000 by four Italians—Alberto Peruffo, Enrico Peruffo, Michele Romio, and Mirco Scarso—via the complex and long east ridge (D), approached from the south. (They proposed renaming it Casarotto Peak after the Italian alpinist.) The 2021 French party most likely made the second ascent of this peak by a new route. Snowy Garmush North (6,048m) appears to have no known ascent.

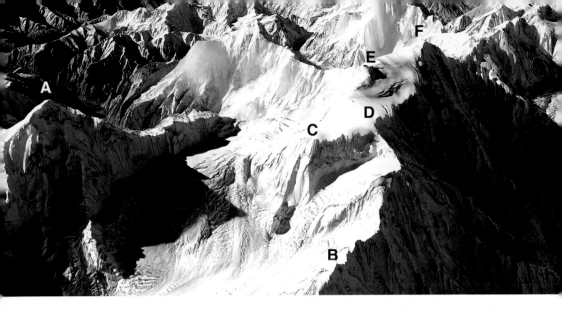

Looking west at (A) Shispare, (B) Darmyani (a.k.a. Needle Peak or Maidon Sar), (C) Passu Diar East, (D) Passu North, (E) Passu Diar, and (F) Passu Sar. *Google Earth Image*

BATURA MUZTAGH

PASSU DIAR, NORTHWEST FACE; PASSU NORTH, FIRST ASCENT VIA SOUTH FLANK; DARMYANI, SOUTH RIDGE

THE BATURA WALL rises more than 4,500m from the Hunza Valley to the south and stretches around 40km without ever dropping below 6,000m. I first set eyes on this playground in 2020, but with the COVID-19 pandemic in full bloom, the climbing season came to a quick end for me. Keen to explore this seldom-visited massif, I returned to Pakistan in the summer of 2021.

On July 11 my good friend Hassan Aljabbal and I started walking west up the Batura Glacier to climb the majestic Darmyani (Needle Peak, a.k.a. Maidon Sar, 6,090m). We gained the Passu Cwm via a new route on the north ridge of Hiriz (5,550m; for a history of both peaks see *AAJ 2018*). At this point, Hassan decided to stay at our high camp while I attempted Darmyani's east ridge, turning back at 5,900m due to dangerous snow conditions.

The following day I turned my focus to the unclimbed south ridge of Darmyani. I gained the ridge via a snow and rock gully at 5,200m and made good progress over mixed ground to a final delicate pitch of UIAA IV and onto the summit.

A few days later I attempted the rock tower of Bublimotin (a.k.a. Lady's Finger, 6,000m) from a camp on the Hasanabad Glacier to the west. I climbed 1,400m on 60° ice, reaching 5,800m by daybreak. Caught out by the power of the Karakoram sun, I found myself climbing a waterfall with blocks of ice hurtling by, so I carved a small hole into the ice and took shelter for the day. Having no food or bivouac gear to continue, I descended.

On September 1, now well acclimatized and carrying 35kg of kit, I set off to repeat Passu Diar (7,295m), which has seen few ascents. [*Generally, these have been from the Upper Passu Glacier and Passu Terrace, finishing up the northeast flank.*] Using skis for the approach, I broke trail through a complicated icefall to reach the Upper Passu Glacier and set up a high camp at 6,500m. On the 11th, I reached the Passu Terrace and continued to the saddle at the start of the southeast ridge of Passu Sar. I then headed back up the northwest face of Passu Diar, climbing a 70° pitch of snow and ice over a serac and then continuing 300m up easy ground to the summit.

A day later, I skinned up the gentle south flank of Passu North (6,884m), making the probable first ascent of this remote peak. [*In 1985, a Japanese expedition reportedly climbed the south flank/ridge of Passu Diar East (6,842m), a southeastern subsummit of Passu North.*]

The Batura Muztagh has phenomenal climbing potential, and the proximity to the Karakoram Highway and the kindness of the local population make it even more desirable. 📗 📷

— JAMES PRICE, *U.K.*

EDITOR'S NOTE: *The Passu peaks have been given various names over the years, but we have used those designated by the Polish cartographer Jerzy Wala on his recent maps, and by the German historian Wolfgang Heichel in his Chronik der Erschließung des Karakorum (Part 1).*

GHUJERAB MOUNTAINS

KARUN KOH GROUP, SAMI SAR (PEAK 6,032M), NORTH RIDGE

COVID-19 APPEARED TO settle down during November, and Takuya Mitoro and I decided to go climbing overseas. It would be our first trip for at least two years. With the summer season in the Karakoram already passed, we opted to try some winter ascents in the Karun Koh area.

Every time I attempted my dream mountain, Shispare (7,611m, climbed in 2017 on my fourth attempt, see *AAJ 2018*), I had gazed north at Karun Koh (variously 7,164m or 6,977m). To be honest, I had not gone there because most of the peaks in that area were below 7,000m. However, given the strong winds and cold temperature of the winter months, this lower area seemed the best place to restart our Karakoram exploration.

Researching the area more extensively, I discovered that Japanese climbers had twice attempted a 6,000m peak about 4km north of Karun Koh, in 2015 and 2016. Peak 6,032m (Peak 243 or Maqbul Sar on Jerzy Wala's sketch map of the Karun Koh Mountains) is at 36°38'55.58"N, 75°04'03.66"E. During the second attempt, Sami Ullah Khan, a climber from Pakistan, had lost his life.

Takuya and I left Japan on December 3 and trekked up the Unakin-i-Gur Valley to a base camp at the end of the tongue of the Unakin Glacier at around 4,200m. Although it was still outside the

(A) Mario Sar (6,210m), climbed in 2019 by a Polish team. (B) Sami Sar (6,032m). (C) Karun Koh (7,164m/6,977m). Red line: The 2016 Japanese attempt, showing Camp 1 (D) and the high point (H), scene of an accident that killed Sami Ullah Khan. Yellow lines: The 2021 ascent, continuing to the summit. *Wataru Takasaki*

Uli Biaho Gallery from the Trango Glacier. The 2014 Ecuadorian route takes a parallel line to the right. Four other routes have been climbed close to the left arête. *Marcin Tomaszewski*

We made our first bivouac beneath the face and the following day started our 11-day climb, reaching the top on December 16. Temperatures down to around -30°C and spindrift made the climb very slow; each day we were able to aid only one or two pitches. The route was 16 pitches, and only four of these were free (up to M7). The remaining terrain was too challenging to be free climbed due to sand-filled cracks or offwidths. We placed nine 10mm bolts for rappelling and hauling.

We climbed capsule-style, with our second bivouac at the top of pitch six. We fixed 400m of rope above this and then set off for a summit push. We had estimated the top to be 70m above the end of the ropes, but fore-shortening misled us, and we had to climb three long pitches, almost 150m. In the upper chimney we found bolts from the Ecuadorian route Freetanga Ecuatoriana (2014), which we joined for 1.5 pitches before climbing direct where the Ecuadorian route moves left.

We named our route Frozen Fight Club (700m of climbing, M7 A3). The climb has no extreme difficulties and offers beautiful, solid, and exposed terrain; it has potential to be free climbed in summer. However, one needs lots of determination to reach the top in winter conditions.

— DAMIAN "DANY" BIELECKI *AND* MARCIN "YETI" TOMASZEWSKI, *POLAND*

PRAQPA RI CENTRAL, ATTEMPTS

FROM MID-JULY TO late August, Martin Sieberer (Austria) and I attempted to reach unclimbed Praqpa Ri Central (7,156m), to the west of K2. Even while approaching the mountain, we noticed "monsoon-like" weather, with elevated temperatures and almost daily precipitation. On the Praqpa Glacier, hoping to find a way toward the sharp northwest ridge, we ground to a halt in water-soaked snow. We camped, hoping to continue if there was an appreciable drop in temperature, but the next day we retreated.

Later we tried the east flank, already climbed to the 7,026m southeast top by Chileans in 2017 (*AAJ 2018*), hoping to continue their route to the main summit. We climbed through the night to reach broad Khalkhal Pass (5,701m) on the east-southeast ridge. After resting the whole day on August 11, we continued at night, but then met unconsolidated powder, which we were unable to protect. In the last few days of the trip, we made another attempt on this route, but the result was the same: Bad conditions forced us down from 6,000m.

Our expedition was not only horribly unsuccessful but also depressing. Climate change is affecting the high ranges of our planet, and the climbing season for 6,000m and 7,000m peaks has now likely shifted to the autumn.

— SIMON MESSNER, *ITALY*

GASHERBRUM II, FIRST SKI DESCENT OF FRENCH SPUR; GASHERBRUM I SKI ATTEMPT

FOLLOWING ACCLIMATIZATION WITH climbs and ski descents in the southern Rakaposhi Range and Eastern Hindu Raj (see p.256), Boris Langenstein, Aurélia Lanoé, Guillaume Pierrel, and I transferred to Skardu, trekked up the Baltoro Glacier, and on June 26 were installed at Gasherbrum base camp at 5,040m. Our plan was to ascend and then ski the rarely climbed French (central) spur on the south face of Gasherbrum II (8,035m).

Our first foray on the south spur, at the end of June, only took us to 6,560m instead of the hoped-for 7,000m. On July 8, we returned to this elevation and spent the night. Deep snow and technical ground prevented us from reaching the plateau at 7,200m next day, and we camped at 6,949m. On the 10th we continued to the plateau; the exit from the top of the spur was a 50° couloir of thin snow over ice, and a rotten rock ridge. We continued a little further and camped at 7,321m.

On the morning of the 11th, snow driven by a westerly wind had buried the tents. Breaking trail through deep snow, we reached the summit at 11:30 a.m. and spent two hours there before starting our ski descent. The snow on the way back to our top camp was horrible. Once there, we decided to keep going. The couloir was the technical crux: There was barely any snow on the top section, and we had to make a 30m rappel to access it. We returned to our 6,949m site, camped for the night, and the following day were able to ski all the way to base camp.

With only a little time left, Boris and I made a lightweight attempt to ski the Japanese Couloir on Gasherbrum I (8,080m). On the 17th we tried to make a summit push of 1,600m, but ground to a halt at 7,720m, too fatigued to make the top that day. We skied from that point with one 30m rappel and the next day were in base camp.

[Top] (A) Gasherbrum II (8,035m), (B) Gasherbrum II East (7,772m), and (C) Peak 7,103m. (1) The Normal (Austrian) Route (1956). (2) Line skied by Thierry Renard in 1985. (3) French Spur (1975). [Bottom] Climbing the French Spur of Gasherbrum II. Across the glacier is the northeast face of Gasherbrum VI and behind it the trapezoidal summit of Chogolisa. *Tiphaine Duperier*

– TIPHAINE DUPERIER, *FRANCE*

EDITOR'S NOTE: *In 1975 a 14-member French expedition climbed the central spur on the south face, with Marc Batard and Yannick Seigneur first to reach the top. This was the second ascent of Gasherbrum II. The first ski descent of Gasherbrum II took place in August 1984, when Patrice Bournat (France) and Wim Pasquier (Switzerland) descended the complete Normal (Austrian) Route on the southwest ridge. The following year Thierry Renard skied the south face from the summit, west of the central spur.*

MASHERBRUM MOUNTAINS

HONBORO MASSIF, BONDIT PEAK, NORTHEAST SPUR ATTEMPT

JAPANESE CLIMBERS TAKAYASU Semba and Shinji Tamura attempted the northeast spur of Bondit Peak (formerly called Muntin and a little less than 6,000m in altitude). After trekking two days up the Kande Valley, they made base camp at 4,430m and started up the glacier, finding soft, deep snow and many crevasses. They made camps at 5,100m and 5,400m, and reached a high point of 5,500m before descending after 30cm of snow fell overnight, increasing the avalanche risk. Their full report is at the AAJ website. 📄 📷

— *INFORMATION FROM* **SHINJI TAMURA**

The Biarchedi group seen from high on Laila Peak to the south-southeast. Ralf Dujmovits and Nancy Hansen followed the route shown in an attempt to reach the Biarchedi South Glacier (hidden), which flows down from (A) Biarchedi I (6,810m) and (B) Biarchedi II. (C) is Biarchedi IV. (D) K2. *Luca Pandolfi*

BIARCHEDI I, ATTEMPT FROM SOUTHEAST

OUR TRIP IN June to attempt unclimbed Biarchedi I (6,810m) can be summed up in two words: bad weather. One day after Ralf Dujmovits and I reached base camp, after a trek under clear blue skies, the weather turned for the worse, and in the 28 days that followed, only three were without precipitation. Luckily, the frequent snowstorms came without wind, and we had enough visibility between storms to make some progress.

Base camp was on a terrace at 4,550m, halfway between the Dalsampa and Huispang trekking camps on the north side of the Gondogoro (a.k.a. Gondokhoro) Glacier. We placed Camp 1 at a safe site at 5,350m, looking across the Gondogoro Glacier to Laila Peak. Above us were two small cols separated by a rocky outcrop. We hoped one of these cols would give access to the Biarchedi South Glacier, flowing down from Biarchedi I and II.

We first ventured to the left (southwest) col at 5,575m, but found a huge cornice running the length of the col, making this option a no-go. We reached the right (northeast) col at 5,650m, but extremely limited visibility did not allow us to see whether we could safely descend the far side. We returned to base camp.

After several days of waiting, six days of good weather were promised. We headed up again with high hopes and heavily laden packs, weaving between many hanging seracs. But after just a few hours the weather deteriorated, and it snowed continuously for the next two days, dumping yet another 40cm. In mostly whiteout conditions, we retraced our route to the right-hand col and waited for visibility that never arrived. Our rather uncertain impression was that we might have to descend 300m of steep terrain to reach the Biarchedi South Glacier. We left without ever having seen the mountain. I do want to thank the Grit & Rock Award for supporting the trip.

There are other potential options for approaching Biarchedi I. There is an east-facing glacier between the mountain and the Huispang camp. Its 300m headwall will likely involve mixed climbing, but this access will land you much higher up the Biarchedi South Glacier. The big problem with this east-facing approach is that it will barely freeze in early summer; later, the icefall could be tricky.

A second option is via the Baltoro and Yermanendu glaciers, then over the Masherbrum La. This would have to be done in early season to maximize snow covering and therefore minimize crevasse problems. We met a group that had just trekked from Askole to Hushe over the Masherbrum La, finishing in early June, so it is possible early in the season. However, it is very long. Hard-core alpinists may find other options directly from the Baltoro Glacier. 📄 🔲 🔍

– NANCY HANSEN, *CANADA*

TAGAS MOUNTAINS

NANGMA VALLEY, PEAK 5,007M (ATTEMPT), ASTERISK

SEVERAL UNNAMED PEAKS line the Nangma Valley, one of which Jonathan Schaffer and I attempted to climb in August. [*This mountain, at approximately 35°21'58.82"N, 76°29'24.54"E, is labeled Peak 19, 5,007m, on Jerzy Wala's orographic map of the K6 Group.*] Our climb on the northwest face gained around 600m and consisted of almost all things: scrambling, slab, offwidth, runouts, goat poop, choss, snow, ice, stuck ropes, and midnight rappels—even a point of aid where I was too lazy to don crampons for an icy bit. What was missing was a summit.

From our high point, an impenetrable slab separated us from glory: nary a divet on which to find purchase, nor a seam to afford protection. With the right wind, I could have peed on the summit. But I didn't, and we went down. We named the route to our high point Asterisk (5.10 A0).

We were in the Nangma primarily to attempt the north ridge of Shingu Charpa (ca 5,900m), and like so many before, did not get to the summit. We made it around two-thirds of the way up the mountain before rime-plastered rock and generally poor conditions thwarted our attempt.

– PETE FASOLDT, *USA*

Approximate line of Asterisk, almost to the summit of Peak 5,007m, seen from base camp. *Jonathan Schaffer*

Looking northwest from the top bivouac, at around 6,000m, during the first ascent of Korada North. The pyramid in the background is Drifika (6,447m). *Tim Exley*

KORADA NORTH AND KAPURA CENTRAL
TWO NEW ROUTES OUT OF THE NANGMA VALLEY

BY WILL LEWALLEN, *U.K.*

ON AUGUST 28, Tim Exley, Tom Seccombe, and I made a one-day walk up the Nangma Valley to establish base camp at around 4,300m, directly below Zang Brakk (4,800m). Despite unsettled weather during the first few days, we managed to establish an advanced base camp at around 5,100m at the start of the East Changma Glacier. We had a forecast for seven days of high pressure starting on September 1, so on the 2nd we walked to advanced base to attempt our initial objective: unclimbed Korada North (6,146m, 35°24'58.32"N, 76°29'29.50"E).

The next day we walked up the East Changma Glacier and then climbed snow slopes that led to the northwest ridge of Korada North, slightly right of the col at the very head of the glacier. After several pitches of mixed climbing on the crest, we decided to retreat after encountering steep, loose rock on the north flank. We returned to base camp that day.

After a day's rest, we regained advanced base with the aim of trying the west face of Korada North. On the 6th, we started up the initial icefields, climbing 700m up to 75° to reach a leftward-trending mixed ramp that led to the northwest ridge. We camped and then, before daybreak next morning, climbed onto the north face, where about 150m of enjoyable mixed climbing led to the summit ridge. A 15m blank slab guarded what we thought to be the summit. Tom coolly balanced up the slab at M5+, and we were soon traversing the final few meters. We made approximately 20 rappels down the line of our ascent to reach the glacier, naming the route Hot Tang (900m, TD+ M5+ 75°).

Six days of unfavorable weather gave us time to relax in base camp, after which we received news of the long high-pressure system we would need to attempt our main objective of the trip, unclimbed Kapura Central (6,530m, 35°25'43.44"N, 76°30'34.71"E).

We returned to advanced base on the 14th and next day climbed back to the col (ca 5,500m) at the head of the East Changma Glacier, which we hoped would provide a smooth entry into the Second Charakusa Cwm. Three rappels and a short walk saw us establish camp just below the west face of Kapura.

Our alarm sounded at 1 a.m. on the 16th. By 3:30 a.m., we were over the bergschrund and climbing the long snow and ice slopes on the lower section of the face. We climbed mostly good ice and névé for 700m, following the line of Wild Wings (Doudlebsky-Holeček, 2008, to Kapura's south summit; see *AAJ 2009*), though our conditions were much better. At the base of a large rock wall, we stopped at 1:30 p.m. Deploying our improvised snow hammock (the footprint of our advanced base camp tent), we settled in our tent for a night under a clear Karakoram sky.

The next morning, after a short traverse left, we entered the top icefield, which we climbed up and left to the base of mixed ground. A short step of 85° ice led to some delicate climbing on melting verglas over

[Top] **Tom Seccombe moving up the M5+ slabs of the summit block on Korada North.** *Tim Exley* [Middle] **The Korada Peaks from the East Changma Glacier. On the left is the 2021 line, Hot Tang, to Korada North. The col at the head of the glacier is hidden at far left. On the right is the 2004 Slovenian Route to Korada South.** [Bottom] **The west face of Kapura showing (1) In the Fire (2021) to the central summit, and (2) Wild Wings (Doudlebsky-Holeček, 2008) to the south summit.** *Will Lewallen (two photos)*

rock (M4+). Above, we reached the upper snow-field, which led to a col with a tower where, somewhat optimistically, we had hoped to stamp out a tent platform. Much to our disappointment, the corniced ice ridge forced us to continue. In search of ledges, Tom left the col, climbing a tricky mixed pitch (M6). It was getting late, and rather than push into the unknown, we chopped a small, sloping ledge. The wind picked up, the ledge was inadequate for the tent, and consequently we spent a sleepless night.

Tim was melting water by 3 a.m. At first light, we could see the summit was close. We were all keen to get there so we could begin heading down. A short tension traverse/pendulum placed us on the final snow slopes, which led after 100m or so to the corniced summit ridge and warm sunshine. Sugar snow led to the top of Kapura Central.

Almost immediately we began to rappel. At the bottom of the second rappel, I watched my belay device tumble down the face. Lots of carabiner brakes and some frozen V-threads near the base slowed us slightly, but 27 rappels and nine hours later, we were back on the glacier. The next day, after a deep, long sleep, we began the tiresome climb back over the col to return to the East Changma Glacier. That evening, six days after leaving, we were in base camp. We named our route In the Fire (1,300m, ED M6 85°). ◙

NOTES ON KORADA AND KAPURA: *Korada North is erroneously marked Lukpilla Brakk (5,584m, Peak 123) on Jerzy Wala's map of the Nangma Valley. Lukpilla Brakk is a peak south of Baintha Brakk (the Ogre), and locals do not recognize the name in the Nangma. Korada South (5,944m) was climbed by a Slovenian team in 2004 (AAJ 2005).*

The peak widely known as Kapura Central (6,530m, the peak climbed in 2021) is probably the same one marked as Thanda Parbat (6,553m, Peak 122) on Wala's sketch map. The main (north) summit of Kapura (6,544m) was first climbed in 2004 by an American-Slovenian party, while the south summit (thought to be at least 6,350m) was climbed in 2008, as noted above.

[Top] Ice runnels on Kapura's west face. [Bottom] Will Lewallen heel-hooking onto the summit ridge of Kapura Central. The trapezoidal peak of Choglisa is visible behind. *Tim Exley (both)*

WESTERN SALTORO MOUNTAINS

PEAK 6,210M, SOUTHEAST RIDGE; DANSAM, NORTH FACE, ATTEMPT

IN JULY I traveled to Pakistan with Eivind Hugaas (Norway) and Nelson Neirinck (Belgium) to attempt the first ascent of Dansam (a.k.a. K13, 6,666m).

The day before jumping onto a plane, we learned that a French team had climbed our planned line on the north face (*see story on p.62*). Our moods sank, yet we also knew they had summited the lower western top, already climbed by a Japanese team in the early 1980s. The main summit, 1km to the east, was still untouched.

From Skardu we drove to the village of Khorkondus and hiked to up the Mingling Valley. On July 7 we established base camp. During acclimatization we scouted the north

Peak 6,210m, showing the upper section of the 2021 first-ascent route, finishing up the southeast ridge. *Juho Knuuttila*

face of Dansam, and it became clear that there were few safe options, as hanging seracs filled almost the entire face. However, we found a relatively safe passage that we felt we could try.

To finish our acclimatization, we made the first ascent of unnamed Peak 6,210m (35°17'22.01"N, 76°48'39.37"E), the most prominent mountain between Dansam and Saltoro Kangri. We first hiked to the glacier south of the peak on July 15, and since we wanted to take it easy and allow the glacier to refreeze during the night, we slept in the open, on top of large, flat boulders at 5,170m. The following morning, we ascended the glacier for a few kilometers before climbing an easy snow couloir that gave access to a higher glacier. We camped at 5,700m and endured the heat of the day.

A little after midnight on the 17th, we began simul-soloing a 60° snow and ice couloir to reach the broad southeast ridge, which we followed to the summit of Peak 6,210m, arriving at 3:40 a.m. We wasted no time in descending, rappelling the icy sections of the couloir. After reaching our camp, we packed and continued down to base camp for an early lunch.

After five days of rest at base camp, we received a forecast for a six-day weather window. On the 23rd we walked to the base of the north face of Dansam, which by this time was plastered with snow. Our idea was again to climb mostly during the night, reaching a spot where we could safely bivouac before the sun hit the face.

We started simul-soloing icefields, roping up when we reached the first difficulties. I led two pitches of almost vertical slush. Poor protection and insecure climbing made the going quite slow. The fact that snow was melting so early in the morning made actual daytime look far from promising.

Nelson led another tricky mixed pitch, and then Eivind took over to aid through a rock barrier. At this point small debris was raining down on us, and it didn't require much discussion to agree to bail. We rapped from our high point at approximately 5,550m and walked back to base camp while huge, wet snow avalanches cascaded down the face. With conditions simply too dangerous, we returned to Skardu. 📷 🔍

— JUHO KNUUTTILA, *FINLAND*

The 1,200-meter south face of Rokapi (Kap Chuli) and the 2021 solo route. The ascent was the second overall and first winter ascent of the 6,468-meter peak. *Roger Nix*

API HIMAL, ROKAPI, NEW ROUTE AND FIRST WINTER ASCENT

FROM DECEMBER 21 to 23, John Kelley (USA) made the second overall and first winter ascent of Rokapi (a.k.a. Kap Chuli, 6,468m, 29°50'52.60"N, 81°2'19.20"E) in the Api Himal. Climbing alone, Kelley established base camp on November 19 at 4,380m, below the south face of Rokapi. After a week of snowfall in early December, he cached gear a little below 4,900m and descended to base camp. He did not return to this cache until the 20th, when he spent the night and then started next day up the south face of the mountain.

Kelley climbed toward the right side of the 1,200m south face, which comprised mixed rock, ice, and snow, to reach a subsidiary summit of 6,050m on the southeast ridge. He bivouacked once on the face at around 5,300m. From the subsummit, he followed the ridge to a col (ca 6,000m) before the main summit and made his second bivouac. On the 23rd he reached the summit after a long day and returned to his bivouac at night. On the 24th he was back in base camp. Difficulties are reported to have been sustained at M4 WI3.

The first ascent of Rokapi was in 1977. A British team approached from the Rokapi Khola to the northwest, establishing a base camp toward the end of September at 3,800m. Despite being slightly epic in character, the ascent of the mountain—a 13-day alpine-style traverse—remains an impressive and little-known achievement for the era.

With only the leader, Dick Godfrey, and Nepali staff left in base camp, Tom Herley and Kevin McLane climbed the west southwest ridge, over a foresummit they named the Merangue, to the main top. Then, returning to the col before the Merangue, they cut back north and descended the northwest face. At one point on the ascent they were avalanched about 150m, while on the descent both fell between 12m and 25m over an ice cliff. They had no food for the last four days, and on the last two suffered many hallucinations. Godfrey and the liaison officer, having given the two up for dead, were just on the point of leaving when Herley and McLane staggered into base camp. [*Additional history of the climbing in this area is included with this report at the AAJ website.*]

– **LINDSAY GRIFFIN**, *WITH INFORMATION FROM LA CHRONIQUE ALPINE-FFCAM*

KANTI HIMAL, MARIYANG, SOUTHWEST FACE AND WEST RIDGE

MARIYANG (6,528M, 29°41'35.29"N, 82°53'13.89"E) is an impressive but little-known summit in the Kanti Himal, on the Nepal-Tibet border west of Danphe Shail (6,103m). It was added to the official permitted list in 2014 and until 2021 had no known ascent, when it became the goal of an eight-member team from the Korean Alpine Rescue Association led by Koo Eun-sun.

On September 27, 15 days after leaving Kathmandu, the team finished its approach up the Tankya Khola and established base camp on the Mariyang Glacier at 5,150m. They climbed a rock face on the southwest side of the peak, fixing 200m of rope and placing a high camp on October 5 at 5,800m. Moving west from this point, they climbed a 200m snow face (fixing 140m of rope) to reach the west ridge, which they followed easily to the summit.

The top was reached on the morning of October 9 by Baek Jong-min, Joung Je-gyun, Jung Jae-Jin, and Ongchu Sherpa (the only Sherpa who climbed above base camp), and on the 10th by Eom Tae-chul, Koo, Lee Myeong Hyi, Lim Jeong-hewi, and Ongchu (again). On this day Koo also traversed solo to the east top. Both parties descended to base camp on their respective summit days. 📷

– *INFORMATION FROM* **RODOLPHE POPIER**, *HIMALAYAN DATABASE, FRANCE*

EDITOR'S NOTE: *The Korean climb appears to have been the first attempt on Mariyang. However, in 1993 an Austrian and German team climbed the sharp and corniced southwest ridge of the peak immediately west (Peak 6,455m, HMG-Finn, 29°41'22"N, 82°52'27"E), which could in the future be referred to as Mariyang West (AAJ 1994). The summit was reached by Franz Kröll and Fritz Mross.*

DHAULAGIRI HIMAL

DHAULAGIRI I, NORTHWEST RIDGE, ATTEMPT

THE UNCLIMBED NORTHWEST ridge of Dhaulagiri is at least 6km in length and around 4,000m high. Although the average angle is not steep and there are long stretches of straightforward snow slopes, the ridge starts with a steep 500m rock buttress. It has been the goal for Horia Colibasanu, Marius Gane (both Romanian), and Peter Hamor (Slovakia) for three years.

The team first attempted the line in 2019, climbing and fixing the rock buttress; they reached a high point of 5,600m before giving up due to very strong winds. Their return match in 2020 was thwarted by the pandemic, which stranded them in Kathmandu.

In 2021, operating from the 4,000m "Japanese Base Camp" and climbing as before without oxygen or Sherpa support, the three reached a high point of 6,000m in early May. At this point, their tent was hit by an avalanche during the night, forcing them to cut through the fabric to escape. Every day the weather had produced clear mornings but snow in the afternoons. With

Dorje Lhakpa II (center) and Dorje Lhakpa (far left) from the valley to the south. The 2021 route on Dorje Lhakpa finished up the sunlit snow and ice face. *Mikel Zabalza*

JUGAL HIMAL

DORJE LHAKPA, SOUTH FACE, AND OTHER ROUTES

AN EXPEDITION TO the Greater Ranges marks the end of the three-year cycle of the Spanish National Mountaineering Team. Here they gain experience with altitude and learn how to operate carefully and safely in remote ranges. Choosing the south side of Dorje Lhakpa for the 2021 expedition of the men's team was not down to chance. I was looking for somewhere little-visited but relatively accessible, with solitude and potential for opening new routes. In 1992 I had tried the north face of Dorje Lhakpa (6,955m, 28°10'25.58"N, 85°46'42.77"E), approaching from the Langtang Valley to the northwest. The valley to the south seemed to meet all my requirements. [*This valley appears unnamed on the HMG-Finn map but flows into the Lagan Khola.*] Only a minor shepherds' path went into the valley.

In early October, after a five-day trek from Botang (1,850m) via Panch Pokhari, Javier Guzmán, Mikel Inoriza, Iker Madoz, Rubén San Martín, Ander Zabalza, and I established our base camp at an idyllic site around 4,200m. The weather was perfect, the conditions on the south face of Dorje Lhakpa excellent, and the cold of autumn had yet to arrive. We made an advanced base at 4,900m and then, to acclimatize, climbed the northeast ridge of Lingsing Himal (a.k.a. Linsin Himal, the 6,074m summit on the watershed ridge between Dorje Lhakpa and 6,143m Urkinmang) to a small point at approximately 5,900m. We bivouacked at 5,300m on the way up and again at 5,600m on the way down. It was a beautiful ridge: snow with a few rock steps of grade V. [*It is not clear if this ridge has ever been climbed in its entirety.*]

Once we were down, five consecutive days of bad weather left 1.5m of fresh snow on the glacier. We then received a weather report that promised a short window with a sharp drop in temperature. Afterward, the wind at altitude would become very strong. Inoriza, Madoz, and I would try the south face of Dorje Lhakpa, while Ander, Javi, and Rubén would try the southwest wall. To 5,800m, our routes would coincide.

Making a trail up the glacier proved painful. My team bivouacked at 5,700m, the others 100m higher at the foot of the face. We set out at 4 a.m. on the 25th in biting cold. A little later we saw the other team back on the glacier: The cold had been too intense and the conditions too poor.

We three continued upward, opening a deep track. When I checked the satellite phone, I saw a message that next day the wind on the summit would be 80km/h and would not decrease in the coming days. We quickly decided to go for the summit that day.

Leaving a tent pitched at 6,100m, we set ourselves a turnaround time of 4 p.m. (It was getting dark around 5:40 p.m.) We stood on the summit at 5 o'clock: It was cold and windy but magnificent.

Bivouac at 5,600m on the northeast ridge of Lingsing Himal with the flat-topped Gurkarpo Ri (6,889m, left) and Leonpo Gang (Big White Peak, 6,979m) rising above the Langshisha Glacier. *Mikel Zabalza*

We carefully descended the upper 500m of snow and ice (55–65°), rappelling the lower section in the dark. The following day we stumbled into base camp, with just a couple of days remaining before the arrival of our porters. However, there was enough time for our companions, despite frostnip in the feet, to open a fine rock route on a peak close to camp that they named Point Sofia (5,300m): Diedro Ziripot (350m, 6c).

We left with smiles on our faces. The experience gained will be used by these guys on further expeditions, which they are sure to make. 📷

— **MIKEL ZABALZA**, *SPAIN*

ROLWALING HIMAL

CHEKIGO, SOUTH FACE TO EAST RIDGE

THE SPANISH WOMEN'S mountaineering team was operating in the Rolwaling at the same time as the men's team was in the Dorje Lhakpa region (*see report above*). Our expedition lasted from the beginning of October to November 5, with "base camp" established in one of the comfortable guest houses in the village of Na at 4,183m.

We first climbed Yalung Ri (5,650m) and went to 6,100m on Parchamo for acclimatization, then sought refuge in Na during a period of bad weather. When it improved, we went for our main objective, Chekigo (6,257m). We wanted to repeat the Alegre-Baró route Sopeti on the south face and climb a more direct start to the French Route on the southeast face of Chekigo

Spanish route on Chekigo (6,257m). See AAJ 2015 for routes to the left. *Marc Subirana*

Sano (6,121m). However, both attempts failed due to the heavy snow deposition.

As our last chance, we opted to try a new line on the right side of the south face of Chekigo, which Mikel Zabalza had noticed during a previous visit. The first half was a rocky buttress, while the second had snow, ice, and seracs at the top. On October 30, Laia Duaigües, Nieves Gil, and I climbed this line in a 22-hour push from a camp at a little over 5,000m (1,000m, TD), reaching the east-northeast ridge but then having to turn back (at around 6,000m) due to strong winds. 📷

— **MARC SUBIRANA**, *SPAIN*

SLOVENIAN DIRECT
THE NORTHWEST FACE OF CHOBUTSE IN THE ROLWALING HIMAL

BY LUKA STRAŽAR, *SLOVENIA*

FROM OCTOBER 28–30, Nejc Marčič and I succeeded on the first ascent of the 1,700m northwest face of Chobutse (6,685m). The peak was first climbed in 1972 via the east ridge/face, approached from the north, by Germans Gustav and Klaus Harder, Peter Vogler, and Wolfgang Weinzierl. On the west side of the mountain, Mingma Gyalje Sherpa made an impressive solo ascent in 2015. [*For a brief history of climbing on Chobutse, see AAJ 2016.*]

We left Slovenia together with Marko Prezelj and Matija Volontar at the beginning of October and made our base camp in the village of Na on the 12th. After thorough acclimatization, during which we climbed Omi Tso Go (6,230m), where we slept two nights at 5,700m, we were ready for the northwest face of Chobutse.

Heading up the lower section of the northwest face of Chobutse. The route continues directly above the climber. *Luka Stražar* [Inset] Upper part of the 1,700-meter Slovenian Route on Chobutse (6,685m). *Pablo Herraez*

Leaving Na at 1 a.m., we started up the face at 5 a.m. The initial slopes proved to be in good condition, enabling us to advance quickly. Then we encountered steep climbing, and at one point had to rappel a pitch due to poor conditions and find an alternative route on thin ice. In the central section we found steep, exposed climbing.

At the end of the first day, we were really lucky to find a good bivouac site at around 5,800m in very steep terrain, where there had been no decent ledges below. Our second bivouac was in a crevasse around 500m below the summit. The climbing on both the second and third day was accompanied by low temperatures and strong winds, creating frequent spindrift.

We arrived on top around 2 p.m. There is very little height difference between the central and east summits, which are about half an hour apart, and to be sure we climbed them both; we estimate the central summit is a few meters higher. We descended the west face of the mountain in the area of Mingma's route and were back in Na by 8 p.m. the evening of the 30th. The Slovenian Direct had difficulties of ED M5 AI5.

In the meantime, Marko and Matija had attempted the New Zealand route on the southwest ridge but turned around at 6,100m due to high winds. On the 31st we began our return to Kathmandu. ◙

PEAK 5,794M AND PARCHAMO, HISTORICAL ASCENTS AND ENCOUNTERS

IN AUTUMN 1996, a small group of friends and I climbed in the Rolwaling Valley. In addition to adventures on new routes, we had other memorable experiences, some of which were so remarkable that it is hard to explain their occurrence through coincidence alone.

First, the climbs. Starting from Na, we set a high camp within striking distance of an unnamed peak at the edge of the glacial plateau leading to the trekking peak of Ramdung (5,930m). [*This is Peak 5,794m, first climbed in 1952 via the south ridge; see AAJ 2015.*] On October 30, Chuck Yax and I climbed eight pitches up the prominent west-facing couloir through steep, unstable snow that we avoided whenever possible by climbing the firm rock of the gully wall. A ramp promised access to the summit, but the snow was chest deep and felt ready to slide. With headlamps on, we rappelled the route and staggered back to our tent 14 hours after leaving.

In November, Kili Sherpa and I climbed 15 pitches up the left side of the west face of Parchamo (6,279m), as recorded in *AAJ 2020*. The recent discovery of my topo and write-up of the climb, along with a recent photo of the face, add some important clarity to that 2020 account. Contrary to what I recalled, the route is in much the same condition today as in 1996, being composed more of rock than snow. Following an excellent rock pitch off the glacier, nine of the subsequent pitches were mixed climbing, weaving up a line of runnels and rock sections to 5.7. We called the 12th pitch Stairway to Nirvana, as it followed a unique series of stacked blocks. From there it was 60° snow to the intersection with the standard route on the north ridge. We descended from there.

Shortly after our arrival at base camp, we had a series of chance encounters with climbers who seemed to have stepped directly from the pages of Himalayan mountaineering history into this secluded valley. It began with meeting a very fit-looking Jean Jacques Asper, who was a member of the 1952 pre-monsoon Swiss expedition to Mt. Everest that nearly made the first ascent.

Next came an equally energetic group of older trekkers from the U.K.; one of them introduced himself as Mike Westmacott, then the Alpine Club president. It dawned on me that we were in the company of members of the successful 1953 British Mt. Everest expedition.

Finally, while on our way to high camp, a white-haired gentleman carrying a wooden-shafted ice axe descended toward us. We discovered the climber was Dennis Davis, whose account of 19 first ascents in the region during the 1955 Merseyside Expedition [*including the first ascent of Parchamo*] was the reason we had decided to come to Rolwaling. It seemed so improbable to be meeting, in a remote corner of the Himalaya, not only the heroes that first inspired me to climb but also a man who was the inspiration for my current expedition. Dennis explained that he had journeyed to Rolwaling to celebrate the 40th anniversary of the expedition. The ice axe had made its return as well. 🔳

– TAD WELCH, *USA*

TENGKANGPOCHE, NORTHEAST PILLAR

OVER SEVEN DAYS in October, Matt Glenn and I climbed the northeast pillar of Tengkangpoche (6,487m; *this formation has long been called the north pillar, but much of the climbing faces northeast*). We acclimatized by sleeping progressively higher up the Thame Valley toward Tashi Lapcha Pass and made our first attempt earlier in the month. On our second day of climbing, I fell while aiding and injured my little finger. We returned to the valley and found a doctor in Thame, who dressed it and gave me antibiotics. We then had mixed weather for seven days, during which the condition of the pillar deteriorated but the state of my finger improved.

When the weather cleared, showing the surrounding peaks buried in powder, another attempt

[Left] Day seven: Matt Glenn plows up the poorly protected final ridge of Tengkangpoche's northeast pillar. This section of ridge had been climbed before by a Russian-Ukrainian team as a finish to their route on the northeast face (*AAJ 2014*). [Right] The upper northeast pillar and the line of Massive Attack. (H) marks the high point of the 2019 attempt. The 2021 team climbed a little farther to the left to pass this point and bivouacked twice more before reaching the summit. *Tom Livingstone (both photos)*

on Tengkangpoche seemed the logical option, as it was steep and clearing of snow quickest. We packed our bags with a feeling of déjà-vu.

On the first day we simul-soloed easy ground and then belayed four mixed pitches to a snow terrace marking the start of the headwall. The next day we fixed 90m up the lower headwall, following the only feasible line of cracks. This was almost exclusively aid climbing on small gear. On day three we ascended the ropes and continued aid and mixed climbing, heading for the snow terrace at the top of the lower headwall. Night caught us before this, forcing a bivouac in a small alcove. On day four we climbed two high-quality mixed pitches to the snow terrace. Although early, we decided to bivouac on this terrace.

Next day we climbed the upper headwall, mostly aiding a rightward-slanting crack system. Soon after nightfall, we bivouacked beneath a rock band that lies just before the start of the final snow ridge. On day six we made it through the exposed rock band and quested up the ridge, which proved slow going due to unsupportive snow.

Day seven—October 30—was our last on the route. We slogged up the remaining snow ridge and reached the summit at 12:15 p.m. We then descended the east ridge, made two rappels on the north flank, and returned to our tea house base camp at Thengbo just after nightfall. We named the route Massive Attack.

— TOM LIVINGSTONE, *U.K.*

NOTES ON THE NORTHEAST PILLAR: *This pillar had seen several previous attempts, with the highest point reached in six days of climbing by Juho Knuuttila (Finland) and Quentin Roberts (Canada) in the autumn of 2019: They stopped at around 5,930m (AAJ 2020) and reported difficulties up to*

5.11 A3 M7 to their high point. In the spring of 2021, Roberts returned with Jesse Huey (USA), but after repeated storms before and during their attempt, they did not reach the previous high point. The two cached a pack containing some gear and food near their first bivy on the route, anticipating they would return for another attempt. For their own second attempt, Glenn and Livingstone opted to use some of this gear, fuel, and food. Near the top of the pillar, Glenn and Livingstone moved left and then angled right along a ramp system to avoid the blank slab that had stopped Roberts and Knuuttila, then continued straight up to the snow ridge. Livingstone posted a four-part story about the ascent at www.tomlivingstone.com.

TENGKANGPOCHE, EAST RIDGE INTEGRAL; TENGI RAGI TAU SOUTHEAST, NEW VARIANT

AFTER TWO YEARS of pandemic, the desire to climb in the Greater Ranges was intense. After the umpteenth postponement of our summer expedition to K2, I remembered Tengkangpoche. It wasn't difficult to assemble a close-knit team: After a couple of phone calls, Roger Bovard, Emrik Favre, Leonardo Gheza, Jerome Perruquet, and Francesco Ratti had agreed to travel to Nepal.

We arrived at our 4,500m base camp, a little further on from Thame village, on October 17, and began acclimatizing immediately. We slept at 5,400m just before a big storm arrived; after the storm, the mountains were covered with a good meter of fresh snow, with the coverage down to 4,500m. A few days later, we decided to look at nearby Tengi Ragi Tau Southeast (a.k.a. Pahamlahaka, 6,141m). Leo, Emrik, and I chose the rocky south-southeast ridge, leading to a shoulder on the east ridge, while Francesco, Jerome, and Roger opted for the snowier east ridge itself.

On the 22nd we left base camp. The rock on the south-southeast ridge proved to be very good, and after an initial sharp section we climbed a conspicuous gendarme with two pitches of sustained UIAA V/V+. We bivouacked above this at around 5,300m; to this point we had seen pitons from previous travel. [*This ridge was first climbed in its entirety, with two bivouacs, by Radek Lienerth and Alexandr Tolok (Czech Republic) in autumn 2003. On reaching the shoulder, they followed the southeast ridge to the summit of Tengi Ragi Tau Southeast. The 1,700m route was named Like a Dhal Bhat (ED1, VII- 75°) and was repeated the following year by three French, who found difficulties up to 6b+.*] Next day we moved right, onto the southeast face, following lines of weakness. Snow conditions were not perfect, and rockfall passed over our heads. From the radio we heard our friends had reached the shoulder, so our escape down the east ridge now had a track in place.

At midday we finally reached the shoulder at a little below 6,000m. Mist began to envelop us. Over the radio, Roger explained they had just set off an avalanche and conditions were delicate. We descended from there, and fortunately all went well; by 5 p.m. we were back in base camp, drinking beer. We named our variant Himalayanos Desperados (1,200m, V+ M5 80°).

After a suitable rest we set off for our main goal, a direct line up the northeast face of Tengkangpoche (6,487m), left of the northeast pillar, finishing up the east ridge. Matt Glenn and Tom Livingstone were climbing the pillar, and I was inspired by their motivation and skill. Our first two days passed smoothly, the biggest difficulties placing solid protection on the hard pitches and deep snow on less inclined sections. There were a couple of pitches of around M6. At around 5,500m, a large avalanche, triggered by the collapse of seracs just below the summit, came down the face. Fortunately, it missed us by 20m. We had estimated our route would only be exposed to serac fall for around 20m, and we now realized that a discharge from one of these seracs could sweep the entire wall. It would have been madness to continue.

Back in the valley, morale was low, and we now had few ideas about what to do with our remaining time. Francesco and Jerome went to reconnoiter the northern aspect of the smaller summits that lie on the ridge between Kwangde and Tengkangpoche. They were pleasantly surprised to see solid ice lines, and a decision was made to try a new route on this face. Arriving at the base, we discovered two obvious parallel lines, both leading to a col where we intended to bivouac. We split into two teams.

Leo and I climbed a beautiful *goulotte*, interrupted in the middle by a vertical rock step that Leo led via an obvious and difficult crack. At 6 p.m. we exited onto the ridge at 5,700m. Emrik, Francesco, and Jerome were just behind, having climbed their own line. (Roger remained in base camp.) By 10 p.m. we had chopped platforms for two tents and were warm after the day's cold exertions. This col marks the lowest point on the ridge between Kwangde Nup and Tengkangpoche. We would later name these two routes Santarai (Cazzanelli-Ghezza) and Settebello (Favre-Perruquet-Ratti). Both were 450m, AI5 (or 5 R) M7 A2.

After waiting for the sun to reach us next morning, by 9 a.m. all five of us were traversing the ridge toward Tengkangpoche, crossing various small summits between 5,800m and 6,000m. The highest was covered with prayer flags, presumably placed by climbers coming from the south. In the middle of the afternoon, at around 6,100m, we set up camp below the final rise of the east ridge toward Tengkangpoche. [*This part of the ridge, approached from the south, was climbed in 1984 by Trevor Pilling and Andy Zimet during the first known ascent of the mountain.*] Here we found sections of fixed rope, left by a French expedition that had attempted the summit a few days previously.

[Top] The east ridge of Tengkangpoche, climbed in 2021 from the north, with two parallel starts. On the left is the Kwangde group. *Radek Lienerth* [Bottom] Seen from the northeast pillar of Tengkangpoche: (A) Tengi Ragi Tau, (B) Tengi Ragi Tau South, (C) Tengi Ragi Tau Southeast, (D) the Shoulder, and (E) Lunag Massif. (1) Southeast Face (Japanese, 1992). (2) South Pillar—Le Pilier du Grand Darbon (French, 2005). (3) Southwest ridge—Le Sourire de Mingma (French, 2004). (4) Southeast ridge—Like a Dhal Bhat (Czechs, 2003). (5) Himalayanos Desperados (Italians, 2021). (6) East ridge, used in descent. *Tom Livingstone*

The following day, helped by the fixed ropes, we climbed quickly to 6,200m, where the ropes stopped and we realized the French had not reached the top. The way ahead was steep and sharp—not extreme but very exposed. Finally, we reached the top and quickly began our descent.

Reversing our route to the 6,100m bivouac site, we then went down to the north, following the descent line used by Nick Bullock, solo, in 2003, after an ascent of the route Love and Hate (D+/TD-) further right on the face. After a couple of rappels, we downclimbed at our own pace and before evening were back in camp. [*The online version of this report includes details of a subsequent speed ascent of Ama Dablam by the author.*]

— FRANÇOIS CAZZANELLI, *ITALY, WITH INFORMATION FROM RODOLPHE POPIER, HIMALAYAN DATABASE, FRANCE*

The Kangchung peaks in October 2015 with their north faces in profile. Kangchung Nup is nearer the camera. The 2021 route on Kangchung Shar and bivouac site are marked. From the col, the team descended south (right) between the two peaks. *Martin Klestinec*

KANGCHUNG SHAR, NORTH FACE AND NORTHWEST FACE/RIDGE, ADA'S HEAVENLY TRAVERSE

AFTER AN ENFORCED "rest year" in 2020 due to COVID-19, I was motivated to return to alpine projects. However, the situation with the pandemic was not favorable in many parts of the world, so I made modest plans. Kangchung Shar (6,063m) and Kangchung Nup (6,043m) are two beautiful mountains, a bit like two Matterhorns side by side but 2km higher.

After arriving in Kathmandu in April, my fellow Czech and old friend Jaroslav Bansky, nicknamed Banán (Banana), and I purchased a permit for Kangchung Nup. It has a beautiful north face and had been attempted by, among other teams, Czech climbers.

In the spring, Nepal was completely lacking tourists. Most lodges were closed, but those that remained open were even more hospitable than usual. During the approach everything went well; I felt great, less affected by altitude than usual. However, before reaching Gokyo, I came down with a headache and diarrhea. We spent two days in a lodge at Gokyo watching snow fall. Banán and I then left our trekking group and through deep snow eventually arrived on the Gaunara Glacier, where we established base camp below the north face of Kangchung Nup.

I spent the next two days at camp with a sore throat and weak body. The clock was ticking. We only had food for six days, and the weather was about to worsen again. If we didn't try the following day we would have to give up. We changed our plans and decided to climb Kangchung Shar.

In the morning of April 27, my legs were shaking, but I didn't feel sick. In 1.5 hours we reached the bottom of our proposed route, which would take us to the broad 5,637m col between Kangchung Shar and Nup. [*This line was first climbed in 2016 by Paul Schweizer and Simon Yates, who reached the col and progressed a little way up the northwest ridge of Kangchung Shar before retreating. Kang-*

chung Shar's first known ascent was in 1984, by Franci Knez (Slovenia), who reached the col from the south and continued up the northwest ridge. For further history, see AAJ 2017.] I quickly lost power while climbing, and Banán ended up leading the most physically difficult pitches and breaking trail through deep snow. At 2 p.m. we set up camp just east of the col. From here we had a superb view of Himalayan peaks, but the faces looked terrible—dry with hard ice. Our continuation route, up the tapering northwest face, had been climbed before, but conditions now were completely different.

Next day we began at 5:30 a.m. and reached the summit around midday. The top was well guarded by several pitches of difficult mixed climbing. Everything was so much harder due to loose snow in corners and over slabs.

After a few photos we quickly began to descend, rappelling to the initial glacier slope. We had not noticed how warm it had become. Whoom! The slope settled: If it slid, there was little chance for us. We reached the tent and decided to pack it and descend the easier original route on the south face of the mountain. Locating the route quickly, we partially downclimbed, partially rappelled to the bottom, arriving at Dranang just before dark. What a day!

On the following day we returned to Namche Bazar and met our trekking companions. The picture was not a happy one. Most were ill like me, and half could not fly back to Europe due to having a positive COVID test. The time for expeditions was not yet right.

Ours was the first complete climb of Kangchung Shar from the north and the first north-to-south traverse. We named our route Ada's Heavenly Traverse (TD+) in honor of the ex-chief of the Czech Mountain Rescue Service, Banán's uncle, Adolf Kleps. 📄 📷

— **ZDENĚK HÁK**, *CZECH REPUBLIC*

AMA DABLAM, WEST FACE, DAMILANO ROUTE AND RAPID ASCENT OF AMERICAN DIRECT

PREVIOUSLY UNREPORTED IN the AAJ was a new route up the west face of Ama Dablam (6,812m) climbed solo on November 9, 1993, by François Damilano (France).

Damilano had reached the summit via the normal route on November 4 while part of a commercial expedition. After returning to base camp, he left camp at 3 a.m. on the 9th and started climbing the west face a little to the right of the American Direct (Dunmire-Warner, 1990). He crossed this route and the 1985 Japanese route to its left, before arcing back to join the American Direct at the upper left end of the Dablam (the conspicuous serac barrier near the top right side of the west face). He then traversed across the top of the Dablam to reach the southwest ridge at 6,600m. It was 4 p.m., he was tired, and had already been to the summit a few days previously. From this point, he descended the normal route to Camp 2 and spent the night there before returning to base.

In November 2021, Zdeněk Hák and Jakub Kácha made a rare ascent of the American Direct on the west face with only two bivouacs. Above the Dablam, the two Czechs finished direct to the summit, following the last section of a line climbed in 1986 by another Czech, Miroslav Smid, solo. Hák and Kácha found sections of UIAA IV/V rock, WI4, and M4/5, suggesting an overall grade of TD+/ED1.

The American Direct, which takes the relatively sheltered rib leading to the left edge of the Dablam, was first climbed over four days by Glenn Dunmire and Chris Warner, finishing at the summit on the first day of the calendar winter, December 21, 1990. Above the Dablam, they slanted right to finish up the final 200m of the southwest ridge. They graded their 1,500m route 5.6 AI4 (*AAJ 1991*). 📄 📷

— **LINDSAY GRIFFIN**, *WITH ADDITIONAL INFORMATION FROM* **RODOLPHE POPIER**, *HIMALAYAN DATABASE*

Marek Holecek and Radek Groh found much drier conditions on the west face of Baruntse than were seen even eight years earlier, forcing tenuous climbing on hard, brittle ice and broken rock. *Radek Groh*

HEAVENLY TRAP
SURVIVING A NEW ROUTE ON BARUNTSE'S WEST FACE

BY MAREK HOLEČEK, *CZECH REPUBLIC*

I FELL UNDER the spell of the west face of Baruntse (7,152m) in 2001 during an expedition to attempt Kyashar, about 20km to the southwest. As I stared at the 1,300m face of interlacing snow, ice, and rock features, I began looking for lines of weakness. Before long, I had identified a clear and distinct path. But I buried the notion of climbing it; some ideas need time to percolate before one's awareness and courage are equal to them.

I exhumed the idea in 2019, when I once again passed beneath the west face of Baruntse. Zdeněk Hák and I were in Nepal to make the first ascent of the complete northwest face of Chamlang. Even before we had returned to the ground, after summiting via our new route UFO Line, I was scheming for Baruntse.

The pandemic put those plans on hold until the spring of 2021, when I teamed up with Radek "Ráďa" Groh. Ráďa is 15 years younger than me, but we had already tested our partnership, climbing a hard route in Peru together in 2019.

For 15 days Rada and I acclimatized as we trekked through the heart of the Nepal Himalaya, crossing several 5,000m-high passes around Gokyo and then over the very high pass of Amphu Lapcha to the Hongu Valley. We arrived at Baruntse base camp on May 13. There was absolute silence except for the cracking glacier and occasional avalanche, and not a soul to be seen. And there, in front of us, was the west face.

This face had only one established route, climbed by a Russian team in 1995. Our line was to the left of theirs and completely independent. A Czech pair had attempted our line in 2013 to around 6,600m but never returned.

Already well acclimatized, we just had to wait for a four-day window of good weather, which took a while. But on May 21, our friend and meteorologist Alena Zárybnická sent us a good weather report on the satellite phone, which sent my blood-pressure sky-high. We packed gear and food for six days and immediately set off up the Hongu Glacier. Our first bivouac was just below an overhanging serac at 5,800m, which offered protection against any "hellos" that might swoop down upon us during the night.

The next morning we started up the 2km-wide face and, from the very first moments, encountered challenging conditions. Our axes and crampon points squeaked into the hard ice like nails on a chalkboard. In recent years, the west face has undergone a major change; a lot of the ice and snow I saw plastered on the face 20 years earlier had melted, leaving only the hardest shell. Looking at the pillar climbed by the 1995 Russian expedition, I can't imagine anyone repeating it in the current conditions.

The terrain stayed difficult throughout the day, and we made pathetic progress. After ten hours of constant front-pointing, we stopped to bivy at 6,200m, about 100m lower than we'd hoped. We dug a small platform into a ridge of solid frozen snow, reminiscent of an organ pipe. The spot was so small that we couldn't lie down, only sit with our legs hanging over the abyss. We draped the tent over us without poles, like a canopy. It was a miserable night.

Good weather greeted us on May 23. We climbed to an ice sheet that led us diagonally left and then continued up hard ice grooves separated by ribs of soft snow. The climbing was monotonously tiring. Thankfully, the hard work paid off, as we made up for our poor progress of the day before. In the late afternoon, we found a small but comfortable space for the tent on a snow rib at 6,500m. Ráďa and I exchanged hardly any words, thinking only of how tired, hungry, and excruciatingly thirsty we were. We soothed our parched throats with tea, stretched out, and went straight to sleep.

May 24 brought the most difficult part of the ascent, a 250m barrier of broken rock. It took us a while to decide where to go. The climbing was technical and slow—which only got harder when it began to snow. We had hoped to reach the ridge, but were forced to bivy again on the face. Fortunately, we found a rocky promontory at 6,900m that perfectly matched the size of our tent, jutting out so the torrents of spindrift flowed by on either side. Once inside, we crawled into our sleeping bags, which had absorbed moisture during the previous nights and then frozen hard; still, it was best to lie down and steam inside them.

I pulled out my satellite phone to find a message from Alena: "Damn, the weather wasn't supposed to change today. It shouldn't have been getting worse until tomorrow afternoon." We had been half a day slower than planned, and the weather had deteriorated dramatically. There were no good options for retreat—the only way down was up. We hoped the weather would allow us to climb the final few tens of meters to the summit ridge the next day, and then we could descend via the normal route on the southeast ridge.

Suddenly, the satellite phone beeped with another message from Alena, bearing worse news. Now the forecast called for the weather to deteriorate even more the next afternoon, and possibly even more the day after that.

On the morning of May 25, it was cloudy with poor visibility, but we had to try to get off the mountain. We climbed the final mixed sections to the ridge and crossed over the summit around 4 p.m., covered in hoar frost, and then descended a bit and set up the tent at 7,100m with impend-

[Top] **Torrents of spindrift by the final bivy site on the face (6,900m).** [Bottom] **The west face of Baruntse (7,152m) showing (1) Heavenly Trap (2021) and (2) Russian Route (1995). The descent was near the right skyline.** *Marek Holecek (both photos)*

ing dread. Strong wind and driving snow hammered the thin tent walls during the night like a military bombardment.

Near dawn on May 26, everything seemed calm: Although the wind raged on, the tent was now completely buried in snow. We dragged ourselves into the storm and moved the tent a few meters. Whiteness all around forestalled any possibility of safe descent. We lay next to each other all day without saying anything.

Finally, on May 27, we felt like our luck might be turning. Around 10 a.m., the wind began to die and the fog started dissolving. We hastily packed the tent. As we started descending along the ridge, the sun shining through a wall of clouds created a diffuse light that was extremely disorienting, like a feeling of total drunkenness. There were no reference points, just shimmering white.

"Ráďa, we can't go on, I don't see anything."

"But we must try to keep going or we'll kick the bucket here, Mára."

"I know it's hard to accept, but there's nothing we can do, we have to wait."

We kept up the discussion until common sense prevailed and we repitched the tent only a few tens of meters lower. Aside from trips outside to free the tent from snow, we waited and prayed. Everything was wet or frozen, and we felt the beginnings of frostbite. Moreover, we were out of food and tea. Thankfully, we still had some fuel to melt snow. We remained tent-bound all of May 28.

The weather eased some on May 29, and we climbed down the sharp, steep ridge, which was covered in deep unstable powder. We managed to descend about 750m by nightfall, before resigning ourselves to a ninth consecutive bivouac. Now very scared about serious frostbite, we slipped into a single sleeping bag to keep each other warm.

Before going to sleep I called our agency to request that a helicopter pick us up the following day. Between our physical state and the high avalanche hazard at the bottom of the face, we needed help. Plus, there was no one left at our base camp and no chance of anyone reaching us on foot with the deep new snow.

May 30 was a beautiful day—finally! We fine-tuned the coordinates with the helicopter pilot, started down again, and he picked us up around 7 a.m., freeing us from our icy hell.

We called our route Heavenly Trap and graded it VI+ M6+ 80°. It is the hardest climb I have done in the mountains. Ráďa and I dedicated the route to our two friends, Petr Machold and Kuba Vaněk, who lost their lives on the same face eight years earlier.

Translation assistance was provided by Lenka Strnadova. The author was interviewed about this climb for the Cutting Edge podcast.

BARUNTSE, WEST FACE, HISTORICAL ASCENT

The first ascent of the west face of Baruntse, by a Russian team in 1995, was reported in the AAJ only with a brief note. This account has been adapted from a longer article published in the 1997 Alpine Journal (U.K.), with permission; the complete article is available online.

Until now, no attempt had been made to climb the beautiful west face of Baruntse, despite the great popularity of this peak. Starting in 1954, when the first ascent of the mountain was made by a New Zealand team, a number of expeditions had reached the summit, but they had all ascended by ridge routes.

Suddenly the links in a chain of ideas came together in my mind, leading up to the possibility of an ascent of Makalu by the west face. A first ascent of the west face of Baruntse would offer our young high-altitude climbers some excellent preparatory experience. Such an expedition also would prepare us for a technically difficult route on an 8,000m peak such as Annapurna. Only then would we attempt the west face of Makalu. The expedition to Baruntse thus was the first stage of a three-year program.

On September 14, a helicopter transported the whole party and all our gear to the mountain village of Lukla. Eight climbers, the sirdar, and Nepali staff set off for base camp, while the three remaining members of the expedition were responsible for transferring the rest of the luggage by helicopter to base camp. The journey on foot took us eight days. Dense cloud in the gorges made flying impossible, and only on September 23, the day after we reached base camp on the moraine of the Hunku Glacier, at 5,400m, was it possible for the helicopter to land near camp.

In order to gain acclimatization and to mark the descent route with wands, all ten climbers ascended the southeast ridge twice to an altitude of 6,200m. It took three more days to find a way through the many-tiered icefall under the west face and transfer equipment to the base of the route at 5,900m. Then it was time to embark on the face.

The composition of the assault team was Valeri Pershin (climbing leader), Evgeni Vinogradski, Salavat Habibulin, Nikolai Zhilin, and Yuri Ermachek. The central buttress of the west face was chosen for the ascent; the projecting part of the buttress gave some hope of protection from [the] rock and ice that fell unceasingly on the face between 11 a.m. and 8 p.m. This kilometer-high face [had not appeared] as impregnable and dangerous in photos as it proved to be in reality.

On October 5 [*after the team had fixed seven rope lengths to the site of the first camp on the face*], the five members of the assault team embarked, taking with them provisions for seven days. The remaining expedition members crossed the West Col to the southeast ridge once more, planning to climb to 6,800m, fixing rope at difficult points and setting up wands to help the assault team to find the descent.

The ascent of almost 1.5km [*climbing distance*] took seven days—days of constant physical and psychological tension. Snow merged into rock pitches, often plastered with ice. Steep, fluted slopes collapsed under your feet and would not consolidate. Every step demanded great physical and nervous outlay. In order to arrange protection, the leader literally had to dig into the snow to a depth of about a meter in order to reach ice or rock where it was possible to place an ice screw or piton. There were no good bivouac sites. Every day, two and a half to three hours were spent organizing tent sites.

Only on the ninth day did the climbers get down to base camp. Dirty and unshaven, with faces blackened by the sun, they smiled as they slowly took off their heavy boots, pulled off their clothes, exposed their thinner bodies to the sun, and shared their impressions, which had not yet had time to fade.

— **SERGEI EFIMOV,** *RUSSIA*

The north side of Chamlang (7,319m), showing (1) the unclimbed north pillar, (2) A l'Ombre du Mensonge (French, 2021) on the north face, (3) UFO (Czech, 2019) on the northwest face, (4) 1990 German ascent to the upper west ridge (fourth ascent of Chamlang), and (5) 1986 Japanese route up the west ridge. *Andy Houseman*

CHAMLANG'S NORTH FACE
A MAJOR NEW ROUTE IN EASTERN NEPAL

BY LINDSAY GRIFFIN, *AAJ*

ON OCTOBER 4, six French alpinists—Charles Dubouloz, Damien and Fanny Tomasi, Aurélien Vaissière, Benjamin Védrines and Symon Welfringer—arrived at a 4,970m base camp in the Hongu Valley, below the north face of Chamlang (7,319m). In 2019, Védrines had attempted the unclimbed north pillar and then climbed the northeast couloir to a 7,240m foresummit on the east ridge of Chamlang (*AAJ 2020*). He was now back with Dubouloz for the main event: a new direct route up the north face. The other four climbers would attempt the north pillar.

Dubouloz and Védrines spent October 1–3 climbing and sleeping on Mera Peak (6,470m). From then until the 9th, when they slept at a previously placed camp below the face at 5,450m, they either rested at base or cached gear at this higher camp, on one day climbing over the berg-schrund to check snow conditions on the north face and leaving a rope fixed (a good precaution, as it happened, because by the time they made their attempt, the slot had opened considerably).

Leaving on the morning of the 10th, the pair simul-climbed the first 300m of the face (55–65° snow) and then pitched more difficult ground between 6,000m and 6,400m, finding the climbing much steeper than they had envisaged. They bivouacked to the left of what would prove to be the crux section and spent a fairly miserable night due to heavy spindrift.

Next morning, they made a rappel to reach the start of the 200m crux section and climbed through it over thinly iced terrain (WI5+ M5+), bivouacking just above at 6,700m. According to Védrines, this was the worst night of his life, as spindrift constantly tried to collapse the tent and came through the walls and into his sleeping bag. The pair had very little sleep. They experienced no wind while climbing the lower and middle sections, but in the upper part had mostly continuous 70–100km/h westerlies, which funnelled spindrift down the north face.

On the 12th they found the upper slopes less sustained (45–50°) and in good condition. At first, they pitched but then climbed unroped, stopping only to belay two mixed pitches of M4 and M5. After eventually joining the last section of the 2019 Hák-Holoček route, UFO, on the northwest face, they arrived on Chamlang's summit at 3 p.m. in strong wind.

Moving fast, the pair traversed over the top and descended to a bivouac at 6,600m on the west ridge by 4:30 p.m. The following day they climbed unroped down the west ridge, finding it sharp in sections ("a little like Lyskamm in the Valais Alps, only steeper"). The pair arrived back at base camp around 1:30 p.m. They named the route A l'Ombre du Mensonge ("In the Shadow of Lies," ca 1,600m, ED WI5+ M5+ 90°, with around 10 sustained pitches of this technical grade in the crux section).

Meanwhile, the other four French had reached a 6,100m camp on the plateau below the north pillar, but had found too much snow for a safe attempt. Instead, they chose to try Hongku Chuli's southwest ridge. On the morning of the attempt, while packing up without wearing gloves, Welfringer badly injured his thumb when a tent pole snapped. After some debate, the four descended to base camp.

On the 15th, with everyone resting in base camp, and knowing that heavy snowfall was on its way, Védrines decided to solo the southwest ridge of Hongku Chuli (6,833m). This mountain is officially unclimbed but may have been ascended from the north in 1952 by the Evans-Hillary-Shipton expedition (the 1954 Hillary expedition climbed Hongku Chuli West from the north), and since then by

unauthorized parties. The southwest ridge, however, was more than likely unclimbed, although it had been attempted in November 2019 by the German guide Luis Stitzinger and his client, Manuel Moeller, who turned back 300m below the summit.

Védrines was able to use his fellow team members' tracks on the 300m west-north-west face of the 6,070m col that gives access to the plateau below Chamlang's northeast side as well as the start of Hongku Chuli's ridge. Above the col, Védrines found mixed ground on the ridge and then a prominent rock section (III). Beyond another col was a beautiful sharp snow arête with a few mixed steps, which led to a 300m-long plateau. Above this were sections of 40° before he reached the summit.

Lacking energy, Védrines began to doubt he could descend the way he had come, and he tried to inspect the west-northwest ridge. As he couldn't see the lower section of this ridge, he returned by his ascent route, and fortunately felt stronger as he lost height and the downclimb proved less difficult than anticipated. The team left base camp on the 16th.

— WITH INFORMATION PROVIDED BY **RODOLPHE POPIER**, HIMALAYAN DATABASE, FRANCE

[Top] Tracks to Col 6,070m and the start of the southwest ridge of Hongku Chuli, which slants up left to the summit. [Bottom] Seen from high on Chamlang, the southwest ridge of Hongku Chuli points toward the camera. *Benjamin Védrines (both photos)*

The Kang Yatze Group from Hangkar to the northwest: (A) Kang Yatze I (6,400m, first known ascent in 1982); (B) Kang Yatze II; (C) Kang Yatze III, and (D) Kang Yatze IV (6,130m, climbed in 2021). *Sonam Yangjor*

LADAKH

KANG YATZE IV, WEST FACE AND NORTHWEST RIDGE

ON AUGUST 1, Sonam Yangjor, Stanzin Wangial, and I made the first documented ascent of Kang Yatze IV (6,130m).

Kang Yatze (commonly called Kang Yissay in the past) is the high mountain group at the head of the Markha Valley; the highest summit is Kang Yatze I (6,400m), with a subsidiary summit to the northwest called Kang Yatze II (6,175m). British climber Mike Ratty, who visited the area twice in the 1990s, noted two more peaks on a southern arm that he suggested should be named Kang Yatze III and IV.

A three-man British party made the probable first ascent of Kang Yatze III (6,310m) in August 2015 (*see AAJ 2016*). After much research and talking with knowledgeable climbers, I concluded that Kang Yatze IV remained unclimbed. However, just as the British did, I have been careful to call our eventual climb the first documented ascent, since there have been many undocumented climbs in Ladakh.

Our climb took three attempts. Aloke Kumar Das and I first tried in winter. We ventured deep into the Markha Valley at the end of February 2021, but at a crucial stage, one of Aloke's almost new plastic boots came completely apart.

I came back in April with Sonam and Stanzin, approaching Kang Yatze IV directly from the Langthang Chu valley. We placed our final camp at 5,400m, but the night before our summit push, we were hit by a fierce storm and eventually retreated.

On July 24 we left Leh to begin our third attempt. Earlier in the year, we had taken a good road constructed during the lockdown in 2020 all the way to Markha. However, in July we could only go partway due to dangerously high river levels. On the 26th, we reached base camp at 4,410m in the Langthang Chu.

On the 29th, we established Camp 1 at 4,950m, where it then rained until late afternoon on the 30th. From a vantage above camp, the west face and northwest ridge of Kang Yatze IV looked long and tedious but doable.

On the 31st, in the rainfall to which we had now become accustomed, we walked to a summit camp at 5,180m. To our great surprise, at 5 a.m. the following day we set out under a starlit sky. The west face was at first steep scree, then ribs of shattered rock, then a snow slope. We arrived on the northwest ridge at 5,800m. Engulfed in dense mist, we ascended the ridge for nearly a kilometer, turning a succession of gendarmes on the west side. At 2 p.m. we were on the north summit (6,130m, 33°44'24.6"N, 77°32'25.9"E; there are two summits that appear to be of equal height). The grade of our route was AD. After a long wait on top for the clouds to lift so we could enjoy the view, we regained our camp at 8:30 p.m. 📄 📷 🔍

— ANINDYA MUKHERJEE, *INDIA*

HIMACHAL PRADESH

LAHAUL-SPITI, FYANLABTE WEST SUMMIT, NORTHWEST RIDGE

IN AUGUST, RAJESH Gadgil, Vineeta Muni, Atin Sathe, Rajendra Shinde, and I explored a branch of the Karcha Valley, where part of the team made the first ascent of a 6,065m peak.

We had set out to explore the Gyundi Nala, but heavy rain and snowfall in the previous weeks would have made it difficult for us to proceed into this valley with loads.

We switched to Plan B, an exploration of the branch of the Karcha Valley leading to the watershed with the Bara Shigri. This branch is named Valley 4 on the Karcha Nala sketch map that appears in *AAJ 2019*. (Some members of the team had explored Valley 3 in 2018.) Base camp was established on August 8 at Gharelu (4,500m), the entrance to Valley 4. On the 11th we made advanced base at 5,000m in the valley and Camp 1 at 5,500m on the east bank of the glacier where it bends to the east.

From there we explored a possible crossing to the Gyundi Nala from the watershed ridge south of Ache Peak. It was steep, with much loose scree and broken rock; a higher snow line earlier in the year would surely make this easier. However, a visit to the ridge between our glacier and the Lion Glacier was most rewarding. The Lion Glacier (visited in 1961 by the British women's Kullu expedition) flows north from Lion Peak (6,126m) before bending west then south around Central Peak (6,285m) to descend into the Bara Shigri. A crossing from our Valley 4 glacier appeared

straightforward. The watershed ridge, with the two glaciers on its flanks and a peak at its southeastern end, looked like a butterfly. We decided to attempt this twin-summited peak (32°15'28.86"N, 77°42'17.59"E).

On August 25, at a camp on the ridge at around 5,800m, we received news of the demise of Vineeta's father, and we both started down to return to Mumbai. The next day, via the northwest ridge, Rajesh, Atin, and Rajendra made the first ascent of the 6,065m west summit of the twin-summited peak [*the summits appear to be roughly the same height*], supported by Lendup Bhutia, Vipin Sharma, and Phupu Sherpa. They named it Fyanlabte ("Butterfly" in Lahauli).

Bad weather prevented further exploration, and the remaining members descended to the road head at Batal. 📄 📷

— DIVYESH MUNI, *INDIA*

On the upper northwest ridge of Fyanlabte ("Butterfly," 6,065m). The glacier to the left is the Lion, flowing into the Bara Shigri; to the right is the glacier of Valley 4 flowing down to the Karcha Nala. In the distance are peaks of the Chandra Bhaga Group. *Rajendra Shinde*

[Left] **Approaching the summit of Mt. Ibex (6,220m), east of Sumdo.** [Right] **Leo Purgyil (6,791m, left) and Reo Purgyil (6,816m) from Jogse to the north.** *Jay Prakash (both)*

FIRST ASCENTS IN SOUTHERN ZANSKAR RANGE

SUMDO LIES ON the banks of the Spiti River, has a large military base, and is an important strategic point between the districts of Lahaul and Spiti and Kinnaur. To its east lie many unclimbed peaks of the Southern Zanskar Range, north and south of the highest mountain in Himachal Pradesh, Reo Purgyil (Reo Purgyol, 6,816m). The mountains east and south of Sumdo and close to the border with Tibet are little visited by mountaineers because of travel restrictions and underdeveloped tourism facilities.

Four self-sustained expeditions by the Sumdo-based Snow Saboteurs military team carried out extensive exploration in part of this area between August 2020 and June 2021.

The first sortie took place August 16–28, 2020, when I led a 17-member team into the area east of Sumdo to try peaks in the Jogse Massif. Jogse (6,362m, 32°01'30"N, 78°43'27"E) is a largely rocky peak. From the summit, a ridge runs in an arc to Jogse South (6,335m), then southeast to Peak 6,401m, and finally to a spur that shoots westward to a 6,220m summit popularly known as Mt. Ibex and climbed many times. Starting on the 27th from a camp at 5,283m, a 10-person team climbed the dry and rocky northwest slope of Jogse to make the first ascent. The team then moved north easily to make the first ascent of Peak 5,873m.

A second expedition took place September 21–October 15, 2020, this time to the probably untouched Rakti Khad Glacier, east of Pooh on the Spiti Highway, well south of Sumdo. Our goals were unclimbed peaks 5,985m and, just to the north, Peak 5,974m, both lying on the border with Tibet and overlooking the latter's Shipki Valley. From Camp 3 at 5,078m, our eight-member team climbed the rocky southwest spur of Peak 5,974m. During a subsequent attempt on Peak 5,985m, by the northwest-facing upper Rakti Khad Glacier, formidable crevasses and ice walls forced us to climb out left from the glacier to reach the north-northwest ridge, about 1km from the summit. We retreated from around 5,900m.

From January 28 to February 10, 2021, we conducted our first winter expedition from Sumdo to explore the Chango Heights. Located close to and east of Chango village, this group comprises three prominent peaks north of the Chango Valley: 5,866m, 6,000m, and 6,215m (all 12 to 13km northwest of Reo Purgyil). Making one high camp at around 4,200m, our 15-member team climbed the west ridge of Peak 5,866m over boulders and scree on February 7, gaining the summit after a strenuous 11-hour climb. The continuation ridge east toward Peak 6,000m was heavily corniced, with steep rocky cliffs to either side. [*Peak 5,886m had been climbed before, though this was certainly the first winter ascent. The two 6,000m peaks of the Chango Heights are unclimbed*].

Our most challenging expedition took place from May 10–June 9, 2021. Our goal was to climb six peaks southeast of Sumdo: Peak 6,401m, Jogse South (6,335m), Mt. Ibex (6,220m), Peak 6,104m, Peak 6,098m, and Peak 5,873m (the last already climbed on our August 2020 expedition). These peaks form an arc around the previously unvisited Newlathang Glacier.

On May 31, three groups made the first ascent of the northwest face of Mt. Ibex. Peaks 6,164m and 6,098m are pimples on the north ridge of Ibex overlooking the Newlathang Valley to the east and were climbed easily, as was Peak 5,873m, via the frozen, snow-covered western slope.

Heavy snowfall then added to the challenge of climbing Peak 6,401m and Jogse South. The ascent of the Newlathang Glacier was a crevasse-laden 10km trek, with avalanche-prone slopes to both sides. A final camp was placed to the south of Jogse at 5,963m. On June 6 a 12-person team climbed the northwest flank of Peak 6,401m to reach Newlathang Col, a broad icy saddle, then traversed the upper east face, finally sneaking onto the south ridge to reach the summit. The team returned to Newlathang Col and from there crossed to the southeast ridge of Jogse South, which they followed to its summit.

The Snow Saboteur expeditions have hopefully showed the mountaineering potential of the Southern Zanskar, where there are still unclimbed summits such as Peaks 6,608m, 6,500m, and 6,230m. At present, however, the border area remains restricted. 🗎 🔲

– LT. COL. JAY PRAKASH, *INDIA*

VARIOUS ASCENTS AND EXPEDITION PLANNING UPDATES

EXPEDITIONS TO THE Indian Himalaya from other countries were nonexistent during 2020 and 2021 due to COVID-19 restrictions. However, from time to time, Indian nationals were allowed to travel within the country.

Winter climbing on the higher peaks in the Indian Himalaya is still in its infancy, but during 2020 and '21, several teams of Indian climbers attempted 6,000m summits. Attempts on Deo Tibba (6,001m) in the Kullu region of Himachal Pradesh (February 2021) and Baljuri (5,922m) in the Eastern Garhwal (December 2020) were not successful. [*Details of these attempts are at the AAJ website.*] In February 2021, Sunil Kumar Raju and White Magic Adventure Travel members Sanjeev Rai and Sunny made the first winter ascent of Kang Yatze II (6,175m) in Ladakh. Approaching via the frozen Markha River and the village of Hangkar, the expedition followed the normal route from the northwest, reaching the summit on February 25. [*See also the report on p.274.*]

Previously unreported, toward the end of September 2019, an expedition from the National Institute of Mountaineering and Allied Sports in the state of Arunachal Pradesh made the first ascent of Kangto VI (6,062m). This is one of the smaller peaks of the Kangto massif, which is dominated by Kangto I (7,042m), the only summit in the group known to have been climbed before.

Planning first ascents in the Indian Himalaya has become easier with the publication of the second edition of the Japanese Alpine Club's (Tokai Section) excellent *Indian Himalaya* (ISBN 978-4-8331-5384-3). This 700-page comprehensive guide covers approximately 2,400km of the Himalaya from East Karakoram to Sikkim. It describes all significant ascents, with many photographs. The main text is in Japanese, but there are 28 excellent sketch maps in English (typically at a scale of 1:300,000). Moreover, an English edition is expected in 2022.

Gaining official permission to climb in India remains challenging. Official approval (or rejection) is often not given until a few days before travel, particularly in the border areas. Fortunately, the Indian Mountaineering Foundation (IMF), which administers the application process, has allowed some recent expeditions to specify not only their preferred area (and peaks) but also a reserve area farther from international borders, thus ameliorating the risks of a rejected application. [*Editor's Note: The online version of this report contains additional information, including useful advice on map resources for the mountains of India.*] 🗎

– *INFORMATION FROM* KEITH GOFFIN, *GERMANY, AND* NANDINI PURANDARE/HIMALAYAN JOURNAL, *INDIA*

Aerial view from the south of (A) Pik Pobeda East, (B) Khan Tengri, (C) Pik Voennyh Topografov, (D) Pik 6,747m (a.k.a. Pik Engilchek), and (E) Chonteren Glacier. (1) Northwest ridge (1965), descended to Chonteren Col in 2021. The Zvyozdochka Glacier, used for the approach to Chonteren Col, is hidden byond. (2) South face (Impromptu (2021). (3) South Ridge (2006). *Chen Zhao, CC BY 2.0, Wikimedia Commons*

THE LONG CLIMB
NEW ROUTE AND TRAVERSE ON REMOTE PIK VOENNYH TOPOGRAFOV

BY DMITRY GOLOVCHENKO, *RUSSIA*

PIK VOENNYH TOPOGRAFOV (Military Topographers Peak, 6,873m) is the third-highest mountain of the Tien Shan. Prior to 2021, only three routes had reached the main summit: the northwest ridge (Vodokhodov, 1965), northeast ridge (Korenev, 2003), and south ridge (Dzhuliy, 2006; *see AAJ 2007*). Our plan was a new route on the south face, left of the ridge climbed in 2006. [*Past AAJ reports have referred to Pik Army Topographers, but "Military Topographers" is a better translation.*]

On August 10, Dmitry Grigorev, Sergey Nilov, and I arrived by helicopter at the standard Khan Tengri Base Camp (4,046m) on the South Inylchek Glacier in Kyrgyzstan. The same day we began ferrying equipment toward the mountain. The Zvyozdochka Glacier was heavily loaded with snow, so it took a week to move us and our gear the 20km to Chonteren Col (5,500m) on the frontier ridge with China, between Voennyh Topografov and Pik Pobeda (7,439m). This week gave us enough acclimatization to make an attempt on our objective.

On August 20 we made four rappels from the col to the Chonteren Glacier and crossed it below the south face of Voennyh Topografov, spotting a line of mostly snow and ice leading to the summit. At the start, we found a crevasse at 4,840m where we could camp for the night. We also fixed our four ropes on the initial section of the face.

Next day we added 13 pitches, stopping at a snow terrace at 5,468m. Although it was a comfortable campsite, the wind was strong and we spent two hours making a snow wall to shelter the tent. On the 22nd we climbed a further 16 pitches to reach an altitude of 6,030m. Although we spent three hours working into the night, we only managed to excavate a poor ledge and were unable to get a good night's rest. Next day the weather was bad and we stopped early, after nine pitches, at 6,382m. Fortunately, there was a big crevasse that was more than suitable for a luxury camp.

On the 24th conditions were still bad, but we climbed 12 pitches and prepared our tent site in a sheltered place beneath a large overhanging rock at 6,657m. We planned to reach the summit the next day, but the weather was so bad that we were only able to fix the four ropes before returning to the tent. We tried again on the 26th. However, after reaching the top of the second fixed rope, Dmitry (Grigorev) felt so unwell that we had to return to our campsite below the rock. Later, in a Moscow hospital, he was diagnosed with a blood clot on a lung; at the time we thought he was experiencing a bad attack of high-altitude sickness.

Fortunately, the following morning he felt better, and as the weather was now good, we continued. We gave Dmitry just two sleeping pads to carry in his pack, and Sergey and I took the rest. Above the fixed ropes, we climbed three more pitches to the summit.

The obvious descent was along the northwest ridge, as this leads directly to Chonteren Col. However, it is much longer than any line from the south. After four hours we had descended to around 6,800m, where we dug out a good ledge beneath a snow mushroom. As we continued down on August 28, we had to stop at times because we couldn't see where to go. At 5 p.m., in strong wind and snowfall, we had to camp at 6,058m, disappointed that we hadn't reached the col.

After waiting through snowfall during the morning of the 29th, we moved down in improving visibility and reached the col by midday, the 10th day after leaving this col to start our climb. We then began our descent toward the Zvyozdochka Glacier. Again, the weather forced us to stop early, at 5,311m, below a large snow wall. On the 30th the weather was amazingly good, so we were able to descend to the glacier and cross it. With one more camp at 4,441m, we reached Khan Tengi Base Camp on August 31. This is a large, fixed camp, but the season had already finished, the last helicopter having left five days earlier. It was totally deserted and, sadly, resembled a huge garbage dump. We discovered some abandoned food, including 100 eggs. These were never going to last until 2022, so we decided to "rescue" them. I have never eaten so many eggs in one day!

The next day, after more eggs, we started down the South Inylchek Glacier, Dmitry carrying just a few items of personal clothing and Sergey and I the rest. That night a huge snowstorm covered us while we were erecting the tent, but on the following day the weather was brilliant—we managed to dry our clothing and sleeping bags, and reached the Mertzbacher Meadow at 3,400m, the first green grass we had seen.

On September 3, following a good trail, we got to Willow Camp at 2,940m, and on the 4th, after crossing the At-Djailoo River, we reached the road—a week after we had started home from Chonteren Col. Before long we were enjoying the restaurants of Karakol.

Dmitry had been lucky: first when the clot went to his lung rather than his heart, and second when he managed to get off the mountain under his own steam without too much damage to his lung.

In all, we had spent nearly a month on this adventure. Our new route, Impromptu (5D or TD AI3), had just over 2,000m of elevation gain and around 3,000m of climbing. 📷

Sergey Nilov climbing into the narrows on the right side of a large serac barrier on the south face. *Dmitry Golovchenko*

Pik Oolong, prominent on the left, from the south. In the distance on the right is the unclimbed southwest face of Kyzyl Asker. *Evgeny Murin*

WESTERN KOKSHAAL-TOO, PIC OOLONG, ATTEMPT

IN 2019 A group of trekkers visited the Kyzyl Asker area and posted pictures of unclimbed peaks that attracted the attention of Evgeny Murin, who had climbed the south pillar of Kyzyl Asker in 2018. In the summer of 2021, Murin, Anton Kulpin, Mikhail Makeenko, and Maxim Vinchevsky (all Russian) drove to the north (Kyrgyz) side of Kyzyl Asker. After a week of rain, they received a forecast for five days of good weather and set out with 35kg packs on a trek of about 40km.

They first went south up the Dzhirnagaktu Glacier and then crossed Uigur Pass at its head (4,631m), traversed southeast to another pass of a little less than 4,800m, and descended the east side onto an unnamed Chinese glacier. This put them at a base camp south of their proposed objective, a border peak of 5,300m to 5,400m at 41°0'44.96"N, 77°18'44.27"E, later named Pik Oolong. Also visible from this camp was the untouched southwest face of Kyzyl Asker.

The south face of Oolong was split by an icy depression, and the team attempted a line on the steep granite walls to the left. On the first day they barely climbed 150m. The cracks were icy and often wide (they had not brought large cams). Discouraged by their slow progress, they retreated to base camp. Poor weather was on its way, so the team headed for home. They hope to return, but with better equipment and the easier approach from China. 📷

— *INFORMATION FROM* EVGENY MURIN, *PROVIDED BY* ANNA PIUNOVA, *MOUNTAIN.RU*

BEU-TSE, WEST FACE AND NORTHWEST RIDGE

IN 2010, THE late alpinist Yan Dongdong explored the southwestern end of the Nyachen Tanglha, where he made the first ascent of a peak named Dongxung (ca 6,100m), a few kilometers to the south of the town of Yangbajain (*AAJ 2011*). He wrote that he hoped climbers would try other mountains in this area.

On October 4, 2020, Gong Heqing, Sun Wang, Wei Libin, and Zhang Chaodong, inspired by Yan's writing, started up a mountain south of Dongxung that they believed to be unclimbed. A large and chaotic west-facing glacier descended from the summit. The trio made three camps on the west face, starting their climb on polished rock to the right of the glacier, then moving up the glacier itself, and finally camping on a steep gravel ridge to the left.

On the 7th they moved up the gravel ridge before descending a 30° ice slope to reach the upper glacier. From here they climbed steeply to the northwest ridge and followed it to a point estimated to be 20m below the summit. Unable to make any belay or protection in the snow, they stopped here. The GPS displayed a height of 6,206m.

The Chinese party referred to the mountain as Ba-Ci-Pu and assumed they were making a first ascent. In fact, the mountain has been known as Beu-tse, with a map height of 6,247m, and was climbed in 2003 by the British team of Derek Buckle, Alasdair Scott, Martin Scott, and John Town (*AAJ 2004*). This expedition operated from the next valley north, climbing a steepening northwest face (70° at the top) to reach the northwest ridge, which they followed to a point around 6m below the heavily corniced top. They estimated the summit altitude to be 6,270m. 🖹 📷

— **XIA ZHONGMING**, *GERMANY*

SICHUAN

TATSIENLU MASSIF, SANPINGFENG, WEST GLACIER AND NORTH RIDGE

IN NOVEMBER 2020, Lu Haichuan, Song Yuancheng, Wan Cong, and Zhang Baolong climbed what they believed to be called Bijiashan, a rocky peak toward the north end of the Tatsienlu Massif [*marked as 5,880m in Tamotsu Nakamura's East of the Himalaya book*]. Over two days, they climbed the west glacier (between this peak and the next peak to the north), which was complicated by crevasses, loose rock, and a steep exit onto the north ridge. The ridge itself was straightforward névé. This climb had been unauthorized, so Lu and Zhang returned in December with Bao Yifei and Wang Xuefeng, and an official permit, and summited on the 18th via the same route.

Although there has been some naming confusion in the Tatsienlu, this peak appears to be Sanpingfeng (5,917m, 30°0'8.08"N, 102° 2'52.50"E), climbed by a similar route in 1996 by Mark Carter, John Chilton, Jia Condon, Steve Must, and Rich Prohaska, all with a Fred Beckey expedition. The Chinese most likely made the second and third ascents of the peak. The name Sanpingfeng was awarded to this summit by the famous cartographer Eduard Imhof and geologist Arnold Heim, both from Switzerland, who surveyed the range in 1930. They named the three northern peaks Yipingfeng, Erpingfeng, and Sanpingfeng, which simply mean First, Second, and Third Peak. 📷

— *INFORMATION FROM* **XIA ZHONGMING**, *GERMANY*

QONGLAI RANGE, SIGUNIANG NORTH, NORTH FACE, ATTEMPT

HE LANG AND Liu Yang attempted the north face of Siguniang North (Yangangzi, 5,900m) in August 2020, planning to traverse the summit and continue up the north ridge of Siguniang (6,250m). In two days, they reached the final snow slope on Siguniang North and began to dig a bivouac site about 150m below the top. However, they soon discovered half a meter of fresh snow on top of a 10cm layer of graupel and, given the obvious avalanche danger, immediately retreated.

The only known prior attempt on this side of the peak was made in 2004 by U.K. climbers Dave Hollinger and Andy Sharpe, who attempted the northeast ridge—the left edge of the north face—but gave up after climbing 200m due to bad weather. The summit of Siguniang North may only have been reached once, via the southwest face (WI4+ M4), by a French team in 2006.

A few days before He and Liu's August 2020 attempt, Chen Hui tried to solo the north ridge of Siguniang. Access to the north ridge is by the complex ice slope between Siguniang and Siguniang North (ascended by the French in 2006). In two days, Chen reached a high point of 5,384m (with three roped-solo pitches up to 5.8 M5 60–70°), but after all-night snowfall soaked his gear at his second bivouac, he descended from there in the morning. 📷

— **XIA ZHONGMING**, *GERMANY*

NEW ZEALAND

Hamish Fleming makes a committing leap over the Copland River on day six of the 30-day enchainment. Five preplaced caches and use of huts lightened the climbers' loads, but only so much. *Alastair McDowell*

THE SOUTHERN ALPS ENCHAINED
ALL 24 OF NEW ZEALAND'S 3,000-METER PEAKS IN A LONG PUSH

BY ALASTAIR MCDOWELL, *NEW ZEALAND*

THE CONCEPT OF linking multiple summits in an "enchainment," birthed in the European Alps, has become increasingly popular. In 2015, Ueli Steck completed a 62-day enchainment of the 82 4,000m peaks in the European Alps, traveling between mountain ranges by bike and descending from some summits by paraglider. More recently, Nirmal Purja's fast enchainment of the world's 8,000m peaks in a little over six months—albeit with extensive use of air transportation—has refreshed the idea in the public consciousness.

This style of mountaineering is well suited to New Zealand's Southern Alps, where individual peaks require only a few days of effort at a moderate altitude, but they can be linked to create a much longer expedition. New Zealand has 24 named peaks above 3,000m, the majority clustered around Aoraki/Mt. Cook, with access to Tititea/Mt. Aspiring 175 miles by road to the southwest. For most New Zealand mountaineers, completing the 24-peak list is a lifetime goal. Only two parties have completed all 24 peaks within a single climbing season, with multiple trips in and out of the mountains: Russell Brice and Paddy Freaney in summer 1976–77, and Erica Beuzenberg and Gottlieb Braun Elwert in the winter of 1989.

My hope was to link all 24 summits in a continuous human-powered effort. For the attempt, I teamed up with Hamish Fleming, a Queenstown-based adventure racer who had only moderate mountaineering experience but exceptional fitness and stamina.

Enchainments like this first require an interesting problem-solving stage, searching for an efficient route to link up all the peaks. Our approach was to start the expedition in the Copland Valley, nearly at sea level to the west of Aoraki/Mt. Cook, cross onto the upper Hooker Glacier, traverse over to the Fox and Franz Josef glaciers, before weaving back via the Tasman Glacier

and Grand Plateau, bagging peaks all along the way. We'd then cycle to Mt. Aspiring National Park to finish. We divided the route into seven phases, caching food at five alpine huts around the park, which would also provide shelter from the regular storms that batter the Southern Alps. Some peaks were climbed in long day trips from huts; others involved multi-day ridgeline traverses (the Hicks-Haast traverse entailed 11 peaks over two days).

We started the enchainment on November 13 and emerged from the Aoraki/Mt. Cook National Park after climbing the first 23 peaks on December 10. This was a moment we had visualized for months, and the three-day bike ride toward Mt. Aspiring (3,033m) gave us time to reflect on what we'd experienced.

What attracted Hamish and me to this adventure was much more than ticking off a list of summits— it was the transalpine nature of the journey through beautiful, isolated places. We were committed to completing the trip in a continuous push, embracing all of the mountain's moods. Although there were four major storms during the month, each lasting several days,

[Top] Fleming traversing over Malaspina (3,042m) at sunset on the Hicks-Haast segment of the enchainment, during which 11 peaks were summited in two days. *Alastair McDowell* [Bottom] McDowell (left) and Fleming setting out on their 30-day journey in the rain. *Beale Manguse*

weather windows always seemed to work in our favour. We experienced magical moments, like gazing up at the huge bulk of La Perouse (3,078m) from the remote Strauchon Valley and falling off the edge of the map into the Times Glacier, with Mt. Elle De Beaumont (3,109m) looming above. Deep physical and mental fatigue, sleep deprivation, and dubious weather challenged us as we sought to complete the final peaks with our days running out.

On December 12, 30 days after starting, we summited Tititea/Mt. Aspiring. We felt very fortunate to succeed at our goal of climbing all 24 peaks by human power. Over the course of the month, a total of 160 miles of mountaineering and 175 miles of cycling were covered, with 67,000' of elevation gain.

In a time when travel opportunities for overseas expeditions are complicated by the pandemic, enchainments can provide the mountaineer with interesting expeditions in their local mountain ranges, where the journey through the landscape is equally as important as the summits themselves. 📷 🔍

ANNUAL HIGHLIGHTS

THE SUMMER OF early 2021 was highlighted by a series of adventurous trips into remote areas of the southern ranges.

In January, Leonard Brockerhoff, Ed Cromwell, Nick Kowalski, and Ben Mangan made the long trek into the Garden of Allah, via the Lyell Glacier, where they climbed two moderate routes on Newton Peak (2,543m). Fruit Salad (15/5.7)ascended seven pitches up a previously unclimbed eastern buttress. Apple Crumble, climbed the next day, follows a grade 18/5.10a crack line up a neighboring western buttress.

The following month, down in the Darran Mountains, Jimmy Finlayson, Olivia Truax, and Sam Waetford climbed Mist Crystals (400m, 17/5.9) on the Kaipo Kid buttress, the northwest flank of Peak 2,072m, adjacent to the main Kaipo Wall. The ascent was made during a multi-day circumnavigation of Mt. Tutoko (2,723m).

Asher March and Rose Pearson made a three-day traverse of the central Darrans, from Cleft Creek to the Donne Valley, and in the process completed a new route (250m, 17/5.9) up the northwest face of Karetai Peak (2,206m). Conor Vaessen and

[Top] Northeast face of Torres Peak, showing God's Zone (yellow, 2004) and Southern Traverse (red, 2021). Arrow marks start of Land Bridge (Denz-Gabites-Perry, 1977), zigzagging up ramps. *Alastair McDowell* [Bottom] **The Itch on Mt. Crosscut's West Peak.** *Steven Fortune*

Maddy Whittaker headed up Mistake Creek to climb a 19-pitch new route on the southwest face of Pyramid Peak (2,295m)—New Zealand Alpine Kids Go Climbing (1,100m, 19/5.10b)—which tops out on the ridge between Pyramid and Ngatimamoe (2,164m).

Further north in the Canterbury area, Bernie Frankpitt, Greg Low, and Grant Piper headed to Cloudy Peak (2,403m) to climb The Whole Nine Yards (16 pitches, 21/5.10d). This route goes from the bottom of the west-facing Hourglass Wall to the top of the Great Prow.

To close out the "summer" rock climbing season, in May, Daniel Joll and Ben Mangan paired up for the first ascent of Dream Liner (700m, 29/5.13) on the Airport Wall, above Milford Sound. Joll, who led the effort to climb Airport Wall's first full route, The Mile High Club (700m, 22 pitches, 5.12d) in 2020, returned with James Hobson for the free ascent of Dream Liner.

Attending the annual Darrans Winter Climbing meet in July, Steven Fortune, Ruari Macfarlane, and Alastair McDowell climbed nearly 1,000 vertical meters up through the Crosscut Bluffs to gain access to the southwest face of the West Peak of Mt. Crosscut (2,203m) and there climbed The Itch (700m, IV, 6 (M5)).

Moving north and into early October, McDowell and Pat Gray made the third ascent of the northeast face of Torres Peak (3,160m) via a difficult and aesthetic variation. Starting up the first five pitches of God's Zone (Jefferies-Uren, 2004), they first broke right and then left up a rock buttress, climbing seven new pitches: Southern Traverse (500m, V,6).

Rounding out the month, Joe Collinson, Will Rowntree, and Sam Smoothy hiked in to climb the East Ridge of Aoraki/Mt. Cook (3,724m) en route to making the second ski descent of the imposing 2,000m Caroline Face; the first descent was in 2017 (*see AAJ 2020*). 📷

– BEN DARE, NEW ZEALAND

FLAT TOP PEAK, EAST FACE, SOULFLY

THE HEAD OF Mistake Creek in the Earl Mountains is seldom visited in winter, at least not by climbers. It's a cold and dark place, but when I first ventured there in the winter of 2020, to climb the south face of Pyramid Peak (2,295m, *AAJ 2021*), my eyes were well and truly opened to the vast potential. One feature in particular had caught my attention: a continuous line of ice runnels and mixed grooves that linked nearly a vertical kilometer up the east face of Flat Top Peak (2,282m).

It was almost a year to the day before I returned. The onset of winter saw my anticipation grow and had me eagerly checking forecasts and monitoring freezing levels. When I thought the right conditions had developed, I hiked into the upper Mistake Creek valley on a brisk July afternoon.

In the morning, a warmthless alpenglow began to reveal the secrets of the coming day as I tentatively climbed the slope beneath the face. A thin accumulation of plastered snow and névé covered the otherwise blank and weathered rock slabs. Above, I could glimpse a hanging curtain of icicles emerging from the half-light. A tenuous frozen link to the unknown ground beyond. The first swing into firm water ice both excited and scared me. Losing all sense of time, I immersed myself in the repetitive rhythm of movement. Swing and kick, step up, and repeat. The face slowly came to life with the arrival of the sun, bringing with it both welcome warmth and less welcome intermittent barrages of falling ice and snow. The rattle and hiss from above a constant reminder for caution.

The solid ice on the lower face gradually transitioned into less consistent alpine névé, thinning as the terrain steepened. Protection for belays and runners became increasingly hard to find and tricky to place. Forgoing questionable security for speed, I left the screws clipped to my harness and began to trail the rope. It was the type of ice that climbs well but leaves you on edge: Delicate placements bite, slip, then bite again, sometimes bouncing and skating off the rock below.

Eventually I entered the upper headwall and scratched my way up a thin mixed groove to reach the exit gully. Steep climbing on fine hooks, often with a veneer of ice overlaying the rock below, was followed by an oddly reassuring waist-deep snow wallow. It's not often that you find solace in plowing a snow trench after 1,000m of climbing, but there is a lot to be said for the simple pleasure of being able to stand upright without using your frontpoints.

Reaching the summit brought relief rather than celebration, and the respite was temporary. While not overly complicated, the descent was nonetheless engaging. The long traverse south takes your breath away in equal amounts due to the otherworldly beauty of the surrounding vista and the unrelenting exposure. I felt blessed to look down on the frozen expanse of Lake Erskine, a view enjoyed only by a fortunate few. Savoring the unparalleled silence of the high mountains on a calm day—it's an experience that we as mountaineers are privileged to enjoy, and is what draws me back time and time again.

Soulfly (1,100m, VI, 6+ or AI5+ R M5) takes a line far to the right of the original east face route (1970) and the East Face Direct (1975), both climbed in summer conditions. 📄📷

– BEN DARE, NEW ZEALAND

BOOK REVIEWS

EDITED BY DAVID STEVENSON

THE NEXT EVEREST: SURVIVING THE MOUNTAIN'S DEADLIEST DAY AND FINDING THE RESILIENCE TO CLIMB AGAIN

Jim Davidson. St. Martins' Press, 2021. Hardcover, 409 pages, $29.99.

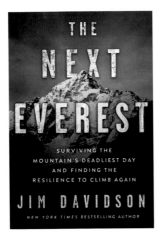

IMAGINE YOURSELF NINE hours into your first acclimatization rotation on Everest, a mountain you had dreamed of climbing your whole adult life, when disaster strikes. A large, deadly earthquake causes massive damage and chaos. By sheer luck, you survive. Others are not so lucky. Nineteen people lose their lives in and around Everest Base Camp. Your expedition is canceled and you walk back down the Khumbu valley, view the devastation of Kathmandu, and eventually arrive home.

Such is the backdrop of Jim Davidson's book *The Next Everest*. Davidson is the best-selling author of *The Ledge* (2011), the courageous story of a difficult self-rescue from a crevasse on Mt. Rainier, the same crevasse that had killed his climbing partner. Obviously, adventure and danger are in his blood. So, when you pick up this book, be ready for a fast-paced, detailed account of one man's experience with the Everest earthquake disaster. Davidson deftly examines multiple viewpoints, using conversations with expedition leaders, medical personnel, and rescue workers to augment his story. He uses his trained geologist's eye to provide details of why Everest Base Camp was so ripe for impact. Intermixed are personal stories of his upbringing, giving the reader context for his climbing motivations. The story flows smoothly.

At first, the book seemed to me to be missing some important context. Right after the 2015 earthquake, when the insatiable attention of the media was focused on Everest, Davidson became a center of attention. He gave live interviews to American news outlets. He was contacted by CNN and Anderson Cooper. What? How did that happen? He was a guided client who hadn't gotten high on the mountain, so why was Davidson a voice for Himalayan climbing? It's only later in the book that the reader begins to understand that Davidson was already a published writer and lecturer, and the picture becomes clearer. Perhaps he is being humble, but a little earlier context would have gone a long way toward heading off the reader's feeling of disorientation.

In the second half of the book, Davidson recounts his return in 2017 for a second attempt on Everest. His journey, as an IMG client supported by a summit Sherpa called PK, is pretty routine, though he provides significant detail, and any aspiring Everest climber, especially one who chooses to use a commercial outfit for support, can learn quite a bit from it. One interesting aspect is his relationship with PK. On summit day, at almost any opportunity—a cold foot, a log jam of climbers—PK wants him to turn back, bringing up the fundamental tug of war between any aspiring Everest summiter and their Sherpa summit guide. There are many reasons a Sherpa guide might advise his client to turn around if things are not going as planned: the guide's desire to return home safely to his family, or perhaps his perception that his client may not be up to the task. Or some other reason. Although Davidson handles this part of the story with dignity and respect, it deserves a more nuanced look.

The Next Everest closes with familiar notions about motivation and overcoming adversity. Many AAJ readers might prefer to get their personal growth insights from self-help seminars or other avenues, rather than from their alpinism. So, when it comes to applying the concept of "The Next Everest" to your life, remember this tale has been told many times before, by many different people, and in many different venues. Not a lot of new ground is covered, and your mileage may vary depending upon your level of experience. If you're looking for a base camp read before an alpine-style ascent on Nanga Parbat, you might want to reconsider. But if you're trying to learn what it's like to summit Everest in the era of modern commercial expeditions, this is a solid read.

— DOUG BROCKMEYER

HIGHER LOVE: CLIMBING AND SKIING THE SEVEN SUMMITS
Kit DesLauriers. Mountaineers Books, 2021. Paperback, 288 pages, $19.95.

EVERY ONCE IN a while, someone attempts a feat so ambitious, it seems nearly impossible. We can't wrap our heads around it. When Kit DesLauriers set out to climb and ski the Seven Summits in 2005, she was ahead of her time. She dared to dream bigger than anyone had before.

Higher Love is an honest and thoughtful account of DesLauriers' endeavor, one she was able to finish in an astonishing two years. Her story is sure to inspire more people, especially women, to climb and ski the world's highest peaks. But more than that, it gives the reader permission to dream, to write down goals and attempt the unattainable.

As a reader, I appreciated the details she provided in terms of logistics and the experience she had on each mountain. In a sense, the book could serve as a guide for a climber attempting to repeat parts of her project. Her book also gives the reader a glimpse into the mind of an elite athlete. Her honesty and transparency about her climbing style and personal approach is refreshing. DesLauriers is straightforward about how she financed her adventure.

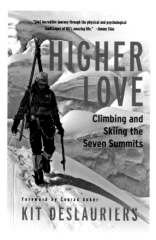

As a woman, I appreciated when she shared the vulnerable moments where she confronts imposter syndrome, as well as the interpersonal dramas that played out on some of the mountains, and especially the conversations with her husband.

Sometimes, her matter-of-fact reporting seems like it was meant to deflect criticism or to answer questions about the style in which she was able to accomplish such an audacious goal. As a woman mountaineer who has had my own accomplishments diminished, questioned, and undercut many times, I can understand why she wrote the way she did. If she hadn't provided all the details, readers likely would have asked for them.

There is not a clear way to combat the double binds that women face in the male-dominated sport of ski mountaineering. (It is another one of the many double binds women have to live in.) If you focus too much on relationships, on the backstory and the emotions, climbers will fail to recognize your accomplishments. Women don't just face the physical and mental challenges of the mountains; there are also cultural barriers to overcome. There's still a societal stigma about where a woman's place is, and many people continue to believe that's not on the top of high mountains.

DesLauriers leans into the double binds as she shares her inner dialogue when she has to think hard about asking for help. At times, I feel like she has to adopt to the masculine norms of leadership in order to be taken seriously. I would've liked to have her lean into her femininity more. I wanted more of the love, heart, and soul. There are moments where the wall around her starts to crack, but it doesn't quite open up all the way to let the reader in.

Kit is a personal hero of mine who paved the way for me to be who I am today. Her contributions to ski mountaineering will live on in history, and *Higher Love* gives the readers insight into how she accomplished them. To climb and ski the Seven Summits in two years, everything needed to line up, not just physically and mentally, but also logistically, culturally, financially, and politically. It took luck, skill, and loads of hard work.

The biggest takeaway is to do it now. Take the moment to write down your wildest dreams and make them happen.

— CAROLINE GLEICH

MOUNTAINS AND DESIRE: CLIMBING VS. THE END OF THE WORLD
MARGRET GREBOWICZ. Repeater Books, 2021. Paperback, 113 pages, $14.95.

MOUNTAINS AND DESIRE is enigmatically subtitled *Climbing vs. the End of the World*. A more accurate subtitle might be *Random Thoughts on the Current State of Mountaineering by a Fangirl* [the author's term] *Trained in Philosophy*. This is a book about climbing as a cultural phenomenon as seen through the eyes of a non-climber. But being a non-climber isn't the problem here; rather, it's her academic training that has led her a bit astray. As in:

> My working philosophy is that climbing is not just something that happens on the mountain's surface, not when the whole world is watching. At least since Mallory, it has taken the form of cultural/semiotic extraction, and this extraction seems to have reached its peak moment.

Cultural/semiotic extraction? Just one of many places in the book where I penciled *WTF?* into the margin. The point I am able to extract here is that she's interested in climbing, now, at the point at which it has become a mainstream activity and plays some kind of role in the culture at large, a phenomenon she traces back to Mallory and its "inauguration of celebrity climbers and celebrity mountains." Mallory's famous and flippant response, "Because it's there," is a kind of announcement, Grebowicz claims, that climbing has an audience, and that fact affects climbing.

The book owes a large debt, mostly acknowledged here, to David Roberts' 1984 essay, "The Public Climber: A Reactionary Rumination." By the time it was collected in *Moments of Doubt* just two years later, Roberts was already defending the friendly accusation that no one had done more to popularize climbing than he had. Roberts' original question was something along the lines of: What does publicity cost in terms of innocence? Climbing that's recorded for the public, Roberts said, is "not the real thing." (Obviously, by the time he collaborated with Alex Honnold on their book *Alone on the Wall*, this opinion had evolved into something else.)

This book is divided into seven short chapters, but I would describe its movement as more recursive than linear. It's also structured, as Grebowicz points out, by the three mountains around which she measures her ideas: Everest, El Capitan, and K2.

Everest, she claims, is "symbolic of a world used up by humans, crawling with amateur adventurers who can afford it and littered with the corpses of those who don't make it down." Much of her discussion of Everest is focused on the use of supplemental oxygen and relies on Everest guide Lukas Furtenbach's assertion that most deaths on the mountain are caused by altitude, and could be prevented by using more oxygen. From there she leaps to the arguable conclusion that "almost all deaths are the fault of expedition companies, not the climbers themselves." This seems a radical oversimplification to me. Yet immediately following that she nicely complicates the issues: "Death by altitude," she notes, "is not exactly an accident since altitude is precisely what climbers seek out." She tempers that with the rhetorical question: "How safe do high-altitude enthusiasts want climbing to become?"

Part of her reasoning stems from her focus on 8,000-meter peak clients and "pro climbers" (guides). She seems unaware that there are other measures of worthy climbing besides altitude. Of course, there are very skilled climbers guiding 8,000-meter peaks. But, for example, if we look at Piolets d'Or awardees, even though climbs in the Himalaya and Karakoram predominate, most are not done on 8,000-meter peaks, nor are most done by Everest guides. She seems to have a limited understanding of what is moving mountaineering forward.

Grebowicz's claim that the "tendency to distinguish between summiting and 'how you play the game'" goes back to Karen Warren's 1990 essay "The Power and Promise of Ecological Feminism" reveals a shockingly limited awareness of our history. Debates about the importance of "how you play the game" have been woven into the fabric of mountaineering from its inception.

She does offer some compelling leaps from the climbing world to contemporary culture: "Because it's there," she writes, "is a symptom of the ever deeper well of uncertainty about why anyone does anything at all." And, "Summiting is not about summiting but can also be a call to re-interrogate and thus re-imagine what one really wants to do with one's time on earth."

For such a compact book, it's packed with a wide range of such big ideas. When I wasn't flummoxed by her opacity or questioning her conclusions, I was impressed by her attempts and ability to find in our still-relatively-small climbing subculture a magnifying mirror to humanity in general.

Grebowicz has a terrific instinct to rely on those whose fingers have accurately taken our collective pulse, like Roberts, who is both prescient and foundational here, but also Steph Davis, whose words may summarize Grebowicz's arguments more succinctly than the author herself is able to articulate: "Perhaps progression [in climbing] means something very different, perhaps it means refining the experience, becoming safer, more elegant, and more aware. Perhaps it means sustainability."

— DAVID STEVENSON

IMAGINARY PEAKS: THE RIESENSTEIN HOAX AND OTHER MOUNTAIN DREAMS

Katie Ives. Mountaineers Books, 2021. Hardcover, 304 pages, $26.95.

THE RIESENSTEINS WERE an invented mountain range, purported to be in British Columbia, that appeared in Summit magazine in 1962. In Imaginary Peaks, Katie Ives unpacks the cartographical mysteries of this hoax, and the unique characters, particularly Harvey Manning, the driving force behind Freedom of the Hills, who perpetrated the prank. Ives locates this moment within the larger context of climbing, literary, and personal history. She immerses the reader in the seemingly endless quest for newly discovered peaks, claims of first ascents, and human desire for blank spots on the map. — Editor

We all have dark nights. We all have dark summits. We all have those cold, desperate slogs to get off a peak, or the moments of terror when the next move is so committing, and a slip is so possible and retreat impossible, that we stuff our rationales deep down. It's been said that perhaps we climbers have short memories, and that's why we keep returning. But I'd argue the opposite.

Before the obsessions, before the certainties, before the knowledge, we were led by imaginings and dreams. Lying on the shag rug of the rumpus room with, as Katie Ives puts it in *Imaginary Peaks*, "scraps of old images that drifted from illuminated manuscripts and sepia-toned maps, tales that slipped from leather-bound volumes and ink-blurred magazine pages…," dreaming of yarding our way up pinnacles, yes, that was painless. Beautiful, too. The sunlight: how it bent. The solidity. The lack of doubt.

This is what Ives has rekindled in *Imaginary Peaks*.

In her retellings, as a fly-on-the-wall of rooms like the Explorers Club library in New York, we watch as friends cook up mountain hoaxes. This is a powerful tool to deflate the overly serious and egotistical, because, "…if modern maps and guidebooks detract from their user's imaginations, you can always shift the peaks around, mix in a few errors and fables, and then see what happens to the people you fool." Because "facts and fiction read the very same way in print."

But look deeper, and before that intention, before the spreading mischievous smiles, even before the first wondering "What if we…" was quietly breached—these were individuals scanning the maps. Smoothed flat by calloused hands, peered at by experienced eyes, pursed over by hardened lips. And in that nascent moment when something caught their eye was a hope. From somewhere deep in the recesses of their childish fascination with maps and mountains, a hope that they would find something everyone else had missed. And a "something" that was not a knoll or a minor ridge, but something hidden and discrete and very, very powerful. And that is where Ives brings us:

> When the world has been fully codified and collated…a sense of loss arises…. It is within this context that the unnamed and discarded places…take on a romantic aura. In a fully discovered world exploration does not stop; it just has to be reinvented…. Hidden geographies are the inverse of lost places; they hint at the possibility that the age of discovery is not quite over.

This dangerous lure, as is all too apparent in this day and age, once the seal on the trust-lamp is broken, that genie is hard to recapture. This book, then, is a guide on how to conduct a hoax, for "what people most desired, it seemed, was folklore, particularly if its content matched what they wanted to hear."

And, ultimately, isn't that what we all want? When we construct these pranks, deep down, it's because we wish someone would do it for us. To lead us out there, with hope of the impossible. A journal description, a map fragment, a clue leading to something just bordering the imagination. That is the fountainhead. That is the vague sunlit memory that launched us all, because the next best thing to finding a treasure map is making a treasure map.

– JERRY AULD

DAMMED IF YOU DON'T

Chris Kalman, with illustrations by Craig Muderlak. Privately published, 2021. Hardcover, 170 pages, $24.99.

AN IDYLLIC, HIDDEN valley. A horde of climbers comes to despoil it. A misguided attempt to preserve the land, whatever that means. Chris Kalman's swift-moving novella treads familiar ground even as it explores a fantastical fictional river valley in Patagonia, surrounded by unclimbed peaks and populated by pumas, condors, and a novel species of salamander.

Kalman is at his best describing Seattle climbers John and Gary making a presumed first ascent up white granite, capturing the moves with prose that manages to feel familiar without cliche. The pair performs "a long and drawn out game of hopscotch," the river below "oxbowed and goosenecked around white beaches."

The story interrogates how the Chile climbing trip of the American duo—one wealthy and white, one not-so-rich and native Coast Salish—launches a series of events that brings climber crowds and destructive tourists to this Shangri-La. That the story's protagonist turns out to be the white and rather clueless climber feels like an admirable challenge on Kalman's part, choosing to follow the rather unsympathetic philanthropist as he flails through the act of protecting the "unspoiled" landscape he introduced to the world. (Smartly, Kalman is quick to interrogate the very colonialist notion of unspoiled wilderness, though indigenous perspective is largely limited to Gary's brief appearance.)

At times it feels as though neither John, who undertakes a scheme to protect the imaginary Lahuenco from either a hydroelectric dam or overuse, nor the author himself, has any real affection for the climbing community. The story is littered with relentless allusions to selfie-takers, drum circle parties in Joshua Tree, and the Disneyfication of Yosemite Valley. But a real understanding of the power of climbing comes through, not only the sport's propensity for destruction of self and environment, but also its sheer ability to connect disparate people and ideas.

Kalman brings real pathos to the appearance and possible extinction of the strange salamander that inhabits the Lahuenco, an amphibian that seems bizarrely out of place in the remote mountains, but whose crawly nature is suited perfectly to the contradictory conditions of a Patagonian river valley. The endangered lizard-like creatures may be as rare as a climber who does not somehow destroy the rock he loves—but when sighted is just as spectacular.

– ALLISON WILLIAMS

THE MOUNTAIN PATH: A CLIMBER'S JOURNEY THROUGH LIFE AND DEATH.

PAUL PRITCHARD. Vertebrate Publishing (U.K.), 2021. Hardcover, 192 pages, £24.

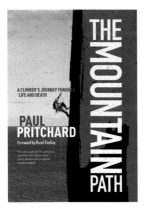

BRITISH CLIMBER PAUL Pritchard's 1998 fall on Tasmania's Totem Pole is one of the most famous accidents in mountaineering history. It left him paralyzed on the right side of his body and became the inspiration for two books. Now, Pritchard has written a third book that concerns the accident, but only peripherally. In it, he takes us on a tour of his thinking and philosophies about climbing as a busted-up old man.

The Mountain Path took Pritchard six years to write, and it contains some outstanding reflections on life, death, pain, disability, perception, misconception, mind games, and, of course, climbing.

Pritchard's first chapter, about freedom, is highly recommended for all readers. Through research and personal anecdotes, he describes why choice can be stressful, and why following a line up a mountain face can become a clarifying experience, freeing us from burdens we are generally unaware of. "With limited choice there is less expectation of a positive outcome," he writes. "We follow a particular sequence of holds up the cliff because it is the only thing we can do.... More choice brings greater expectation. Greater expectation leads to frustration and negativity."

Pain is an important theme, and Pritchard's struggles against his dogged physical state see him dive deep into the philosophy of pain: whether it really is a thing, how it can be offset by the mind, and some treatments that require moving toward a state in which we view pain without "prejudice," that is, as just a thing that exists without value. "This was the profound moment that I realized that by being non-reactive I could simply observe my pain compassionately, as though it were not my pain but someone else's," he writes. "A good feeling, a bad feeling, it didn't make any difference. They were both impermanent manifestations of subatomic vibrations."

From a philosophy for pain, death follows. In 1993, five years before the Totem Pole accident, Pritchard himself experienced a form of death when, after a bone-crunching fall, partner Glenn Robbins could not revive him nor find a pulse for several minutes ("...back then I wrote that this had been 'the most beautiful part of all my life. Utterly final' ").

Death should come naturally, he writes. The event should not pollute with our bodies "...stuck with needles, with a snorkel stuck down our trachea." Modern humans have "the most important time in our lives: our precious last moments on the Earth" taken from us in unnatural ways.

He argues death should be an easy transition because, in essence, we are a part of a greater universe, we are a part of everything around us. And this really is the point of understanding *The Mountain Path*. The people, places, worlds, and universe around are just part of us and we are a part of it. Judgment is unnecessary, and forgiveness and understanding are the keys to success for life and death and whatever life and death might encapsulate. It's a very heady path that Pritchard lays out for us, but one that is beautiful in its simplicity.

On a more basic, fun-climber level, *The Mountain Path* periodically dips into the rise of 1980s British rock stars who lived, like Pritchard, for climbing, often under meager circumstances. No good climbing book would be *sans* action and Pritchard delivers when, 18 years after his accident, he climbs the Totem Pole a second time. It's an arduous journey, but it ties his philosophizing into a nice package, at the heart of which is adventure.

Ultimately, Pritchard pulls himself back to reality in a concrete way to which every climber can relate: "As long as I am moving forward on the path, skyward on the mountain path, I am content. I am content to be on this road always, to not ever arrive. And this is of great consolation. Though, sometimes, especially at night, I do still ask the darkness one question. 'What the hell am I doing here?' "

– CAMERON M. BURNS

TO BE A WARRIOR: THE ADVENTUROUS LIFE AND MYSTERIOUS DEATH OF BILLY DAVIDSON

Brandon Pullan. Rocky Mountain Books (Canada), 2021. Paperback, 248 pages, $28 (CAN).

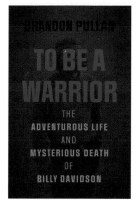

IN THE YEAR 2000, the young author Brandon Pullan is on his first trip to the Canadian Rockies, and after long days of climbing, he reads Chic Scott's book *Pushing the Limits* by headlamp in the back of his truck. The history of Canadian mountaineering mentions hundreds of climbers, but one stands alone: Billy Davidson gets four pages while most climbers get a paragraph or two. As quickly as Billy arrives on the Canadian climbing scene, he leaves.

By 2005 the author has finished college, moved to the Rockies, and on Christmas Day meets up with Scott and two others to drink Guinness and listen to stories. He asks how he can meet Billy Davidson. He learns of Billy's mysterious death the previous year from either suicide or murder. Scott tells Pullan if he wants to know about Billy he'll have to talk to Urs Kallen, one of Billy's best friends.

A few weeks later, Pullan is at Kallen's home for a dinner of Alberta beef and Okanogan wine. Obviously Kallen was impressed by Pullan's fire and says, sure, I'll tell you about Billy, but first you have to write another book for me. Kallen and Dave Cheesmond had been collecting material for a "best routes" book for the Canadian Rockies, modeled after a Swiss book. When Cheesmond was lost with Catherine Freer on Mt. Logan in 1987, Kallen lost his mojo for the project and turned it over to Pullan. That book would become *The Bold and Cold: A History of 25 Classic Climbs in the Canadian Rockies* (Rocky Mountain Books), published in 2016. Pullan then turned his pen toward Billy Davidson.

Kallen guides Pullan, gives him Billy's journals, and points him to people and places where he can find his story. They climb together and the author repeats almost all of Billy's ascents, including the classic and difficult CMC Wall on Yamnuska, which Davidson climbed with Kallen in 1972.

Billy Davidson's mom left him at a Calgary orphanage when he was six. The orphanage was a good place next to a forest, and the Rockies were right there. He started writing and drawing in a climbing journal when he was 12.

After climbing, Billy ends up on the West Coast, living off the land in an ocean kayak. His drawings became paintings, which he sells, and he lives this nomadic adventurous life for 28 years until his mysterious death.

Pullan set out to write the story of Billy Davidson, and he did that and so much more. The book tells the history of the Calgary Mountain Club and its exploits on Mt. Yamnuska. It takes us to Yosemite, where Billy and a group of Canadian climbers do significant early ascents. Billy admits in his journal on his way to solo Tis-sa-ack on Half Dome that he's doing it for fame.

Painting by Billy Davidson

The book wanders between excerpts from Billy's journals and Pullan's narrative. Drinking, tobacco, drugging, and worn wool sweaters permeate the pages. The author sugar-coats no words and the humor is all climbing-centered: "They wasted the day getting wasted. They started earlier than normal the following morning because they were out of smokes, beer and weed and wanted off the wall."

To Be a Warrior sings. After three readings it still sings. The images of Billy's paintings sing the loudest. Hopefully the book becomes a Canadian classic like Joni Mitchell's "River" or Neil Young's version of Ian Tyson's "Four Strong Winds."

Davidson wrote many poems, and I leave this review with the end of one:

If only Yam could talk, what a tale it would tell—the countless epics; sweat, blood; the noisy passage of this boorish lot.

– JAMES P. SWEENEY

THE THIRD POLE: MYSTERY, OBSESSION, AND DEATH ON MOUNT EVEREST
MARK SYNNOTT, Dutton, 2021. Hardback, 416 pages. $29.

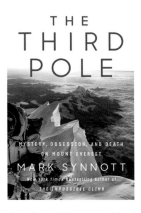

ANY ARMCHAIR MOUNTAINEER knows that Sir Edmund Hillary and Tenzing Norgay are credited with the first ascent of Everest on May 29, 1953. If you've dabbled much in Everest history, you probably also know that George Mallory and Andrew "Sandy" Irvine died in their effort to summit the mountain—an effort that made it tantalizingly close, if not more—in 1924. What I was only dimly aware of before reading *The Third Pole* is how much mystery remains concerning Mallory and Irvine's high point, and therefore the truth behind possibly the biggest first ascent in climbing history.

Synnott's book attempts to answer a series of questions, each of which leads to another, like false summits along a mountain ridge. Did Mallory and Irvine reach the top of Everest—the so-called "third pole"—29 years before Hillary and Norgay? If so, did Irvine capture the moment with the camera he almost certainly carried with him that fateful day? Could it be the camera is still with Irvine's body, and that the film is still viable? And if so, could the greatest mystery in mountaineering history be solved by finding Irvine's body?

Spoiler alert: Synnott didn't find the answers to these questions. But what he found along the way is, in my opinion, far more interesting.

You've probably seen Nirmal Purja's 2019 photo near the top of Everest, with a Disneyland-esque conga line of climbers all vying for the summit along a precipitous serrated ridge. Synnott calls this "the day Everest broke," and he provides an insider's perspective to the occurrences of that day. Indeed, Synnott's experience provides an overarching glimpse into the entire industry of climbing on Mt. Everest, an enterprise that has long struck me as an amalgamation of all the worst elements of climbing: colonialism, capitalism, racism, one-upmanship, hubris, and pride. It's a part of climbing I've seldom had much interest in, or anything nice to say about. If a book about Everest has a target audience, I—in spite of the fact that I'm a climber of close to 20 years—could not be said to be part of that group.

And yet *The Third Pole* vastly exceeded my expectations. Not only did I enjoy reading it, but also I actually found myself yearning to join that absurd procession, gasping for Everest's rarefied air (or from O2 tanks, anyway) from the top of the world. Synnott's pacing was perfect, and the storytelling suspenseful. But the real magic in the book is that it made me long to do something I judged others for doing in the past. In other words, it put me in someone else's shoes.

Synnott's book struck me as deeply truthful. The truth is, it forced me to see my snarky opinions about Everest and its climbers for what they really are: prejudices. I have not been to Everest, nor met many of its suitors, and as such, have no legitimate basis for judging them. Synnott *has* been there and met them, and the impression he relays is far more positive than the critical narrative that has predominated among climbers of mine and Synnott's ilk for as long as I can remember.

Climbing on Everest is a deeply conflicted, deeply problematic industry. Synnott doesn't shy away from that—he leans into it. But even with oxygen, fixed lines, and Sherpa guides, Everest is far from easy. Neither a summit nor survival is guaranteed. No matter who the suitor (including Synnott), there's still very much a question of whether any of us has the mettle to climb the third pole, and return home safely. In that sense, the specter of the summit is just as beguiling today as it was for Mallory and Irvine nearly 100 years ago. That, at least, remains the same.

Synnott was on the mountain to try to find Sandy Irvine, his camera, and the answer to a longstanding riddle. But when push came to shove, he decided to pursue the summit in spite of all manner of complications—including the possibility that doing so might jeopardize the very purpose of the mission. I find that telling, but what precisely it tells me, I won't say. Like Synnott, I'll leave it to the reader to decide. [*Note: In April 2022, The Third Pole was issued in paperback ($18), with a postscript that presents very intriguing new information about the potential whereabouts of Irvine's camera. Hint: It may be locked away in a vault in China.*]

– CHRIS KALMAN

IN BRIEF

THERE AND BACK: *Photographs from the Edge* (Ten Speed Press, $50) collects a "best of" compilation of climber Jimmy Chin's (of *Meru* and *Free Solo* fame) spectacular photographs. Patrick Dean's **Window to Heaven: *The Daring First Ascent of Denali, America's Wildest Peak*** (Pegasus Books, $27.95) tells the unlikely story of the first ascent of Denali led by the Episcopal minister Hudson Stuck. Vanessa O'Brien's **The Greatest Heights: *Facing Danger, Finding Humility, and Climbing a Mountain of Truth*** (Atria/Emily Bestler Books, $27) tells the story of a wealthy client's success on guided 8,000-meter peaks, including becoming the first American woman to summit K2. Best known to readers as a climber, Rick Ridgeway's **Life Lived Wild: *Adventures at the Edge of the Map*** (Patagonia

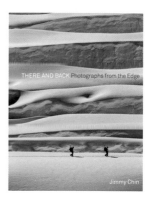

Books, $30) expands the reader's view to see the author as explorer, conservationist, friend, and family man. **Structured Chaos: *The Unusual Life of a Climber*** (Vertebrate Press, £14.95) is past Boardman Tasker winner Victor Saunders's third volume of memoirs. **Kangchenjunga: *The Himalayan Giant*** (Vertebrate Press, £24), finished just before Doug Scott passed away, describes the 1979 second ascent, alpine-style, of the sacred mountain Kangchenjunga.

IN MEMORIAM

Some of these tributes have been edited for length; the complete text and additional photos are at the AAJ website: publications.americanalpineclub.org.

Isherwood Collection

DANA JOAN ISHERWOOD, 1936 – 2021

AFTER A YOUTH and early adulthood in the flatlands, Dana's peregrinations brought her to the Sierra Nevada, where she learned to climb and met an explorer named Bill Isherwood. Dana had loved before—she even had two daughters—but Bill swept away all who came before him. Months after they met, he took her to Peru, where they joined a team aiming to summit the Nevado Huascarán, Dana's first major expedition.

Dana fell in love with the climbing life. She wasn't a tall woman, but she had broad shoulders, large Hobbit feet, indomitable lungs, powerful hands, and an iron will. She didn't reach Huascarán's summit, but she did stand on top of nearby Maparaju, and she was learning and getting stronger.

Not long after Peru, Dana and Bill were on Glacier Point Apron in Yosemite Valley when they met two women, one of whom, Arlene Blum, shared that she wanted to climb Denali but had been told by a travel company that women could not go beyond base camp. Right there, Arlene and Dana hatched a plot for a team of women to climb Denali—unassisted by men.

In June 1970, six "Denali Damsels" flew to base camp on the Kahiltna Glacier. Not long into the climb, the expedition leader, Grace Hoeman, became ill with altitude sickness, yet she refused to turn back. Shepherded by the other climbers, Hoeman reached the summit, but soon after fell unconscious. The climbers wrapped the woman in a sleeping bag, then lowered, dragged, and carried her down. Ultimately, they all descended safely. Blum would later say, "Dana was very strong. I remember her climbs because of her strength. She was [also] a great organizer."

After Alaska, Dana enrolled in a Ph.D. program in geology at the University of Colorado. Women scientists were rare, but Dana didn't let that stop her; science was another great reason for heading to remote, frigid places. She made three trips with Bill to Baffin Island, where Bill was also doing research. The two finished their dissertations and graduated together in 1975.

The Isherwoods returned to California and took jobs at Lawrence Livermore National Laboratory. Dana led an investigation into groundwater transportation of radioactive material from underground nuclear tests. During vacations, she climbed. In 1978, she led a team of Americans to attempt Pik Kommunizma (now Ismail Somoni) in the Soviet Union, then made another attempt the next year. Through the '80s, she joined expeditions to the Caucasus, China, and Pakistan. In the fall of 1985, Dana was chosen for a one-year assignment working for Senator Al Gore as legislative assistant for energy issues. It was a challenging job, but hard work was Dana's superpower.

In 1993, Dana received a diagnosis of breast cancer. She underwent treatment and recovered. When Lawrence Livermore decided to downsize its workforce, she grabbed the buyout and retired in order to travel and climb. In November 1996, she joined a group of breast cancer survivors with their sights set on Mt. Vinson, the highest peak on the Antarctic continent. The climbing team did not reach the summit, so two years later Dana joined a different team and made a second attempt.

In 1997, Dana began traveling to Tibet in trips organized by a small nonprofit, Kham Aid Foundation. This led to her becoming director of KhamAid's education program. Each spring and fall, she flew to Chengdu, China, and boarded public buses to make an arduous weeklong trip to visit schools. Eventually, she persuaded Bill that they should move to Beijing. She started learning Chinese and undertook many self-guided trips with Bill around the region.

After returning to the U.S., the Isherwoods moved to Washington and continued to travel throughout the world. Bill told their friends, "Our trips have gotten tamer as we get older, but we still get out there and have fun."

In the course of working, traveling, and studying in the Buddhist world, Dana had collected many treasures: paintings, statues, even protection yarns personally blessed by the Dalai Lama. In her last years and months, she gave them all away. She will be remembered for her strength, kindness, and indomitable spirit.

– PAM LOGAN

DAVE JONES, 1956 – 2021

Steve Chardon

A LEGENDARY DESERT climber, Dave Jones, 65, unexpectedly passed away at his home on December 27, 2021. He was much too young. Born in Connecticut, Dave graduated with a degree in geology from Dartmouth College in 1978. Moving to Tucson, he received his master's degree at the University of Arizona. He began climbing in college and continued actively for more than 40 years.

Dave did much of his geology in Mexico, where he discovered some of the country's largest gold deposits. He had unique experiences as a geologist, including surviving two helicopter crashes and rowing through the Grand Canyon with no prior rafting experience.

Dave was a strong, bold, and talented all-around climber. His adventures took him to Canada and Alaska, where he made fast ascents of Mt. Edith Cavell, Mt. Robson, and Mt. Huntington. He climbed many walls in Yosemite, including some obscure ones, but his real passion was the walls of Zion, where he made over 20 big-wall first ascents, as well as many shorter climbs. These include the classics Spaceshot, Shune's Buttress, The Vigil, Silmaril, Chastity Crack, and others. Two of his early wall routes were the canyon's first A5 climbs: Empty Pages and Wages of Sin. On the latter, which he climbed with Steve Chardon, Dave stacked and equalized RURPs (pre-beaks) to get up thin sections with ground fall-potential.

Many of these classics included offwidth cracks, which at the time were avoided by most climbers because of the lack of wide-crack protection in the 1980s. His adventurous, bold leads on climbs like Golden Years (5.11 C2), Lovelace (5.10 C1), Rites of Passage (5.11), Cowboy Bob Goes to Zion (5.10 A2), The Vigil (5.11), and others were legendary. Mike Anderson, a leading modern free climber in Zion, said of Golden Years, "Pitch six is the hardman pitch! It's a slanting offwidth that you really have to commit to. It just goes to show that there was some pretty impressive free climbing being done in Zion in those years."

With boundless energy, Dave climbed four new wall routes in Zion during a two-week trip in the 1980s. In 2007, he climbed two first ascents in a four-day weekend. Together, we finished a nine-pitch route on Mt. Moroni, and the next day he prodded us to do a new line next to the Watchman. Dave loved scoping new routes in Zion Canyon, having a great eye for beautiful lines, and he had strong ethics about preserving the fragile sandstone and keeping bolts to a minimum.

Another passion was caving. Dave made many trips to the Guadalupe Mountains and the Lechuguilla Cave in New Mexico, where he mapped out new sections of that beautiful and unique cavern. At the time of his death, he was preparing for a major caving expedition to Mexico.

Dave was an excellent climbing partner, as he was very confident, positive, funny, and patient. He was a solid alpha. Although Dave was plenty aware that he was not the best climber around, he liked to joke about himself and his efforts as "valiant, heroic, and virile". When you asked how he was doing, he would say, "Great—getting younger and better looking!" He was a great writer and storyteller, as well as being skilled at the guitar.

I will never forget his famous "I told you so" smile when I arrived at a belay after climbing something excellent that he had discovered. His unique personality, enthusiasm, knowledge, and friendship will be sorely missed.

– BRIAN SMOOT

Sally Leversee Collection

RICHARD LEVERSEE, 1958 – 2022

The climbing community and many friends have been and remain saddened by the passing of Richard Leversee on January 12, 2022. Although the term Stonemaster is somewhat overused, Richard embraced the ethos, and will be sincerely remembered as one. Thankfully, Richard's first ascents are still with us—as both lasting memory and fine legacy.

It all began when Richard—a geeky high school freshman—signed up for a climbing class in Pasadena, California. Attempting to escape the Los Angeles suburbs, Richard first sought solace in backpacking. Boundlessly bored, Richard's heart intuitively realized that climbing was the next step. After his first climb, at Mt. Pacifico in the Angeles National Forest, Richard was hooked. His soon-to-be-famous energy and inspiration were placed into overdrive when, that same year, the 1972 Chouinard Equipment catalog was released. The pivotal clean climbing revolution had begun, and Richard was all in. With fresh and audacious challenges, climbing became religion and the climbing community became Richard's tribe.

His teen life was typical: Avoiding family functions, every opportunity to climb was taken instead. Nonetheless, epiphany came when "forced" to participate in a family holiday at their cabin in Camp Nelson, California. An ensuing hike to the Needles was magically empowering—befitting the Magician, Witch, Warlock, and Sorcerer's vibrations found there. With advancing technique and energy, Richard soon became the area's first resident climber.

In due time, Richard met E.C. Joe at Dome Rock in 1975. Richard was on a new route when E.C. and friends passed below "ROCK!" After dodging Richard's plummeting bolt kit, E.C. soon discovered that he and Richard were kindred spirits. Their simpatico enthusiasm and infectious momentum led to many fine and coveted backcountry climbs. Two of Richard's own favorites, reflecting his core wilderness commitment and high standards, are Archangel on Cherubim Dome and Crystal Bonsai on Bubbs Creek Wall. The following timeless routes are also worthy of any bucket list: White Punks on Dope and Imaginary Voyage at the Needles, Close to the Edge, Windjammer, and The Spectrum at Dome Rock, and The Sun Also Rises at Patterson Bluff.

Equally, the pair shared a desire to preserve history, without sacrificing adventure; their co-authored *Stonemasher Rockclimbing Guide to the Kern River Canyon and Environs* (1983) accomplished that vision and helped preserve the boldness and ethical quality of classic routes.

Although Richard planned to teach English, he again followed his heart as a Chouinard Equipment sales representative. This 13-year run was a fine opportunity to expand opportunities for adventure—now a very natural part of Richard's soul. During these years, Richard was at the top of his game, highly respected for his climbing, skiing, snowboarding, and photography. Naturally, as time passed, priorities changed, as happens to us all. Despite his passion, Richard became weary of life on the road. So, he followed his heart once more and wisely chose to spend his time with the love of his life, his wife, Cari. He left his outdoor pursuits and found equal reward helping people heal as a massage therapist.

What a fine legacy is left to embrace—following your heart with dynamic energy, to do what you love. The memory of Richard's adventurous enthusiasm—whether in or out of the mountains—will always be a brilliant and haunting force. No matter in tempest, diamond sky, calming starlight, or enchanted cloud, the rock eternally remembers as well. It too has been forever changed by Richard's touch and passing—quietly whispering back, if you listen. To discover this legacy and the soaring freedom created, climbing any of Richard's prolific and bold Sierra Nevada routes will suffice.

– E.C. JOE *AND* DAVID OHST

CESARE MAESTRI, 1929 – 2021

CESARE MAESTRI WAS born in Trento, Italy, in 1929, where as a child he began to climb the walls of buildings and electrical poles—more than a few of these ascents resulted in falls, scratches, and hospital visits. During World War II, the young Maestri joined partisans fighting the Germans. After the war, Cesare's father sent him to Rome to study the history of art, but after two years, unsatisfied, he returned to Trento. It was then that Maestri began to climb in earnest, as a way to escape the daily societal stresses in the aftermath of the war.

According to many sources, he climbed about 3,500 routes in his life, a third of them solo. The Dolomites were his stage: In 1950, at the age of 21, he burst onto the scene by soloing Via Preuss at Campanile Basso. His first solo ascents of the Solda-Conforto Route (650m, 5.9 A2) on the Marmolada and the Guides' Route on the Crozzon di Brenta, both in 1953, were world renowned. In the style of Paul Preuss, he descended many routes without ropes, down-soloing them after he free soloed to the top; he down-soloed routes up to UIAA VI (about 5.10-) on Crozzon di Brenta and Sass Maor. He made a solo winter ascent of the southwest ridge of the

Matterhorn. The list goes on. Maestri also mastered aid climbing and started inventing new gear suitable for hard climbs in the Dolomites, including aid ladders with metal steps, special pitons, and lighter ropes. He used any means necessary—including bolts—to establish new direttissimas. On the one hand he loved Preuss' pure style, but on the other he embraced extreme aid climbing. He loved the "persona" ascribed to him and gave dramatic accounts of his climbs, and for the general public he became known as the "Spider of the Dolomites"—a volcanic, contradictory but also very human character.

Maestri's many accomplishments were overshadowed by the controversies around his two climbs on Cerro Torre in Patagonia. In 1959, he claimed he had reached the summit via the east and north faces with Toni Egger and that, while descending, Egger was wiped out by an avalanche. Doubts soon arose, and Maestri issued a whirlwind of ferocious polemics against the growing chorus of detractors. He returned to Cerro Torre in 1970, this time on the southeast ridge, where he placed hundreds bolts using a heavy gas-powered compressor—which he left hanging on the wall—and descended from just below the summit mushroom.

For the rest of his life, Maestri refused to explain more about his 1959 Cerro Torre story, which is not accepted by today's climbing community. Tragically, the Cerro Torre controversy entangled Maestri like a spider caught in his own web. But his many critics sometimes went too far, exaggerating his transgressions and crossing the boundaries of common sense and respect. In my personal journey of reading and learning about this complex character, the following passage, from Maestri's book *Two-thousand Meters of Our Life*, is how I shall remember him, as it captures both his divisiveness and passion:

I have always been an advocate of the principle according to which every mountaineer should be free to go to the mountains as he pleases: day or night, with pegs or without, to find God or deny him, for comfort or despair. By doing so we would have as many forms of mountaineering as there are people who go to the mountains, and no single form would preclude or lessen any of the others.

— FEDERICO BERNARDI

Nikki Smith

RICK REESE, 1942 – 2022

RICK REESE WAS a great friend, humble, understated, honest, and so full of life. He had the ability to inspire us and lead us forward. He carefully balanced his zest and daring with common sense in the mountains. Approaching a mountain route with Rick gave us a certainty that he would climb strongly, safely, and joyously. And that he would show deep appreciation of the mountains, the sky, and nature.

In the late 1950s, the Alpenbock Climbing Club was the epicenter of climbing in Salt Lake City, and Rick pushed the limits in forging new routes in the canyons of the nearby Wasatch Range. In 1962, with Ted Wilson, he made the first ascent of The Great White Icicle, long before ice climbing was popular, as well as spectacular rock routes like Crescent Crack, Pentapitch, and Flashdance. Rick's National Guard unit was called to active duty for a year in the early 1960s, but after his service, his ascents spread. In 1963 he and Fred Beckey pioneered the Beckey-Reese East Face Direct on Day Needle in the Sierra Nevada. In the summer of 1964 he became a Jenny Lake ranger in the

Tetons, where he and the team performed mountain rescues, including the famed North Face rescue on the Grand Teton in 1967. After the Tetons, while still in graduate school, Rick and his family spent the summer at Mt. Rainier, a mountain he had loved since he climbed it at age 16

But Rick was not just a climber. He met his wife, Mary Lee, while studying philosophy at the University of Utah. They moved to Denver where Rick worked on his Ph.D. at the University of Denver, doing his research on dangerous revolutionary conditions in South America. They then moved to Helena, Montana, where he taught at Carroll College. Their two children, Paige and Seth, were born there.

Inspired by the mountains of the West, and also greatly influenced by the climbers, explorers, and conservationists who came before him and had worked tirelessly to protect places like the Tetons and Yellowstone, Rick and his family moved to Yellowstone National Park after his teaching career, where he created the Yellowstone Institute in the Lamar Valley in 1970. Building upon the work of his mentors, in 1983, Rick co-founded the Greater Yellowstone Coalition, now the leading conservation group fighting for the protection of this incredible 4.5 million acre ecosystem. Rick went on to co-create the Yellowstone Business Partnership. In publishing, he founded both the Utah Geographic series and the online Mountain Journal.

Moving back to Salt Lake City, he conceptualized Utah's Bonneville Shoreline Trail and worked for years to complete it. Were it not for Rick's tireless and tenacious work on behalf of these magnificent, globally recognized mountain landscapes, there is no question the West would be a much diminished place today, and all of us, and future generations, would be poorer because of it. In 2022, the American Alpine Club recognized Rick's accomplishments by awarding him the David Brower Award for environmental stewardship.

Along with being one of the most important Western conservationists of our generation as well as a bold, tenacious, and accomplished climber and ranger, Rick was a beloved husband, father, brother, grandfather, and dear friend to so many people. We will all remember Rick with the quote of Geoffrey Winthrop Young: "I have not lost the magic of long days: I live them, dream them still. Still am I master of the starry ways, and freeman of the hill." Indeed you are, Rick.

– RALPH TINGEY, TED WILSON, *AND* PETER METCALF

HERBERT AUGUST RICKERT, 1926 – 2021

IN A GESTURE befitting how he lived his life, close to nature and its poetry, my father, Herb, chose the harvest moon, September 20, 2021, for his departure. His focus around the appreciation of nature, both in its raw elements and its lyric forms, and in what he saw as the poetic synchronicity within it, was rooted in a profound well of literature, art history, mythology, and natural history; his spark was most lively when weaving together these strands, giving resonance to kinships he recognized.

Herb's early life was spent exploring the woods around Cleveland with friend Don Eckelberry, formative in shaping his interest in nature and art. While studying engineering on the GI Bill at the University of Kentucky, he met Willi Unsoeld. They began climbing on nearby cliffs and took glee in scaling campus edifices. This grew into trips out West to the Rockies, Tetons, and Cascades.

Susanne Pestel

When World War II ended, Herb traveled to Switzerland to study; he also worked with Ernst Feuz at the Swiss Foundation for Alpine Research, testing and developing mountain equipment.

In 1949, Herb, Willi Unsoeld, and Englishman Laurie French embarked on an attempt on 6,596-meter Nilkantha in the Garhwal Himal. To fund their trip, the trio worked an entire winter in a Swedish iron foundry, then spent weeks aboard a cargo ship, peeling potatoes en route to India to earn their keep.

Always a minimalist and improviser in the mountains, he never did need a stove, hardly graduated from his tube tent even for snow camping, and often preferred to repose directly on the ground or needles. In the mid-1950s, he walked the John Muir Trail without a sleeping bag by means of an insert he'd sewed for his jacket that allowed him to rest by day and hike by night, subsisting on oats and raisins and cold instant coffee.

Out of teaching basic English courses at UC Santa Barbara grew Herb's idea of a wilderness writing class. From the mid-1960s to early '70s, he taught this celebrated course and took groups of bright-minded, thirsty students on free-form outings in the High Sierra through all seasons. Taking this spirit into the chapter of his life as an older father, a period of free-flowing family outings to the mountains and thousands of foot-miles across Europe followed, quietly and steadfastly supported by my mother, Susanne Pestel.

Just as Herb was perpetually immersed in study, he was also devoted to the practice of art and music. He saw these, along with time spent in the mountains and nature, as an expression of honoring and preserving wildness in the world and the human spirit and soul. As a writer, he excelled in the letter form; in art, at sketching. In exception to his minimalist equipment, he had no hesitation to carry his fiddle to a summit in celebration of a composer's birthday or a solstice or equinox.

In the later years of life, Herb took greatest pleasure in being with his family in the mountains, watching his grandson, Finn Zeugswetter, grow into his own love for nature. And he cheered and studied along vicariously on his daughter Hjördis' and then partner Bernd's mountain-driven life.

Nearly half a century after his footsteps on the John Muir Trail, he walked the remaining Pacific Crest miles at age 80, with a wistfulness to the ending of a cheerful theme. Into his old age, Herb retained boyish impishness and exuberance, remarkable balance and spring to step, taking to spontaneous dance with his dogs; delightfully off-keel with quip and larking remark; at times erupting in body-trembling glee at a literary passage or some mischief. And always yodeling and joyfully waving at reuniting and at bidding good-bye!

– HJÖRDIS RICKERT

DAVID ROBERTS, 1943 – 2021

I WAS TEN when I first met the writer and mountaineer David Roberts, who was sitting at my parents' kitchen table with Jon Krakauer and another friend. Huge wire-rimmed glasses framed David's face, adding intensity to an already owl-like gaze, and the expression "does not suffer fools" would have come to mind if I'd known it. My mom whisked me upstairs and I tried to eavesdrop the adult conversation below—climbers talking about climbing.

Some time later, my dad crept into my room while I was sick with a fever and gave me David's first two books—*The Mountain of My Fear* and *Deborah: A Wilderness Narrative*—and I read both in a single day. Mountains unfolded in my bedroom. From then on, I harbored a secret dream—more than anything, I wanted to do what Roberts did.

Apart from his fellow Harvard alum Bradford Washburn, no one explored more unknown

Mat-Hale

terrain in Alaska than David did. His very first Alaskan expedition, as a 20-year-old in 1964, yielded a new
route on Denali, the Wickersham Wall. In a decade of
fevered exploring, he completed new routes or first
ascents of remote peaks on an annual basis, most of
which are still sought after by alpinists. His finest
achievement was his last serious climb in the range,
the Southeast Pillar of Mt. Dickey, one of the largest
and most imposing granite walls on earth, which David
ascended over three days in 1974 along with Galen
Rowell and Ed Ward. On their third day of climbing,
thousands of feet above the Ruth Glacier, a threatening storm settled over the range. Rain turned to snow.
With the team's single pair of crampons and an ice axe,
Roberts led into the gale over verglassed loose rock. It was a brilliant bit of alpinism.

Memorialized in *The Mountain of My Fear*, Mt. Huntington's Harvard Route is Roberts' best-
known Alaskan achievement, but the tragedy that ensued when Ed Bernd fell to his death on the
descent haunted David his entire life. Yet the route's modern popularity attests to its elegance,
to the line Roberts and his young companions so cannily divined from Bradford Washburn's
photographs.

Bernd's accident on Huntington also launched Roberts' writing career; in just nine days, he
churned out *The Mountain of My Fear*, a slim volume that, at first, struggled to find a publisher,
though the book soon attracted the attention of critics who knew little about climbing but a lot
about good writing, notably the British poet W.H. Auden, who told Roberts that "your book is
one of the finest of its genre I have ever come across."

David's journalism spanned more than a half-century; his diverse palette led him to write biog-
raphies of figures as disparate as the American short story writer Jean Stafford and the Australian
explorer Douglas Mawson. As a freelancer, he wrote about Jeff Lowe's solo ascent of the Eiger,
the ruins of Ancestral Puebloans, the sordid lives and horrid deaths of polar heroes. Upon retir-
ing from Alaskan alpinism, he turned his obsessive zeal to the desert Southwest, tracking down
Puebloan sites and tracing, with admiration, the ways of these ancient climbers. He published
more than 30 books and countless articles—a staggering body of work.

To the maddened chagrin of other writers, David wrote clean, clear stories without hesitation,
the speed and clarity with which he clacked out copy astounds me still. He laughed imagining
his friends laboring over word choice and fretting over sentence structure, the way a boulderer
might struggle on a particular sequence of moves.

Despite profiling hundreds of people, David's writing shone most when turned inward, when
it examined his own struggles with death, with tragedy, with the lingering questions of why climbers and explorers seek out risk. He was not the first adventure writer to tackle these subjects,
but his prose was strong and stark enough to endure, to become part of our collective canon, to
tackle his trauma head on. These contributions changed the landscape of adventure literature.

Despite our early meeting, I did not speak to David again until after I graduated college. Before
two friends and I attempted Mt. Deborah in Alaska, I reached out for beta with trepidation; he
replied the same day, and soon sheafs of archived AAJ articles and photographs pinged into my
inbox. The fire always burned bright with David.

When I sent him a story I'd written about our failed expedition, he encouraged me to keep writing. I was not the only person who benefitted from his enthusiasm and shrewd, unyielding insight: far from it. David taught writing at Hampshire College in the 1970s, and there he realized the potential of a young Jon Krakauer. Later, he plucked writers from Banff workshops and helped them secure book deals or introduced them to editors. He loved the craft of writing; if he couldn't write a story, he hoped someone else would, and he'd share it with enthusiasm when it came out.

When David was diagnosed with stage IV throat cancer in 2015, the urgency and pace of this writing increased and he produced some of his finest work. With his wife, Sharon, by his side, he documented the fears and physical ailments of this disease. In this short time, despite endless hospital visits and a plethora of complications, David finished three more books. *Limits of the Known* is my favorite of these, burdened with questions about the deaths we all must face, yet soaring with hope and wonder for what we call adventure.

Even in poor health, David climbed, too, marching to cliffs and rock gyms as best as he was able, never ceasing to quest upward. Partners and confidantes were as important to him as the wild places he'd been, and many of these recent trips were completed with Matt Hale or Ed Ward or Jon Krakauer, climbers from his Alaskan expeditions a half-century ago. He adored holding court at Banff dinner parties or evenings at his house in Watertown.

Most important to David was Sharon, who provided the perfect foil to David's staccato lines of questioning. A professional psychoanalyst, she softened his journalistic edges. Over the last few years of David's illness, Sharon worked tirelessly to care for him while he kept writing. Never once did I see her waver.

David once joked that his obit's lede should read: "He died after a feeble and pathetic battle against cancer." The truth, of course, is that no one peered into that abyss with more courage or grace.

— **MICHAEL WEJCHERT**

This tribute is adapted from a longer article published at adventure-journal.com on August 26, 2021.

MUHAMMAD ALI SADPARA, 1976 – 2021

ALI SADPARA was first and foremost a great alpinist and not "simply" a high-altitude porter (HAP). He had the ambition to create a new generation of strong climbers in Pakistan and to replicate in his country a tourism industry similar to the one in Nepal. This is why he so often collaborated and climbed with foreign (especially Nepali) friends.

Even coming from a very poor region and family, Ali was very open-minded. He was humble and ambitious at the same time, with the right balance of these two traits. In the mountains, he was always so happy and enthusiastic, and in the Pakistani climbing community, he was a charismatic and much-loved figure.

Ali had climbed many of the 8,000-meter peaks, including four ascents of Nanga Parbat. It was of course a great privilege to realize with him and Alex Txikon the first winter ascent of Nanga Parbat in 2016. I will forever remember those days in the tent during our climb, and it was incredible how gentle he was with Tamara Lunger (who was ill and stopped less than 100 meters below the summit of Nanga Parbat), and in general how respectful he was of women. He was really a great ambassador for his country and Pakistan's northern areas.

We had ideas and plans for future climbs together, but then came the K2 tragedy in early February 2021, when Ali, Juan Pablo Mohr, and John Snorri never returned from their summit bid. However, for sure, Ali's death did not end his influence on Pakistan's new generation of climbers. Now, for example Sirbaz Khan is attempting all of the 8,000-meter peaks, following the Ali Sadpara example, and he frequently remembers and thanks Ali for his influence. Ali's son Sajid is also trying to follow his father's example and career. He had a very proactive mentality, and this is why he is considered the "father" of modern mountaineering in Pakistan.

We will miss him a lot , but I'm sure that many young Pakistanis will continue the work that Ali Sadpara started.

— SIMONE MORO

JOLENE UNSOELD, 1931 – 2021

Unsoeld Collection

FORMER CONGRESSWOMAN, MOUNTAIN climber, and lifelong adventurer Jolene Unsoeld began climbing with the Mazamas in 1949, her first ascent being the south side of Mt. Hood in logging boots with caulked soles. In the summer of 1950, after her first year at Oregon State College, she did the WyEast route on Mt. Hood and then climbed Mt. Shuksan. She met her future husband, Willi Unsoeld, that fall at OSC; she always said that he had fallen in love with her GI mountain pants, she with his Aladdin mountain stove—as well as his storytelling around the campfire. They got engaged on the top of Mt. Saint Helens.

Their first summer together as a married couple in 1951 was in the Grand Tetons, where Willi was hired as a guide. Thereafter, she got to climb every other summer, between each new baby that came along. Her climbs included the first ascent of the Direct North Face of the Grand in 1955.

The "fierce intimacy of marriage," as Jolene put it, and family life were of utmost importance to the parents of Regon, Devi, Krag, and Terres. They were able to manage through long separations, including Willi's expeditions. But the three years of Peace Corps in Nepal, where Willi was assigned as deputy director, were for Jolene an "ideal match for Bill and me: adventure, service, and full involvement of the whole family," as she wrote in her memoir, *Wild Adventures We Have Known*, published in 2016. Jolene flourished: raising four kids in a foreign land, teaching English, and working to help local Nepali women.

When the family returned to the United States, they lived first in Andover, Massachusetts, where Willi was deputy director of Outward Bound. In 1970, the Unsoelds returned to the Pacific Northwest, where Willi became a founding faculty member of Evergreen State College. Jolene joined the local chapter of the League of Women Voters and the Coalition for Open Government. She registered herself as a lobbyist, occupation: "Professional meddler, unpaid."

The following years included the death of daughter Nanda Devi in 1976, when she fell ill on the mountain she was named for, and Willi's death in an avalanche, with that of a student, Janie Diepenbrock, while leading an Evergreen college group in 1979 on Mt. Rainier.

Jolene became a spokesperson for the value of risk. In 1979, just four months after losing Willi, she was the keynote speaker at the annual conference of Association for Experiential Education. She spoke of her losses but also of the importance and understanding of why we take risks. She elaborated on the topic again as keynote at the annual Wilderness Risk Managers Conference (WRMC) in 1994. "I understand our need to avoid the inevitable moment that comes to us all—death," she said. "But to control death is to control the life—and that's a kind of life Bill and I would not have wanted to live."

Jolene was elected to Congress from Washington state and served from 1989 to 1995. As a congressperson, she was an early progressive, backing environmental and feminist causes and pushing for government transparency.

From the 1990s to 2017, in addition to writing two autobiographies, Jolene would go on two-week adventures each year with her daughter Terres. Her last climb was an ascent of Kilimanjaro with Terres in 1995.

Let us conclude with more of Jolene's own words, from her speech at WRMC: "When tragedy strikes, we can't just sit around and feel sorry for ourselves. We have to rise up and make something of our life—for no other reason than to keep ourselves from drowning in grief—but for a very much better reason of trying to make the world a better place—so when it is our turn to go, we can rest easy—knowing that somehow, in our own little way, we made a difference…. I cannot say I know what wild adventure awaits us on the other side. But I am open to all possibilities."

– JED WILLIAMSON *AND* TERRES UNSOELD

GEORGE WHITMORE, 1931 – 2021

IN THE SPRING of 2020, legendary climber and conservationist George Whitmore, 89, texted a friend about November 12, 1958, the day he and partners Warren Harding (1924–2002) and Wayne Merry (1931–2019) completed the first ascent of The Nose on El Capitan. "I am now the last man standing, and the wolves are circling," Whitmore wrote in his text. "Probably don't have much time left. In the meantime, I get satisfaction from questing after unreachable stars." On New Year's Day, at a hospice facility in Fresno, California, Whitmore, weakened by complications from COVID-19, finally reached those stars.

Climbing El Capitan ranks with the most unlikely tasks a human can ever do. Even with the space-age technology and Olympic-caliber fitness of modern climbers, scaling El Capitan is never a sure thing. In 1958, it was revolutionary.

Warren Harding, Bill "Dolt" Feuerer, and Mark Powell began the climb on July 4, 1957. Whitmore, then 27 and recently discharged from the Air Force, was working as a pharmacist down in Fresno. As Harding and company slowly climbed higher up The Nose, leaving fixed ropes behind them, Feuerer abandoned the adventure and then Powell went down with an ankle injury, leaving Harding without a partner. Wayne Merry, a leading Valley climber, quicky signed on to share the leading; Rich Calderwood was recruited to help haul loads. Whitmore joined the team in September 1958, with 2,000 feet to go.

Whitmore was a seasoned scrambler and peakbagger who'd climbed mountains in the Andes and throughout the Sierra Nevada, but had little meaningful experience with cutting-edge rock climbing. (Few people did in the late 1950s.) However, Whitmore's fitness, tenacity, steel nerves, and his yen for "unreachable stars" proved indispensable. Hauling on a big wall is grievous work, even today with ascenders and pulleys, but nothing compared to the nightmare of hauling bags in 1958, which Whitmore was tasked to do, single-handedly, during the final days of the summit push. (Calderwood had had to bail, in order to save his job.) Harding's famous and epic all-night push over the summit headwall was only made possible when Whitmore—battling a storm—prusiked up waterlogged ropes with a fresh supply of drills and bolts, fetched from Camp 6, 650 feet below.

The Nose was Whitmore's first and last big technical rock climb, but his contributions to the world, and all of us on it, were only beginning.

According to Nancy, his wife of 42 years, Whitmore retired from the pharmacy in the early 1970s to focus on conservation. He was involved with the Sierra Club in local, state, and national campaigns, serving as chairman of the Fresno-based Tehipite Chapter. El Capitan had taught Whitmore to think big and to act boldly. So, he did.

From the late 1960s through the early 1970s, Whitmore spearheaded efforts by the Sierra Club to prevent Disney from developing a ski resort at Mineral King. The project was halted, and the site became part of Sequoia National Park. Whitmore's tireless lobbying helped establish the Kaiser Wilderness in 1976 and the California Wilderness Act of 1984. These added 1.8 million acres into the National Wilderness Preservation System, including present-day Ansel Adams, John Muir, Dinkey Lakes, and Monarch wilderness lands. He helped protect Mono Lake and prevented a proposed highway over the Sierra in the San Joaquin River corridor.

As a staunch ally of the Friends of Yosemite Valley, Whitmore helped the group win a decisive court victory in the 2000s against the National Park Service that halted development near the Merced River. Whitmore was also instrumental in nixing a proposed dam project on the Kings River. "What means most is that protection is now complete from Tioga Pass Road in the north to Sherman Pass Road on the Kern Plateau in the south," Whitmore told *The Fresno Bee* in September 1984. "It is the longest stretch of de facto wilderness in the lower 48 states."

Whitmore's nephew, Randy Fisher, asked him a few years ago if he would put his El Cap climb on the top of his list of accomplishments. Whitmore told him he wasn't sure he'd even put it on the list.

"He was a climber, but that was secondary," said his wife, Nancy. "His love of the wilderness is the most important legacy that he left us."

— JOHN LONG

This tribute is adapted from a longer article published at Patagonia.com.

NECROLOGY

In addition, we remember the following AAC members who passed away in 2021.

FRANK ALLING	STEVEN FURMAN	BRUCE MARSHALL
MARCIA BILBAO	WILLIAM HAUSER	PAUL NELSON
LESLIE BUCKLAND	THOMAS JOHNSTON	RICHARD ROSENDAL
DR. THOMAS COPE	LEE LANDKAMER	MASON STANSFIELD
GISELLE FIELD	MAX LENAIL	WILLIAM STRAKA

INDEX

Compiled by Eve Tallman & Ralph Ferrara

Mountains are listed by their official names. Ranges, geographic locations, and maps are also indexed. Unnamed peaks (eg. Peak 2340m.) are listed under P. Abbreviations are used for the following: Cordillera: C.; Mountains: Mts.; National Park: Natl. Park; Obituary: obit. Indexed photographs are listed in bold type.